Movement for Actors

Movement for Actors

Edited by NICOLE POTTER

06   05   04   03   02   5   4   3   2   1

Published by Allworth Press
An imprint of Allworth Communications, Inc.
10 East 23rd Street, New York, NY 10010

Cover and interior design by Annemarie Redmond

Cover photo credits (clockwise, from upper left): Margolis Brown Theater Company, *The Bed Experiment*, conceived and written by Kari Margolis and Tony Brown, photo: Jim Moore; Theater Ten Ten, *King Lear*, 1998, directed by Rod McLucas, fight direction by Joe Travers, Jason Hauser (Edmund), Andrew Oswald (Edgar), photo: Sascha Nobés; Shakespeare and Company, Sarah Hickler, Rebecca Perrin, Mary Conway, Susan Dibble, photo: Stephanie Nash.

Page composition/typography by Sharp Des!gns, Lansing, MI

ISBN: 1-58115-233-7

LIBRARY OF CONGRESS CATALOGING-IN-PUBLICATION DATA
Movement for actors / edited by Nicole Potter.
p.   cm.
Includes bibliographical references and index.
ISBN 1-58115-233-7
1. Movement (Acting) I. Potter, Nicole.
PN2071.M6 M59 2002
792'.028—dc21
2002004246

Printed in Canada

For my parents, Maren and Macy Potter,
and my baby brother, Professor Dan Potter

I must offer my thanks to Tad Crawford and Bob Porter, Allworth's publisher and associate publisher, who allowed me to run with this idea; to my professional colleagues in theater and academia, who were generous with their time and their advice; to my contributors, of course; and to those members of Allworth's excellent staff who were instrumental in seeing this through to fruition: Jamie Kijwoski, Liz Van Hoose, Michael Madole, and, most especially, Kate Lothman.

Contents

PART SIX: INSIDE OUT AND OUTSIDE IN
197

PART SEVEN: MOVING FORWARD
227

Introduction

A long time ago, my brother and I used to make up plays that we would produce by enticing the neighborhood kids with promises of glory and then enslaving them in endless rehearsals on my grandmother's front porch. At that time, I had no training as an actress, and whatever I chose to believe seemed true enough to me. My sense of truth was not disturbed when my brother wrote an opera about a woman who lived in a bathtub (a wheelbarrow turned on its side, for the purposes of the Porch Premiere), and whose death scene required that she slide down the drain with the bubbles.

Some time later, I went to theater school. My training started with the Method, as so often happens in this country, and I was inculcated with a mistrust of work that I perceived as starting from anywhere other than wherever I perceived Method acting as starting from (personal Truth, I think). I codified what I learned into a strict set of rules, thus providing myself with a narrow and brittle idea of what was right and what was wrong, what was good and what was bad. I fancied that I was becoming more discerning, because I grew to dislike nearly everything, including my own ideas. This was a problem, for while I enjoyed being able to analyze the work I saw from a specific point of view, I missed the trust in my own ideas. It was as if I had two parallel tracks going: On the one hand, I had this (to me) amorphous technique, which I couldn't quite figure out how to practice myself, and on the other hand, I had my once beloved and now muzzled inspiration. The two were never going to merge.

While I was thus engaged in honing my critical ability, I happened to see both Andre Gregory's *Alice in Wonderland* and Lee Breuer's *Shaggy Dog Story*. Here were plays that defied my perception of "the Laws of Good Theater." They had schtick, they had style, they looked as if they had been created by kids on a rainy day in a junk-filled attic, and they felt True. Of course, the actors in Manhattan Project and in Mabou Mines had far more technique than I did, and their evocation of child's play was a deception—a deception of simplicity, the best kind in art. Why was this work so enthralling, and why was it so beyond anything I could conceive of? My conclusion? I was missing something, a turnoff somewhere. There had to be a way for my divergent pathways to become one.

What I was missing, what most novitiates are missing when they begin the arduous and ecstatic pilgrimage into a performing life, is the ability to synthesize. Discipline and spontaneity, knowledge and instinct, technique and inspiration—how do you reach the place where these are integrated? At last, a sudden, laughably simple insight: The body is the instrument. The crossroads exist within the body.

Which is why, to make a long story short, this book has been created. In performance, the actor's body, and all that it entails—alignment, shape, senses, impulses, sounds, gestures—tells the story. If the body is the place of synthesis, it is as important for the student, teacher, and director to be aware of an array of approaches as it is for them to have knowledge of diverse styles of theater and acting techniques.

There are many—although by no means an exhaustive catalog of—body and movement disciplines contained in this eclectic collection. Some writers included here offer insights into the discipline of a historically well-known master teacher, and some have synthesized their training and their experiences and gone on to create unique methodologies. Yet each one brings his or her own singular perspective and ideas to movement for actors. Many of these approaches intersect with and build upon each other, although the contributors—performers, teachers, directors, choreographers—may ultimately veer off in very different aesthetic directions. Still, I think all of them would agree that the pleasure in seeing a polished performer fully realize a mask or execute precise choreography is equal to the satisfaction derived from watching an actor who fully utilizes her teacup to express her disapproval of her scene partner or who sweeps the floor with conviction, allowing her feelings to be displayed (or artfully masked) through this action.

After reading a book about acting technique, I have often come away inspired but with little idea of implementation. How to go from the page to the work (the body)? Because of that, I wanted to put together a book both stimulating and pragmatic. My knowledgeable and generous contributors worked hard so that this book would be a compendium of both the practicable and the inspiring, and I hope that you will use it as a cookbook of movement techniques. It is for teacher, student, and director. I hope that you can look here when you are discontent with your work and find something that will make the proper diagnostic pop into your head, or that an exercise will suddenly strike you as the perfect lead-in or segue. Or perhaps you will find a particular discipline that so intrigues you that you decide to pursue it well beyond the pages of this book.

NICOLE POTTER

PART ONE

A Little History

PREVIOUS PAGE: *Chaplin, dancing his joy in* The Floorwalker—*a moment before being knocked down yet again.*

Biomechanics: Understanding Meyerhold's System of Actor Training

Marianne Kubik

Movement is the most powerful means of expression in the creation of a theatrical production. Deprived of words, costumes, footlights, wings, theatre auditorium, and left with only the actor and his mastery of movement, the theatre would still remain theatre.

—Vsevolod Meyerhold in 1914[1]

The end of the last century witnessed the resurrection of a technique for physical actor training that was first uncovered at the very start of it. Russian pedagogue Vsevolod Meyerhold (1874–1940)[2] developed a system of acting based upon the premise that "any art is the organization of material," and in the art of theater, the actor is "at one and the same time the material and the organizer of it."[3] He coined the term "biomechanics" as it applies to acting and used it primarily as a teaching tool, or a means to an end, although what often came out of his classroom work was directly inserted into his highly stylized productions.

Fortunately for Meyerhold, both Imperial and Soviet Russia were receptive to his work throughout most of his career, appointing him to directorships with the Imperial State Theatre (1908), the State Higher Theatre Workshops (1921), and the State Institute of Theatre Art (GITIS) (1922). By 1926, his theater company, one of several he had founded, was officially recognized as the Meyerhold State Theatre, and his work was hailed by some as "Revolutionary Theatre in the Name of Meyerhold."[4] While Meyerhold pledged allegiance to Bolshevism, however, he held greater personal allegiance to his art and theater pedagogy. He was interested in the socialist propagandist plays of the period because of what they offered him in his exploration of new theater forms and in the advancement of his career. Once propagandist writers began to lose their literary spark, Meyerhold moved on to material that explored more innovative theatrical ideas, going beyond constructivism toward formalism and the avant-garde.

The political tide began to turn against him in 1934, when Stalin mandated that the only acceptable form of Soviet art would be socialist realism, which Meyerhold the artist had moved well beyond. By 1936, he became victim to a vicious political campaign that pitted artist against artist in an attempt to abolish formalism and force allegiance to socialist realism. Both Meyerhold and his theater came under public attack, and in 1939, he was arrested by the Soviet government, interrogated, tortured, and forced to falsely confess rebellion against his country's ideology. Awarded the title "People's Artist of the Republic" a decade before,[5] Meyerhold was shot in prison in 1940 and never referred to publicly for over thirty years. To Stalinist Russia, it was as if he and his achievements disappeared from history.

Meyerhold's influence lived on secretly in the work of two former students: Sergei Eisenstein, the Russian filmmaker, and Nikolai Kustov, the actor in the famous photographs brought to the United States by Lee Strasberg in 1934. Western practitioners had to rely on these stills, past accounts by foreign visitors to Meyerhold's classes, and scant writings on the subject to define the concept of biomechanics, let alone utilize it in actor training. Biomechanics began to earn a reputation for being a static technique, where the actor moves like a machine, and it certainly held little strength against the widely popular Method approach.

In 1972, the Moscow Theatre of Satire assumed great political risk by inviting Kustov to train a select group of actors in the still-forbidden technique. Gennadi Bogdanov was one of eight students who received formal training from Kustov for three and a half years until his death. Bogdanov is currently the only one of the original eight who teaches biomechanics, and he is, therefore, the closest living link to it as a practical technique.

I had the opportunity to study twice with Bogdanov and Nikolai Karpov,[6] in 1993 at the Institute in Meyerhold's Theatrical Biomechanics hosted by Tufts University and in 1995 at the Moscow School of Theatrical Biomechanics hosted by the Russian Academy of Theatre Arts (formerly GITIS, of which Meyerhold was founding director). My understanding of biomechanics as a system of actor training comes from my research and analysis, my formal training in the practice of the technique, and my incorporation of it into my courses for American actors. One can never duplicate the work of Meyerhold, and an attempt to do so would be for the sake of historical reconstruction. His ideas, and his practical instruction, however, live on in the work of those who teach and study biomechanics in order to understand the limitless possibilities of physical communication as applied to acting in the twenty-first century.

THEORY AND TECHNIQUE

There is a misconception that Meyerhold is the antithesis of Stanislavsky. Although Meyerhold left the Moscow Art Theatre in 1902 because of artistic and personal conflicts,[7] he and Stanislavsky maintained a mutual respect for the other's artistic endeavors throughout their careers. What Meyerhold learned from Stanislavsky is that every dramatic action requires justification; what he discovered for himself was a different means to the same end. He felt that Stanislavsky focused on developing the inner life of the actor at the expense of the physical. Actors inherently knew how to think, feel, and remember, believed Meyerhold; what they could not realize for themselves was how to dramatically express such thoughts and emotions through their body and voice. This was an actual skill in need of development.

Meyerhold trained his company of actors in a variety of physical skills to provide a solid awareness of balance, control, and expressive ability in the acting instrument. By 1915, his "Studio Programme" consisted of classes in ballet, music, athletics, gymnastics, fencing, juggling, pantomime, diction, and vocal production. With his students, he developed a series of exercises that applied this foundation work specifically to theatrical performance. Influenced by science, technology, and kinesiology, he established an entire system based on the creation of efficient and effortless stage movement. By 1922, this system was publicly known as "biomechanics," the analysis of the mechanics of the acting instrument in order to fully integrate it into performance. What follows is a description of the ideas behind the system, delineated in no particular order of importance, as they are all interrelated and essential to one another.

The Actor Has a Dual Personality

Meyerhold was influenced by the acting theory of Constant-Benoit Coquelin, who believed in the "dual personality" of the actor: "He has his first self, which is the player, and his second self, which is the instrument."[8] Meyerhold "borrowed" Coquelin's formula for acting verbatim, stating that $N = A_1 + A_2$, where N is the actor who is made up equally of two selves, A_1 and A_2. A_1 is the first self, the player of the instrument; it represents the metaphysical actor, or the conceiver of the idea. A_2 is the second self, the instrument played upon; it represents the physical actor, or the executor of the idea. While the muscles of the metaphysical actor (A_1) are stretched and strengthened through an ongoing process of self-discovery, life experience, and the imagination, the muscles of the physical actor (A_2) require a more conscious stretching and strengthening through intense physical training.

In rehearsal, it is the A_1 who determines what the A_2 will execute. In performance, it is the A_2 who allows what is behind the A_1 to come through. In other words, once the actor has consciously choreographed his movement to his character intention, it is then the movement that provides the form through which the character emotion flows. Otherwise, the emotive performance by the actor becomes a cathartic experience for himself alone; the audience cannot experience the actor's intention, no matter how much he means it, if it remains locked inside an unskilled body and choking out of an underdeveloped voice.

Meyerhold believed that, because art represents not a copy of life but the dramatic truth in it, art must be a conscious process, with the actor making choices about how his intention is best to be expressed: "The art of the actor consists in organizing his material: that is, in his capacity to utilize correctly his body's means of expression."[9] The actor is at the same time the organizer of his material and the material itself.

Movement Is the Result of the Work of the Entire Body

A visitor to Meyerhold's class in 1933, André Van Gyseghem, observed that an actor "must be able to use his whole body as an instrument to play upon. His mind and body must be in complete harmony. What he understands with his mind he must be able to express with the movement or non-movement of his body."[10] In order to achieve this, the actor's body must be in a constant state of equilibrium, continually making adjustments in order to find maximum expressiveness. The slightest move of an arm, or even a finger, causes a shift in the scales of balance and counterbalance, and the rest of the body must find the most efficient adjustment to maintain equilibrium, which is why "when the tip of the nose works, so does the entire body."[11]

In life, a body can be in a state of balance; on stage, it must be in a state of equilibrium. A body in balance is a stable force, an aesthetically pleasing integration of the equal and opposite influences acting upon it; it is what Eisenstein referred to as a static pose. A body in a state of equilibrium is alive and dynamic, even in repose, continually moving in reaction to the forces acting on it and inside of it, playing between the balance and counterbalance; it is what Eisenstein called a *raccourci*. This is a conscious act, as both the A_1 and A_2 of the actor must remain in a constant state of readiness, prepared to work against the forces of gravity and momentum to maintain dynamic expressiveness. It is movement working with countermovement; it is equilibrium.

The Body Is the Machine, the Actor the Machinist

If one looks at how the musculoskeletal system of the human body is designed to provide a useful system of levers and counterbalance, one will see that the essence behind each movement as Meyerhold devised it is inherent to the body. He did not invent it; rather, he accurately surmised it through both careful observation of the body in space and through his own natural instinct for movement. His logical and scientific mind made connections between the human body and the physical world around him, which is why he was readily influenced by American industrialist Frederick Winslow Taylor's study of "motion economy" on a factory production line. Meyerhold connected Taylor's model of the skilled factory worker to the Soviet concept of a "new worker" of the theater, believing that one must observe in both the absence of superfluous or unproductive movements and correct positioning of the body's center of gravity, rhythm, and stability.[12] Taylor's "work cycle" became Meyerhold's "acting cycle," involving a studied relationship between movement and rest that would enable the worker, and Meyerhold's actor, to produce the most efficient performance with the least degree of effort.

Combining Coquelin's idea of the dual personality with Taylor's system of worker efficiency, Meyerhold compared the A_1 and A_2 of the actor to the machinist and his machine. If a factory worker can learn to work with his machine efficiently, then the production line is an effective one. If the actor can uncover for himself the complex workings of his own machine, his acting instrument, then his dramatic actions will be equally effective while particular to the work of the performer. Add to this the human capacity for thought and emotion, and the human machine in performance excels beyond any other.

The acting cycle is not foreign to life, observed Meyerhold, but sorely neglected on the stage. Because he saw theater as theatrical rather than lifelike, he concluded that every theatrical moment should be executed to its fullest. Through a careful study of the muscular coordination and system of levers already inherent in the human form, the actor can make the job of moving, gesturing, and speaking more effective by initially making it more efficient. He can then choose how to manipulate his movement, because he has already trained his body to execute what his mind and emotions ask of it.

The Actor's Art Lies in the Extremely Strict Coordination of All the Elements of His Work

Once the actor has an awareness of the mechanical principles of the body and can apply these principles to every action, he moves beyond work toward expressive play. Achieving such level of play, however, requires careful study of kinesiology and the diligent breaking down of the movement to analyze its process. When an action is broken down into its separate parts, the muscles are learning a new way of moving and require repetition and exaggeration to establish muscle memory. Only when this muscle memory is achieved can the movement be reassembled or synthesized. Meyerhold described this process musically: "When an exercise is broken up into small elements it must be done staccato; the legato will appear when the exercise is executed as an unbroken flowing whole."[13] A musician learns the music phrase by phrase, practicing intricate measures in isolation before reassembling them into an unbroken whole. So, too, must the actor.

This process is similar to Stanislavsky's scoring of a script. Careful analysis of the script in rehearsal enables its detail to be uncovered. When reassembled for performance, the distinctive beats uncovered in analysis are neither blurred nor static; rather, each beat communicates with such precision how the next beat is to be executed, to seamless effect.

VOCABULARY

There is a fundamental law of human movement whereby, when one wishes to make a movement in a certain direction, one initially makes a movement in the opposite direction before proceeding forward and passing through the point of origin to the intended goal. Although it is more obvious to some actions—bringing a hammer up before coming down onto the nail or taking a few steps backward in order to run and jump over a small stream—"[t]he unexpectedness begins the moment it is pointed out to you that this organic law applies always, everywhere, and to all kinds of phenomena."[14] Eisenstein described this law with a diagram similar to the following:[15]

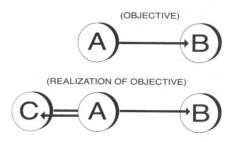

(OBJECTIVE)

(REALIZATION OF OBJECTIVE)

This diagram illustrates first the actor's intent for a movement from point A to point B (the A_1 of the actor), and then what his instrument inherently does in order to achieve the intention (the A_2 of the actor).

Meyerhold further observed that there exist three basic parts to every action: the preparation for the action, the action itself, and the precise end of the action. These are designated in the diagram as the path from A to C, from C passing through A to B, and B itself, respectively. These elements create the acting cycle. Meyerhold was able to demonstrate through his students' work that this acting cycle is embodied in every gesture and every line, and because it is cyclical, the end of one action should lead directly and smoothly into the next.

Meyerhold developed a vocabulary for the acting cycle in order to offer students a communal reference point in their analysis. None of the terms has more significance than the others, but none can be omitted from the acting cycle. Below is a transliteration of the Russian terms into the Roman alphabet, as well as an IPA transcription for proper pronunciation.[16] Bogdanov and Karpov insist that the Russian terminology be retained because of the semantics behind the literal translation of each word.[17]

CYRILLIC	TRANSLITERATION	IPA TRANSCRIPTION	TRANSLATION
отказ	otkaz	aṭˈkʌẕ	a refusal, a reversal
посыл	posyl	paˈsʉɫ	a sending out, to, or away
точка	tochka	ˈṭotʃkə	a point or dot
стоика	stoika	ˈstoika	a stop or stance
тормоз	tormoz	ˈṭorməs	a brake
пауза	pauza	ˈpauẕə	a pause or interval

Otkaz: "A Refusal, a Reversal"

The *otkaz* is the preparation for the action and one of the most difficult elements to master. It is a reversal of the action, or more precisely, a movement directly opposing the action (the path from A to C in Eisenstein's diagram). We bend our knees in order to jump; we inhale in order to speak or blow out a candle; we raise our fingers in order to strike a chord on a piano; we open our eyes wide in order to close them tightly when we sneeze. These recoils go against the main action and are inherent in every physical action, no matter how subtle: "One cannot shoot from a bow without first drawing back the string," Meyerhold was fond of telling his students. The *otkaz* is the body's organic way of collecting the energy required for the action, holding onto it in anticipation for the "point of excitability," or the point at which the body senses is the right moment to execute the action.

Meyerhold also referred to the *otkaz* as the "pre-action," because it subtly indicates to the audience the action that they are about to see and, therefore, makes the perception of the entire movement more complete. For example, when we can sense the actor's intake of breath, we subconsciously surmise that he is about to blow out the candle before him. We are prepared for it, even without recognizing it, and can more completely enjoy the moment. The audience will not be conscious of this, but it is not its job to be so. That level of awareness falls to the actor, and without it, he is merely doing things on stage; it is not performance.

Posyl: "A Sending Out, To, or Away"

The *posyl*[18] is the execution of the main action intended. On Eisenstein's diagram, it is the path from *C* to *B*, passing back through the point of origin, *A*. Just as a ball thrown by a pitcher, the energy collected and held in the body during the *otkaz* is released and sent in the direction of the action, with the degree of intensity necessitated by the action. Because it passes back through the point of origin, the *posyl* is seen by the spectator as the path from *A* to *B*, but containing the dynamic energy collected from the *otkaz*. Without this energy, the *posyl* begins from a dead point. For example, when it is difficult to understand the first few words of an actor's line, it is because he is not building up the energy for the line until halfway through it; he has not utilized the *otkaz* to his advantage.

Tochka: "A Point or Dot" or *Stoika:* "A Stop or Stance"

The *tochka*, or *stoika*, is the precise end of the action, and it is best understood as the period at the end of the sentence. The path from *A* to *B* has an end, which is *B*, and it is the actor's job to clarify what and where that point is. If an archer shoots an arrow at a target, the precise moment the arrow makes contact with the target is the end of the action; if this action ends too soon, the arrow falls short of the archer's intention. Often, an unskilled actor will allow the end of his lines to trail during performance. In this case, the intended line is falling short of its target, the communication of the idea to the audience; it might fall close, but close is not precise enough for the stage.

Stoika can be used interchangeably with *tochka*, and it provides another way of looking at point *B*. It refers to the end of the action as a full stop, requiring a solid stance that incorporates the entire body, regardless of whether the action was a whole-body movement or simply a gesture.

Tormoz: "A Brake"

The *tormoz* is necessary so you don't crash-land when you stop the movement of your body. It is the body's reorganization of its equilibrium in preparation for a stop or change of direction. Just as a driver applies the brakes of the car when approaching a stop sign, the actor must apply his system of brakes upon approaching his target, or he will overshoot it. It is not simply a matter of slowing down, however, as that will change the dynamics of the action.

A simple exercise to discover how the *tormoz* is essential to the action is to run full-speed toward a cube or block and, without stopping, jump up and land directly on it. If the body does not apply its brakes in time as it makes the change in direction from forward to up, then momentum will continue to carry it forward, and the actor will fall forward off the cube. If he slows down too soon, he loses the dynamism of his forward motion as well as the energy to jump up.

An actor can never consciously manipulate his movement by speeding it up, slowing it down, or changing its direction if he allows himself to yield to the laws of gravity and momentum. Even when the

Movement for Actors

actor is executing a movement in the direction of gravity—falling to the ground, for example—he must apply the brakes in order to control his equilibrium and communicate the action as he consciously intends it.

Pauza: "A Pause or Interval"

The *pauza* is the space between the first action and the next, or the break between the *tochka* and ensuing *otkaz*. The moment after the car comes to a complete stop, it returns to idling and remains in a state of readiness as it awaits the next application by the driver to the gas pedal. Although it appears a non-action, the pause is never devoid of the play between balance and counterbalance; the brakes are applied, not the keys removed from the vehicle. Finding this in the body, however, involves a more subtle process than the *otkaz*.

The most basic parallel to this idea is when you ride an elevator. As it arrives at the intended floor, it slows down slightly (*tormoz*) before stopping and settling into the correct position for the doors to open. That settling reverberates in you, the passenger, a bit and marks the *pauza* before the next action of the doors opening.

As another example of this principle, imagine wearing a long velvet cape that drags along the floor behind you as you walk. Whenever you stop walking, it takes a moment for the cape to settle behind you. If you were to run and stop, the settling would be great; if you were to slowly glide to a stop, the settling would be gentle. The settling, however, is inherent to wearing the cape, because it is an extension of your body and follows behind your movement. This moment of settling happens within the body as well, because the extensions of energy emanating from the torso begin to settle when the body comes to a stop. In the *posyl,* the body is moving against the laws of gravity and momentum. In the *pauza,* it is still, but it is not in a static pose.

An illustration of the collaborative roles of this vocabulary is the action of pitching a ball to a catcher. There is the windup, counter to the direction of the batter (*otkaz*), leading into the step forward, the sending of the ball and full extension of the torso and arm, ending just as the ball leaves the hand (*posyl*). The pitcher's body remains active, while the energy in the ball begins to dissipate as the ball nears the catcher (*tormoz*). The moment the ball meets the catcher's glove marks the end of the complete action (*tochka*), and the pitcher, whose arm is usually still extended, can feel this connection with the ball even though he is no longer attached to it. The pitcher can, in fact, feel the *tormoz* even before the ball leaves his hand; without it, he would not be able to manipulate his movement and release the ball at the exact point he intends. Finally, the energy of this action dissipates for both the ball as it settles into the glove, and the pitcher as he feels this connection from the mound (*pauza*).

EXERCISES

One set of biomechanical exercises trained the actor to find equilibrium in space at all times while pushing the limits of his own natural movement. Another set was designed by Meyerhold to instruct the actor about the vocabulary of the acting cycle. Finally, the etudes were a culmination of Meyerhold's principles to test the actor's application to performance. With the exception of the etudes, the exercises do not have precise names, and I therefore refer to them by the main *posyl* of the exercise. Meyerhold taught all of his exercises in a group and felt strongly that the actors should maintain group awareness even while executing individual movements so that there was no chance of self-indulgence, which he felt had no place on the stage.

Balancing the Stick

Meyerhold used balls and sticks (batons) often in his work to promote awareness in the actor of the extension of his energy and of the continual shift in equilibrium. Take a stick (¾" in diameter by 4') and balance one end on both the middle and index fingers of one hand. Try transferring the stick from finger to finger while still balancing it, or toss it up and catch it on the fingers of the other hand. Try balancing it on the elbow, nose, chin, foot, or knee. Try walking while balancing, then running, sitting, squatting, or lying down.

The stick is an extension of the arm, which is an extension of the torso via the upper and middle back muscles. The stick, therefore, is the ultimate test of balance in the body, for if the stick falls, the body is not in equilibrium. The actor can determine even the subtlest changes in his balance by watching the upper end of the stick for any tipping or swaying. Unless there is a complete release of tension from the torso through the arm and hand, there will not be a solid enough equilibrium to balance the stick for very long.

Allow that which is inherent in the body's mechanics to assist you in this exercise. Widen your stance, with one foot slightly forward to bring your center of gravity closer to the floor and expand your tripod. Bend your knees, so that they are ready as springboards to move the feet when needed. Keep your body underneath the stick as much as possible, so that your alignment can assist your sense of balance. Exhale as thoroughly as possible to release any muscles in the neck, shoulders, or elbows that tend to overwork during this exercise. Finally, have fun with the exercise, because it is through a sense of intricate play with the stick that we learn and respond to the "choices" it makes in dialogue with our own equilibrium.

Stomping the Feet

This is one of the simplest exercise with which to understand the integration of the three basic elements of the acting cycle: *otkaz, posyl,* and *tochka.* Lift the right foot with the intent of stepping down into the floor. Place the ball of the right foot strongly on the floor, followed by the heel. Alternate left and right sides continually until you find an organic rhythm to the movement. Be careful to lift the leg and foot energetically but only as high as you need to execute the main action of stomping the foot down. You will execute stronger movements and find better balance and support by using your knees as springs, releasing tension in your torso and grounding your center.

Once the stomping becomes familiar in the body, you can begin to break it down into its acting cycle of *otkaz, posyl,* and *tochka.* The action (*posyl*) is stepping down on the ball of the foot, but in order to do so, you must first lift the foot in preparation (*otkaz*). The *otkaz,* lifting the foot, acts as a pickup beat to the downbeat of placing the foot down, and together, they are counted as "and one." The heel meeting the floor marks the very end, or period, of the action (*tochka*) and is, therefore, separate from placing the ball of the foot down. Together, the *otkaz, posyl* and *tochka* are counted "and one, two."

Movement for Actors

Return to a firm stomping of each foot into the floor, utilizing this count as you lift the right foot, place the ball, then the heel; lift the left foot, place the ball, then the heel; and so on ("and one, two," "and one, two," etc.). A tendency to speed up means that the heel is not making solid contact with the floor, and you are passing through the *tochka* of the action rather than clearly defining it.

Moving to a Point

The addition of the *tormoz* and *pauza* to the acting cycle is better understood with this exercise. Fix your eyes and face on a specific point across the room; perhaps it is a poster on the wall, a speck of dust on the floor, or a ceiling light. Walk determinedly to that point and stop as close to it as you can, bringing your arm and hand up like a crossing guard would signal "stop." It is important that the action of this "stop" signal be initiated from the torso through the shoulder, elbow, and hand. The hand does not come upward in front of you but outward, as if you are firmly and slowly pushing the space in front of you: "Stop." Repeat this action with another point, then another, until you feel comfortable with the action. Your movement will feel more organic if you inhale before you walk to each point.

In this exercise, the preparation (*otkaz*) is not the turning of the head to look at the point, but the moment just before you take your first step toward it—the moment of inhale. It is a subtle recoil from the intended direction—like drawing back the string before shooting from the bow—and it needs to be exaggerated until it becomes ingrained in both the body and mind.

Following the recoil, or *otkaz,* is the *posyl* of walking directly to the point. The "stop" sign you make with your hand is a signal to your body that this is the very end of your action, which is why it is essential that you feel this gesture in the torso: specifically, the back muscles. It is a precise end, as if the hand meets an imagined wall—a period to the sentence of walking across the space (*tochka* or *stoika*).

As you begin to bring the arm out, this signals in the body the preparation for the stop. There is a natural slowing down in the body before the stop, and this is what Meyerhold referred to as the *tormoz,* or "putting on the brakes." Once you take your last step and stop, there is a settling in the body that goes on, a slight reverberation. The end of this reverberation marks the *pauza,* or pause, after the action. The body does not relax, as it needs to remain ready to move toward the next point.

Sending the Ball

This exercise applies the acting cycle to partner work. Stand facing your partner with a child's rubber play ball in your hands, holding it just below chest level in front of you. Using equal force in both arms, send the ball along a straight path directly to your partner, aiming just below his chest. Your partner should catch the ball with both hands and send it back to you in the manner just described. Repeat continually, sending the ball only along this path (i.e., not tossing underhand, overhead, or making one-handed throws).

This exercise may seem elementary, but any change in rhythm, speed, or number of balls too early in the game is likely to cause the ball to drop or the body to tense. There is also a tendency to stop the energy of the ball, like a catcher does with his mitt. In this exercise, allow the energy sent to you from your partner to continue through your catch.

To determine what this "energy of the ball" is, step aside for a moment instead of catching the ball and watch where it goes. It will travel beyond you until it, perhaps, meets a wall or loses its momentum. This same energy is blocked every time you catch the ball abruptly. Instead, embrace the ball soundlessly and literally step back a few paces until you have actually received the energy of the ball. When you can determine the exact moment when the energy is completely received by you, you have found the *stoika*. The *pauza* is the moment between your receipt and your release, when you transfer the energy of the ball toward your partner, stepping forward. The energy behind the ball is like the energy of a line, an emotion, even an eye contact onstage; it is the dialogue between partners so in sync that the ball never falls nor makes a sound.

The *Daktil'* (дактыл)

Meyerhold created a series of short biomechanical studies, which he called etudes. They are compositions built around a technical basis and executed both for the practice of the technique and for their artistic value, much like the etudes developed for a musician. Each tells a simple action story, such as "Shooting from the Bow," "Throwing the Stone," and "Stabbing with the Dagger," and contains a series of prescribed movements designed to incorporate "all the elements of stage movement and mind-state which Meyerhold demands of every actor."[19]

Every etude is preceded by and concludes with a similar exercise called the *daktil'*.[20] The *daktil'* acts as the bookends to the etude, or as the *otkaz* and *tochka* of the grand *posyl*. Within three seconds, the actor moves from a neutral stance to a state of physical and mental readiness with the weight centered strongly over the balls of the feet, which Meyerhold felt was much more active. The *daktil'* focuses both the A_1 and A_2 of the actor, reminds the actor of the need for balance and counterbalance, and establishes synchronicity between partners or among a group. When executed *en masse*, a single clap that is slightly off the rest, in rhythm or even timbre, is obvious. The *daktil'* is often executed repeatedly by new students before moving on to the etude, until the group finds unified precision.

Meyerhold borrowed the term from verse poetry (dactyl), where it refers to a metrical foot consisting of one stressed and two unstressed syllables, as in the word "butterfly." So, too, is the meter of the *daktil'* in biomechanics. The stressed syllable involves a sending upward of the torso and arms, followed by two precise claps as the actor centers his energy. The intent of each "syllable" differs, and the second two are slightly shorter than the first, like two quarter notes following one half note.

The *daktil'* is not difficult to copy, but it is challenging to sort out its usefulness as a preparatory exercise. Its significance as a key example of biomechanical principles gets lost in fairly generic descriptions of its execution. As an experiment, I asked one of my students to attempt to recreate the *daktil'* based on recorded information,[21] without my assistance. I then asked her questions that might guide her to discover the reasons behind what she was doing and, therefore, make the movement more organic to her body, without actually telling or demonstrating for her. After significant discussion and analysis, she was able to execute the *daktil'* fully and with precision and uncover the essence of the dactylic rhythm. The following is the result of our experiment. The description of the execution is based on the technique I learned from Bogdanov.

The Daktil'

1. Begin in neutral stance, feet hip-width apart (figure 1). Bring the arms back in preparation, and allow the spine to curve and the knees to bend in response (figures 2 to 3).

Imagine jumping up as high as you can, as if your fingertips could brush the ceiling. In order to execute this, you would first need to bend at the knees, to prepare this jump by moving counter to the direction of the jump. You would probably inhale, lower your body, and take your arms behind you. In so doing, you are collecting all your energy in preparation for springing up. You would also find a certain lift in the knees and feet, readying them as springboards for the jump. It is as if you were making a minuscule jump, a pre-jump, before the main one.

Fig. 1. Neutral stance.   *Fig. 2. Inhale.*   *Fig. 3. Prepare.*   *Fig. 4. Gather energy.*

2. Bring the arms in front of the body in a large arc (figure 4). Continue the shape of this arc as the hands begin to ascend in front of you toward the ceiling. When the arms are almost parallel with the floor, begin to release the heels as the eyes and head face upward, followed by the arms and torso extending up as high as they will reach (figure 5).

Now, execute the jump you just imagined, exhaling as you do so and using your arms to help you lift upward. Experiment with scooping with your hands and arms versus swinging them; you will find that the action of scooping assists you better in gaining height and maintaining balance in an upward direction. Imagine sending up confetti

Fig. 5. Extend upward.   *Fig. 6. Collect energy.*   *Fig. 7. Clap downward.*   *Fig. 8. Extend.*

| *Fig. 9. Rise upward.* | *Fig. 10. clap again.* | *Fig. 11. Extend down.* | *Fig. 12. Ready stance.* |

*with you as you jump, watching it as you release, so that it falls in front of and not behind you. Once this jump feels comfortable, alter it by extending as far as you can without actually jumping up. Allow your heels to release if they want, but stay connected to the floor with the balls of your feet. The high point of this extension should feel like a moment of suspension where the energy has not been released through the ceiling, as it is when you jump. This moment of suspension is the end (*tochka*) of the stressed syllable in the* daktil'; *it also marks the preparation (small* otkaz*) for the first of two unstressed syllables, the claps.*

3. Bring the hands downward and inward (figure 6), allowing the elbows to bend and spine to curve as the body gathers around its center point. When both hands near the body's center (stomach-pelvic region), bring them together in a downward clap, extending the hands and arms toward the floor (figures 7 to 8).

Once your arms are extended toward the ceiling, reach for the edge of an imaginary sheet hanging midair. Pull down on the sheet, as if trying to release it. This action should naturally involve your torso as well as your arms and hands. Let your hands meet for just a moment, as if gathering the sheet, to strengthen the energy you are sending downward in one strong clap. The hands do not clap inward but downward, like pushing down strongly through water with the palms of the hands.

4. Rise up until almost standing (figure 9), then repeat the clap and downward extension of the arms as described above (figures 10 to 11).

This clap acts as a "second chance" to send out any energy you missed the first time. It is a check-in for yourself, to see that you are focused and balanced. It is most useful when executing the daktil' *with a partner or as a group; if the first clap is off, the second usually brings everyone together. Be careful not to rush through this clap, but to give it the same rhythm as the first. Both claps mark the unstressed syllables of the entire* daktil'. *The main action is the sending of all your energy upward and, before it can release from your body, containing it in the two claps: half note, quarter note, quarter note ("and 1, (2), 3, 4").*

5. Rise to standing, allowing the spine to uncurl with the movement. Place the weight of the body over the balls of the feet, which will cause the body to lean slightly forward (figure 12).

Movement for Actors

Most of your energy should now be directed forward and downward by the action of the hands clapping in front of you. When you rise up to standing, keep your feet planted as the central line of your torso recovers the extension it found in the "jump." The body is now in equilibrium, with energy moving at the same time upward and downward. Continue to focus your weight more on the balls of your feet as you rise, and feel the weight of the downward pull in the hands as the torso travels upward. When standing, the heels have the same freedom as when executing the "jump," the knees are flexible, and the aligned body inclines slightly forward. This is your energized stance, your state of readiness.

In the *daktil'* demonstrated by Gennadi Bogdanov, which was passed down from Kustov, the heels of the feet barely leave the ground on the upward extension. Robert Leach states that the "feet remain firm on the ground,"[22] while Alma Law maintains that the actor should be "on the balls of his feet."[23] Archival photos and films offer differing views, and it becomes challenging to assess the historical accuracy of this point. When actually executing this extension, it is difficult to completely involve the torso unless the heels can release a bit from the floor; otherwise, there is a sense of the feet being too planted into the ground and holding back the energy. If on full *relevé*, however, the degree to which the actor can send the energy upward lessens because of issues with balance.

Photos courtesy Matt Jacobson

NOTES

1. Law, Alma H., and Gordon, Mel. *Meyerhold, Eisenstein and Biomechanics: Actor Training in Revolutionary Russia.* Jefferson, N.C.: McFarland & Company, Inc., 1996, 23.
2. Robert Leach accurately views Meyerhold as a pedagogue, which he defines as a "teacher, a researcher and a practitioner in one." (Leach, Robert. *Vsevolod Meyerhold.* Cambridge, Mass.: Cambridge University Press, 1989, xiii.)
3. Law, 136.
4. Leach, 23–24.
5. Braun, Edward. *Meyerhold: A Revolution in Theatre*, Iowa City: University of Iowa Press, 1995, 188.
6. Karpov audited Kustov's classes in 1974, and he and Bogdanov have often team-taught courses in biomechanics.
7. Meyerhold was becoming disgruntled with the lack of opportunity for him at the Moscow Art Theatre, and the MAT with his revolutionary ideas. When the company reorganized in 1902, Nemirovich-Danchenko and Stanislavsky did not invite Meyerhold to be a shareholder. Meyerhold subsequently resigned and started his own company in Kherson.
8. Coquelin, Constant-Benoit. *The Art of Acting.* New York: Columbia University Press, 1926, 5.
9. Braun, 173.
10. Law, 234.
11. Law, 135.
12. Braun, Edward. *Meyerhold on Theatre,* London: Methuen, 1991, 198.
13. As recorded by Mikhail Korenev. Law, 138.
14. For details regarding this phenomenon, see Sergei Eisenstein's essay, "On Recoil Movement," in Law, 193.
15. Law, 193.
16. I am indebted to Maia Kipp (University of Kansas) for editing my transliterations and to Paul Meier (University of Kansas) for providing the International Phonetic Alphabet (IPA) transcriptions.
17. Some practitioners assert that Meyerhold's terminology is slightly different than Bogdanov's, but as I understood from both institutes I attended, this is the original terminology and usage.
18. Often transliterated as *pacil*. According to Russian-born scholar Maia Kipp, the accepted transliteration following the guidelines set by the Library of Congress would be *posyl* (personal interview).
19. As observed by André Van Gyseghem. Law, 234.
20. Often transliterated as *dactyl*, which is how it is used in poetry. According to Russian-born scholar Maia Kipp, the accepted transliteration following the guidelines set by the Library of Congress would be *daktil'* (personal interview). See also note 16 above.
21. I am indebted to Laura Sternberg for her work on this experiment, based on descriptions by Robert Leach (Leach, "Meyerhold and Biomechanics," 46–7) and Alma Law and Mel Gordon (Law, 103–5).
22. Leach, "Meyerhold and Biomechanics," 46.
23. Law, 103.

Michael Chekhov, Psychological Gesture, and the Thinking Heart

Floyd Rumohr

I first encountered the work of Michael Chekhov as a first-year graduate student at Temple University in 1985. My teacher, Kevin Cotter, had such a profound impact on me that I began immediately to apply the work. Within only two weeks, I was spellbound by its effectiveness and a bit awed by its ease, having previously been subject only to the internal sufferings of the Method actor. I wondered why I had never heard of a "psychophysical" approach before. By 1988, I had applied the technique to critical acclaim in several Philadelphia performances, which resulted in a few requests by my peers to teach them. With more experience as a practitioner than a teacher, I wasn't quite sure how to go about it, though I thought I might as well give it a try. My handful of students at that time evolved into a six-month waiting list by the time I arrived in New York City in 1990. Their confidence in me provided opportunities to improve my teaching and test some of my ideas.

As demand for private coaching increased beyond capacity, I struggled with a central question: What am I training these artists to do? Having recently graduated from a world-class conservatory program and landed an agent who was primarily focused on television in the New York market, I realized that my best years in the theater could quite possibly be behind me. I wasn't a good enough singer or dancer for Broadway, and the handful of classical theater companies in New York paid very little, if any thing at all. So, was I to spend my late twenties doing commercials for Chevrolet, which paid more for two days' work than I made in an entire year in the theater?

I struggled with this idea. Was I to "train" actors very much the way I was trained, which ultimately constituted overkill, given that I really didn't need that level of training to do commercials or daytime TV? What was I training them for? To be unemployed? To wait tables? After a time, I found it difficult to take their money when I knew they were struggling to survive.

Some of my more ambitious students approached me about forming an ensemble. This sounded like a good idea, but I was not so sure that New York City needed yet another new theater among the three hundred and fifty that already existed off- and off-off-Broadway. Our emphasis on the work of Michael Chekhov would certainly distinguish us, but I wasn't convinced that would be enough.

After some discussion among the actors, drawing upon my six years of experience at Theatre for a New Audience, and turning to Mr. Chekhov's suggestion that the creative spirit grows stronger within us when we do things for others without a "selfish note in it," we decided to offer artist residencies to three New York City public schools free of charge. Following training workshops that developed their teaching skills, the actors visited the schools to teach aesthetic skills and rehearsal strategies in partnership with public school teachers once each week for several weeks. The pilot project was such a success that it has evolved into one of the most comprehensive and successful arts-in-education programs currently in the United States, reaching nearly four thousand teachers, children, and their families in all five boroughs of New York City, with pilot activity in Florida and Pennsylvania. The program, called "Stages of Learning®," was inspired by Mr. Chekhov's artistic principles and employs artists trained in his approach.

MR. CHEKHOV AND HIS TECHNIQUE

Any approach to acting, let alone a psychophysical approach, lends itself to misinterpretation or confused application, particularly when that application is derived from the written word. For this reason, I will focus on the meaning of "psychophysical" and its relationship to psychological gesture, which is an amalgam that embodies nearly all of the separate components of the Chekhov technique. Not to say that what you read here is beyond interpretation, but my intention is to clarify our terms, provide an overall framework for psychophysical development, and attempt a written description to an approach, which is indispensable to a good teacher.

Perhaps one of the aspects of Mr. Chekhov's work that is the most compelling is that he was an actor first—not just a good one, but a great one. In a 1993 letter to me, Bobby Lewis described him as "the greatest actor I ever saw." He is known currently in the Soviet Union as "the acting genius of the century." Mr. Chekhov, a consummate actor who experienced the ebb and flow of success and deprivation, sought to "go beyond" the playwright and the play to embody the character in the most profound ways.

Michael Chekhov joined Konstantin Stanislavsky's Moscow Art Theatre in 1912, at the age of twenty-one, and within months was invited into the First Studio, where he appeared in walk-ons and later in major roles. Between 1913 and 1923, Chekhov's reputation as a creative and independent thinker increased dramatically.

In 1923, Chekhov became the director of the Second Studio of the Moscow Art Theatre upon Stanislavsky's request. Soon, his innovations became a threat to the Soviet government, and he was denounced in 1927 as an "idealist" and mystic. Moscow newspapers cited Chekhov as "a sick artist" and "alien and reactionary." In 1928, director Max Reinhardt invited Chekhov to emigrate to Germany. For seven years, Chekhov "wandered"[1] in Austria, Berlin, Paris, Latvia, and Lithuania, pursuing his lifelong quest to create his own troupe and method of actor training. Upon the invitation of Sol Hurok, Chekhov came to America, where he met Beatrice Straight, who generously supported Chekhov's vision.

By 1938, Chekhov's method had been established. In the fall of 1941, the Chekhov Theatre opened a New York studio on 56th Street in New York City, but was unable to sustain itself without the financial assistance of Beatrice Straight.

Between 1943 and 1954, Chekhov starred in nine Hollywood films. In 1945, after receiving an Academy Award nomination for his role as the psychoanalyst in Alfred Hitchcock's *Spellbound*, Chekhov resumed teaching his technique to young Hollywood actors. Marilyn Monroe, Jack Palance, and Anthony Quinn were among his students. In 1955, Michael Chekhov died of heart failure in his Hollywood home. Today, there are dozens of organizations exploring his technique all over the world.

In Chekhov's technique, the "internal" and "external" are inexorably linked, so much so that separating them would be more an academic exercise than artistic expression. Such separation might be necessary for discussion and training, but the stage bares the inevitable truth every time: If the actor cannot reconcile the unification of the "inner" and "outer," his acting is likely to be strained, unimaginative, and flat.

"Psychophysical" refers to the unification of the body with all that lies within it, though it may appear at times, and indeed it can be true, that the body and soul can be independent of each other. The "soul" is that intangible reservoir within us that acquires experiences: They can be imagined, thought about, or actually experienced. Like a savory stew, the soul acquires ingredients upon which the spirit will work.

The "spirit" is that which uses the body to take action, drawing upon the resources of the soul. The spirit "amalgamates, condenses, and draws conclusions," which the soul cannot do.

For actors, the soul, spirit, and body are in constant interplay, inhabiting each other in space, neither one before or after the other, like sea waves rippling into that which came before and all that follows. The soul and spirit require the body to express these ripples, which we might refer to as *sensations of feelings*.

Chekhov would suggest that movement awakens "sensations" of feelings. Sensations are physical responses to stimuli, like goose bumps. The goose bumps call up feelings, *some from real life and others from the imagination*. These sensations draw out feelings. The relationship between sensation and feeling might at first seem insignificant, but nothing could be further from the truth.

On stage, movement is sometimes visible, reaching the audience through their eyes. Other times, the movement is invisible and directly penetrates their hearts, such as in the case of sensations that flare out beyond the stage. The latter is still movement, even if the actor is not visibly moving. This is so because the actor is "radiating" at every moment. For example, when sitting, the actor is not a frozen statue, but living within that shape. As the actor lives in space, pauses become loaded with waves of imaginative impulses richer than any single memory could provide. Imagine a character sitting in an icy room on death row. The possibilities for sensations, inner gestures, and radiations are numerous and possibly infinite.

The body is capable of expressing an array of psychological values if we involve it from the inside, even if these values are so plentiful they defy intellectual inquiry and analysis. Such inquiry implies a possible distinction between the "inner" and "outer"—at least in the beginning. When practicing staccato movement, which is sharp, abrupt, we should try to experience this quality inwardly, even though we begin it outwardly. What is it like inwardly to experience any part of your body moving in a sharp way? What is it like psychologically to change thought patterns abruptly or think in a black-and-white way? Perhaps start with one body part, such as a hand or arm. The sharp movement will eventually awaken inner thoughts and impulses appropriate to that quality.[2] Eventually, the whole body must be incorporated. New feelings and sensations should not be limited only to those areas of the body that are already within your awareness and in tune with your imagination. You might have a habit of practicing a staccato quality in your arms because you're good at it or because it feels the most comfortable. That's fine for now, but eventually, you must awaken this quality in your whole body if you want to have access to the widest possible range of expression, which includes inner or "psychological" gesture, a hallmark of the Chekhov technique.

Great acting is comprised of movement, or "gesture," at every moment, but you need not explicitly develop gestures for every moment unless you want to. This is because you are intuitively already doing them when you are acting at your best. Any good performance is physically alive at every moment; the performer is radiating energy even when at rest; as Martha Graham said, we are still dancing inwardly even when we are still. Generally, psychological gestures, or "inner gestures," are helpful when you get stuck on a moment that just isn't working or the character's core is elusive. The "core" emerges from the question, "Who is this character?" The answer usually lies in the archetype of the character.

ARCHETYPES AND PROTOTYPES

Archetypes are forms, symbols, or images that have universal meaning and inspire an original model, or prototype. The prototype, in the case of an actor, is the character he creates.

Archetypes appear in our dreams, works of art, and historically in aspects of our culture, especially in such things as paintings, literature, and religious representations. The ancient Greek root *arche* means "the first." "Type" means to "imprint or impress" or "pattern." These impressions, as the psychologist Jung discovered, arise spontaneously from the unconscious in the form of images. "Because they appear as universal, collectively owned images, their symbolism evokes similar feelings, raises similar issues, and constellates similar behavior wherever they arise and enter into the life of an individual or a culture,"[3] notes Robert A. Johnson.

Imagine, for example, the archetype of the Warrior. We might see an image immediately, even if we have no experience with one, almost as if it were imprinted on our consciousness. The Warrior, Prisoner, and Skeptic are types, but human beings are made up of combinations of types, making us many-faceted, as in the following example from Johnson:

> Years ago a young graduate student came to work on his dreams with me, and a masculine figure began to appear repeatedly in his dreams. The student spontaneously invented his own name for this friendly male companion that showed a universal character. He called him "the tribal brother." The dreamer and his tribal brother lived among a tribe of Vikings in an ancient age in Europe.
>
> In some dreams he and his companion were warriors and went to battle together. In others, they were healers. In one they discovered a radiant and magical woman in a white robe who became the dreamer's consort. Together, they went through all the struggles and numerous discoveries of young manhood. The dreamer's friendship with his inner figure was so close, and felt so real, that he felt lonely whenever he had to go for many days without seeing him in his dreams.[4]

This archetype, as with all of them, is psychologically complex. For the actor, archetypes can be powerful tools to inspire a character prototype and its inner life, because such archetypes will spontaneously awaken sensation in the body. The sensations are what the body remembers and can repeat—feelings are less reliable and harder to recreate. You can try to command yourself to experience a feeling on the stage, but the result will probably be inartistic and marginally successful at best. But you can ask your imagination to show you the archetype of the Warrior. Often, the result is (1) a strong image that describes the "outer," (2) sensations resonating throughout your body that fill the "inner," and (3) a character prototype that is uniquely your own.[5] Other examples of archetypes include the Star, Magician, Addict, Lover, Prostitute, Prophet, and Clown. In order to awaken sensations, you will have to practice imagining them—an exercise that will become more fun than labor if you do it often enough.

Your imagination will respond if you can ask questions in the spirit of play. Ask yourself, "Who is my character?" Remember, you are going for the character at its core. The Prisoner on death row, for example, might have a way of walking or mannerism that is particular to his personality. Archetypically, he is the Prisoner. Elements of behavior and personality can be added later. It's important to begin with the character at is core: the root, the impulse. Think of it as the original impression of who the person is. Be careful of layering on personality traits too soon, because it is possible that you will limit the character to preconceived notions born of habit rather than imagination. The *sequence* of the work is important here: Start with the archetype and then layer on the personality.

Begin by looking at the first three or four things the character *does* in the script. Romeo, for example:

- Stays out all night with Rosaline
- Greets the Friar in the early morning and professes his love
- Denounces his love of Rosaline upon seeing Juliet at a party

The unfortunate trap that many young Romeos fall into is that of the Lover—a dull and unimaginative response to the facts that Shakespeare gives us. At a recent workshop on archetypes, several of my ethnically diverse colleagues came up with the following possibilities for Romeo:

- Alley cat
- Gambler
- A Playa
- Snoop Doggy Dog
- Tomcat
- Businessman
- Salesman
- Peacock

What wonderful responses to a character who has been around for four hundred years! To you, some of them might be stereotypes, which are usually preconceived and oversimplified ideas of the characteristics that typify a person or thing. Don't be alarmed if you think in stereotypical terms, but seek to go more deeply before you start to make choices about the personality of the character. You may not agree with the above responses, but that's okay. Your unique imagination will create something entirely your own if you let it. Imagine the witches in *Macbeth*. They appear, hail, cook, conjure, and predict—among other things. What do you see? Certainly the Prophet is among the possibilities—quite a different direction than what we might think of as a more stereotypical witch.

Once you have a sense of who the character is (the archetype), imagine yourself as the character, and walk around the space asking, "What do I want?" Pay close attention to what your body is doing. Let's imagine the Prisoner. Is your body opening, closing, clutching, pushing? Even the smallest movements of the fingers should be considered. Does the movement suggest some sort of a push, as if the archetype wants to escape?

Whatever the body is doing should be favored over any discussion of the topic. Don't try to label or talk too much about what is happening. If it's a push, then it's a push. Keep it simple. Behavioral movement, such as scratching, smoking, etc., can be layered on later. It's the purity of your initial impulse that produces inner gesture.

GESTURE

Once you have an archetype that feels right to you, and you have a sense of what your character wants, then your body is probably already trying to tell you something. If you're not careful, however, the "sneaking and sniffing" analytical mind, as Chekhov cautions, could put a stop to it and kill sensation.

What is the "sneaking and sniffing" weasel that Chekhov refers to? It's anything that kills your enthusiasm for creative play—a thought or impulse, probably born of some inhibiting habit, that prevents you from experiencing new sensations in your body. Its power over us can be strong, suggesting thoughts like, "I'm not good enough," "That actor is so bad, and because of him, I can't concentrate," or "My belly is too big, and I hope nobody sees it." This side of your psychology can play a major role if you are unable to focus on the positive, the imaginative, what you like about this or that actor or yourself instead of what you don't like. Insecurity with any part of the body can result in enough self-criticism to inhibit the creation of your own character prototype—killed forever because of a critical impulse arising from an agenda that is anything but creative.

The "Higher Intellect,"[6] as Chekhov points out, is born of the heart and does not have the destructive quality of the "cold, calculating mind." This "thinking heart" is the companion of the creative spirit and should always be invited to participate in the process. The Higher Intellect is curious, helpful, and supportive. Its analysis is exacting, but gentle, deferring to the synthesizing power of the creative spirit.

Movement for Actors

Chekhov never intended for our acting to be brainless. In fact, if it were, our choices would lack clarity. But the intellect must have a supportive quality in order to be effective in our creative work.[7]

Assuming the calculating mind has been subdued, in favor of the Higher Intellect, begin moving about the space, guided by the impulse from what your character wants. A teacher or playmate is particularly helpful at this point, because you will need feedback as to how and in what ways your body is responding. Pay particular attention to those seemingly meaningless little movements that might express the want. A small opening of the chest area might suggest, for example, that your character wants to expose his or her heart, or to "open." Imagine such an impulse coming from our archetypal Prisoner. Here, we would have a character who perhaps has committed violent acts and yearns to admit or reveal something in the deepest recesses of his soul. I can't help but be reminded of Sean Penn's exquisite performance in *Dead Man Walking* when I imagine the archetype this way. A full exploration of the impulse will provide you with the information you need to determine if "opening" is the artistic choice for your portrayal.

While working on *A Midsummer Night's Dream* with two actors of the Chekhov Theatre Ensemble, for example, I asked the actress playing Helena what she wanted in order to invoke the inner gesture. She provided a long and detailed answer, going on and on until I eventually just stopped her and said, "All that might be true, but tell me in one word or less what she wants." Her brain, having toiled over a complicated intellectual answer, didn't have enough information to be succinct. Her body, however, responded immediately, spontaneously, and visibly. At least to me.

Her arms and fingers were clearly pulling—the movements were very small, but they were there. At first, she didn't understand how the tiniest pulling of her fingers had anything to do with Helena, until she realized that Helena wants Demetrius—she needs Demetrius so much that the Addict came to mind as an archetype. Imagine that! Helena as the Addict. I'm sure most people would not traditionally approach it that way, but if you penetrate into the core of who she is, you might discover that the Addict could be a possibility, depending on how your director is thinking of her in the context of the production as a whole.

Now, the actress needed to experience the essence of pulling him toward her, but not with just her fingers.

The task before us now was to develop a gesture that embodied the essence of "pull" in her whole body. Her feet remained flat on the ground—important so that the shape of the gesture can easily be repeated without going off-balance. We started the movement in the opposite place of the "pull" in order to give us the greatest polarity.[8] Her arms were pushed outwardly with her torso full front. Her feet were about three and a half feet apart. Starting from this position, she then "pulled" with her arms, shifting her weight onto her back foot, as she released a sound: "Ahhhhhhhhhhhhhh."[9] After a bit of side coaching, she eventually involved the whole body, including her head.[10]

When she eventually had a gesture that seemed right to her, we worked on the shape, tempo, and quality of the gesture, until it inspired her as she said, "I want Demetrius." We discovered that a staccato quality seemed truer to her than a more legato quality, even though legato was more sensual, which might have been our choice had we remained at the surface level of the Lover.

It is important to play with a gesture a bit before rejecting it, because the answer might lie in how it is done as much as in its shape. Repeat the gesture at least three times, radiating at the end of each form and inviting the voice along. You can start out with a release of sound, such as in "Ahhhhhhhhhhh,"[11] allowing the gesture to color the voice. Let the voice evolve to language—"I want Demetrius"—and then play with other lines of text with the gesture. With each successive radiation, the gesture will become more powerful and awaken stronger psychological values within the voice and body.

Repeat the gesture at least three times, pausing at the end of each repetition to allow the radiations to flow through you. Walk around the room, see yourself doing the gesture inwardly, and now, speak some of your lines. You might discover that doing the gesture inwardly becomes more powerful than physically doing it. Imagine Helena as described above: as the Addict, inwardly pulling, professing her love with a need that burns—quite a different rendition than we might expect from a syrupy lover.[12]

Once the actor generated the essence of "pull" through repetition and radiation of her gesture, she awakened a desperation and urgency in the character that was as amusing as it was heartbreaking. Allowing breath to release with each subsequent pull, the actress evolved onto solid sound and eventually speech through her gesture. Her resulting performance was remarkably complex and emotionally rich— all emerging from the embodiment and simplicity of "pull." The "pull" was a distillation of more complex elements.

When her "pulling" Helena was combined with the "pushing" Demetrius, we were able to stage the scene in forty-five minutes. The actor's imagination created the inner life, and her body awakened sensations of feelings that were complex and compelling. Because the actors had approached the underlying psychology of the scene through gesture, rather than through an emotional memory or personal substitution approach, they were able to step out of the play and back into their everyday lives without harm to their personal psychology.[13]

This approach served us well when we had only four weeks to stage *King Lear*, which some scholars consider impossible to stage, even with an infinite amount of rehearsal time. Not only was it possible, the Ensemble received an Off-Off-Broadway Award, which cited the outstanding acting, among other distinctions.

By distilling characters or scenic moments to their core gestures, you can achieve performances that are so psychologically complex that it would take reams of paper to describe them. In Helena's final moments in the scene before Demetrius rejects her, the actress radiated hope, despair, desperation, loss, rage, confusion, and decisiveness in her fleeting moments, as we experienced her yearning need for him. Were I to ask her to feel all of these things, she probably would have failed—not to mention that the process would have been as unpleasant as it would be ineffective.

GETTING STUCK

The invariable question arises when working with movement: What's wrong if my gesture doesn't awaken anything in me? There are two possibilities that I have seen over the years: (1) the archetype, gesture, and rhythms, tempos, or other qualities need to be modified until you feel some sort of inspiration, or (2) you are not sufficiently "in your body" to experience the gesture, and some preliminary work needs to be done.

The former is easier to deal with, because a few adjustments, often minor, could awaken you in entirely new ways. If you aren't "in your body," there could be a stiffness brought on by years of habitual use of the body. If this is true, then it is too soon for you to engage in psychological gesture: Releasing extraneous tension in the body should be priority one. There are many good approaches to do this through conventional movement trainings (such as Alexander or Feldenkrais), which make wonderful introductions to the basic exercises of Michael Chekhov. Every effort should be made to inhabit your body, or "be in your body," while doing the basic exercises or engaging in other movement training.

"In your body" means that every aspect of your inner world coexists with every aspect of your outer world. The body is constantly acquiring knowledge, expressing feelings, and awakening sensation in the whole body: toes, feet, back of legs, inner thighs, and the oblique muscles that are often neglected. Our world has become so civilized that we often forget that we inhabit our bodies for only moments on the spectrum of time. If you spend a lot of time sitting down with your legs crossed, find a way to hang upside down and pretend to be a bat.

BASIC EXERCISES

The basic exercises are essential to establishing and maintaining psychophysical alignment. They encourage the imagination to stream through the body, awakening areas that might be stiff or not particularly expressive. As a visual artist's palette contains many colors, so, too, must an actor's body and voice comprise a palette of "psychological values." Without this kind of psychophysical development, the actor might fall victim to, "But Mr. Director, I *am* feeling the inner life of the character," and the director responds, "But Mr. Actor, that's not what's coming across."

The actor's job is not to feel, but to *express and embody* all aspects of character in a theatrical context. How can he do this if the character wants to move in a legato way and the actor is only able to express himself through staccato forms? Not only is it impossible, but interminably frustrating for actor, director, and audience.

Basic exercises used at the Ensemble to develop psychological values and best enable inner gesture include:

- Staccato and legato
- Flying, floating/flowing,[14] molding, radiating
- Expansion/contraction
- Ease, form, beauty, and the whole

Because the basic exercises and atmospheres are thoroughly explained in *To the Actor* and its subsequent incarnations, I will describe the following exercises in order to provide an idea of our particular approach to them.

Staccato

Begin by moving one part of your body in a sharp way. Invite another part of the body to join in, and then another, until the whole body is involved. Blink the eyes in a staccato way; twist the torso, reach with the arms, open the legs, and lengthen the spine. Breathe and release sound. What is the experience like? What sensations and feelings accompany the movement? What kinds of sounds come out of you? Variations include adding language in improvisational circumstances.

Legato

Begin by moving one part of your body in a smooth and seamless way.[15] Invite another part of the body and then another, until the whole body is involved. Blink the eyes in a legato way; twist the torso, reach with the arms, open the legs, and lengthen the spine. Pay particular attention to the lower body, and invite it to move seamlessly. Breathe and release sound. What kinds of sounds come out of you? Variations include adding language in improvisational circumstances.

Contraction as Sensation

Make your body as small as you can by placing your forehead on the floor, arms and hands flopped to the side.[17] Imagine yourself as tiny as you can. Allow breath into your body and release sound. What is it like to be so small? What sensations are awakened in your body?

Expansion as Sensation [16]

Make your body as big as a shining star—arms, legs, and face spread apart. Allow breath into your body and release sound. What is it like to be so large? What sensations are awakened in your body?

Contraction/Expansion as Gesture

This time, begin with your two feet flat on the floor; weight distributed so that you can move with ease. Make your body small in a way that feels comfortable for you. Allow the sensations of contraction to awaken, but do not squeeze your muscles. Then, grow the body into expansion, and end the gesture with the sensations of expansion. You can play with the tempo, rhythm, and other qualities. Try it slow, fast, staccato, legato, heavy, light, and so on. How do the different qualities affect you inwardly? Repeat the experience, but start in an expanded way and move to a contracted shape. How does the movement of "closing" affect the experience?

It is important for me to reiterate that the use of breath and voice evolved over time at the Ensemble and is a departure from Chekhov. We have found that, without an integrated approach, actors are often able to fulfill the character in the body but not the voice. The result has been that voice and speech processes have had to "catch up" to reflect the complex psychological values developed in the body—a dichotomy that is frustrating and avoidable. Perhaps it is helpful to think of the voice as emerging from a complex array of muscles, some of which are small and most of which are internal but no less absent from the whole body than any other part of us.

FINAL TIPS

Chekhov never intended for psychological gesture to be performed onstage. Like the technique of F. Matthias Alexander (a contemporary of Chekhov), psychological gesture is intended as a "means-whereby" to enable the fullest possible expression.[18] This "means-whereby" is particularly important to note: Ultimately, any technique should liberate you to be brilliant and inspired. It must never be used as a substitute for your talent, but, like any good technique, must be used to *enable* it. You might find there are roles that you play brilliantly with little such development. But you will need a technique to inspire you for roles that are less accessible. Even then, your goal should be to play the character, the scene, the play as beautifully as possible—with audacity, imagination, and theatrical truth—using the technique to enable such expression and never as a substitute for it, which is perhaps the greatest example of the partnership between the "inner" and the "outer."

If you are going to undertake the Chekhov work, it will be necessary to train with a good teacher. Most artists cannot derive all that they need to from books, not even Mr. Chekhov's. That said, some things to keep in mind when working:

- Approach character through archetypes. It is likely to lead you to a unique prototype.
- Do movements from the inside. What sensations, feelings, and impulses are awakened within you when you are moving? Use your body in entirely new ways. If it feels strange or odd, then you're exploring new territory (just don't hurt yourself).
- Release breath and sound. Though Mr. Chekhov precluded voice and speech from his work until his collaboration with Rudolf Steiner, our work at the Chekhov Theatre Ensemble has shown that integrated breath awareness is as much a part of the psychophysical process as any other part of the body. Do not force breath out, manufacture language, or indulge an impulse to make the release audible: *Breath should stream out of and through the body as a result of the movement*, similarly to the way a sigh comes out from an impulse of relief. It might be a good idea to do some of your Chekhov exercises with a voice and speech teacher with whom you have worked to see what he or she has to say about it.

Psychological gestures should:

- Be archetypal and involve the whole body.
- Generally involve two feet flat on the floor.
- Be well-shaped with a sense of beginning, middle, and end.
- Involve breath and sound.
- Embody the character as a whole, a fragment of it, or a moment in the scene.
- Be performed inwardly when acting.
- Be repeated three times in succession with radiation between each repetition.
- Inspire you.

If your psychological gesture doesn't inspire you, change it or get rid of it until you find something that does. Play with its rhythms, tempos, and qualities. You might discover that the same shape dramatically changes in psychological values with the smallest adjustment.

- Let your imagination soar above common bounds, but do not extend yourself beyond that which you can do with a feeling of ease. You're not competing.
- Invite your Higher Intellect into the process to help you make artistic choices.

Inhabit and trust your body with every aspect of your consciousness. It will reveal and express entirely new renditions of even age-old characters if you can recognize and develop your impulses. The body desires, in the words of Leonardo da Vinci, to "dwell with the soul, because without the members of the body the soul can neither act nor feel."

Thank you to Kelly Ellenwood, Jerry Homan, and Joe Hoover for their assistance in the preparation of this article.

NOTES

1. Laurence Senelick. ed. *Wandering Stars: Russian Emigre Theatre, 1905–1940* (Studies in Theatre History and Culture). Iowa City: University of Iowa Press, November 1992. Michael Chekhov chapter by Deirdre Hurst du Prey.
2. Sometimes, characters will move with the opposite quality of that which would describe their inner life. A character could be outwardly staccato, but inwardly legato—moving with a sharp quality, but thinking in a languid way.
3. Johnson, Robert A. *Inner Work: Using Dreams and Active Imagination for Personal Growth.* San Francisco: Harper & Row Publishers, 1986.
4. Ibid.
5. Actors sometimes skip the first two steps of archetypes and prototypes, particularly when playing classical roles. They often get stuck trying to re-create or mimic other artists' prototypes, such as with Marlon Brando's prototype of Stanley Kowalski in *A Streetcar Named Desire.*
6. From Michael Chekhov's 1955 Hollywood Lecture Series, Lincoln Center Library.
7. Think of this as a symbiotic inner relationship, similar to those relationships we have on the "outside" that make the most profound experiences possible. In a recent yearlong project at P.S. 145, Brooklyn, for example, I was teaching theatrical skills, strategies, and processes in partnership with public school teachers in grades three, four and five. In my role as "artist," I focused on direct instruction and experiential activities that reinforced them. The classroom teachers and Jane Remer, researcher and evaluator, served the project as the wise "scientists" who made curricular connections, helped me to include age-appropriate vocabulary, and offered suggestions to improve the process. One such suggestion was that I teach the fifth grade first, fourth grade second, and third grade last in order that I could "rehearse" my lesson and internally edit by the time I got to the third grade. I marveled at the simplicity of the idea and how it might never have occurred to me had I not had the benefit of these "wise scientists."
8. Polarity is ending the gesture in the opposite place from where you began it. When working with polarity, it is important to consider levels above and below, as well as in front and behind. This provides the greatest psychological power to the movement.
9. The use of sound is a departure from Chekhov, but essential for the actor to express the inner gesture through the voice as much as through the body.
10. The head must be incorporated in a way that contributes to the shape of the gesture. If your head is reluctant, you're probably thinking too much.
11. Be careful of manipulating the voice. Let it stream out as a result of the movement.
12. I have nothing against lovers, but it really is not a compelling approach for either Helena or Demetrius, given what each of the characters does.
13. In Stanislavsky's "Method," a personal substitution approach to conjuring feelings has often resulted in mental instability of actors who attempt to recall memories from their pasts—"cold dishes of yesterday," as Chekhov refers to it. A little-known fact is that Stanislavsky favored the "theory of physical actions" close to his death—an approach that is akin to Chekhov's "psychophysical" technique.
14. There is some disagreement about whether Chekhov meant "floating" or "flowing." Deirdre Hurst du Prey doesn't recall a distinction, his book cites "floating," and I was trained in "floating." Some Chekhov teachers insist on "flowing." Both legato in quality, floating and flowing are distinctive: floating more buoyant and flowing more streaming. Each artist, however, will have to discern for his or herself how and in what ways they are distinguishable.
15. Pay particular note of any part of your body that is jerky. Work with that area of the body until you can move it in a seamless, legato way. Allow a smoothness into areas of the body that are jerky or staccato. You might need to release age-old habits in order to do this.
16. Some teachers have referred to Expansion/Contraction as a "psychological gesture." This is true when *moving* from one shape to the other, as described in the subsequent exercise. I recommend, however, that the *sensations* of each are fully experienced prior to moving from one to the other.
17. This shape discourages the impulse to move. The focus here should be on experiencing the *sensations* of the form.
18. Alexander, F. Matthias. *The Resurrection of the Body: The Essential Writings of F. Matthias Alexander.* Boston: Shambhala Publications, 1986.

Theatrical Stillness

Mary Fleischer

In an anthology devoted to the subject of movement, it seems only fitting to explore the theatrical potential of stillness. Ranging from fixity to transcendence, the experience of stillness onstage for both performer and audience heightens our awareness of the duration of the present moment. The most emblematic word of the last century may well have been "faster," but the absence of visible movement—stillness—holds an enduring fascination. Just consider the popularity of street performers who pose as "living statues": Our curiosity is piqued to look for signs of life—breathing, a blink, a slight swaying or flinching—to give away their artifice. Stillness abstracts physical form, while asking us to reconsider what it is to be alive, sensate, and human.

Theater is the art of time: We expect something to happen, to exhibit change, to take its course. How we perceive the quality of a particular slice of time is determined by the particular rhythms and tempos a performance establishes through the movements of actors and visual elements, the ebb and flow of language, music, and sound, and, most importantly, the synergistic combination of elements. Stillness can connote a wide range of emotional states—from calm, meditation, exhaustion, sleep, dream, and trance to extreme attitudes of rigidity and panic. From an actor's studied hesitation to a telling stage picture frozen in tableau, stillness throws into relief the whole notion of time onstage—it compels us to consider what brought us to this present stillness and to anticipate a release into the future, into action, once again. The stillness of the body in live performance has a particular resonance, since that body occupies the same time and space as the audience and our experience of rhythm and tempo are related to pulse and emotion. Our connection to the performer is a kinesthetic one, as we watch a body not unlike our own breathing and held in space, still in a dynamic relationship to gravity.

Like silence, stillness is a grounding or blank canvas from which a production springs and can remain a dynamic and expressive element. In rehearsal, we need to locate a still point from which to perceive a movement or blocking sequence, and our memory of stage movement usually takes the form of a series of frozen or cumulative pictures we unconsciously select to remember. Stillness has been likened to the Japanese aesthetic concept of the spaces between the lines of a visual design being as important as the lines themselves—seeing the lines as borders for the spaces. Thus stillness can be used to create a kind of theatrical punctuation or accentuation. Frequent or irregularly occurring stillnesses may yield an uneasy effect, for example, while regularly spaced still intervals might have a more ritualistic or steady mood. Many actor-training methods of the twentieth century value stillness as a starting or "centering" point. Jacques Copeau stressed that actors should work from a "neutral" departure point, a state of readiness:

> To start from silence and calm. That is the first point. An actor must know how to be silent, to listen, respond, keep still, begin a gesture, develop it, return to stillness and to silence, with all the tones and halftones that those actions imply.[1]

From the work of Copeau's student, Etienne Decroux, Anne Dennis further elaborates:

> An actor without skills finds stillness very difficult . . . such a technique implies a prepared, breath-
> ing, concentrated actor, with clear intentions, permitting the action to be sustained in the inaction.
> Stillness commands great power and authority in the theatre space. An actor must learn how to use
> it. Stillness gives clarity to relationships. It brings focus to a moment or rest to the end of a thought
> (much as a full stop does in diction). It gives the audience space in which to take in the process
> leading up to and causing an action; stillness permits the transitional moments to be seen.[2]

The contemporary director JoAnne Akalaitis has explored stillness as a punctuation to movement and has
developed what she calls a "stopping-and-starting" aesthetic in her projects. She is interested in a style
where actions, scenes, and even characters come to a complete stop, and then something entirely new
begins with a fresh attack. The stopping is motionless but energized and allows time for the actors physically to "understand what it means to stop."[3]

TABLEAUX VIVANTS

Perhaps the most obvious form of performing stillness is representational posing, which can be traced
back to antiquity. *Tableaux vivants*, the frozen arrangements of costumed performers, were used to
reproduce scenes from religion, art, and literature throughout theater history. The medieval church displayed tableaux from the Bible in procession, and allegorical tableaux were a popular form of entertainment and an important component of the Renaissance masque. As a means to heighten moral themes, the
tableau vivant became a major technique to culminate the acts of nineteenth-century melodrama. In
recent years, tableaux have most often been employed in musicals. The 1969 Sherman Edwards–Peter
Stone musical *1776* culminated in a frozen-in-time enactment of the famous Pine-Savage painting of the
ratification of the Declaration of Independence. Stephen Sondheim and James Lapine's staged Georges
Seurat's pointillist painting *A Sunday Afternoon on the Island of La Grande Jatte* as a stunning tableau
vivant for their 1984 musical *Sunday in the Park with George.*

The *pose plastique*, in which performers imitated classical art, was popular throughout the nineteenth century in various forms, as troupes toured Europe and America and performers became a feature
of cabaret and music hall performance. The form could also be considered a rather risqué attraction. In
1894, a heated public controversy arose over the display of "Living Statues" at London's Palace Theatre
for a mixed audience. Here, women who were scantily clad in muslin (which was sculpted to their corset-
ted bodies by applications of plaster of paris) re-created well-known paintings with such titles as
"Ariadne" (picturing a naked woman on the back of a lion) and "The Polar Star" (depicting an almost
nude woman standing on a pedestal and holding above her head an electric lamp).[4] Stillness exposes the
body to close scrutiny, and its lack of action, of forward movement, allows the audience to "read" the
static image at its own pace and follow its own train of thought. Hence, these "Living Statues" created quite
a scandal, which summoned judgments from the major critics of the day, including George Bernard Shaw,
Max Beerbohm, and Arthur Symons. Depending on what side of the controversy you were on, the stillness
of these plastiques either distanced and tamed their erotic power or provided languorous and corrupting
opportunities for the male gaze.

While plastique performers at the Palace may have commanded little respect, the American Genevieve

Stebbins elevated the art of statue posing to express "universal truths" as exhibited by Greek statuary, and her work influenced several early modern dancers, notably Isadora Duncan and Ruth St. Denis. Stebbins developed the ideas of a French teacher of acting and aesthetics, François Delsarte, and his pupil Steele Mackaye into an activity that she believed would produce both physical and spiritual benefits:

> Artistic statue-posing is not mere external imitation of Greek marble. It is something infinitely greater. It is a creative work of intellectual love . . . a spiritual aspiration toward a superior and definite type of beauty, in which lives and moves a human soul.[5]

For the Delsarteans, stillness was a product of "dynamic opposition" and "harmonic equilibrium," where the legs, torso, and head are all in counterbalance with one another, and corresponded to an ideal of "moral pose."[6] As Nancy Lee Chalfa Ruyter has shown,[7] Stebbins started by studying statues and photographs for models and, unlike other Delsarteans, developed a style of performance that presented posing as a series of images in which transitions into and out of the poses were of equal interest:

> Stand in front of a large mirror and attempt to make yourself a living duplicate of the picture . . . whenever a series of statues is gone through, one form must gradually melt into the other by the following rules: (a) Regarding each statue as an attitude expressing an impression, the rules of transition of attitude and gesture should be carefully observed, such as the arm moving in an opposite direction to the pointing of the hand; (b) harmonious balancing of arm to arm; (c) preparatory movement in opposite direction to intended attitude; and, finally, rhythm of movement in harmony with character of statue or emotion depicted.[8]

Stebbins was exploring the different qualities that stillness can take on, depending upon where and how it occurs in a movement sequence. Like mask work, the use of stillness makes the performer aware of the expressivity of her total body. Moving in and out of stillness means shaping tensions and impulses to increase or decrease gradually, or to start and stop in a more abrupt fashion. The particular kind of transition into or out of stillness helps to define to a large degree the emotional temper of the stillness itself: the stillness just after stopping or just before starting, the stillness of resisting movement, the stillness of withdrawal and meditation, the stillness of waiting and anticipation.

AVANT-GARDE INNOVATIONS

The theatrical avant-garde of the early twentieth century was drawn to the powers of stillness, in tandem with a renewed interest in the human body. Reacting against the excesses of nineteenth-century acting styles, of Romantic histrionics and period melodrama, many reformers sought to abstract and depersonalize the actor's performance and to reconceptualize it in terms of visual art, music, and dance.

Responding to the materialistic qualities of modern life, the symbolist theater strove to regain a lost wholeness through unearthing links to myth and ancient rituals, exploring border states of consciousness, and experimenting with sensory correspondences, or synesthesia. They evolved an acting style that was stylized and static, movement was slow and hieratic, and the iconography of painters from the emerging Nabis group (including Paul Bonnard, Eduard Vuillard, and Paul Sérusier) greatly influenced the look of the actors' gestures and poses. The use of scrim and evocative lighting on a mostly bare stage helped to integrate the actor into the whole decor, and a simplification of means was employed to evoke an inner reality rather than illustrate an objective one. In 1891, Paul Fort announced that performances at his Théâtre d'Art in Paris would henceforth

conclude with the mise-en-scène of a painting of a new school which has not yet been exhibited publicly or which is still in progress. The curtain will be raised for three minutes to show the tableau vivant. Actors and models will represent the immobile and silent figures. . . . The combination of scenic music and perfumed scents relevant to the subject of the painting will prepare and subsequently perfect the artistic impact of the work. . . . As Baudelaire stated, the perfumes, colors, and sounds are in reciprocal correspondence.[9]

Although the staging of these symbolist tableaux didn't become a regular practice as Fort had wished, his experiment of utilizing a still image as a focal point for a multisensory performance raises interesting questions about how our senses interrelate. While vision might dominate as we contemplate a fixed image, the suspension of forward time that stillness offers allows for the freer interplay of other senses and "reciprocal correspondences."

The stillness evoked by contemporary painting also inspired the playwright and theater reformer W. B. Yeats. Early in his career as a playwright, Yeats investigated how poetry could interact with other arts of the theater. Although the Pre-Raphaelites created paintings and portraits with specific subjects, Yeats was most drawn to the flat, two-dimensional, stylized elements of their work and the remote and timeless qualities they evoked. As Elizabeth Loizeaux has pointed out,[10] Yeats imagined his early stage pictures as paintings and associated them with the works he admired, first those of his father, J. B. Yeats, and later especially those of Dante Gabriel Rossetti, Edward Burne-Jones, and William Morris. He often saw Pre-Raphaelite paintings as frozen moments of drama and sometimes worked from favorite paintings when writing plays. Yeats perceived that stylized gesture and stillness could convey symbolic meaning in performance, as he witnessed in Sarah Bernhardt and De Max's performance of *Phèdre* in 1902:

For long periods the performers would merely stand and pose . . . I noticed, too, that the gestures had a rhythmic progression. Sarah Bernhardt would keep her hands clasped over, let us say, her right breast for some time, and then move them to the other side, perhaps, lowering her chin till it touched her hands, and then, after another long stillness, she would unclasp them and hold one out . . . until she had exhausted all the gestures of uplifted hands. Through one long scene De Max . . . never lifted his hand above his elbow . . . Beyond them stood a crowd of white-robed men who never moved at all, and the whole scene had the nobility of Greek sculpture, and an extraordinary reality and intensity.[11]

Yeats's call for stillness had other implications about the body and inner life. Influenced by the occult belief that the unconscious could be tapped by keeping the body still, Yeats revered those

who follow the old rule [and] keep their bodies still and their minds awake and clear, dreading especially any confusion between the images of the mind and the objects of sense; they seek to become, as it were, polished mirrors.[12]

The image of a still body as a mirror to the unconscious connotes a border state of awareness between waking and dream, living and dead. Allied with stillness is the idea of the trance state, where the body serves as a kind of mask pointing to possession by multiple inner selves and forces. Yeats believed that true tragic art would bring his audience to "the intensity of trance."[13]

Gordon Craig called for the gradual replacement of the actor by an "Über-marionette," which "will not compete with Life—but rather will go beyond it. Its ideal will not be the flesh and blood but rather the body in Trance."[14] Craig was particularly struck by Isadora Duncan's use of stasis, which she credited to having learned from Eleonora Duse and Ellen Terry and which was the chief virtue of the marionette.[15] Throughout the modernist period, theater artists were enthralled by automata, puppets, marionettes, and mime as an emphasis on a language of the body eclipsed the primacy of spoken language. Puppets and shadow plays were an important component of cabaret entertainment, and particularly at the first Russian cabaret, the Letuchaya Mysh (or "Flying Mouse"), in Moscow. As Harold Segel has described, the cabaret's founder, Nikita Baliev, developed a unique variation on "living statues" called "living doll" performances, in which elaborately costumed actors composed frozen pictures as puppets, marionettes, or dolls. At a certain point, they came to "life" by singing, dancing, and speaking, only to return to their immobile state.[16] The appeal of these performances was the striking contrast between the still and animate actors, and the skill with which the actors made the transitions.

Maurice Maeterlinck, one of the first playwrights and theorists of symbolist drama, also wrestled with reconceiving the physical theater to serve his poetic and spiritual visions. Maeterlinck went considerably further than Craig and recommended that

one should perhaps eliminate the living being from the stage . . . Will the day come when sculpture . . . will be used onstage? Will the human being be replaced by a shadow? a reflection? a projection of symbolic forms, or a being who would appear to live without being alive?[17]

Neither Craig nor Maeterlinck were really trying to get rid of the actor, but were looking for an expanded grammar of physical expression in which the performer functioned as a pliable, artistic medium. Maeterlinck rejected the "tragique des grandes aventures" as superficial and diversionary and argued for a "tragédie immobile," where

an old man, seated in his armchair, waiting patiently, with his lamp beside him . . . motionless as he is, does yet live in reality a deeper, more human and more universal life than the lover who strangles his mistress . . . I shall be told, perhaps, that a motionless life would be invisible, that therefore animation must be conferred upon it, and that such varied movement as would be acceptable is to be found only in the few passions of which use has hitherto been made. I do not know whether it be true that a static theatre is impossible. Indeed, to me it seems to exist already.[18]

For Maeterlinck, the stillness and silence of a static theater opened a window to spiritual and mysterious forces that control human life and helped to create simple characters of universal significance. Almost half a century later, Samuel Beckett created a drama that, like Maeterlinck's, pared down action and character to create highly compressed and static images for the human condition. Vladimir and Estragon's waiting is reinforced by the stage direction, "*They do not move*," occurring at the end of each act of *Waiting for Godot*. Other Beckett characters are stilled by physical images of degenerating life:

Hamm's parents are planted in dustbins, Winnie is buried to her neck in a mound of sand, and the adulterers of *Play* are immobilized in funeral urns.

Vsevolod Meyerhold's early work concentrated on techniques to move beyond realism and to develop a stylized directorial style that could do justice to the new plays of Maeterlinck, Hauptmann, Schnitzler, and others. Konstantin Rudnitsky describes what Meyerhold called his "motionless" theater as

> a theatre of slow, significant, profound motions . . . in which the plastic form of the acting was intended to give not a plastic rendering of human motion in real life (as the Moscow Art Theatre tried to do), but the slow "music" of motion in harmony with the hidden spirit of the play. The plastic form was subordinated to the musical rhythm of the motion, not to its real-life logic. Sometimes, at especially significant moments of the action, the actors suddenly froze. At such moments, human faces and bodies became living sculptures.[19]

When Meyerhold directed Maeterlinck's *The Death of Tintagiles*, he sought an artistic synthesis of design, music, and acting. A pattern of stylized poses and gestures were employed to express "an exterior calm that conceal[ed] volcanic emotions with everything light and unforced."[20] For his production of *Hedda Gabler* in 1906, Meyerhold abstracted Ibsen's realistic setting to a shallow downstage playing area, influenced by the ideas of Georg Fuchs. Movement was reduced to a minimum, and much of the action was immobilized, as when Hedda and Loevborg are alone for the first time in Act II:

> Throughout the entire scene they sit side by side, tense and motionless, looking straight ahead. Their quiet, disquieting words fall rhythmically from lips which seem dry and cold. Before them stand two glasses and a flame burns beneath the punch bowl . . . Not once throughout the entire long scene do they alter the direction of their gaze or their pose. Only on the line "Then you too have a thirst for life!" does Loevborg make a violent motion towards Hedda, and at this point the scene comes to an abrupt conclusion.[21]

Meyerhold used this trance-like stillness so that the audience members would feel as if the characters were directly speaking to them, and they would be acutely aware of the slightest changes in expression, thereby intuiting hidden emotions.

Directors and actors working in an expressionist style also used stillness to abstract the actor's performance. While naturalistic actors employed gestures and facial expressions to give their performance a lifelike quality, the expressionist actor selected and essentialized body positions and gestures to project strong emotional states. Such focused concentration yielded the intense stare and absorbed stillness we associate with expressionist acting, and the use of stillness set off expressionism's intense vocal style. David Kuhns has cogently pointed out that there was a strong connection between vocal dynamics and physical stasis in expressionist acting, as he describes regarding a production of Paul Kornfeld's 1920 play, *The Seduction*:

> Movement . . . appears to have been a matter of symbolic posturing. Such poses as that of the crucifixion, or the arms raised high, or arms held at the side, were not merely arbitrarily chosen signs . . . They were the physical means of throwing vocal expression into relief by establishing a physical tension of expressive contrast with the voice. While the actor waxed eloquent for two or three pages

he apparently would assume a pose and hold it. In such moments, Expressionist physicalization became literally sculptural.[22]

A major director of the time, Leopold Jessner, devised a system of multiple acting levels on a bare stage ("Jessnertreppen"), on which stylized gesture and facial expression were set off in stark relief to project inner vision. His staging compelled a kind of statuesque performance and a convention whereby an actor could move and gesture only when speaking his own lines; everyone else onstage had to remain frozen in pose and not react to the speaker. These groupings were said to have "the stiffness and symmetry of primitive effigies. They strove for the effect of a relief."[23]

As seen with several twentieth-century movements, the stillness of the actor is often described as "statuesque," and as such brings allusions to antiquity and a pantheon of classical characters. Even though a production might not use specific classical characters, an overlay of myth and the impulse to discover analogies can all be implied by still, archaic poses. Very early in her dance career, Isadora Duncan was inspired by Eleonora Duse's use of stillness and presence, which created a kind of mythic stature, as she witnessed in the actress's performance in Pinero's realistic drama, *The Second Mrs. Tanqueray*, during a scene of suicidal despair, Duncan recalls that Duse unexpectedly

> stood quite still, alone on the stage. Suddenly, without any special outward movement, she seemed to grow and grow until her head appeared to touch the roof of the theatre, like the moment when Demeter appeared before the house of Metaneira…In that supreme gesture Duse was no longer the second Ms. Tanqueray, but some wonderful goddess of all ages . . . I said to myself, when I come on the stage and stand as still as Eleonora Duse did tonight, and, at the same time, create that tremendous force of dynamic movement, then I shall be the greatest dancer in the world.[24]

Introducing statuesque or still figures into a context where we expect life-like movement fascinates and can create a sense of mystery and unease through blurring divisions between divine and human, living and dead, art and life, body and soul. Their stillness increases our curiosity about the interior impetus for the gesture and heightens our search for clues in the outward form the body takes. As Freud noted,[25] there is an "uncanniness" or eeriness about inanimate objects coming to life. The image of a stilled performer is partly familiar in that we know that this is a human actor, but is unfamiliar in the performer's degree of stylization and the duration of the pose. Caught between the familiar and the unexpected, stillness can feel "strange" and provoke questions about "liveness."

CONTEMPORARY DEVELOPMENTS

Performance art of the 1960s and 70s emerged from visual art, and so had a natural affinity for stillness. The body again became a direct medium of expression, as conceptual art and happenings put emphasis on the direct experience of time, space, and materials. One subgenre was known as "Living Sculpture," as artists themselves became the art object. Perhaps most well-known from their many exhibitions were Gilbert and George, who, dressed in identical gray business suits, their hands and faces painted gold, silver, or red, performed a vaudeville-inspired series of poses in response to music or taped commands. In another variation, the painter Stephen Taylor Woodrow created "Living Pictures," which comprised live models attached to a wall of a public building, their bodies and clothes completely painted over in gray or black from hair to shoes, to create a kind of live sculptural frieze that lasted from six to eight hours at a stretch.[26] An emphasis on stillness in performance art allows us to take our time to experience the work, and to contemplate our own thoughts without being pulled along by plot or action. Anthony Howell observes that "stillness is probably the key factor which brought about this difference between performance and theatre, between reading the presented text and developing a mental *subtext* during the event."[27]

Can a performer ever be totally "still"? Inspired by John Cage's infamous musical composition *4'33"*, in which pianist David Tudor sat before a piano without playing for the length of time indicated by the title, Paul Taylor created a dance composition entitled *Duet* (1957), in which he stood still and another dancer sat still for the entire duration of the piece. Louis Horst reviewed *Duet* in *Dance Observer* with a blank column, only indicating the date and place of the performance.[28] While there was no intentional movement occurring, *Duet* asked its audience to meditate on its own stillness, to think about being alive and breathing as a balance of dynamic forces, and heightened its awareness of the present moment.

Tableaux were again popular in the theatrical avant-garde of the 1970s onward. Writing about the work of Lee Breuer, Richard Foreman, and Robert Wilson, Bonnie Marranca emphasizes the importance of still tableaux as the "chief unit of composition" in what she calls the "Theatre of Images":

> Tableau has the multiple function of compelling the spectator to analyze its specific placement in the artistic framework, stopping time by throwing a scene into relief, expanding time and framing scenes . . . the stillness of tableau sequences suspends time, causing the eye to focus on an image, and slows down the process of input. This increases the critical activity of the mind . . . it also regulates the dialectical interplay of word and image.[29]

Stillness is an often-used technique in contemporary theater to delink text, movement, sound, and image—the opposite of what we expect in a conventional, realistic performance. This separation of theatrical elements increases an audience's awareness of the present moment and heightens the metatheatrical quality of a performance.

New opportunities for creative applications of digital technologies in performance continue to challenge our ideas about movement and stillness. Virtual-reality setups usually demand that the viewer keeps still while moving through digitized environments. The technique of "motion capture" records the movements of a live performer at a high rate of speed—essentially a "stillness capture"—for later digital treatment. Working in tandem with digital designers, choreographers have used motion capture as a means to wed technology to live and virtual dancing. Merce Cunningham was one of the first choreographers to create dances in a computer environment with animation software, but with the use of motion capture, he has been able to transpose the movements of individual dancers onto virtual figures that are projected into an actual environment to "dance" with live performers (*Biped*, 1999). And Bill T. Jones created *Ghostcatching* (1999), a video "virtual dance installation," that is based in his own motion-captured movement.[30] Jones muses that

> These virtual creatures, dancers if you will, are spawns of mine. They are not me. . . . These creatures will interact with each other and they will choreograph themselves. They will move like their great-great-ancestor, Bill T. Jones, but they will not look like him.[31]

Taken to the next level, as digital designer Paul Kaiser has envisioned, "emergent dances" could be generated from algorithmic processes and a kind of "motion alphabet" derived from motion capture.[32] Once again, it can be seen that stillness, as utilized in motion capture, abstracts physical form, and poses questions about what it is to be alive and moving. Ilya Prigogine, the physicist known for his work in chaos theory and who finds in art new models for nature, has characterized our era as a convergence of times and spaces in a "time without measure" of stillness:

> What we have in mind may be expressed best by a reference to sculpture—be it the dancing Shiva or in the miniature temples of Guerrero—in which there appears very clearly the search for a junction between stillness and motion, time arrested and time passing. It is this confrontation that will give our era its uniqueness.[33]

NOTES

1. Jacques Copeau, quoted in Rudlin, John, *Jacques Copeau*. Cambridge, Massachusetts: Cambridge University Press, 1986, 46.
2. Dennis, Anne. *The Articulate Body: The Physical Training of the Actor*. New York: Drama Book Publishers, 1995, 53.
3. JoAnne Akalaitis, quoted in Saivetz, Deborah, *An Event in Space: JoAnne Akalaitis in Rehearsal*. Hanover, New Hampshire: Smith and Krauss, 2000, 53–54.
4. Stokes, John. *In the Nineties*. Chicago: The University of Chicago Press, 1989, 76–81.
5. Stebbins, Genevieve. *Delsarte System of Expression*. New York: Dance Horizons, 1977, 461.
6. Zorn, John W., ed. *The Essential Delsarte*. Metuchen, N.J.: The Scarecrow Press, 1968, 162–163.
7. Ruyter, Nancy Lee Chalfa. "Genevieve Stebbins and American Delsartean Performance." In Foster, Susan Leigh, ed. *Corporealities*. London: Routledge, 1996, 70–89.
8. Stebbins, Genevieve. *Delsarte System of Expression*, 459. (See note 5.)
9. Paul Fort, quoted in Deak, Frantisek, *Symbolist Theater: The Formation of an Avant-Garde*. Baltimore, Md.: The Johns Hopkins University Press, 1993, 142.
10. Loizeaux, Elizabeth Bergmann. *Yeats and the Visual Arts*. New Brunswick, N.J.: Rutgers University Press, 1986, 89.
11. Yeats, W. B. "Samhain: 1902." In *Explorations*. New York: Macmillan, 1962, 87.
12. Yeats, W. B. "*Per Amica Silentia Lunae*." (1917). In *Mythologies*. New York: Macmillan, 1959, 344.
13. Yeats, W. B. "The Tragic Theatre" (1910). In *Essays and Introductions*. New York: Macmillan, 1961, 245.
14. Craig, Gordon. "The Actor and the Über-marionette" (1908). In Rood, Arnold, ed., *Gordon Craig on Movement and Dance*. New York: Dance Horizons, 1977, 52.
15. Eynat-Confino, Irène. *Beyond the Mask: Gordon Craig, Movement, and the Actor*. Carbondale, Illinois: Southern Illinois University Press, 1987, 70.
16. Segel, Harold B. *Pinocchio's Progeny* Baltimore: The Johns Hopkins University Press, 1995, 72–73.
17. Maeterlinck, Maurice. "Small Talk—the Theater" (1890). In Dorra, Henri, trans. and ed., *Symbolist Art Theories: A Critical Anthology*. Berkeley: University of California Press, 1995, 145.
18. Maeterlinck, Maurice. "The Tragical in Daily Life" (1896). In Sutro, Alfred, trans., *The Treasure of the Humble*. New York: Dodd, Mead and Company, 1911, 105–107.
19. Rudnitsky, Konstantin. *Meyerbold the Director*, George Petrov, trans. Ann Arbor, Michigan: Ardis, 1981, 66–67.
20. Vsevolod Meyerhold, quoted in Braun, Edward, ed. and trans., *Meyerbold on Theatre*. New York: Hill and Wang, 1969, 54.
21. Ibid, 68.
22. Kuhns, David F. *German Expressionist Theatre: The Actor and the Stage*. Cambridge, Massachusetts: Cambridge University Press, 1997, 128.
23. Alfred Polgar, quoted in Kuhns, 199. (See note 22.)
24. Isadora Duncan, quoted in Cheney, Sheldon, ed. *The Art of the Dance*. New York: Theatre Arts, 1969, 121.
25. Freud, Sigmund. "The 'Uncanny'" (1919). In *Writings on Art and Literature*. Foreword by Neil Hertz Stanford, California: Stanford University Press, 2001, 193–233.
26. See Goldberg, RoseLee. *Performance Art from Futurism to the Present*. New York: Harry N. Abrams, 1988, 167–69, 207–208.
27. Howell, Anthony. *The Analysis of Performance Art*. Amsterdam, Netherlands: Harwood Academic Publishers, 1999, 10.
28. See Jowitt, Deborah. *Time and the Dancing Image*. Berkeley, Calif.: University of California Press, 1988, 312.
29. Marranca, Bonnie. *Theatrewritings*. New York: Performing Arts Journal Publications, 1984, 81.
30. See De Spain, Kent. "Dance and Technology: A Pas de Deux for Post-humans," *Dance Research Journal*, Summer 2000, 32(1), 2–17.
31. Bill T. Jones, quoted in De Spain, 14. (See note 30.)
32. De Spain, Kent. "Digital Dance: The Computer Artistry of Paul Kaiser," *Dance Research Journal*, Summer 2000, 32 (1), 23.
33. Ilya Prigogine, quoted in "West Turns East at the End of History," *New Perspectives Quarterly*, Spring 1992, 9(2) *www.npq.org*.

Teaching Charlie Chaplin How to Walk

Dan Kamin

PITTSBURGH, 1991

I was preparing for the debut of my new solo show, *Confessions of an Illusionist*, when the call came from Hollywood. Robert Downey, Jr., researching his role as Charlie Chaplin in Richard Attenborough's upcoming film, had come across a copy of my book, *Charlie Chaplin's One-Man Show*. "I think you may be the only person who can help me pull this off," he said.

I knew why he thought that. Parts of my book read like an instruction manual on how to play Charlie Chaplin. Facing the daunting challenge of portraying the man who was arguably the greatest comedian, filmmaker, and, some would say, *actor* of the twentieth century, Downey, even then notorious in Hollywood as a brilliant but undisciplined bad boy, realized that for once, he couldn't get by on *chutzpah* and native ability. This time, he needed a number of highly specific physical acting skills. Within a couple of weeks, he flew to Pittsburgh, and we began the task of preparing him for his role. Eventually, I was hired by the production, both to train Downey and to create several of the film's comedy sequences.

To put my work on the Chaplin film into a meaningful context, I will first offer a short account of how Charlie Chaplin inspired me to become a movement artist and the training that helped me to do so. Then, I will examine in some detail how movement, comedy, and meaning are intertwined in the films of Chaplin and his great colleague, Buster Keaton.

PITTSBURGH, 1966

Certain moments of our lives illuminate the landscape of our existence in such a way that nothing ever looks the same again. For me, seeing my first Chaplin film was such a moment.

I was in college at Carnegie Mellon University (CMU) at the time, studying graphic and industrial design. Before I saw the film, I couldn't even have told you what Chaplin looked like or named a single one of his films. So I was unprepared for the impact this ancient film from 1925 had upon me. I had never seen anything like it. The film's comedy sequences seemed spontaneous, yet at the same time, precisely choreographed. Chaplin seemed like a real and endearing character, yet he sometimes moved like a marionette. *The Gold Rush* was a very funny comedy, yet its themes were greed, murder, cannibalism, and loneliness, expressed in poignant scenes that were worlds apart from the maudlin "sad-clown" schtick I'd grown up watching Red Skelton and Jackie Gleason perform on television. In the film, a cabin was blown to the edge of a cliff by the force of a gale. I felt just as helpless against the force of the film.

As I walked out of the theater that night, I could hardly have imagined the life I was walking into. Instead of moving forward into my career as a designer, I was being blown backwards into the vanished world of Chaplin's mimetic art. I found myself devouring what books I could find on the subject, but they offered little insight into the question that haunted me—*why did that old film still have such power? What were its secrets?*

Then, I saw a man named Jewel Walker perform his solo mime show on campus. Like Chaplin, he used precise, choreographed movement to create scenes; like Chaplin, he created memorable comic and dramatic moments; and like Chaplin, he delighted the audience with strange and wonderful physical skills. This man, it seemed to me, held the key to Chaplin's art! I was elated to find that he had recently been hired as a movement teacher by the world-renowned drama department on my campus.

But then, as now, it was a jealous department. Outsiders were summarily turned away. To my delight, however, I found that a good teacher is powerless before the enthusiasm of a student. Jewel generously welcomed me, and so began my off-the-record apprenticeship. I illegally audited his classes, worked lights at his performances, and generally hounded him. Sometimes, I would accost him in the middle of the crowded campus and demand that he demonstrate a movement—which he would cheerfully do, whereupon, I'd rush off to the full-length mirror in the student union bathroom to practice.

Gradually, I learned that Jewel's lineage was impressive. He had studied acting with Lee Strasberg, Herbert Berghof, and Vera Soloviova of the Moscow Art Theatre. But his primary mentor was a French mime named Etienne Decroux. Jewel had come to CMU following a four-year stint in Decroux's American company.

Decroux, famous mostly as the teacher of Marcel Marceau, had created the movement technique and most of the illusions that Marceau popularized. He redefined theatrical mime in the twentieth century and is justly regarded as the "father of modern mime." At the heart of his system were what Jewel called "articulation" exercises, a way to move the body along precise geometrical lines. Movements of the head, neck, upper trunk, and so on are isolated and then combined into movement scales, comparable to the practice of playing musical scales. It is a system of great complexity and elegance. For Decroux, this basic work led to the highly trained, articulated bodies capable of performing his mime pieces, some of which resembled a kind of theatrical cubism. For me, the exercises provided a way to understand, execute, and see movement more clearly.

Following my time at CMU, I studied with a number of other movement teachers, but none who influenced me more than Dr. Dorothy Nolte. In the 1950s, Dorothy became one of the first disciples of Ida Rolf, whose physical alignment technique, called Structural Integration or "rolfing," accomplished postural change by a series of deep massage treatments. The goal was to achieve an alignment similar to that taught in the better-known Alexander Technique. Dorothy, a movement teacher, came to believe that the same results could be achieved without the often-painful rolfing process or the lengthy training period of the Alexander work. She developed a series of subtle exercises that move the various hinges of the body to create dramatic changes in alignment and called her system Structural Awareness.

I sought Dorothy out because of a whiplash neck injury that for a year had made my life a daily ordeal. Within two weeks after learning her exercises, the pain of the injury lifted, and a new disciple was born. Again, I found that Dorothy bowed before my enthusiasm, and she and her associate, Dr. Rachel Harris, trained and certified me as a teacher of Structural Awareness, which deepened my understanding of the work. Structural Awareness reinforced all the articulation and physical characterization work I had done with Jewel, enhanced my awareness of the postural aspect of body language, and gave me a daily regimen that greatly increased my personal comfort. An additional benefit was that, with its focus on the body mechanics of everyday life, Structural Awareness helped me to separate movement for art from movement for life, an important distinction that can be elusive for new theater artists.

As my performing career developed, I continued to find inspiration in the work of Chaplin and his great silent film colleagues, Buster Keaton and Harold Lloyd. Luckily for me, their work was more generally available now, for it was part of the general revival of interest in film as an art form. Colleges everywhere began offering film studies programs, and bookstores began filling with serious new works on film. However, despite the many excellent new books that appeared, I still was not finding the book I wanted to read on Chaplin. So finally, between engagements, I wrote it myself.

IOLA, KANSAS, 1997

While on the face of it my book was arcane in the extreme—a movement analysis of Charlie Chaplin—it had positive repercussions on my life and career that continue to this day. It put me in touch with an international community of Chaplin scholars and fans, opened doors to performance and lecture opportunities both here and abroad, and ultimately led to my working in the medium that had inspired my stage career in the first place.

In 1997, I was asked to give a talk contrasting Chaplin's physicality with Keaton's. Keaton was born in Piqua, Kansas, a tiny town that subsequently blew away in a storm. Iola, a slighter larger town ten miles down the road, survived the storm and commemorates his birth with an annual Keaton Celebration. The following comments are adapted from that talk.

The World of Chaplin and Keaton

The two greatest visual comedy thinkers of the twentieth century were hard at work honing their performance skills by the time the century began. Keaton was only five and Chaplin eleven, but they were already veterans—Keaton had started performing virtually from birth, and Chaplin not long afterwards. Each mastered a rich repertoire of physical techniques that included knockabout comedy acrobatics, a smattering of dance, and a specialized form of physical acting known variously as mime, pantomime, and dumb show.

Keaton and Chaplin were born into a world bursting with popular entertainment, including burlesque, medicine shows, circuses, "legit" theater, opera, operetta, dance, melodrama, musical revues, and minstrel shows. They absorbed influences from all these forms and would draw upon and parody them in their stage and film careers. But their primary education came from the stages of American vaudeville and British music hall, where they were able to study closely the luminous personalities who dominated the popular stage. From this fertile tradition sprang not only Keaton and Chaplin, but comedians such as the Marx Brothers, W. C. Fields, Sid Caesar, Danny Kaye, Milton Berle, and Jack Benny—in short, the performers who would define and dominate American comedy for the first half of the century.

It was a fabulous training ground. Keaton and Chaplin learned by experience in front of thousands of audiences how to use movement to create characterization and comedy. Audiences could be kind or cruel, and the feedback was instant and undeniable—laughter or catcalls. Keaton performed with his parents as The Three Keatons, and Chaplin honed his skills for seven years with Fred Karno's Speechless Comedians, then the leading comedy mime troupe in the world. By the time they were in their early twenties, both had embarked on their film careers. Ironically, their success in cinema contributed to the decline of the stage tradition that spawned them.

Since film was silent, both these troupers were uniquely equipped to enter the new field. But the new medium frustrated expectations. Many great stage stars bombed, and previously unknown performers such as Mary Pickford achieved fame and fortune on an unprecedented scale. Keaton and Chaplin were among the lucky few who managed to translate their stage skills to the silent screen. Because these little men are the twin giants of silent film achievement, their films have been endlessly analyzed. But seldom do writers focus on the physicality that is, after all, the source of their continuing appeal. It's my premise that Chaplin and Keaton's differing physicality not only defined and circumscribed the characters they played, but led directly to the content and comedy of their films.

The Usual Suspects

We'll begin investigating this claim by placing Chaplin and Keaton into a kind of police lineup. Bodies can be classified as roughly linear, circular, or rectangular in shape. *Ectomorphs* are linear—skinny or stringy-looking people, like Woody Allen, Marty Feldman, or Basil Rathbone.

When you watch them, your eyes are often drawn to their extremities, their hands or feet; their movements tend to be either delicate or nervous-looking. Their opposites are *endomorphs*, people like John Candy or Oliver Hardy, who are fleshy, rounder. Their movements seem to emanate from deeper inside their bodies, and they can look powerful, lumbering, or sluggish. When an endormorph moves delicately, like an ectomorph, it has an incongruous, comic effect—think of Hardy's signature tie-twiddle or the balletic hippos in *Fantasia*. Endomorphs are often bottom-heavy. The third body type is the blocky *mesomorph*, the classic he-man type. We can trace a direct line of mesomorphic leading men in movies from Keanu Reeves to Clark Gable to Rudolph Valentino.

Keaton and Chaplin were short men, about 5'6", but Keaton weighed about fifteen pounds more than Chaplin, which points us toward one essential difference between the two: Despite his portrayal of a comic antihero, Keaton actually has the heroic physique of a mesomorph. Typical of mesomorphic males, his musculature is highly developed—undoubtedly from the family knockabout act, known as the most violent in vaudeville history. Chaplin, on the other hand, is slight, with a proportionally small upper half. His ectomorphic body is unusually proportioned, with a very large head, short arms, and small hands and feet.

Both men learned to use their physique to maximum advantage. Most obviously, they capitalized on their small stature by pitting themselves against larger, stronger antagonists—in those days called "heavies." The David-and-Goliath theme became central to their films. In Chaplin's *The Cure*, for example, an endomorphic masseur casually looks Charlie over by rapidly twisting him back to front as though he's weightless. Charlie's body moves as a unit, unresisting. The effect is reinforced when Charlie sits down on

LEFT: *Keaton working on his form in* Battling Butler. RIGHT: *Chaplin: Chaplin and the sadistic masseur in* The Cure.

Chaplin's graceful tramp and Keaton's angular vaudevillian.

a cot and the man flips him onto his back with a flick of the wrist. Charlie's body position remains unchanged as he flips backward; while anyone else's feet would remain on the floor, Charlie's legs stay up the air in "sitting" position, as though the blow was too powerful and swift to allow for the normal counterbalancing action of the hip joint. In these few movements, Chaplin deftly establishes the masseur as an irresistible force. Later, Charlie watches in alarm as the man sadistically pummels a frail-looking "patient," painfully folding the emaciated wraith in two before tossing him into the pool like a beanbag chair. Rubbing his hands in anticipation, the masseur approaches Charlie, whose tense leg movements clearly convey his alarm. In one of Chaplin's most delightful sequences, Charlie eludes the brute's clutches by turning the massage into a wrestling match.

At the beginning of his film career, Keaton pits himself against similar Goliaths, but his acrobatic athleticism comes across so strongly that we rarely feel the kind of physical intimidation Chaplin was able to convey. So, to increase the menace of his adversaries, Keaton made them larger and more numerous. Thus, while Charlie tangles with countless individual cops throughout his films, in *Cops,* Keaton is pitted against literally hundreds of cops. In his feature films, Keaton grapples with mobs of angry brides, whole armies, and ultimately ocean liners, locomotives, and natural disasters such as windstorms and floods.

Clothes Make the Man

Since the 1950s, few comedians have worn distinctive costumes or makeup; Paul Reubens' Pee Wee Herman stands out as an exception. But for silent-era comedians, costumes and makeup virtually defined character, none more effectively than Chaplin's Tramp costume. That remarkable and evocative juxtaposition of mismatched clothing gives us important clues to the character that wears them. The shabby dress clothes seem to have come from different owners, since every article is a different size. They are discards—found objects—suggesting both the wealth of their previous owners and the trash bins they were consigned to. Chaplin's carefully trimmed mustache, bamboo cane, and comically fastidious demeanor further reinforce the implied gulf between wealth and poverty. This derelict assumes the airs of an aristocrat.

Another dichotomy evoked by the costume is youth versus age. Even young children, seeing Chaplin's Tramp image for the first time, know instantly that this is a *funny* man—a child dressed up in grown-up clothes, with his large head (proportionally like a child's), mop of unruly hair, too-small hat and coat, too-big baggy pants, and those huge, out-turned shoes. Chaplin capitalizes on this association with playful and mischievous behavior. Remarkably, in only his second film, Chaplin discovered the costume that embodied the conflicts—wealth versus poverty, youth versus age, and large versus small—that he would spend the rest of his career exploring

In addition to expressing his inner character, Chaplin's costume and makeup have an eye-catching, graphic quality that set him apart on the crowded movie screens of 1914. Even in long shots, his distinctive, dark silhouette allows him to stand out from the other actors with cartoon-like clarity. And his square black mustache acts like a bull's-eye, drawing your eye to his dramatically whitened, expressive face.

Keaton's costume, not so easily caricatured as Chaplin's, emphasizes straight lines and angles rather than curves. It's baggier and less form-fitting than Chaplin's. While Chaplin's tight coat outlines his trunk (an expressively important portion of Chaplin's body, as we will see), Keaton's vest and jacket hang down loosely. Chaplin's large pants drape in such a way that we're aware of his spindly legs beneath, but the crotch of Keaton's pants comes down almost to his knees, disguising his muscular legs. The plainness and angularity of his costume are reinforced by Keaton's unsmiling, straight-across mouth and long, heavily lidded eyes and topped off by the double horizontal lines of his squat "porkpie" hat. While his jacket, vest, and clip-on tie suggest street apparel, the funny hat, baggy pants, and big shoes link him to the stage more than real life. Audiences of the period would have seen Keaton's costume as that of a vaudeville comedian. Chaplin's costume and makeup believably connect him to the real worlds of derelicts and men-about-town.

While contemporary audiences ascribed talismanic comic power to Chaplin's costume, it was, of course, through movement that both he and Keaton brought their characters to life.

Posture and Movement—From the Top Down

Chaplin holds his head in an unusual way, directly above his body. This was an unusual postural choice, because most people hold their heads slightly forward. On the other hand, in that era, the wealthy, restricted by high, stiff collars, held themselves more upright than the middle and lower classes. Charlie's assumption of a rich man's prideful carriage was inherently comic, adding an intriguing and unlikely air of dignity to his indigent wanderer.

By contrast, Keaton thrusts his head forward. This off-center head position not only reinforces the angularity of his costume, but also has the effect of directing our attention away from his body toward the object of his attention, an appropriate choice given the character's continuing attempts to figure out a baffling world.

Chaplin's regal head position continues into the upright carriage of his trunk. Turning, he spirals smoothly around his center line to avoid bending his spine. His fluid motion lends him a graceful, self-confident quality, which he occasionally exaggerates by tilting his pelvis back, which in turn causes his chest to elevate in the theatrically bravura stance of a ballet dancer.

The self-contained, confident aspect of his character led Chaplin to a bold performance technique: He often looks directly at the camera, and therefore at us, the audience. Acknowledging the audience was quite common on the variety stage, but only a few film performers have used the device—Oliver Hardy and Groucho come to mind. Chaplin, however, made the most extensive and subtle use of it, notably in his great Mutual series of films in 1916 and 1917. While the other characters in his films are trapped in filmic reality, unaware of the existence of an audience watching them, Charlie repeatedly acknowledges us with laughs or glances. Paradoxically, this has the effect of drawing us deeper into the action of the films by making us coconspirators in Charlie's adventures. It is one of the keys to Chaplin's strong rapport with audiences and imbues his films with a warm, intimate quality.

Keaton's little man never acknowledges the film audience. He's too busy trying to fathom what's going on around him. On the other hand, Keaton as director often acknowledges the audience by playing with the conventions of filmic storytelling. In *One Week*, a young woman is bathing and drops her soap onto the bathroom floor; a hand discreetly covers the camera lens as she reaches to get it. In *Our Hospitality,* the mansion Buster thinks he has inherited turns out to be a shack. As he gazes at it in disbelief, Keaton inserts a shot of a real mansion house exploding.

When Keaton turns, unlike Chaplin, his head always gets there ahead of the rest of his body. Leading with his head gives Keaton's character an immature, awkward demeanor, reinforced by his chest, which he modestly folds forward. This awkwardness is particularly evident when Keaton touches people and things. His touch is invariably shy and hesitant, nowhere more so than in the many comically awkward courtship scenes in his films.

While sight and hearing connect us with the world at a distance, touch is personal, direct, intimate. In contrast to Keaton, Chaplin touches himself and other characters often and with ease. When he hugs a woman, his hands travel down her back like butterflies, inviting us to share his sensual delight. Chaplin's courting scenes, at once bold, tender, and comically inventive, are among the high points of his films.

Continuing our journey downward, we finally arrive at those oversized shoes—slapshoes, as they were called then. Now, shoes that are four or five inches longer than your feet make it impossible to walk normally, because when you bend your toes, the extra length tends to trip you up. How Chaplin and Keaton solved that problem is very telling. Chaplin turns his feet out, opening his legs. He walks by bringing the side of his foot forward, eliminating the problem of bending his toes and resulting in a kind of penguin walk that's at once awkward and strangely graceful, like a ballet dancer lumbered with clodhoppers. It was an archetypally funny walk, easy to imitate, and one of the signature movements that was celebrated in the many Chaplin imitation contests and songs of the period. Chaplin was to develop the comic implications of his walk in the many incongruously graceful moments that fill his films.

Keaton, on the other hand, keeps his feet wide apart and rigorously parallel, even pigeon-toed. To avoid the extra shoe leather, instead of bending his knees as he walks, he kicks his legs out straight from the hip. The resulting jackknife movement, his top half bobbing forward to balance the stiff-legged movements of his bottom half, makes him resemble a hinged toy. Buster exploits this angular, mechanical quality by occasionally freezing, statue-like; often, his body makes an oblique line in apparent defiance of gravity, such as his signature position of leaning forward and scanning the horizon, his hand shading his eyes.

The way both men run reveals still more about their characters. When Chaplin runs, his head bends backwards, as though forced by inertia or the wind to trail behind. It's a very sensual stylization, making us feel the forces at play on his body. Keaton simply rockets along, with no extraneous movement at all. All traces of hesitation and awkwardness vanish as Keaton becomes a streamlined running machine. This transformation neatly crystallizes one of the key Keaton themes: Buster's identification with mechanical objects (more on that later).

Moving into Character

Critic Andrew Sarris pointed out that Keaton and Chaplin represented the centripetal and centrifugal tendencies of slapstick, and indeed, the energy in their films does travel in opposite directions. The motivating forces in Keaton's films are centripetal, coming from outside his character and buffeting him about, while Charlie's strong needs provide the force that sets his films in motion.

We're aware of Charlie's needs because his whole body responds to his thoughts with the sensitivity of insect antennae. Nowhere is this better illustrated than in a lovely, brief scene—no more than thirty seconds—from *Easy Street,* which we will examine in some detail.

A sign catches Charlie's eye as he walks past a police station:

POLICEMAN

WANTED

AT ONCE

As though drawn magnetically, Charlie revolves back toward the sign and walks over to peer at it more closely. Turning to face the camera, he gives a slight shrug and starts to walk off. But again, he stops and turns toward the camera, points his finger at himself, and returns to scrutinize the sign even more closely, bending toward it and placing his hands on his hips. Once again, he turns to face the camera, shifting his weight and biting his forefinger in indecision. Finally, he gives a determined tug at his vest and coat and turns to step up into the station. But his courage falters in the face of the large, unmoving policeman who fills the doorway, and he walks off to the side, snapping his fingers in an "aw, shucks" gesture and biting his forefinger. Working up his courage, he pulls back his shoulders and goes for the door a second time—and for a second time shrinks away. Agonized, he faces the camera. He twists around to look at the sign a couple more times, chewing his finger. Finally, marshalling all his inner resources, he gives himself an encouraging slap on the chest, tugs his coat firmly down, pulls back his shoulders, and plunges in past the surprised cop.

Shot full-figure and in a single take, the scene reveals Chaplin's ability to "speak" with every part of his body. Most actors of the period would have played the scene primarily with a series of puzzled head movements, perhaps scratching their heads. The pattern of Charlie's movement toward and away from the door dramatizes his indecision much more vividly. The comedy emanates from the delicate rhythmic play of Charlie's faltering intention. Chaplin draws the viewer in further by playing much of the scene directly to the camera. Not only does he look at the camera, he also presents his trunk to it openly. Opening one's trunk in this way indicates a trusting, nothing-to-hide attitude and constitutes, along with his direct gaze, a further invitation to share his adventures. Chaplin uses his trunk to subtly, even subliminally, deepen his direct communication with his film audience. This small scene demonstrates how Chaplin's mimetic art was able to sweep across world cultures, for his incarnation of thought transcends language barriers. It is both crystal clear and choreographically pleasurable to watch.

Several directorial devices serve to further clarify the action for the viewer. The cop never takes his eyes off Charlie, despite the fact that Charlie only acknowledges him during his few moments in the doorway. The cop is framed in the doorway, which in turn is framed squarely in the center of the film frame. A single step leads to the doorway—a big step, as we discover, for Charlie. The sign, prominently displayed next to the doorway, reads POLICEMAN WANTED AT ONCE. The smaller size of "at once" lends a desperate, pleading tone—perhaps they'd even accept a vagrant like Charlie? Thus, literally everything in view helps to make Charlie's dilemma tangible. The sign beckons to him, and the door stands invitingly open, if only he can overcome the obstacles presented by the step, the cop, and his own ambivalence.

The circular, composed quality of his gestures and the sinuous choreography of his movements reveal why critics have long labeled Chaplin balletic. In fact, his films are peppered with comic ballet dancing, climaxing in his memorable dance with a globe in *The Great Dictator*. Even though he's not overtly dancing outside the police station, Chaplin links himself with ballet by drawing our attention to the formal and florid qualities of his movement. Expressively, however, his movements are far richer than the standardized gestural vocabulary found in most ballet performances. He finds ways to make common-place gestures, such as pointing to himself or shrugging his shoulders, compelling both dramatically and choreographically. Even such a mundane movement as peering at the sign becomes interesting to watch because of the way he counterbalances the sideways tilt of his trunk with an opposing tilt of his head.

Generally, we Americans distrust ornamentation and preening in our movement. While Charlie moves in ornate, interlocking circular patterns that draw our attention to his center, Buster's gestures are far plainer. They are eccentric, flung away from his center, drawing our attention away from his body. Keaton's offhanded movement quality makes his character seem distinctly American. Keaton was well aware of this and capitalized on it by portraying classic American types, such as a Civil War soldier and the son of a steamboat captain. It's worth noting that in his feature films, he often abandoned his famil-iar costume (although not his slapshoes) for period clothing or formal wear, in both of which he looks strikingly handsome, rather than comic. But his audiences understood that whatever his costume, Keaton was playing slight variations on the same character.

Or rather, on the same two characters. For the awkward Buster we have been describing invariably becomes an action hero. In *Sherlock, Jr.*, for example, Buster is a movie projectionist who'd like to become a detective. Eventually he does, but only in a remarkable dream sequence in which he walks into the movie he's projecting to perform amazing feats of derring-do. In real life, Buster is a wash as a detec-tive. However, by the end of the film, through no fault of his own, he wins his girl, who joins him in the projection booth. She expects a kiss, but he knows what to do only by stealing glances at the actors in the film he is projecting. Only in his bursts of action—in this case only in his dream—does Buster move with confidence.

Visual Puns

Chaplin generally moves with great confidence, but it's a false front, for he has to cope with a hostile world. Finding ways for him to cope led Chaplin to his most imaginative comic motif: transformation gags, or visual puns. Chaplin's films seethe with inventive transformations of objects and movements. For exam-ple, in *The Vagabond*, Charlie wants to rescue a woman who's being beaten by a brutal gypsy, so he picks up a thick branch and heads across a bridge. Another of the gypsies approaches from the opposite side— and Charlie instantly, instinctively pretends to be fishing. When the gypsy looks over Charlie's shoulder to see his "catch," Charlie deftly knocks him out with the log. There are two kinds of visual pun here: Charlie's log becomes a fishing pole, and the movement of yanking the fish out of the water becomes a knockout conk.

Chaplin's two most celebrated transformations occur in *The Gold Rush*. In the first, starving pros-pector Charlie cooks and eats his shoe. While most actors would focus on the disgust of having to eat an old shoe, Chaplin takes the scene much further by treating the shoe as a gourmet feast, eating the laces like spaghetti, sucking the "juice" from a bent nail, trying and trying to break it like a wishbone. Based on a true incident, the scene resonates with the truth that, to a starving man, a cooked shoe *would* be a feast. Later, Charlie is asked to give an after-dinner speech to the dance hall girls he's invited to a painstak-ingly prepared New Year's Eve dinner. Too shy to speak for himself, he impales two long bread rolls onto forks and transforms them into a pair of legs and feet, which perform a funny, graceful vaudeville dance on the tabletop.

This delightful sequence moves to quite another level when we realize that the dancing limbs Charlie conjures from the forks and rolls are a tiny replica of his own spindly legs and big shoes, and his own head becomes the giant head of a puppet Charlie. He has improvised a spokesman. And the gag takes on still greater depth when we remember the earlier scene in which Charlie had eaten his shoe. First a shoe becomes food, and then food becomes a shoe. Then the comedy of the scene transmutes to sadness when it turns out that Charlie's guests have never actually arrived. Charlie has fallen asleep waiting for them. Suddenly his social triumph evaporates—the brilliant dance was just a dream. This is visual thinking and storytelling of the highest order.

Keaton also uses visual puns, but often Buster-the-character is not in on the joke. At the beginning of *The General,* the locomotive engineer is going to visit his girlfriend, and two worshipful boys follow in single file behind him. Buster's girl then joins the line to become the caboose of this human train. Buster-the-character is oblivious to this; it's the director's joke, and the perfect beginning to a film that stresses how inexorably Keaton is linked to his beloved locomotive. Later in the film, when the cowcatcher of the moving train gently scoops Keaton up as he's clearing logs off the tracks, we understand that man and train are as one. This gag, incidentally, like much in Keaton, is impossible to fully appreciate except on a large screen.

Another example: *Cops* begins with Buster saying farewell to his sweetheart, apparently from behind the bars of a jail cell. But when the camera cuts to a long shot, we see that he's not inside a jail cell, but outside the gate of her estate. Keaton-the-director has again found a perfect opening for his film, for by the end, Buster will be chased by the entire police force and ultimately jailed. And once more, the joke is played on Buster-the-character by Keaton-the-director.

Chaplin, as a director, serves Charlie the character. Nothing transcends Charlie's character, his personality, and his active role in driving the plot of his films. Buster, on the other hand, is passive, activated only by the forces and plot machinations that director Keaton unleashes on him. Buster's stoical, often puzzled facial expression makes perfect sense in the light of that vision. The exception to Buster's passivity is his amazing mechanical aptitude, which results in numerous Rube Goldberg contraptions, complete with ingenious transformations. For example, in *The Scarecrow,* Buster has totally mechanized breakfast; everything becomes something else, including the tabletop, which swings up onto the wall at the end of the meal to become a sampler that reads: WHAT IS HOME WITHOUT A MOTHER? Keaton's wit was dry and unsentimental.

In one instance, Chaplin appears to have borrowed a Keaton transformation gag and expanded upon it. In *The Navigator,* Buster gets his foot caught in a rope attached to a small cannon. The fuse is burning down, and Buster's panicky movements trying to free himself have the perverse effect of keeping the cannon pointed at him. The following year, in the snowbound cabin of *The Gold Rush,* two large men struggle over a rifle, and the barrel somehow always points at Charlie, who scampers wildly around trying to avoid it. Both scenes are very funny, but the Chaplin scene is richer. Buster could stop at any moment and free himself, but Charlie can't control the situation. It's as if the two men struggling over the rifle are in a different movie than Charlie; for them, it's a melodramatic life-and-death struggle. Add Charlie, and the tragedy turns into slapstick comedy. This ability to merge the comic and tragic, as indicated above in the description of scenes from *The Gold Rush*, is one of Chaplin's greatest achievements. Or was; the nakedly emotional quality of Chaplin's films is out of key with many modern viewers, while Keaton's mordant vision seems bracingly fresh.

Drunk and Disorderly

Comparing Chaplin and Keaton brings up a terrible irony. While alcohol ruined Keaton's career, it basically made Chaplin's. Chaplin's signature stage role was as a rich drunk, and he is drunk in many of his films—sometimes throughout whole films, such as the virtually solo *One A.M.*, in which the task of making his way upstairs to bed occupies the drunk for the full twenty minutes of the film. *The Idle Class* features Chaplin in both his guises, as the Tramp and a rich drunk. Even though drunkenness as a subject for comedy makes some modern viewers uncomfortable (Keaton's innocent use of black performers has a similar effect), in these scenes, we can watch Chaplin's physical virtuosity in its purest form, as he does battle with gravity and his own altered perceptions. His imaginative transformations of the world now work against him. Chaplin played the drunk by the simple expedient of being unable to steady his center line, so basic actions such as lighting a cigarette become bravura triumphs over a world spinning out of control. Drunkenness, and the related state of being dazed from a blow to the head, enabled Chaplin to exploit his great skill at choreographing the comedy of incompetence.

Drunk or not, in many films, Chaplin is comically incompetent at what he's supposed to be doing, but unexpectedly super-competent at other tasks. In both *The Rink* and *Modern Times*, for example, he's a disaster-prone waiter, but a brilliant roller skater. Through this comic alternation of competence and incompetence, two additional Chaplin themes emerge: the intolerability of most kinds of work for Charlie and his perpetual status as an interloper, outsider, or imposter.

Although he rarely played the drunk on screen, Keaton was Chaplin's equal at depicting comic incompetence. But Keaton's incompetence serves a very different purpose than Chaplin's, for it sets off the dramatic change he undergoes in each of his feature films. Just as the brilliant comic of the 1970s, Andy Kaufmann, created a nerdy persona to set off his dazzling Elvis impersonation, so in Keaton's silent features, Buster changes before our eyes, becoming a masculine hero who saves the day with amazing displays of physical prowess and daredevil feats that leave even modern audiences gasping in admiration. I should say *especially* modern audiences, since Keaton's expert filmmaking allowed for no suspicion of stunt doubles or special effects; the danger in his films is palpably real, and audiences are in awe of him because of it. There's been nothing comparable in film since.

In the spectacular finales of his films, Buster-the-character and Keaton-the-author-director finally merge, for the overwhelming physical virtuosity of his performances matches the lean brilliance of the writing and directing. Buster's distinctive machinelike run explodes into dazzling acrobatic pyrotechnics that reveal his total mastery of motion, machinery, and the forces that had earlier thwarted him, including his own awkward body. The climactic thrills and comedy now come from Buster's outrageous super-competence.

This very American Horatio Alger theme of overcoming impossible odds and performing miraculous feats with courage, pluck, and a bit of luck undercuts Keaton's otherwise fatalistic presentation of a character buffeted by forces outside his control. But the endings of the films, while upbeat and emotionally satisfying, don't negate the pervasive dark mood of what came before. We're reminded of that mood by Buster's unsmiling acceptance of his triumph, as he had earlier accepted defeat.

Keaton was known as "The Human Mop" in his family's knockabout stage act, which consisted largely of Buster's aggravating his father to the point that the exasperated soul would start throwing his son around the stage. He would hurl young Buster high onto a painted backdrop, from which the lad would slide down into a graceful somersault. For Keaton, acrobatic prowess on stage led not only to spectacular, explosive falls on screen, but to acrobatic stunts on a scale impossible for the stage. Like Chaplin,

Keaton successfully integrated his physical skills with a profound cinematic vision, in his case, a vision of man buffeted by a world of immense, powerful, and finally indifferent forces. Modern audiences respond to his stoical beauty as he pratfalls on the edge of oblivion.

Chaplin became the twentieth century's icon of comedy because his "coping mechanisms" are ingenious, bold, and graceful responses to an inhumane society. Because this strange outsider does cope—imperfectly, but with incredible panache—he earns our admiration, affection, and gratitude.

All the thematic richness in the films of Keaton and Chaplin is conveyed through the movement of their characters on the screen. For Keaton, the mysterious workings of women and machinery—including the machinery of the motion picture camera—inspire him to superhuman physical feats.

Chaplin often finds his inspiration in the sheer joy of movement itself. Initially just a grace note lending an incongruous élan to the Tramp, movement soon becomes inseparable from the meaning of Chaplin's comedy. Two deceptively simple examples will suffice to illustrate this. In *The Pawnshop*, Charlie hoists himself onto a curb by yanking himself up by the seat of his pants. And in *The Cure*, a revolving door spins him through the lobby and up the stairs. The first gag allows Charlie to demonstrate his insouciance through his casual disregard of the law of gravity; in the second, he achieves the effect of falling upstairs by exaggerating the force of momentum. Like Keaton's great action sequences, these are uniquely filmic gags, neither of which would work as well in a live performance. Chaplin-the-director has found the perfect framing and film speed to convey the mimetic illusions, playfully bending the laws of physics for comic effect; Chaplin-the-performer's exquisite body control and physical style make the gags viscerally delightful to watch.

Chaplin and Keaton appeared together on screen for the first time in Chaplin's last American film, *Limelight*. By then, both had lost their great audience; Keaton's silent masterpieces were all but forgotten, and Chaplin, while he retained his wealth and artistic independence, had become a pariah in America. In the film, the two play washed-up music hall comedians who reunite for a comeback performance. Since the film was made in 1951, Chaplin had to bracket the hilarious physical comedy sequence as a period piece. The world had moved on, and the era of purely visual comedy entertainment in motion pictures had passed.

HOLLYWOOD, 1991

"I want you to correct me when I'm eating. How would he hold a *fork*?" Thus, Robert Downey, Jr. began his short, but intense course in becoming Charlie Chaplin.

Robert, although he bore a striking facial resemblance to Chaplin, was physically quite unlike him. Taller, with the strong musculature of the typical mesomorph, Robert, at least in terms of movement, is a typical product of the late twentieth century. When he sat down, he slumped down. He stabbed at his food and chewed with his mouth open. His movements were tense, coarse, bound. It would be a challenge to get him to move with Chaplin's distinctive choreographic grace and fluidity. Luckily, Robert proved to be an eager and hard-working student. He had to be, for we had only a few weeks to effect his transformation.

Given Chapin's excellent posture in both his life and his films, Structural Awareness was an ideal way to begin our work. Robert was struck by the powerful effect these subtle exercises had on him and how directly they applied to the task at hand. In Structural Awareness, breathing is an important conceptual and physical tool to move the body toward the desired alignment, and soon the phrase "breathe up your line" became our daily mantra. For Robert, achieving an acute awareness of his center line was critical;

not only did he have to alter his own slouchy posture to become the regal off-screen Chaplin, but he had to learn the Tramp's deft, quicksilver postural changes.

In my own performing work, I had never sought to replicate Chaplin's routines or character. After all, I'm 6'3", working in a different era, in a different medium, and with my own artistic axes to grind. Nor had I ever tried to teach anyone to act like Chaplin. But because I am an ectomorph, certain of Chaplin's movement qualities come naturally to me, including a kind of loose-limbed relaxation. As soon as I began working with Robert, this loomed as a central issue, for Robert found it hellishly difficult to achieve. Like most people, he confused a relaxed body with a collapsed body. Robert, who could fall asleep at the drop of a hat, found the idea of maintaining a relaxed state while standing in an aligned posture paradoxical.

The problem became even more apparent when Robert attempted to walk like Chaplin. While Chaplin's walk is often caricatured as a penguin-like, stiff-legged gait, in fact, it's an extraordinarily centered and flowing movement. Trying to walk like Chaplin, Robert looked like he was wearing a suit of armor.

To break down that armor, we made relaxation an important part of our daily regimen. I used every technique I knew, and made up more, to loosen him up. We did endless physical improvisations. In the end, Robert did his walk in only two scenes of the film. Walking out of the makeup room after donning his Tramp costume for the first time, he "discovers" his walk as he strides toward the set. This part of the scene was shot about a dozen times, and Robert nailed it just once. Luckily, that was enough.

Then, Charlie/Robert continues onto the set, where he proceeds to improvise, turning a conventional scene into the first Chaplin comedy. The scene we filmed, in which Charlie disrupts a wedding party, was not based on an actual Chaplin film. For our purposes, Chaplin's early years of artistic development had to be compressed into this single scene. I created it, as much as I could, in Chaplin's style, quoting specific gags here and there.

To prepare Robert for the filming, I began adding to our daily relaxation and alignment work exercises that isolated key Chaplin movements. I was determined that Robert resemble Chaplin more than superficially, that he move with Chaplin's characteristic fluid precision. These qualities were apparently automatic with Chaplin at all times, as we could see from newsreel footage we acquired of Chaplin out of character. I studied these films intently, finding moments to review and work through with Robert. Soon, I *was* correcting the way he held his fork. At the same time, I began working out the various comedy scenes and incorporating them into our routine. The amount of repetition required to master some of these movements surprised Robert, an excellent but instinctive actor.

Along with that deceptively simple walk, we put in endless hours on Chaplin's drunk act. In his autobiography, Chaplin had recorded Sennett's disappointment when he met Chaplin for the first time out of makeup. Chaplin was twenty-four and looked about eighteen, and Sennett wondered if this solemn youth could possibly be the funny drunk he'd seen on stage. In the film version, Chaplin demonstrates his identity and comic virtuosity to Sennett by launching into a drunken improvisation. Because Robert repeatedly fell into my arms during rehearsals for this scene, I ended up playing the part of the Keystone Kop he draws into the action. He knew I wouldn't drop him. Although Robert proved fearless and adept at falling, it was much more difficult for him to achieve the delicate disorientation of Chaplin's drunken movement. By focusing on the wavering center line of the drunk, Robert became more adept at maintaining the erect and relaxed posture of the off-screen Chaplin as well.

Robert's filming schedule was grueling, for he appeared in virtually every scene shot for the next several months. Whenever possible, we would begin the day with warm-ups and steal moments during lunch breaks and setup changes. But our primary work now had to be accomplished during the shooting itself. Luckily, Robert and I had established an excellent rapport, and much could be communicated nonverbally. I would shift my head slightly backwards, and he would nod and make a global postural change; I'd shake my arms, and he would relax into a more fluid movement.

To my mind, one of the most successful moments in the film was our re-creation of a scene from *The Immigrant*. This was the only scene in which Robert appeared in black-and-white footage that replicated the original. When it was shown to Chaplin's daughter Geraldine, who played her own grandmother in the film, she thought she was seeing an actual film clip of her father. This was heady praise, indeed.

But more meaningful for me was the chance to travel back to a time when movies told their stories through movement. The Keystone Studio had been reconstructed with scrupulous accuracy in the middle of an orange grove in Fillmore, California, about an hour from the snarled traffic of the movie capital. It was almost laughably spartan, consisting of just a row of dressing rooms and a tower from which Mack Sennett kept watch over the multiple films in production on the huge, open-air stage. The sunlight on the stage, filtered through large, muslin diffusers high overhead, was soft and watery. I spent hours there rehearsing with Robert and the other actors, and more hours alone, sitting under the magical light of early cinema. The October air was filled with the pungent smells of fall and the newly constructed sets. Antique, hand-cranked movie cameras sat poised upon their tripods, waiting for the action to begin again . . .

Though its glory days ended when the movies learned to talk, physical comedy is still very much with us. Talented physical performers continually emerge, though none has so far displayed anything like the virtuosity and comedic vision of the great silent clowns. They could hardly be expected to, for the silent comedians flourished during a unique historical moment, a brief thirty-year span when movement and film technology merged to become the world's most popular art form. Since then flashes of visual wit have enlivened stage, film, and television productions, but the form our next great era of movement art will take is unclear. Meanwhile, we can be grateful that the silent comedy masterworks survive, a legacy that will continue to delight and amaze the public, and inspire new generations of writers, directors and performers.

Keaton photos from Patricia Tobias Collection.

PART TWO

Body Basics

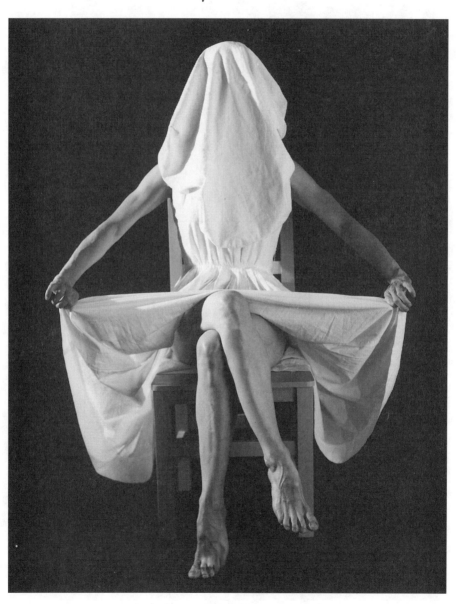

The Feldenkrais Method®

Alan S. Questel

Movement is life. Without movement life is unthinkable.

—Moshe Feldenkrais

The Feldenkrais Method is a unique blend of science and aesthetics. Pioneered over fifty years ago by Dr. Moshe Feldenkrais, it is based on our innate human capacity for lifelong development and growth. It is the means to moving beyond our self-imposed limitations and uncovering our untapped potentials. While our ability to move more efficiently is definitely enhanced, movement is simply the medium for cultivating more effective ways of sensing, thinking, feeling, and knowing. Through movement and the use of attention, self-image is refined, sensory acuity is heightened, and natural curiosity is evoked. As you will discover, it is a process that brings the conceptual into the realm of experience. It is based in learning and gaining insight into how we have "learned how to learn." Through the recognition of how our whole self is involved in everything we do, we can learn to more easily bring our intention into action. The method continues to find growing recognition and wider applications throughout the arts and the sciences.

THE DEVELOPMENT OF THE METHOD

Dr. Moshe Feldenkrais was an extraordinary individual, a Renaissance man with a broad range of knowledge and a true original thinker. He emigrated from Russia to Palestine (now Israel) at the age of thirteen. Working as a laborer and mathematician, he eventually earned degrees in mechanical and electrical engineering and received his D.Sc. from the Sorbonne in Paris, where he assisted Joliet-Curie in early nuclear research. He studied with Professor Kano, the developer of judo, and was one of the first Europeans to earn a black belt in the martial art in 1936.

An avid soccer player as a young man, he destroyed his knees in his dedication to the sport. This disability became the source for his inquiry into human functioning and consciousness. His interest was captured by the fact that some days one knee would hurt, then on other days the other knee would hurt; sometimes both knees hurt, and sometimes neither. At the time the medical profession offered him little hope, so he set off on his own journey. Based on the assumption that "on the days my knees hurt, I must be doing something different," Moshe began to investigate what he was doing and how he was doing it.

While developing an understanding of his own self-use, one of his favorite pastimes was to watch the children playing in the waiting room of his wife's pediatric practice. He observed that while the children had an intention to move toward something—let's say a toy—they were more involved in the actual process than in achieving their goal. While getting the toy was the initiation of the action, the texture of the carpet or the negotiation of a step was what held the child's interest. Retrieval of the toy might or might not be the end result.

It was this kind of attention that Moshe brought to his personal exploration. Drawing from his extensive range of knowledge in movement, learning theory, neuroscience, physics, and psychology, Dr.

Feldenkrais made revolutionary discoveries regarding self-image, the ability to function more ecologically, and our capacity to become more who we imagine ourselves to be.

Functional Integration® is the first modality Feldenkrais developed. Later, he created Awareness Through Movement®. It is these modalities that comprise the Feldenkrais Method.

FUNCTIONAL INTEGRATION® AND AWARENESS THROUGH MOVEMENT®

Functional Integration (FI) lessons are a hands-on, noninvasive, and interactive process where the practitioner uses what he feels and sees to guide a person to a more diverse, more whole, and more well-organized use of herself. The person, referred to as a student, is fully clothed and is usually lying down or sitting. What occurs is tailor-made for the student and is the direct result of the interaction between the practitioner and the student. The applications of this modality range from orthopedic and neurological difficulties to professional athletes, dancers, actors, musicians, and everyone in between who has the desire to improve and grow.

Awareness Through Movement (ATM) lessons are a series of guided movement sequences that people are led through verbally, either in groups or individually. There are over a thousand lessons, and they are done slowly and gently, usually lying down or sitting (some standing), with an emphasis on reducing effort and developing awareness. The student's attention is directed by the practitioner to areas of herself that may be other than the ones she usually attends to, to bring about a more complete sense of what she is doing and how she is doing it. The results are improved breathing, increased range of motion, reduction of pain, a greater sense of well-being, and feeling more connected with oneself.

WHY MOVEMENT?

Feldenkrais observed that within us there is a continuous stream of thinking, feeling, sensing, and moving or acting. We may not be aware of these things going on at times, but if we really focus our attention, we will find that these processes are ongoing. A change in any of these aspects of the self potentiates a change in the others. It is certainly possible to change how we think, how we feel, how we sense, and how we move. The question becomes, how can changes be accessed and sustained?

To change how we think presumes we know how we think. It can be done, but since the evaluation of how we think is through our thinking, it is easy to trick ourselves.

To change how we feel presents a different kind of dilemma. We first have to know what we are feeling and how we come to feel it. Our feelings are quite changeable from one moment to the next. Do we really understand how a change in them takes place?

To change how we sense is probably the most obscure. To understand how information comes into us and how we process it requires a lifetime's study. The stimuli that influence this kind of processing are so varied that it is almost impossible to keep track of them and their interrelationships.

To change how we move is immediate. We know it in that moment. It is something concrete, something that is observable, not only to ourselves but often to others as well.

MY OWN JOURNEY

I was an actor, attended SUNY College at Purchase, and had the good fortune to work with people like Jerzy Grotowski (The Polish Theatre Laboratory) and Paul Sills (Second City and Story Theatre). But as a living, well, it wasn't a living. I had been introduced to the Feldenkrais Method through my acting teacher, George Morrison, but to be honest, I didn't think much of it.

Not until I hurt my back while I was wallpapering George's bathroom (it *was* a living). He recommended I see a Feldenkrais practitioner—so off I went to see a chiropractor. The chiropractor didn't help, so I tried Feldenkrais. My immediate response was that it was a waste of money. The guy obviously didn't know what he was doing. He barely touched me and wasn't doing anything near where the pain in my back was. I stood up at the end, and I had absolutely no pain. I could easily straighten up. I said to him, "What did you do?" He replied, "You did it." I said, "No, really, what did you do?" And again he said, "Really, you did it." So, now I thought, okay, it's a secret!

Well, it didn't end there. Two days later, I was driving on the FDR Drive in New York (the equivalent of a pinball machine for cars), when I suddenly noticed that I wasn't getting angry when people were cutting me off. Not my usual response; all I could think of was that in some way, it was related to the Feldenkrais lesson. I returned for another session; even though I had no more pain, I was hoping to gain some insight into what he was doing with me.

The second lesson in no way resembled the first. I was in a different position, and while the overall quality of how he touched was the same, the ways in which he moved me were completely different. At the end of the session, he told me to get up when I was ready. I slowly moved my head left and right indicating no. He said to me, "No?' And I said, "No." He asked my why, and I explained that I didn't want to go where I was going. I was on my way to give an estimate for a carpentry job at my uncle's office, and at that moment, all my feelings about doing that kind of work crystallized into a very clear and quiet "no."

Subsequently, I returned for a third lesson, after which I decided I wanted to learn how to do this work, thinking I would much prefer to do this, rather than carpentry, to support my nascent acting career.

I can honestly say I had no idea what I was getting into. After four years of study, I began my practice of the Feldenkrais Method, and it is all I have been doing ever since. My work with actors developed over the years with assorted groups, in different universities, and for several years, at a wonderful laboratory in the New Actors Workshop in New York City. The synthesis of the Feldenkrais Method and its specific applications for actors has become somewhat of a specialty of mine, but as you will see, working with any Feldenkrais practitioner will provide you with the means toward becoming more embodied.

APPLICATIONS FOR THE ACTOR

In addition to personal development possibilities it offers to all, this method has several significant applications for the actor, the first being "the tuning of the instrument." Most actors spend a great deal of time getting themselves in shape or learning how to move more in the way they think they should (or worse yet, how someone else thinks they should). This sort of training has its place, but it offers a very limited understanding of what is really available to us in terms of really tuning our instrument. The way in which we use ourselves is so intrinsically related to our habits that the more we work out or exercise, the more we become the same. When we take on a particular style of movement, we tend to "layer it" over ourselves and most often need to use a great deal of energy to maintain it. In the end, we actually begin to narrow our expressive range.

To my mind, "tuning the instrument" is to prepare it to play *any* piece. Maybe it is even more accurate to say that it is to be able to *be* any kind of instrument, as the need presents itself. The body, as a source of expression, is so recognizable by others that we can see a silhouette of someone at a distance and know who he is. What we want is the ability to produce a shift that is significant enough that we are not recognized—and at the same time be able to fully inhabit ourselves.

Expanding Our Self-Image

While I was teaching theater games in an acting and improvisation class at Princeton University, what stood out for me is that people tend to repeat the same sounds and movements. Kind of an ironic discovery to make in an improvisation class. It almost becomes predictable as to who will do what. At the time, I was just beginning my studies on the Feldenkrais Method and decided to try it out with these acting students. I began to observe something quite remarkable. I would begin with a theater game, then teach the group an Awareness Through Movement lesson, then return to the same theater game. After doing the ATM, they were doing completely novel sounds and movements. Different uses of themselves emerged spontaneously. It didn't end there. Throughout the semester, they continued to develop news ways of moving and interacting.

Following is a mini–ATM lesson to give you a taste of the Feldenkrais Method. It is possible to read this yourself and do the movements, but it would be better if you had someone slowly read it to you. Whether you do it yourself or have it read to you, really pause after each instruction to consider what it is you are feeling. Some of the questions posed won't have answers; still, take some time to ponder them.

A Taste of ATM

Sit in a chair and simply notice what you can about how you sit there. Don't change or correct anything, simply observe what you are doing. Maybe observe how your weight is distributed, notice the shape of your back, is it rounded or arched or maybe you're not sure. Where are your feet placed? Are they under you, in front of you, someplace else?

Sit at the edge of the chair and feel what sitting here feels like. What is the shape of your back? Where are your feet placed? Slowly come to standing, observing what you can, and return to sitting. Do this several times slowly and gently, listening to yourself throughout.

Come in and out of the chair again, but this time look up the whole time. Do it several times and observe how your feel.

Now, do it keeping your eyes looking down the whole time. What does this feel like? Different? Can you name a few differences?

Sitting at the edge of your chair, move your feet an inch or two further underneath you. Feel what that is like. Does it change anything in your sitting? In the shape of your back? In how you are balanced? With your feet in this new place, come up to standing a few times. Go slowly, so you can pay attention to what you feel. Is it any different, not only in terms of how you move, but also in terms of how you feel internally and how you imagine you would be perceived by others?

Keeping your feet placed as they are, get in and out of the chair with your eyes looking up. Observe if this changes anything in the shape of your back, in your balance.

Now, do it with your eyes looking down. Notice any differences that this presents for you. Pause and rest for a moment.

Move your feet another couple of inches further under you, and again, come to standing and back to sitting a few times. Has this changed anything in how you sense yourself? Do you get up more easily? Quicker? Are you more unstable or more mobile? Could these both be the same thing?

With your feet in the same place further under you, get in and out of the chair looking up a few times and then looking down. Does it influence the way you get in and out of the chair?

Pause and rest for a moment.

Come back to sitting on the edge of your chair and, this time, place your feet a couple of inches further in front of you from where you initially started, and come to standing and sitting a few times. What is this like? Is it preferable?

Do the same thing looking up and then looking down, sensing where you feel any differences.

Move your feet a couple of inches further out from where you last placed them and continue to come to standing and sitting. What is this like? Can you still get out of the chair? Do you feel heavier doing it? Do different parts of you come into action?

Again, play with where your eyes look as you get in and out of the chair with your feet placed here. Note where you sense any differences.

Pause.

Return to where you initially placed your feet, and come to standing and back to sitting a few times. Is it different? Does your attention move to other places in yourself? Do get in and out of the chair differently? Do you feel lighter, heavier, or something else?

Before you did this exercise, did you ever consider the placement of your feet or where you looked and how these might influence your movement, its quality, or how you feel doing it? If you felt lighter or more mobile with your feet more under you, or heavier or more stable with your feet placed further out, could you imagine this being a choice that might influence your characterization?

Repetition, Repetition, Repetition, Repe . . .

One of the greatest challenges an actor faces is having to say the same lines and repeat the same behavior night after night after night. How do we do it again and keep it alive, vital, and interesting, both to ourselves and the audience? Anything that is repeated has a good chance of becoming mechanical. There is a bit of a paradox here, as we hope to be familiar enough with what we are doing that it isn't taking all of our attention, and yet not so familiar that we become bored while doing it.

It often comes down to where we place our attention that helps us remain present with what we are doing. Our ability to have a mobile and fluid attention that can bring us back (or forward) into the present moment is what we need to develop.

While performing my "great role" as Yakov in Chekhov's *The Seagull*, I was waiting for the cue for one of my six lines. Irina Nikolayevna was speaking; in the meantime, I was looking at Nina Zarechnya and internally pondering her name, repeating it over and over to myself in a kind of singsong way. Suddenly, I heard my cue from Irina Nikolayevna: "Here is a ruble for the three of you." My response was supposed to be "God bless you, Irina Nikolyevna." What came out was "God bless you Irina Ni!" I was about to say Irena Ni-na Zarechnya. Of course, there was an awkward pause, maybe not even noticeable to the audience. I could argue that, if I had more lines with more meaning, I might have been more attentive, but I think not.

The vast amount of associations and the infinite number of places our mind can carry us makes it unreliable resource for bringing us back to the here and now. Processes like meditation can help, but when onstage, we need something more immediate. Our kinesthetic sense is also quite rich, and while it, too, may distract us, the immediacy of it is more likely to connect us to where we are and what we are doing.

Suppose that during a scene, you placed your feet differently as you got out of a chair; and as a result of that, you moved more quickly toward the actor you were speaking with; and as the result of that, he responded by shifting his weight back or even taking a small step backwards. If your awareness is focused so that you are attentive to these details, you will find that both of you are more present, even if it's the four hundredth performance. Of course, this needs to occur within the parameters of how the play was directed and blocked. To be able to sense subtle distinctions, rather than having to change whole pieces of behaviors, not only keeps the play intact, but also allows for a deepening of the experience night after night. Through a more refined understanding of how we move, and the enhanced ability to sense ourselves, we can more effectively remain present with what we are doing.

Taking Better Care of Ourselves

Part of our ability to use ourselves well as "an instrument" is to be able to tolerate new and varied uses of ourselves. Many actors end up sustaining injuries, perhaps because they are performing in a long-running show and because of how the character needs to move. When we take on a new physical characteristic, we generally approach it from the point of view of the audience: How will they see it? While this is necessary, the characterization is often taken on without an understanding of how a person might have actually developed such a physicality. Whether we are taking on a limp or a hunched back, the expression of these traits must be created through the use of our entire selves. If it doesn't incorporate one's whole self, the audience usually doesn't believe it.

To take on a limp means much more than taking on a limp. Has the playwright determined the cause of the limp? Is it an old injury or a new one? Is the injury in the foot, the knee, the hip? The answers to all of these questions will create a different use of self.

Any injury results in compensatory actions that can often lead to other difficulties. The kind of compensatory actions one takes on depends on old habits. These determine what we do and how we do it. The unveiling of our habits is one of the core investigations we pursue in the Feldenkrais Method. The more we come to know what we are doing, the more we will be able to do what we want. When we can understand what our arms do, how our head turns, how we distribute our weight in relation to a limp, we will have created something that will be recognized as an organic part of who we are portraying. This kind of understanding produces degrees of reversibility, so when we come off stage, we can return to ourselves, as a choice, and help prevent unnecessary injuries, both onstage and off.

Embodiment and Presence

What do we mean when we speak of becoming more embodied? When you see someone who appears "more embodied," what makes it recognizable? How do you know when you are more embodied?

The words to describe these experiences are not so easy to come by, yet the experiences themselves are recognizable to us all. In these moments, we could say we are more connected to ourselves; we know what we are feeling, and we can feel ourselves more fully.

To be more present onstage is to have more presence. The ability to fill a space so that an actor is seen and heard by the audience and other actors comes naturally to some, but can be developed by all of us. Through the Feldenkrais Method, we can learn to more fully inhabit ourselves in a sensory way.

How does this happen? We could say that in doing the Feldenkrais Method, we are practicing our sensations. It may sound odd, but it isn't something we typically do. We can take the time to quietly listen to what we feel and to let the sensations of some of the more unknown parts of ourselves slowly emerge. This results in the ability to feel ourselves more, while expanding our self-image.

Clarifying Our Personal Processes

The quality of the environment created by Feldenkrais practitioners is central to the method. It is one of safety, where one is free to make mistakes and explore without having to succeed. Placing ourselves in an environment where we are free from the normal constraints—of being good or doing something well— allows us to experience ourselves at a level that we don't normally attend to. It does not mean we are free from the constraints we impose on ourselves. In fact, when doing the Feldenkrais Method, it is quite common to find that we have quite an internal dialogue: *How am I doing? Am I doing it right? What should I be feeling? Others are better than me. I am better than the others.* The internal dialogue that shows up is reflective of what we do in most situations. The difference here is that there is no great importance placed upon succeeding or achieving a particular movement. We have the chance to witness what we do and discern if it is helping or hindering our intentions. Generally in life, we do not take the time to make these observations. Here, we can investigate how we bring ourselves to a situation, begin to make new distinctions, and start to choose those that serve us more.

LIVING IN THE UNKNOWN

Awareness Through Movement lessons parallel the creative process. In the creative process, we spend a great deal of time in the unknown and engaging in a process that unfolds unto itself. While we may know this, it is something difficult to trust. When we are faced with the unknown, our tendency is to find something known. We are not so comfortable hanging out here. What we need is a safe place to let this happen. A large part of the structure of many ATMs is that we don't know where we are going to end up or how we are going to get there. This puts us in the unknown and gives us time to get accustomed to ourselves in this experience. The more we place ourselves in this type of environment, the more we can find increasing comfort in not knowing and all the feelings that accompany it.

Creativity

In working with actors, I always start out asking the same question: What is the actor's job? The most agreed-upon answer is: to tell the story. The next question I pose is: What is the actor's second job? This answer is usually more debated, and I have yet to hear an answer that I think describes something as essential as "telling the story." So, what am I thinking?

Before answering this, let's for a moment look at how we view others whom we consider more talented, better actors, or more creative than ourselves. What makes talented actors different? Their capacity to express themselves through their voice, their movement, their use of words? All of these are part of their ability to tell the story and are certainly part of what makes them talented. To do this, however, they have to do something else as well.

Most directors I have known appreciate actors who come in with ideas, actors who think for themselves and are willing to stretch. This is not as simple as it sounds. We make choices all the time, but to come up with new ones, original ones, ones that exist outside of our habits is not so easy.

The Feldenkrais Method increases our options and creates more choices for how we do things. Any time someone has taught us the "right" way of doing something, a limitation has been imposed upon him. Not that there aren't "right" ways of doing many things, but most often, the "right" way eliminates further investigation and squelches creativity.

This line of thinking then begs another question: How many possibilities do we need to have a choice? I've heard many answers—two, ten, one hundred? Most people say two, but actually, one variable implies two. That is, with one choice, I can do it or not do it, so it really is two. But is that really a choice? That means onstage, I can behave in a particular way or not. To really have a choice, we need at least three possibilities. With three, we have a much better chance of not feeling stuck. With five or ten choices, we can really begin to explore.

Let me share an instance of how I began to understand this.

The part of Yakov, in *The Seagull*, was the smallest part I ever had. In the beginning of the play, Masha and Medvedenko are having a conversation, while somewhere else, Yakov is building a stage for the play within the play. They don't know he is there, until Yakov interrupts them. There were no directions from the script as to the nature of this interruption. As Yakov, I burst onto the stage, screaming, having just hit my thumb with a hammer. It was the most obvious intrusion I could think of, and it made sense, as I was in the process of building something.

I had quite a bit of time before we returned to rehearsing the scene and I could make my entrance again. An interesting thing occurred during all that time with nothing to do. I came up with another idea. When I heard my cue, I ran about in frenzy, pretending to be chased by bees. More time passed until my next opportunity to enter, and lo and behold, something else came to me. This time, I stumbled onto the scene, laughing and laughing, as if I had just heard the funniest joke, and abruptly stopped, embarrassed that other people were around.

This time, the other actors were shocked. They did not anticipate another variation in the interruption. My small moment began to take on new meaning, as the director began repeated rehearsing of my entrance. Each time, I did something new. I would accidentally toss something and go to retrieve it; I had a sneezing fit; I came out just to observe my handiwork as a builder. By this time, the actors playing Masha and Medvedenko were becoming quite annoyed. What was this scene about anyway? The play was not the story of a servant making an entrance. They were central to the scene, and they were being ignored.

But the director saw something. I was in the process of creating. In that moment, I had accessed something seemingly intangible, but it would be many years before I would understand it. What was I doing?

I was discovering choices, creating choices, acting on my choices.

Here was a situation where I wasn't very concerned with my part. I felt freer to experiment. In most of our situations in life, we don't feel this degree of freedom. What is needed is a place to evoke this. A place where we can begin to observe how "important" we make things and a place where we can feel free to make as many mistakes as we can without any repercussions other than discovering our greater creative potential.

Let's do a more complete ATM. As before, I would recommend that you have someone read this to you, or record it on a tape to listen to. I'll start with guidelines as to how to approach this process.

Preparing for the Lesson

- Use a mat or blanket to lie on—something that allows you to lie comfortably on the floor, without excessive padding.
- Always move slowly and easily.
- Let your own sense of comfort and pleasure be your guide.
- Do only what you can do with ease—do not push or strain.
- As much as you can, let what you are *actually* doing be okay, rather than what you *think* you should be doing.
- Rest as often as you need to. This means to take a break when you feel your attention starting to wander or if you feel yourself increasing your effort or not breathing.
- Follow your attention gently. If you drift off, simply come back and start again.
- The repetition of movements is to provide you with the chance to make observations. Do them as an exploration, not as an exercise.
- The directions are in reference to yourself—for example, *up* is always in the direction above your head, not necessarily to the ceiling, and *down* is always in the direction of your feet.
- If you have any discomfort, make the movements smaller and slower. If discomfort still continues, try imagining the movements.
- There is generally no wrong way to do these movements other than hurting yourself or others.
- There is also no right way to do these movements. This is not meant to confuse you, but to free you from the constraints of trying to do them "correctly."
- If you get confused, slow yourself down, and notice what you are doing in the moment. If you discover that you have been doing a movement differently than I described, congratulations! You just learned something.
- Make mistakes.
- Be inept.
- Be curious.
- Be kind to yourself.
- Stay in the process.
- Enjoy yourself.

ATM Lesson

Lie on your back. Observe what you notice about yourself. Is your attention on your thoughts? Your feelings? Your sensations?

Bring your attention to how you are lying on the floor. Can you feel spaces between yourself and the floor? Where are they? Maybe there is a space behind your knees, your ankles, your neck, your shoulders, your lower back. Maybe in only some of these places, maybe in other places not mentioned.

How do the two sides of yourself compare to each other? Is one side longer or shorter? Wider or narrower? Higher or lower? Thicker or thinner? Do you have some other way of discerning some difference between one side and the other?

Bend your knees, and place your feet so they are "standing." Notice if where you have placed your feet feels stable and easily supports your legs.

Lift the right side of your pelvis a little bit away from the floor and back again. Do this slowly ten to fifteen times. How do you do this? What do you feel when you make this movement? Where do you feel it?

Now, lift the right side of your pelvis by pushing your right foot into the floor. Do this slowly ten to fifteen times. Is this different from what you initially did? Does this feel different? Is it harder or easier?

Now, lift the right side of your pelvis by rolling the left side of your pelvis toward the floor to the left. Do this slowly ten to fifteen times. How does this differ from your previous movements?

Now, imagine that there is a ribbon tied around your right knee and someone is gently pulling that ribbon downward and to the left, so that it starts to lift the right side of your pelvis. Do this slowly ten to fifteen times. Is this any different from the previous ways of lifting your pelvis?

Straighten out your legs and rest. Observe as you rest: What does lying on your back feel like now? Are there any differences compared to when you first lay down?

Bend your knees again, and put your feet in standing position. Explore the different ways of lifting the right side of your pelvis. Find the easiest way for you. You can combine the different ways if you like. Lift the right side of your pelvis the very first way you lifted it. Is it your preference?

Straighten out your legs, rest, and observe how you lie on your back.

Bend your knees again, and put your feet in standing position. Place your left arm, palm up, on the floor, diagonally up to the left (about 45 degrees from your head, where it can rest comfortably on the floor). Slowly and gently, begin to lengthen your left arm in the direction it is pointing, and bring it back to where you started. Do this slowly ten to fifteen times.

Continue lengthening your left arm, and at the same time, begin to lift the right side of your pelvis (in whichever way is easiest for you). Think of connecting these two movements so they become one, as if lifting your pelvis lengthens your arm or that lengthening your arm lifts your pelvis. Do this slowly ten to fifteen times.

Straighten out your legs, rest, and observe how you lie on your back now.

Come back to the same position. Lengthen your left arm as you lift the right side of your pelvis. Begin to roll your head to look at your left hand as you do these movements. Roll your head back to the middle as you lower your pelvis and shorten your arm. Do this slowly ten to fifteen times, again trying to connect these movements.

Straighten out your legs and rest. Is the floor telling you something different than when you started?

Come back to the same position. Lengthen your left arm as you lift the right side of your pelvis while you roll your head to look at your left hand. As you look at your left hand, begin to move your chin toward your left hand. You can also think of this as sliding the back of your head toward your right shoulder. Go slowly, and find out how you can make all of these movements part of the same action.

Straighten out your legs, rest, and sense any differences in how you contact the floor.

Come back to the same position, and do the same movement. As you do this movement, begin to lengthen your right arm downward. Can you make this part of the whole movement? Does including this arm bring more of your back into action?

Straighten out your legs and rest.

Bend your knees, and put your feet in standing position. Slowly lift the right side of your pelvis and see what it is like now. How does it compare to when you first lifted it? Lift the left side of your pelvis only two times, and notice any differences between the right and left sides.

Keep you feet standing, and *imagine* that you are lifting the left side of your pelvis in the three different ways you explored earlier.

Bring your right arm overhead, diagonally up to the right, palm up (about 45 degrees from your head, where it can rest comfortably on the floor), and imagine that you are lifting the left side of your pelvis as you imagine lengthening your right arm.

Continue imagining this movement, and add the movement of your head, turning to the right, with your chin going toward your right hand.

Finally, add the imagined movement of your left arm reaching downwards.

Imagine the whole movement. Starting with an imperceptible amount of movement, begin to actually do the movement. Notice any differences between what you imagined and what you are doing. If it is different, go back and imagine it with this new information.

Straighten out your legs and rest.

Bend your knees and put your feet in standing position. Gently lift the left side of your pelvis and find out what it is like now. Lift the right side a few times and feel how they compare.

Keep your knees bent and bring the left arm diagonally upward on the floor, as you had it earlier, and the right arm diagonally downward alongside you, both with the palms up. Begin to lift the right side of your pelvis, lengthen your left arm upward and your right arm downward, and look to the upward hand. As you bring your pelvis, arms, and head back, switch to the other side. Lift the left side of your pelvis, and lengthen the right arm upward and the left arm downward, and look to the right hand. Begin to go from side to side, observing any differences or similarities.

One last time, with your knees bent and feet in standing position, lift one side of your pelvis, and think of the different ways of initiating the movement. Do you have a different sense of how you might choose to lift it? Has incorporating more of yourself in this action helped clarify how you do it?

Lengthen your legs, and sense how you are lying on the floor now. Has it changed from the beginning? Do you notice different things? Slowly roll to your side, and come to standing. Walk around, and find out if anything is different in your movement. How do you sense yourself? What is your experience in your walking?

If you are having a different experience of yourself, let it run its own course. Try not to hold on to any sensations (even if you prefer them), and let yourself observe any other differences you may feel throughout the rest of your day or evening.

EXPERIENCING THE CONCEPTUAL

The ATM lesson you just explored provided you with the chance to sense yourself differently, not only in your sensations, but also in your attitude toward yourself and the world. For many, it is an unusual experience to do slow, gentle, and seemingly inconsequential movements that can produce such a shift in one's sense of oneself.

There is, however, more here than may meet the eye. Prior to the lesson, I spoke of the actor's second job, an essential part of being creative: developing the ability to create more choices. The lesson itself could be taught from many perspectives. It could be taught as a way to evoke a greater use of your whole self, reduction of effort, more connection through yourself, and gaining insight as to how to make and develop choices.

Part of my intention in offering this particular experiential lesson is to give you the experience of choice. *Experiencing* a concept or idea allows for another kind of understanding than does reading about it.

Feldenkrais himself took great pride in the fact that he could create circumstances, through movement, where an idea could become an embodied experience. To make the abstract concrete is a kind of learning that is not so prevalent in our culture. Most of our learning is informational—facts and ideas that we take in through books, lectures, and other media, where we listen to someone else tell us what we should know and understand.

Real learning, the kind we all experienced as children, comes from our ability to make distinctions and create new relationships to the world we live in. Through this kind of learning, we can develop a sense of self based on an internal criteria and an inner authority.

We have touched on many applications of the Feldenkrais Method for the actor, both in theory and practice. Whether the movement explorations were fascinating or only mildly stimulating to your curiosity, I encourage you to seek out a local practitioner to have a live experience of the work. For a practitioner in your area or a guild in another country, please see appendix A for contact information for the Feldenkrais Guild of North America and Feldenkrais Resources. In addition, there is plenty of material available if you choose to continue to explore the work on your own, including books, CDs, and audio- and videotapes.

Alexander Technique and the Integrated Actor: Applying the Principles of the Alexander Technique to Actor Preparation

Teresa Lee

An integral being knows without going, sees without looking, and accomplishes without doing.
—Lao-tzu

In Stanislavski-based actor training, it is often said that the actor's aim is to live truthfully moment to moment onstage in the imagined circumstances of the character. All too often, excess tension in the actor causes overefforting, which interferes with his availability to subtle expressions of intentions and emotions. The Alexander Technique offers a means whereby acting students may prepare themselves to truthfully embody a character and create authentic moments of action on the stage. Its relevance in the preparation of performers is recognized by such leading actor-training institutions as Juilliard School of Performing Arts, The Performance School at the University of Washington, Dell'Arte School of Movement, The Royal Academy of Dramatic Art, The Stratford Shakespeare Festival, and many others who have certified Alexander Technique teachers on their faculty.

An actor develops and relies on inner and outer resources, such as sense memory, analytical skills, voice, and body. In his book *The Use of the Self,* F. M. Alexander wrote, "Human activity is primarily a process of reacting unceasingly to stimuli received from within and without the self."[1] The same can be said of the actor's process. He is constantly responding to internal and external stimuli during a given performance. The actor's ability to free himself from unconscious habitual responses will allow the actor to listen and respond in the moment of *being* in the given circumstance of the character. In other words, how an actor uses himself determines his functioning onstage. This idea is at the heart of Alexander's work. "Use determines functioning," called "Alexander's Law" by Frank Pierce Jones,[2] was referred to by Alexander as "the Universal Constant."[3]

DEFINING THE TECHNIQUE

The Alexander Technique has similarities to other movement studies that focus on mind-body integration, such as yoga, Feldenkrais®, and t'ai chi. To arrive at what F. M. Alexander called "conscious control of the individual" is central to all of these studies. The difference is that, unlike yoga and the rest, the Alexander Technique is not considered a movement discipline unto itself. It is, rather, an approach to learning, or more accurately "unlearning," applied to any activity. The Alexander Technique is a simple, practical method for consciously engaging in our moment-to-moment lives with improved ease and efficiency. Alexander Technique International defines it as "an indirect method of improving human use and functioning. Practice of the Technique promotes a continually improving coordination, support, flexibility, balance, and ease of movement."[4] F. M. Alexander worked with this process over the course of approximately sixty years, developing it into a widely used technique for kinesthetic re-education.

In order to understand the Alexander Technique, it is important to realize that Alexander's investigations were born from the same needs and impulses we all have—the *desire to do* something (the stimulus) and the unconscious impulse to use too much *effort* in the process of the *doing* (habit.)

> *The essence of the Alexander Technique is to make ourselves more susceptible to grace.*
> —Michael J. Gelb

DEVELOPMENT OF THE ALEXANDER TECHNIQUE

F. M. Alexander, born in 1869 on the northwest coast of Tasmania, Australia, was an actor who kept losing his voice when he was in performance. He sought medical help but found his condition could not be cured by medical treatment, so he took matters into his own hands and began an investigation that took place over a number of years. Alexander simply observed himself in a three-way mirror and methodically studied everything he was doing in the act of speaking. He examined his habitual behaviors and discovered he had a pattern of tensing that resulted in the distortion of several primary relationships in the structure of his body. He determined the most important of these relationships to be the relationship of the head to the neck region of the spinal column. When he introduced the mental stimulus to speak, he noticed that he pulled his head back, down, and forward in relation to his spine in his *effort* to project his voice forward.

No problem, just stop the tensing patterns, right? That's what Alexander thought initially, but when he tried, he realized it was not that easy. He did manage to stop pulling his head back and down to some extent, thus virtually eliminating the "sucking in of breath" and the depression of his larynx that had contributed to his vocal problems. This seemed to be easy enough until he tried to do it consistently in the act of reciting. So, he attempted to *put* his head forward, which, in turn, pulled his chest forward and shortened the length of his torso. He realized that when he tried to change the patterns he had observed in the act of speaking he had actually only compounded the old patterns, or habits, with new patterns of tensing.[5] Alexander was still in the act of *doing* with misdirected *effort* in response to a *stimulus*. Alexander referred to this dynamic as *end-gaining*, the "immediate, habitual response to a stimulus— to go directly for a certain end."[6]

Herein lies the problem: Habits *seem* effortless, because they are unconscious yet familiar. They seem "natural," because that's what we are used to. Alexander realized that our sensory perception of how we *use* ourselves in activity is not reliable. In his Victorian vernacular, he called it "a debauched sense of kinesthesia." Alexander was able to eventually proceed without the overefforting of his habits by replacing his unconscious habitual thinking with a new conscious constructive thinking process, which he called *the means whereby*. This process involved mentally letting go of the desire to speak, what he termed *inhibition*, and redirecting his attention to himself as a *whole* "in such a way" that he could allow the inherent *primary control* in his body to be engaged.[7] In Frank Pierce Jones's book, *The Study of the Alexander Technique: Body Awareness in Action*, he describes *primary control* as "F. M. Alexander's discovery that the dynamic relation of the head and the neck promotes maximal lengthening of the body and facilitates movement throughout the body."[8] Through this process, Alexander experienced an overall improvement in his *use*—*use* meaning the "the total pattern of behavior in the ongoing present," according to Jones.[9] As Alexander's *use* improved, so did his breathing and his voice. He gained notoriety for his performances, with audiences particularly admiring the quality of his voice. Other actors began to come to him for lessons, and by the mid-1890s, he was engaged in a thriving practice of teaching both performers and non-performers about his discoveries.

In London, in 1930, Alexander established the first training course for teachers of the Alexander Technique.[10] The work of F. M. Alexander has influenced such notable figures of our time as John Dewey, Aldous Huxley, George Bernard Shaw, Sir Charles Sherrington, and Professor Raymond Dart. Alexander was clearly ahead of his time in Western culture, for he based his whole technique on the notion that "it is *impossible* to separate 'mental' and 'physical' processes in any form of human activity."[11]

> . . . knowledge of the self is fundamental to all other.
>
> —Frederick Matthias Alexander

APPLYING THE PRINCIPLES OF THE TECHNIQUE

Michael J. Gelb, author of *Body Learning: An Introduction to the Alexander Technique,* describes the Alexander Technique as "the experience of gradually freeing oneself from the domination of fixed habits."[12] How does one go about using the Technique to achieve this freedom? The guiding principles of the Alexander Technique may be summarized as:

- Use and Functioning
- Expanded Field of Attention
- Sensory Appreciation
- Inhibition

- Unity of the Human Organism (Self)
- Primary Control
- End-gaining and Means Whereby
- Conscious Direction

The principles of the Technique are relatively simple—*using* the principles presents the challenge. Part of the challenge to teachers and students of the Alexander Technique is that these principles are not employed in any particular order. Unfortunately, there are no "steps," no "exercises," no "procedures." Alexander coined a phrase, "all together, one after the other," when describing how he employed his directions for the process of improving his use in activity.[13] This is one way to describe the kind of thinking an Alexander teacher must engage in when working with a student.

As an Alexander teacher, I must consciously direct my own thinking about my use as I work with my hands to help students direct theirs. John Dewey called this "thinking in activity."[14] Years of practice and hands-on work with many teachers have helped me to become aware of my own "fixed habits." Those teachers have guided me toward a generally improved quality in the use and functioning of my *self*. This is what I aim for with my students. Alexander Technique International states, "The Alexander Technique is the only method of improving human use and functioning which (1) teaches an indirect method of consciously preventing interferences with one's best use and functioning, and (2) the only method where its teachers consciously use these principles at the same time they are teaching the Technique to others."[15]

Here is an example of how I might work with students using the principles of the Alexander

Technique. The majority of my teaching is in a university undergraduate theater program. Students enter my classroom much the way they might enter any other university classroom. They are either dragging in with the weight of the world and all their stresses, or they are bouncing off the walls with chitchat. Either way, they are entering the classroom environment with unfocused "social energy."

Constructive Rest

I usually begin my performance classes with "constructive rest." It is sometimes referred to as "lying down work" or "the Balanced Resting State procedure."[16] This is actually something Alexander did with students later in his teaching.

Constructive rest consists of a person consciously lying on her back with feet on the floor and knees raised, the semi-supine position, in order to allow unnecessary tensions to ease and the back to regain its length and width. It is recommended that a small stack of books—sometimes one is enough—be placed under the back of the head, where the head is supported by the spine, in order to encourage release from downward pressure. During this work, I will give verbal "directions" to help expand students' attention and bring their awareness to their present state of being in their environment. I quite often talk them through the kind of *directional* thinking Alexander employed to indirectly encourage the freeing of their *primary control*:

> Without interference, notice your breathing, . . . the gentle rise and fall of your stomach as you allow the breath to come in and out of your body. Let your neck be free. Allow your head to release forward and up so that your back may lengthen and widen. Let your shoulders release into the floor. Sense the space and freeing in your hip joints—widening across the front and back of the pelvis. Notice the space between your ribs as they move. Allow the muscles of your neck to free, releasing any undue tension . . .

The kinesthetic experience is also enhanced by subtle hands-on guidance during this floor work. The use of my hands in teaching is specific, clear, and intended to guide the student in her conscious directional thinking. Once the students change their relationship to the floor by coming to standing, we proceed with the class activities, usually starting with a more traditional actor "warm-up." During the warm-up, I monitor students' habitual responses and encourage them to keep their awareness of themselves and their environment (*expanded field of attention*). I challenge them to notice their impulses and inhibit uncontrolled responses until they pause to organize their thinking (*inhibition* and *conscious direction*).

One-on-One Work

Alexander Technique is student-centered. What happens in a lesson is determined by the needs of the individual student. Although it is possible and somewhat effective to work in a large group, it is my experience that it is *most* effective to work one-on-one with a student in order to guide the individual through awareness of her tensing patterns and to encourage release. In one-on-one work with students, common issues frequently emerge. These may include shoulders "slouching," rounding in the back, neck and lower back pain, pressure and pain in the knees, inability to allow the arms to just hang freely, lack of centering often caused by overefforting with the limbs, and breathing tensions. I may begin by noticing if a student is "pulling down" in her head-neck area or in an opposite pattern of overefforting by "pulling up." I will work with the student to help her develop a kinesthetic memory of the dynamic primary relationship of letting the neck be free, the head to go forward and up, and the body to follow "all together, one after the other." To put it simply, when the neck muscles are released, the head will balance itself, thus allowing for lengthening of the stature and widening through the back. After working hands-on with a student, I will watch and notice changes in the quality of her expressivity. I will usually then ask her for feedback about what she experienced. At such a moment, the dialogue might go something like this:

TEACHER: What happened?
STUDENT: It's hard to put into words!
TEACHER: Does anything feel different?
STUDENT: Yes. I feel lighter.
TEACHER: Lighter. How? Can you say more about that feeling?
STUDENT: It's like I'm just standing here with no effort. I feel like I could do anything!
TEACHER: Good! Has anything else changed?
STUDENT: Yes. I feel like it's easier to breathe. I'm taking deeper breaths.

The dialogue could continue in this way, or this may be all the student is able to verbalize about the kinesthetic experience. In the beginning, it is often difficult for the student to find the words to describe such an unfamiliar feeling. The longer I work with students, the more language they develop to describe their experiences. Typically, students will experience an overall feeling of kinesthetic lightness. They usually also experience a sense of being connected, more of an integrated whole rather than disconnected parts. Arms and legs become integrated with the torso, and they engage in a more naturally balanced relationship with the gravitational forces at play with their bodies. The ease in breathing that was mentioned above is a very common response. In addition to the benefits of enhancing the authenticity of their characterizations, the technique offers the benefit of improving the use of their physical and vocal instrument by simply improving their breathing.

The Alexander Technique is also helpful in developing a clearer understanding of the truth of the way the human body functions. This will aid in an actor's development of his physical character. In a recent coaching session, I worked with a young acting student who was playing a character in her seventies. She came to me seeking help with developing the walk of her character, "Miss Emma." Miss Emma was supposed to be suffering from arthritis in her hip joint. When I asked Andrea to show me what she had come up with on her own, she demonstrated the stereotypical cliché of old age, with hunched-over posture and generally stiff movements. I asked her to point to where her right hip joint was. She put her hand generally around the top of the pelvis, but admitted she was guessing. I first worked hands-on with her to improve her sensory appreciation and kinesthetic understanding of where her hip joint was. We then worked with what it would mean to be compromised in that joint—how one might compensate for pain and stiffness in that particular area. The result was a series of *specific* choices that communicated a much more clear, believable physical character. She was also freer in her whole body, especially her torso, which allowed for more breath support for her voice.

What a piece of work is man! how noble in reason! how infinite in faculty! in form and moving how express and admirable!

—William Shakespeare

ACTING WITH EASE

Just as Alexander discovered that the interfering habits he had developed around the act of speaking were amplified when he began to "recite" onstage, so are all "fixed habits" that young performers bring with them in their initial attempts to "act." If the fixed habits of the actor are interfering in her daily life, they are amplified threefold when she attempts to convey a character on the stage. The less these habits interfere with the inherent directionality of actor's use and functioning, the more the true self is revealed. The quality of her actions becomes more authentic. Stanislavski included a discussion of this idea in his book *Building a Character.* In a dialogue between the frustrated student and the Director, Tortsov, the student asks, "What is the matter? What are you trying to extract from us?" The Director replies with an illustration of a white piece of paper that was cluttered with lines and ink splotches, upon which one is asked to "put a delicate pencil sketch." The Director continues:

> . . . In order to do this you must first clean the paper of the superfluous lines and spots which, if they remain on it will blur and ruin your drawing. For its sake you are obliged to have a clean sheet of paper.
>
> The same thing takes place in our type of work. Extra gestures are the equivalent of trash, dirt, spots.
>
> Unrestrained movements, natural though they may be to the actor himself, only blur the design of his part, make his performance unclear, monotonous and uncontrolled.[17]

Stanislavski's advice, as spoken through Tortsov—"Every actor should so harness his gestures that he will always be in control of them and not they of him"—could very well have been given by F. M. Alexander himself!

An actor's habits are not just physical habits leading to disorganization of the body, commonly thought of as "bad posture" or extraneous gestures. Remember that this technique relates to the psychophysical phenomenon. Often, an actor's attention is dominantly fixed on the act of performing, or *end-gaining* in Alexander terms. Her response to the idea of being "judged" by the audience or to her own inner "you're not good enough" demons results in performance anxiety. These thinking patterns manifest themselves into binding physical tensions: neck tension, increased heartbeat, sweaty palms, raising of the shoulders, lifting and gripping in the chest, tensing in the lower back, tensing in the hands, arms, and legs, and lifting of the chin and head in an effort to overcome the other tensions. Psychological tensions, such as not listening to other actors, forcing emotions, and disconnection from the material, also occur.

How does one use the Alexander Technique to become a better, more integrated actor? The same way one uses the Alexander Technique in one's life. As a result of studying this work, I have made profound changes in the way I do almost everything. Don't get me wrong, I still have a long way to go! I don't live every moment of my life with total awareness and ease. But I had many destructive habits to change, and change is an ongoing dynamic process. Just as many theater artists have, I came from the school of

Movement for Actors

"no pain, no gain." Theater training requires hard work in a highly disciplined, rigorous environment. Performing artists must be able to meet the demands of their profession with strength, stamina, versatility, tenacity, and sensitivity. It was difficult for me to believe that I could accomplish more with less effort. I think it is hard for any of us to accept this idea. We are not taught this in life. We don't win the trophy for running the race with the least amount of effort; we win it for running the fastest and finishing first!

And what about creating a character? Isn't that what acting is all about? How can an actor be his "true self" while becoming a believable character? This is perhaps the greatest dilemma an actor struggles with on the journey to mastering his craft. Simply stated, the truth of the character is veiled by the underlying interferences of the actor. An actor always brings a part of himself to every character. The character is filtered through the Self of the actor. Phyllis G. Richmond of Southern Methodist University summed it up quite well when she wrote, "The actor's consciousness supports the character's consciousness by taking care of the conditions that free the actor to act and the character to be."[18] When these "conditions" are attended to, the results are what I call an integrated actor. His performance is perceived by the audience to be effortless, unselfconscious, and authentic.

In a recent coaching session with a student who was preparing a monologue for an audition, I observed many "superfluous gestures" and mannerisms that interfered with the honest communication of the text of her piece. I worked hands-on with her to help her become more connected and grounded with her performance. Here are Caroline's reflections on her experience:

> I'm the kind of person who exerts a lot of extra energy that I sometimes don't need or use. I have a hard time connecting with my body and being connected to my space. During one particular session with my teacher, we worked on an audition piece. She talked me through certain Alexander Technique concepts, and she helped me find my relaxed and aligned body. For the first time ever, I felt connected to the floor. After that session, I performed my audition piece in a truly honest way. It was the first time I had done it that way, and it was amazing! I was honest with my audition from that day forward.

Acting is all about choices. The actor must be free in herself to make those choices. The Alexander Technique teaches that we have choices in our conscious thinking. It is only in our unconscious, habitual thinking that choices do not exist. "When we consciously inhibit, we create a space in which choice can operate."[19] That space in which choice can operate allows for the moment of living truthfully onstage.

Pause . . . listen . . . choose.

NOTES

1. Alexander, F. Matthias. *The Use of the Self.* Long Beach, Calif.: Centerline Press, 1989, 23.
2. Jones, Frank Pierce. *Body Awareness in Action: A Study of the Alexander Technique.* New York: Schocken Books, 1979, 45.
3. Gelb, Michael J. *Body Learning: An Introduction to the Alexander Technique,* 2nd ed. New York: Henry Holt and Company, 1995, 25–26.
4. *Alexander Technique International. An Operational Definition of the Alexander Technique: ATI Professional Development Committee Report (Task A),* online, *www. ati-net.com/ati-pdca.htm,* May 23, 2000.
5. Alexander, 4–19.
6. Alexander, 15.
7. Alexander 5–19.
8. Jones, 196.
9. Jones, 196.
10. Gelb, 18.

11. Alexander, 1.
12. Gelb, 1.
13. Alexander, 16.
14. Alexander, 16.
15. ATI online.
16. Gelb, 161.
17. Stanislavsky, Konstanstin. *Building a Character.* Elizabeth Reynolds Hapgood, trans. New York: Theatre Arts Books, 1981, 69.
18. Sontag, Jerry, ed., *Curiosity Recaptured: Exploring Ways We Think and Move.* San Francisco: Mornum Time Press, 1996, 119.
19. Park, Glen. *The Art of Changing: A New Approach to the Alexander Technique.* Bath, England: Ashgrove Press, 1991.

An Introduction to Laban Movement Analysis for Actors: A Historical, Theoretical, and Practical Perspective

Barbara Adrian

Laban Movement Analysis (LMA) is a theoretical framework for observing qualitative and quantitative changes in movement, ranging from conversational hand gestures to complex actions. This system of movement analysis was developed by Rudolph Laban, an Austrio-Hungarian dancer, choreographer, teacher, philosopher, theorist, and writer, whose life spanned from 1879 to 1958. He is still considered the most important movement theorist of the 1900s. He observed how the human being moves as its physical condition, environment, cultural issues, and communication with other bodies and the universe at large affects it physically and emotionally. He exploded the study of movement beyond the world of the professional dancer. He developed a process whereby expressive movement can belong to all of us, not just a gifted few moving in codified sequences for applause. In fact, the first line of his book *The Mastery of Movement* is "Man moves in order to satisfy a need."[1] This author can't think of a more universal actor-centered training concept than one based on "satisfying a need."

The Russian actor, director, teacher, theorist, and writer Konstantin Stanislavsky (1863–1938) conceived the best-known and universally taught acting technique in this country, the Method. Principally, Stella Adler, Lee Strasberg, and Harold Clurman disseminated the Method, or Method acting, in the United States through the Group Theatre beginning in the 1930s. Method acting, a reaction against the artificial theatrical styles of the day, resulted in an acting technique based on "naturalism." Its premise is to work from the inner emotional life of the character toward the outer form as it is affected by the character's wants and needs. Later in his research, however, Stanislavsky became less enamored of trying to pinpoint the emotional life of the character based on "feelings" and more interested in developing the concept of the "physical action" that would potentially express the inner life of the character through behavior. He felt that concentrating solely on the emotional life was flawed due to its inherent unpredictability, making a repeatable performance elusive at best. Stanislavsky said, "Do not speak to me about feeling. We cannot set feeling, we can only set physical actions."[2] A "physical action" is any move that is calculated toward achieving a goal or satisfying a need. In Laban's vocabulary, this is the equivalent of elevating a move from functional toward expressive. For instance, an actor may decide his character will move from sitting to standing. If the actor determines that the purpose of this move is to intimidate the other character, then moving from sitting to standing is no longer just functional but an expressive move or "physical action." LMA is a process by which the actor can become so precise in his physical choices that he optimizes the possibility of revealing the story to the audience in ways unique to the character and the circumstances.

Because Laban observed that we satisfy our needs, whether functional or expressive, through movement, he, like Stanislavsky, was interested in the natural or organic movements of everyday life—that is to say, how the body moves in the real world accomplishing real tasks. Laban's expanded vision for movement training led him to observe man in relation to nature, in the workplace, during religious rituals, and at play. He came to believe that embedded in the body's natural rhythms was the potential for expressive movement and that each individual had a *right* to opportunities to explore this potential. Consequently, in spite of Laban's profound contribution to German Expressionist dance, working with LMA's principles and concepts is not about developing a rarified system of movement but is an inclusive celebration of the human movement potential embracing all body types, physical conditions, and cultures.

THE BIRTH OF BESS: BODY, EFFORT, SHAPE, AND SPACE

Laban's genius brought into view for us the underlying principles that support the concepts of Body, Effort, Shape, and Space (BESS). Each of these can be perceived as a container for our authentic movement. In this context, I am using the word "container" to mean a flexible holder of goods. A flexible container is an important part of this metaphor, because there is nothing fixed or rigid about exploring BESS. Body, Effort, Shape, and Space interact and play upon one another while maintaining the separateness of individual containers, thus providing us with clear and distinct ways to observe and experience movement. The Body is the container for our breath connection, alignment, flexibility, strength, stamina, and balance. Effort contains our impulses to move based on our attitudes toward the Effort Factors: Time, Weight, Space, and Flow. Shape contains how these attitudes are articulated through the Body. Space is the container for our environment, which includes architecture, objects, and people, not to mention our universe. The component parts of BESS interact with one another in the following ways:

- Shape is dependent on the Body in order to be responsive to inner and outer stimuli, allowing the full expression of an inner attitude to manifest.
- Space acts on the Body, influencing our inner attitudes and resulting in an Effort Action.
- The Body, following the impulse of our Effort Action, influences Space through Shape.

Around and around these concepts or containers go, turning in on each other, forming a complex interrelationship that begins with the impulse to move. Being responsive to the impulse, whether it initiates in Body, Effort, Shape, or Space, is an integral part of the actors' craft, and LMA provides a practical, nonjudgmental process for actors to honor their authentic responses to the world and all it contains.

Effort: The Storyteller

The concept Effort refers to our inner attitude toward the Factors of Weight, Space, Time, and Flow, and this attitude in turn creates behavior. Each of these Factors can be expressed along a continuum, book-ended by two Effort Elements:

- Weight = *strong* ↔ *light*
- Time = *urgent* ↔ *sustained*
- Space = *direct* ↔ *indirect*
- Flow = *bound* ↔ *free*

It is the range of exertion between the extremes of the two Effort Elements where qualitative changes in movement take place. Naturally, because we are complex creatures, most of our physical actions are a combination of Elements that are overlapping and sequencing with each other. But the question LMA asks is, "What in this action is *most* salient? Is it the Time, Weight, Space, or Flow? Or is it a combination of several in equal proportions? If not in equal proportions, which Factors are secondary and tertiary?" If

Table 1: Effort

FACTORS: weight / space / time / flow

ELEMENTS: Light ↔ Strong / Inirect ↔ Direct / Urgent ↔ Sustained / Bound ↔Free

- Light: Indulgent/expansive intention in weight. Delicate or fine touch.
- Strong: Fighting/condensing intention in weight. Having an impact.
- Indirect: Indulgent/expansive attention in space. Flexible, multi-overlapping foci.
- Direct: Fighting/condensing attention in space. To the point, aimed, blunt.
- Urgent: Fighting/condensing decision in time. Spark-like, excited, rushed.
- Sustained: Indulgent/expansive decision in time. Leisurely, prolonged, endless.
- Bound: Fighting/condensing emotions or continuity. Careful, restrained, controlled.
- Free: Indulgent/expansive emotions or continuity. Abandoned, uncontrolled, unlimited.

STATES: A combination of equal parts of two Effort Elements

- Weight + Flow = *Dream State:* Light/Free, Strong/Free, Light/Bound, Strong/Bound
- Space + Time = *Awake State:* Indirect/Sustained, Direct/ Sustained, Indirect/Urgent, Direct/Urgent
- Time + Weight = *Rhythm State:* Sustained/Light, Sustained/Strong, Urgent/Light, Urgent/Strong
- Space + Flow = *Remote State:* Indirect/Free, Indirect/Bound, Direct/Free, Direct/Bound
- Time + Flow = *Mobile State:* Urgent/Free, Urgent/Bound, Sustained/Free, Sustained/Bound
- Weight + Space = *Stable State:* Strong/Direct, Strong/Indirect, Light/Direct, Light/Indirect

DRIVES: A combination of equal parts of three Effort Elements

ACTION DRIVES: Equal parts of Space, Weight, and Time. *Only Action Drives are provided with individual names for each combination:*

- Strong Weight + Direct Space + Urgent Time = *Punch Action Drive*
- Light Weight + Direct Space + Urgent Time = *Dab Action Drive*
- Strong Weight + Indirect Space + Urgent Time = *Slash Action Drive*
- Light Weight + Indirect Space + Urgent Time = *Flick Action Drive*
- Strong Weight + Direct Space + Sustained Time = *Press Action Drive*
- Light Weight + Direct Space + Sustained Time = *Glide Action Drive*
- Strong Weight + Indirect Space + Sustained Time = *Wring Action Drive*
- Light Weight + Indirect Space + Sustained Time = *Float Action Drive*

TRANSFORMATION DRIVES:

- *Passion Drive* = Weight + Time + Flow
- *Vision Drive* = Time + Space + Flow
- *Spell Drive* = Weight + Space + Flow

we combine two Effort Factors in equal proportions, we are moving in a State. If we combine three, we are moving in either an Action Drive or a Transformation Drive (see table 1). The Action Drives are the aspect of LMA that actors are commonly exposed to, because they find them immediately accessible toward promoting the physical manifestation of their actions and objectives.[3]

Because the material is richer and far more varied than the Action Drives suggest, I have chosen to use as examples an actor's evolution toward two Transformation Drives. The difference between the two is that an Action Drive combines the Factors of Weight, Space, and Time while a Transformation Drive substitutes Flow for one of the other Factors.

In the following examples, I will be evolving the movement choices from emphasizing a single Effort Element to emphasizing two Effort Elements (State) to climaxing with three Effort Elements (Drive).

Example 1: In this scene, the character has ten minutes to lounge in a bathtub. Consequently, the actor's attitude toward Time is likely to be *sustained*. Example 2: In this scene, the character has ten minutes to find her lost keys and get thirty blocks downtown; therefore, the actor's attitude toward the same ten minutes is likely to be *quick* or *urgent*. The given circumstances[4] and the objectives are completely different for the same amount of time. Let's add to Example 1, that during the bath, the character is listening to some wonderful music, which influences the actor to wash herself on the Free Flow side of the Flow Factor continuum. If I add that the character has a maid to clean up, then the actor may choose the extreme of Free Flow, most likely resulting in a very wet floor. The actor is now using two Effort Factors, Time and Flow, which constitutes in LMA terms the Mobile State. If the actor emphasizes a third Element, bringing it into equal rather than secondary or tertiary play with Time and Flow, she will enter a Drive. Let's say that the character is described as "bathing as if it were a sensual experience," then the actor would choose to heighten the Weight Factor and perhaps specifically the Element of Light Weight. Balancing equally the importance of Time, Flow, and Weight Factors, the actor will enter what LMA calls a Passion Transformation Drive. The equal use of three Factors simultaneously is reserved for the "extraordinary" moments in life, when the stakes are rising (such as climaxing a sensuous bathing experience), while single Effort Elements and States describe most other ordinary, daily-living activities.

To develop Example 2 further, let's say the character needs to find her keys and get downtown in ten minutes, but she has also hurt her back. Consequently, the actor's relationship with Flow must be *bound* to give the appearance to the audience of trying to prevent further injury, while maintaining an *urgent* relationship with Time. The actor is again in a Mobile State, but in this example, she is emphasizing Urgent Time and Bound Flow, which are at the other end of the spectrum from Sustained Time and Free Flow described in Example 1. To let this evolve into a Drive, the actor needs to bring one more Factor into prominence. Since this character is looking for her keys, the environment is likely to be important to this event, so the actor begins to value Space as much as she is valuing Time and Flow. Taking in the whole room at once and then pinpointing where the keys might be will express her relationship to the Space Factor. The actor is moving along the Space Factor continuum between the Effort Elements of *indirect* and *direct*, while simultaneously having an *urgent* attitude toward Time and a *bound* attitude toward Flow. This combination of equal parts of Time-Flow-Space is called a Vision Transformation Drive and, as with the Passion Drive, gives the appearance to the audience that the stakes within the scene are very high or extraordinary.

In each example, the Effort Elements are interacting either simultaneously, sequentially, or are overlapping each other, influencing the body to move in and out of single Effort Elements, States, and Drives, creating a rich and varied movement sequence around bathing or hunting for the keys. What is important to the actor is not whether she can name a specific State or Drive, but that she understands the *specificity* that can be produced by physicalizing what is most salient in a given beat.[5]

Determining how to physically express the scene requires a certain amount of analysis. LMA provides a lens through which the actor can look at a scene and, through exploring BESS, make succinct, repeatable physical choices that are calculated toward achieving an objective and reflect the character's emotional state. Consequently, LMA, like any valuable movement process, stimulates the imagination and promotes moving on impulse while going a step further and addressing how to craft a performance.

Choosing which Effort Elements may be predominant at any given time is based on the character's physical body, the environment, given circumstances, needs, and objectives, thus helping the actor become physically articulate to the audience. Likewise, Effort can also be an interesting leaping-off point for developing character. For instance, an actor may determine her character, in relation to the other characters in the play, tends toward a very *direct* relationship to the environment and the objects or people in it. If the actor pursues this, she will discover something about who the character is and will be prompted to ask questions like, "When in the play does my character begin to move toward *indirectness*? What does this cost her? What makes her begin to change?" It is also possible to develop a character from the inspiration of a Drive or a State. For instance, an actor playing a king may experiment with *sustainment*, *directness*, and *lightness* (Glide Action Drive) as the baseline for his movement. Once this "baseline" is established, the actor can begin to find out when these Elements are not in equal play as well as when the character begins to bring in moments of Urgent Time or Indirect Space or Strong Weight. In most plays, the character is being forced, or coaxed away, from his baseline or "affinities," and that is why we watch. What is important to remember is that all these Elements are manifesting or being observed in relation to something or someone else.

The effective use of LMA for actors requires that the actors learn who they are as movers before embarking on character development. It is within LMA's scope to educate actors to their affinities and give clarity to where they fit into this puzzle of the moving man. It also gives actors the means to experiment with diversifying and expanding their movement potential by bringing the Elements that are more fragile or elusive, sometimes called "disaffinities," into the foreground. In fact, LMA is such a dynamic means toward personality assessment and self-awareness that Effort Elements and Factors are studied in many dance therapy programs. Its rich information can give the therapist insights to her patients' characters and problems as well as a means to help them, through movement, to literally "change their minds." In addition to self-awareness and discovery, LMA for actors is meant to stimulate the actor's imagination, make room for metaphor, and connect actors to their impulses. For instance, even a simple arbitrary choice to move with an emphasis on Strong Weight will begin to affect the actor and invite vivid imagery as the dance among Body, Effort, Space, and Shape takes form.

Shape: The Link between Effort and Space

Laban began with the concepts Body, Space, and Effort. Shape was developed as a concept when Laban worked with Warren Lamb in England on aptitude assessments for British Industries during World War II. Shape refers to the body's "plasticity," which allows it to adapt to Space and access it. Another way to think of Shape is as the link between Effort and Space. Bridging the content of our inner world to the outer environment, Shape adapts our body to the architecture, objects, and people. Laban observed that the Body tends toward four basic shapes: Ball-like, Pin-like, Wall-like, or Screw-like. These shapes can apply to a single body part, several parts, or the whole body, making this concept a wonderful leaping-off point for character exploration. For instance, an actor who is experimenting with Shape may determine that a Ball-like Shape best expresses his character's tendency to live in a world closed around himself, letting very little in or out; or that a Pin-like Shape emphasizes that his character values clear thinking. Depending on the context, a Pin-like Shape, with its severe verticality, could also suggest superiority, narrow-mindedness, or even a military school background. *Context* is an essential ingredient for exploration, because while there is a range of "personality traits" particular to each Shape, it is only in direct relation to the context of the play and the other characters that the implications are made clear and clichés or assumptions can be avoided.

In addition to Ball-, Wall-, Pin-, and Screw-like Shapes, there is a more sophisticated aspect to Shape called Modes of Shape Change, and they also provide rich fodder for imaginative explorations. Shape Flow is a term that refers to the body's communication with itself. In this Mode of Shape Change, the Body is relating toward and away from itself, with the breath as the baseline. Shape Flow determines if the Body will *Lengthen* or *Shorten*, *Narrow* or *Widen*, *Hollow* or *Bulge*. The Directional Movement Mode of Shape Change describes the Body relating to the Space through either *Spoke-like* or *Arc-like* moves. Directional Movement happens when the Body's goal is to form a "bridge" between itself and the people or objects in the environment. The Shape of this "bridge" determines if the Body will move *Upward* or *Downward*, *Side Across* or *Sideward Out*, *Backward* or *Forward*. Directional Movement, while usually accomplished with a limb or combination of limbs, can also include the whole body. The Mode of Shape Change called Shaping or Carving describes how the Body adapts to the environment by moving between an inner-outer orientation to itself and the Space. Initiating in the trunk, it is usually expressed through the whole body by molding or contouring the body around the objects and people in the environment. It is also the most complex of the Modes of Shape Change, as it forms a three-dimensional relationship between self and the outside world as opposed to the two-dimensional relationship formed in Directional Movement. During the Shaping or Carving Mode, the Body may *Rise* or *Sink*, *Enclose* or *Spread*, *Retreat* or *Advance*.

There is a direct correlation between human developmental patterns from birth to early childhood and the Modes of Shape Change. The infant is all about the "self" and lives in Shape Flow patterns. The baby's first gestures attempt to bridge into the environment, reaching for the toy or Mommy's finger, mak-

---

Table 2: Modes of Shape Change and Developmental Patterns

SHAPE FLOW: It is all about the self with the breath as the base-line. Infants are engaged in this self-to-self communication. Shape Flow manifests as: *Lengthening/Shortening, Narrowing/Widening, Hollowing/Bulging.*

DIRECTIONAL MOVEMENT: Two-dimensional goal-oriented movement that forms a bridge between the self and the environment as in a young child reaching for the bottle. Spoke-like/Arc-like Directional Movement includes: *Upward/Downward, Side Across/Side Open, Backward/Forward.*

SHAPING/CARVING: Three-dimensional movement that creates an inter-active relationship with the outside world. The most complex of the Modes of Shape Change and therefore the most sophisticated relationship a child develops in regards to Shape because it is "process-oriented" rather than "self-" or "goal-oriented." Shaping/Carving includes: *Rising/Sinking, Enclosing/Spreading, Retreating/Advancing.*

Effort Graph with Shape Affinities

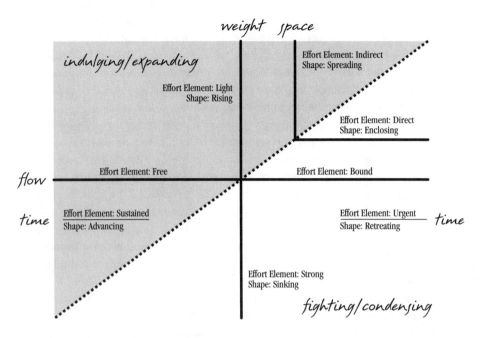

weight   space

indulging/expanding

Effort Element: Indirect
Shape: Spreading

Effort Element: Light
Shape: Rising

Effort Element: Direct
Shape: Enclosing

flow   Effort Element: Free   Effort Element: Bound

time   Effort Element: Sustained   Effort Element: Urgent   time
        Shape: Advancing   Shape: Retreating

Effort Element: Strong
Shape: Sinking

fighting/condensing

ing Spoke-like or Arc-like Directional Movement. As the baby learns to adapt and develop an interactive relationship between himself and the environment, he enters Shaping or Carving Mode (see table 2).

Shape can be potent material for discovering a character's communication style, based on how the actor imagines the character's early childhood development. For instance, a character that gestures predominantly with Directional Movement has a very different background and agenda from a character that gestures mostly from Shaping/Carving. A character that uses predominantly Directional Movement might be aggressive, inflexible, ready to fend off an attack, grabbing for all she can get, or functioning as an authority figure. Conversely, a character who gestures more with Shaping/Carving may value taking in all points of view, thus emphasizing the character's adaptability and cooperative nature. Or perhaps the character is someone who prefers to avoid conflict at all costs; in that context, the nonthreatening aspects of the Shaping/Carving Mode would come into focus. An actor who is emphasizing Shape-Flow may discover that she is constantly touching her own body, adjusting her jacket, hair, and makeup with little awareness of the other characters or outside world. If this becomes a character trait, the audience is likely to experience a character that is self-absorbed, only willing to satisfy her own needs. Again, it is within the *context* of the whole that the actor and audience will understand the implications of making any of these choices a signature for the character. As with Effort, exploring the impact of Shape on character can explode the actor's work as she discovers when, where, why, and how a character moves away from or toward her Shape preferences. Additionally, as with Effort, if an actor explores moving while emphasizing one of the Modes of Shape Change, usually in a short time, her imagination will catch fire, and imagery and metaphor will abound.

Shape is a powerful container for the actor's Effort life and is the outer reflection of her emotions. Shape is dependent on the Body to be able to express the character's Effort life and is influenced by the

Space. There is an aspect of Shape that interacts very closely with Space called Spatial Pathways and Tensions. The awareness of the interaction of Effort and Space with Shape illuminates the effect different Pathways through Space can have on the character, as well as how much and what kinds of Tensions exist between the character and any given object or person. These Spatial Pathways and Tensions have been developed in LMA as *Central, Peripheral,* and *Transverse* Pathways or Tensions. One can think of this as the Effort life determining if the Body will move through Space Centrally (the correlative to Spoke-like Directional Movement) or Peripherally (the correlative to Arc-like Directional Movement), or take a more circuitous Transverse Pathway (the correlative to Shaping/Carving) to its destination.

Inclusive in these Pathways, though not necessarily mirroring them, are the kinds of Tensions that exist between the Body and the environment. Depending on the context, a character that enters a room Centrally may be viewed as someone that knows what she wants and goes for it directly. The statement, "I want that!" may describe this mover. A character that tends toward the Periphery may be witnessed as one who keeps things at a distance and herself on the outer edge of the circumstances. "I will observe all that goes on but not dirty my hands or involve myself," may describe the Peripheral mover. If a character tends to Transverse through the space, she may be someone who values inclusiveness by demonstrating how she likes to touch on all aspects of a problem or circumstance. A character statement for the Transverse mover might be, "I want to understand everything and everyone that is here." Imagine what varied and enticing movement patterns would emerge through an exploration of Pathways.

To summarize thus far, Effort contains the impulse to move, Shape is the manifestation of the impulse, and Space is what the Body is acting upon. Of course, since this is an interactive dance of sorts, it is also important to note that, likewise, Space is acting upon the Body, which in turn affects the Effort life and, therefore, the Shape that manifests.

Space Harmony: The First and Last Frontier

Laban's concept of Space is perhaps the most elusive and stimulating of the four concepts. I have thus far described Space by referring to the architecture and what is contained within it and with the description of Spatial Pathways and Tensions.

Laban, due to his studies of astronomy and the crystalline forms, began to formulate that there is no such thing as "empty" space. He believed that Space has a life, and that life is movement. The Spatial Pathways act on the Body, and the Body acts on them, influenced by the various Spatial Tensions. Additionally, he identified "pulls" in Space that one can "ride" on, like a wave in the ocean. It is perhaps not an accident that we sometimes say that we are "pulled" toward a certain place, or "pulled" toward a certain person. It is not uncommon to hear acting coaches say to an actor, "Take a moment and feel where you are being pulled. Then move there." LMA is a study in learning to feel and respond on impulse to the pulls between our inner architecture (inside the body) and the outer architecture, which may be a stage set, a room in our home, a field, a forest, or even the universe itself.

In the initial stages of rehearsal, actors are sometimes asked to improvise their blocking.[6] The hope is that the play will block itself "organically," through the actors' sensitivity to the needs of their character and knowledge of the environment. It is believed that movement derived from such a process will read more truthfully than if the moves are applied to the actor by the director. Sometimes this works; often it doesn't—but regardless of how the blocking is arrived at, the actor must be able to "fill it" with intention, elevating the "moves" to "physical action." The actor needs to understand the qualitative difference to her character toward achieving her objective if she delivers her speech walking downstage or upstage, or if she is placed high above the stage or sitting on the stage. Even stage right and stage left produce qualitative and functional differences. These concerns are addressed through Laban's theories on Space Harmony, in which he likens Spatial Pulls to musical harmonies or chords. Each point in Space has an affinity that corresponds to Body, Effort, and Shape. For instance, the right arm reaching diagonally across the body toward the down left corner of the stage will influence the actor to use Direct Space, Strong Weight, and Sustained Time (Press Action Drive), with the Directional Mode of Shape Change of *Downward* thus completing the "chord." An actor who has learned to access such harmonies is more likely to be physically responsive to improvisational opportunities, because she will be alive to the impulses that Space provides for her. This is not to say that the actor feeling the chord struck by Body, Effort, Shape, and Space couldn't choose to manifest the opposites or disaffinities. In fact, this should be encouraged, because, as in music, we don't always want to be in a major key.

To develop a practical application for his theories on "spatial pulls," Laban developed movement sequences called Scales. As the body moves through a Scale, it passes through points in space that describe one of the following platonic solids: Cube, Octahedron, or Icosahedron.

Cube   Octahedron   Icosahedron

Theoretically, the body organization that results from moving with the spatial pulls from point to point produces a harmonious interaction among Body, Effort, Shape, and Space. Since Laban was convinced that spatial pulls are inherent in nature, he believed that practicing the Scales would unite the body, mind, and spirit to become harmonious with the universe. Whether or not the actor becomes "one with nature," learning and practicing the Laban Scales has much the same practical benefit that practicing the musical scales has for the musician. Laban's Scales serve as a tune-up for the actor's instrument, developing flexibility, balance, strength, and stamina, while warming it up to be responsive to the interplay of Body, Effort, Shape and Space.

Body: The Doorway to Expressiveness

To be expressive, the actor's body must be physically capable of reflecting or making actual in movement all that has been described in this chapter. This will not be possible unless the actor develops his breath support, alignment, stamina, balance, and flexibility, which requires Body-level training. During Laban's era in Germany and England, the chief means for Body training through LMA was dance. In the United States, however, the Body-level work that is taught along with LMA is usually based on Bartenieff Fundamentals. The Fundamentals are a body reeducation system that encompasses the functional aspects of movement, based on the principles of Breath Support, Dynamic Alignment, Core Support, Spatial Intent, Weight Shift, Initiation and Sequencing, Rotary Factor, Effort Motivation, and Developmental Patterning.

Irmgard Bartenieff, a student of Laban's in Germany, fled to the United States with the advent of World War II. Unable to get work as a dancer, she reeducated herself as a physical therapist and became a pioneer in the development of dance therapy. While at the Rusk Institute during the 1940s, her development of the Fundamentals made a significant contribution to helping polio victims regain mobility.

Bartenieff originated the LMA professional training program in the United States in 1965 and founded the Laban/Bartenieff Institute for Movement Studies in 1978. Because she was Laban's student, Bartenieff Fundamentals consciously incorporate Laban's themes, making it a perfect marriage.

While the cornerstone of Body training among CMAs (Certified Movement Analysts) trained in LMA in the United States are the Bartenieff Fundamentals, the training does not use this system exclusively, and it certainly does not end with the Fundamentals. What else is included in the Body-level training is dependent on the background of the certified LMA practitioner-teacher, as well as the goals, interests, and physical limitations of the actor. Consequently, the training may also include dance, gymnastics, martial arts, or yoga. It may also incorporate other body reeducation systems, such as Pilates, Feldenkrais Method®, or the Alexander Technique, to name a few possibilities.

BESS-R: ACKNOWLEDGING RELATIONSHIP

Initially, Laban's concepts only included Body, Effort, and Space, which he arranged as a trinity. His coworker, Warren Lamb, helped to add Shape to the mix, and the pic-

 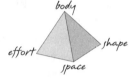

ture became a tetrahedron. While relationship has always been the lens through which we observe how Body, Effort, Space, and Shape affect each other, it is only in recent years that Relationship has been given formal acknowledgment. As every actor knows, telling a story is dependent upon creating relationships. The relationship of the actor to the character, to the events of the play, the environment, the other characters, and the audience defines the theatrical experience and is why acting is often defined as "reacting." LMA's acknowledgement of Relationship as an equal partner with Body, Effort, Shape, and Space underscores the symbiosis between LMA and acting. In each practical example previously cited, there was a specific Relationship drawn among the Body, Effort, Shape, and Space Factors, which made the story visible to the reader. Likewise, it is the actor's ability to forge these Relationships and clearly articulate them in his body that reveals the story to the audience.

LABAN'S LEGACY

Relationship exploded Laban's stable tetrahedron, yet it is the very plasticity of this analysis system that has allowed it to survive and grow to accommodate our changing world and many professional needs. The LMA material has been developed and adapted to support psychologists, architects, occupational and physical therapists, artists, and athletes. I believe it is not hard to see how its rich material can be adapted to support the actor as well. Given the theoretical complicity between the concepts of LMA and the "naturalism" that is so highly valued in actor-training programs, it is curious that Laban Movement Analysis has not become the gold standard for movement training in colleges and conservatories, the way that Stanislavsky's Method has for acting. I believe there are several reasons for this.

The first reason, and perhaps the most surprising, is, in spite of the deeply practical nature of LMA, Laban has also been linked to the occult, which was born of his interest in observing the relationship between movement and the rituals of many eastern and western religions. In his adolescence, he was introduced to the Sufi dervish dances and their powerful trancelike states. This awakened in him an unshakable belief in the magical potential of movement. In his adult life, his relationship with the occult is marked by his association with the Rosicrucians, who practiced a life based on the mystical properties of art and idealism. Additionally, he established a "movement commune" at Ascona, Switzerland

(1911–1914), which gave him a place to explore this mystical potential of movement with a group of students while living a free, bucolic life. His Rosicrucian studies and the experiments that began at Ascona, together with his strong mathematical and architectural background, were finally synthesized in his theories of Space Harmony, which he began writing about in 1939, and were culminated in his book, *The Language of Movement* (Choreutics), published posthumously in 1966.

Sensitizing the body to be receptive to inner and outer forces of energy leading to psychic experiences is a presence in all his work, but also present was an effort to balance the practical with the spiritual. His insatiable curiosity, rich imagination, and connection to nature made him an ideal artistic explorer to open new frontiers in movement theory and application. Truly a man of his times, he was steeped in a classical education of language, science, and math. Before becoming a dancer, he did advanced studies in art and architecture and subsequently became deeply influenced by Hermann Obrist, Wassily Kandinsky, and the music of Arnold Schoenberg. Laban also admired Isadora Duncan and Emile Jaques-Dalcroze for their groundbreaking approaches to movement and used their work as a backdrop to examine his own ideas.

Laban's ideas were fueled by a concern that man's movement potential was being seriously compromised by industrialism, which was moving man away from the land and into factories. Consequently, Laban believed that movement for *all* would be man's salvation from the quotidian of factory work. This belief began his legacy of choreographing movement choirs with laborers of all types. In the instance of the Craft Guilds of Vienna in 1927, he choreographed 10,000 performers, of whom only 2,700 were dancers. As Laban's fame grew during the 1930s, he became the head choreographer at Berlin State Opera and choreographed for Siegfried Wagner (Richard's son) at the Bayreuth Festival and for Richard Wagner's opera *Tannhauser*. Laban was also a consummate teacher and mentor. Among his famous students were Suzanne Perrottet (prior to her work with Laban, she was the star pupil of Dalcroze), Mary Wigman, Dussia Bereska, and Kurt Jooss. His name spread as his disciples began to open Laban schools in Switzerland, Italy, France, Poland, and England. Even so, there were many that looked askance at his free-love lifestyle and cultish ways.

The second reason that Laban training remained underappreciated in the United States for so long is his "German connection." I have already mentioned Wagner, for whom he had great admiration. In many ways, Laban was apolitical, and survival was always uppermost. He lived from hand to mouth most of the time, often in ill health, and suffered from frequent bouts of depression. He juggled supporting a wife, children, lovers and their children, Laban schools, and a dance company, while lecturing at conferences and writing on his theories. So, when Hitler, whose regime was impressed with Laban's charisma and reputation in German dance, asked him to be director of German Dance Stage, he opted to stay in Germany, rather than flee as Kurt Jooss, Bartenieff, and most of his company did. The regime soon turned on him, however, when in 1936, he prepared a movement choir of one thousand participants for the opening of the Olympic games. Dr. Goebbels viewed the dress rehearsal and banned the performance, accusing Laban of celebrating the individual.

With increasing pressure on him to toe the party line, Laban finally fled Germany in 1937, arriving in England, sponsored by Mr. and Mrs. Elmhirst of Dartington Hall, where Kurt Jooss and most of the Essen Laban School had taken refuge. After World War II, the public's rejection of anything German helped stall the spread of LMA, and within Germany, Hitler's regime had completely devastated the arts for generations to come, making any timely recuperation to their former groundbreaking glory in dance and art impossible.

The third reason is that in dance-training programs throughout the world, Laban may be best known for Labanotation, which is a detailed system of recording movement of the whole body as a three-dimensional instrument that puts it in relation to other moving bodies and the space surrounding them. An experienced notator can record not only every move the body makes right down to minute moves of the little finger, but the emotional content of the movement as well. Only for a small segment of the population would it not be a laborious task to learn all the symbols and rules, and in any event, notation would not be a useful tool for the actor. When Laban's name or LMA is mentioned, it is often Labanotation that the individual is familiar with, and this is not a sensible reason to include LMA in an actor's training.

The fourth reason, and perhaps the most potent today, is that Laban had no intention of devoting his time and talents to the development of any one profession or art. Intermittently throughout his career, he worked specifically with actors, but he also worked with many other professionals. He used dance and dancing as a way of exploring and developing his theories, but it was never intended to be just for dancers either. The scope of Laban's ninety-seven published books and articles is indeed daunting, but even more impressive is the scope and breadth of the resulting applications that this author believes were born out of Laban's commitment to education. He poured his energies into educating anyone who would listen: dancers, actors, occupational and physical therapists, grade school teachers, psychotherapists, blue-collar workers, architects, athletes, and painters.

Consequently, how the material was used became the sole domain of his students, and Laban openly encouraged and supported this diversity. It has always been up to the practitioner to develop her relationship to the material and make it applicable to her needs. This has resulted in many exciting uses of the material in actor-training programs as well. Since there is no prescribed way to present the material to actors, the movement coach is unencumbered to develop it, experiment with it, and adapt it to her students' needs. This is both its strength and weakness with regard to it being widely used in training programs. While worldwide, there are pockets of CMAs meeting to develop LMA tools specifically for actors, there is not a history of tried-and-true exercises for actors as there are in acting, voice, speech, and other movement processes. Consequently, the danger is that the theoretical base will remain just that, an idea of what Effort is, or Shape, or Space.

For beginning actors in particular, LMA movement coaches must temper the analytical aspects of the material and cull out the means by which their students will interact with the material on a visceral level, therefore supporting actors in responding moment to moment to their impulses and igniting their imaginations.

Finally, it is interesting to note that it is virtually impossible to spot a Laban-trained actor, because the goal is not to achieve (because it doesn't exist) a "Laban style." This inherent universality is one of its greatest strengths, because it makes LMA not an end in itself but a support for actors to know who they are as movers, expand their movement potential, and become their most expressive and imaginative selves.

NOTES

1. Laban, Rudolph. *The Mastery of Movement*. Boston, Mass.: Plays, Inc., 1972, 1.
2. Toporkov, Vasily. *Stanislavsky in Rehearsal: The Final Years*. Christine Edwards, trans. New York: Theatre Arts Books, 1979, 160.
3. Terms credited to Konstantin Stanislavsky. "Action" describes what the characters are doing to achieve what they want, which is their "objective."
4. A term credited to Stanislavsky to describe the situations in which a character finds him- or herself.
5. A term credited to Stanislavsky to describe a single unit of action of indeterminate length within a phrase of a scene.
6. A term that refers to when and where the actor will move on the stage.

Breathe Before You Act

Caroline Thomas

When it was suggested that I write about the connection between voice and movement, I thought, "Oh boy, here we go!"

The voice part didn't worry me, but movement is the area of acting that I find most difficult to write about, talk about, even think about. It was certainly the weakest link in my own training and early thespian forays. When I was in college, I appeared as Titania in *A Midsummer Night's Dream*. The actor playing Oberon compared my walk to a football player's. In the 1970s, when we were participating in the outdoor workshops that were so much a part of avant-garde theater training, running was required as a form of meditation. For me, it was a cause of agony. My Achilles tendons frequently cramped up, I fell to the ground, and the men would be obliged to hoist me onto their shoulders for the homeward trot. In spite of the fact that for many years now, I've been teaching voice and movement as integral parts of acting training, these early traumas made me feel I hadn't the right to embark on a scholarly dissertation, to bore people with my half-baked, experimental ideas, to show people I'm a fraud who teaches because she can't do. On the other hand, I like to think of myself as one who throws herself into "dangerous" artistic challenges; I'm afraid of being a coward; I wouldn't want to let the editor down after having said I'd do it; and I need to write this so my students will have a document of what they're studying. There seemed to be so many more reasons for than against. . . .

My insecurities grew incrementally with each day that I made another excuse not to get going. A very kind student, wearying of my complaints, brought me great tomes from the Performing Arts Library. Here were tales of Stanislavsky's clashes with insurgent collaborators and of how Meyerhold was murdered for his artistic ideals by the very Communist government he had fought so hard to put into power. I almost envied them their battles with hostile outside forces. My wars were usually with personal demons. I put the tomes away, dusted off my journals, and plunged into accounts of my own early struggles with the muse. There was petite Mme. Fedro, our fiercely elegant Polish Mistress of Movement at The Royal Academy of Dramatic Art (RADA), glaring with icy disgust at the chaos of my long, wayward limbs, which refused absolutely to incorporate the concept of grace. Reviewing my introduction to the Meisner Technique, I recalled how I loved to show a rude, aggressive side in the "repetition" work, but somehow could feel nothing beyond the pleasure of "getting it right." Method-style Sense Memory exercises stirred my deepest feelings by bringing back long-forgotten misery—it worked so well when I practiced in my apartment. I thought about my frequent success with acting class techniques, followed by the frustrations of trying to combine techniques with one another, or doing anything at all when actually faced with a script.

By now, I was on a collision course with my past, feverishly rereading notebooks that concerned the next phase of my training when I traipsed back and forth between the United States and Europe. At one moment, I was spinning in the Polish forest with Jerzy Grotowski until I fell flat on my face; at another, I was chanting and expressing myself through the "plastiques" in Tree of People at the Teatr Laboratorium in Wroclav. Of course, I had retired to the "sleeping room" hours before the others, who finished in the first streaks of dawn and went to celebrate with a breakfast of Polish sausage. Memories flooded back of Stevie Borst down at the Performance Garage teaching us how to layer physical elements of character. But when I performed a monologue from *Fuente Ovejuna*, by Lope de Vega, in front of the class, having matched each beat of the text with a physical state, all the spontaneity was gone, and I felt like a performing seal.

Here and there, moments of fulfillment brought a little sunshine to this otherwise cloudy trip down memory lane. While working on Lady Macbeth with Andre Gregory, I was able to discover some genuine impulses, even to the point of having demonic dreams. Later, under the direction of Robert Wilson, I learned to articulate Greek text, out of which grew elaborate gestures and vocal patterns for the role of the Nurse in *Medea*.

All this research, and particularly the soul-searching in my old notebooks, reminded me of the question that teased me endlessly in those days: Why was I able to "be in my character" occasionally, when most of the time, my experience of acting was just a bunch of fascinating possibilities leading to a dead end of fear and numbness? There was a specific reason for the problem, but I couldn't perceive it. It was my body that was causing the trouble. It was unreliable, to say the least, stubbornly erratic about its involvement in my efforts to act. How and why it failed to connect was a blind spot, a thing that could not perceive itself. I couldn't live physically in my characters or they in me, unless a brilliant director was on hand to maneuver me through the loophole in my own misperception. I knew about "bodywork" but hadn't the faintest idea what it meant for an actor to "be in her body." I was a Puritan from New England; perhaps that had something to do with it. I could identify my body in various modes like pain, pleasure, motion, but not as an entity on its own, going through a whole gamut of sensations. The truth was that whenever possible, I kept my body out of conscious consideration. I could only think about complex levels of awareness; matters of feeling were consigned to unconsciousness. Whatever awareness I had of my body was filtered through my mind first.

Having perused all my notebooks, I moved on to the point when I switched from acting to teaching and, sometimes, directing and playwriting. Working behind the scenes gave me autonomy and the opportunity to search for ways to solve the problems for others that had so bitterly plagued me when I was acting. I eventually came up with the Integrated Acting Process. I called it a "process," because it endlessly reinvents itself and is alternately maddening or exhilarating, or both at once.

But here I was now, nothing on paper yet, plunging deeply into a reassessment of my past. I was spending weeks reading, obsessing about the integrity of my research, besieged by nightmares about students I had never seen before performing scenes from plays I had never heard of. I took special note of everything that was happening in my classes and in my life, searching for a way to capture my vision in words.

THE "FOOTBALL" ANALOGY

Finally, an absurd visual concept began to emerge. I saw myself, decked out in helmet and huge shoulder pads, hugging a football and attempting to carry it across the last nine yards and over the finish line. The ball was held so closely that it felt physically attached. It was like a second version of myself, embodying the totality of the work, and like myself, it included body, voice, mind, and heart—or feeling. But it was more than the sum of its parts; it was, in itself, a work of art, and it required the action of carrying it over the finish line to validate it. All the resistance I encountered, nearly insurmountable as is usually the case with the last nine yards, came from within myself. This time, I had to take the ball all the way, no excuses about Achilles tendons, no help from stalwart young men.

This ridiculous metaphor refused to go away, so I decided to define my terms and particularize the four components of my "football": body, voice, mind, and feeling. The body is composed of flesh, bones, muscles, nerves, and so on—things we can see, or look at in an anatomy diagram. The voice comes out of the body and involves, among other things, the diaphragm muscle, air moving up the windpipe and passing through the voice box, bouncing off the resonators, through the opening of the jaw, and out through the mouth. This is still possible to comprehend as a physical manifestation, but since air flows through different locations in the body while various muscles actively or passively facilitate its passage, it is a difficult concept to visualize. For most of us, therefore, the voice seems less concrete than the body. The mind is even more mysterious. Although we think of it as synonymous with the brain, it connects with the rest of the body, which can't operate without it. Feeling is the most confusing, and a matter of heated dispute among actors, as to its origin and location. Is feeling derived mainly from the mind, from the body, or from both? We notice that the location of a feeling is often different from its place of origin. For example, someone hurts our feelings in the morning, and by the afternoon, we have a headache. It would be difficult to make an exact diagram of the connection between the "emotional reaction" of hurt feelings and the "physical response" of a headache. By the way, such a diagram, even if it were possible to make, wouldn't be very helpful, since many actors are not particularly logical and scientific.

Speaking of not being logical and scientific, I would like to mention the soul, for those of us who believe in its existence. To describe its relationship to this work, however, would require an essay devoted entirely to that subject alone.

Body-Voice-Mind-Emotion

Our principal focus is the relationship between voice and movement in the theater. Since, however, this writing is intended for actors, any discussion of body and voice must include mind and feeling. All four elements are inseparable, and their conjunction is impossible to get at directly, hence this choice of an approach that is circular rather than linear. I decided to test the clarity of my ideas by creating a dialogue with my students; that ought to be very helpful and, I thought, a really democratic way to go about things. But the next problem immediately arose: I'm ready to talk, but are my students ready to listen? Even the most diligent student loses focus and hardly ever has questions when I try to explain how my system of ideas is put together, how all the little pieces cuddle up and make a nice design (football). They laugh at my jokes, at least, but they haven't the vaguest idea what I'm talking about. Watching their struggle, I can't help but remember my training: a technique I could understand in theory, in practice worked only partially, if at all. It was always the process I did not comprehend intellectually in which my work could remain "alive" and make intuitive leaps between the "mental," "vocal," "movement," and "feeling" factors. Are the processes of "conceptualizing" and "doing" mutually exclusive? In other words, can we only "think" what we don't "feel," and "feel" what we don't "think"?

My Journey

For a long time, it had been in the back of my mind that I should put my teaching system into words. Students have, in fact, requested a manual or written guide to support their comprehension of the material. But finding a structure of organized thought from which to start writing made this task agonizingly difficult. On the other hand, it would be uplifting if an explanation could be found that would resonate with conviction and clarify through truth. In the meantime, I felt like an actor who hadn't formulated the way to play a character and was relying on instinct. I still had to find a coherent manner in which to explain the integration of the seemingly "physical" elements (voice and body) with the seemingly "psychological" ones (mind and feeling). I say "seemingly," because the "physical" doesn't work without the "psychological," and vice versa.

There was another hitch. To be honest, I had always had a terrible time trying to decipher other people's testimonies, written or otherwise. I remembered Grotowski's writings and his lectures in New York in the 1970s. He was a genius, but it was impossible, then, for me to understand anything he said, except in vague, intuitive ways. Although pretending otherwise, many actors at that time, especially Americans, seemed to have the same problem. I remember Grotowski's battles with students who attended his lectures at Hunter College. The great man would take aim with his incisive Polish wit at what he judged to be obstreperousness and ignorance, while the students became increasingly incensed at what they perceived as ridicule in the face of their quest for knowledge. Reading books about acting methods has usually put me to sleep. I always figured if I couldn't learn it in class, I wouldn't be helped by reading about it. Voracious reading of other kinds, both relating to theater and on other subjects, has been helpful. Not everyone, however, is like me. For some, reading at home can form an organizational basis for the work in class. I also remembered a curious fact: that I had picked up a lot about voice training, yoga, and Alexander from books. The difference lay in the "facts" available in the descriptions of physical exercises in books about voice and body training, whereas acting texts seemed either mired in theory or excessively precise.

So, after giving up on the words of other time-honored teachers and inventors of methods, how could I stick my head into the same noose and attempt to describe this "integration" of mine. It was a thought that paralyzed the will. I had spent so many years working on acting by myself, and later teaching and collaborating with students, there seemed to be so much to formulate. Within myself, I had created a place of understanding, where body, voice, and mind, and feeling (hopefully, soul, as well—I have to say it) could link and transform themselves into art. Some students in classes could "catch" this "linking" from me, while others might benefit from the "Meisner piece" or the "voice piece." And all the while I was doing my research and soul-searching, the deadline for this essay had gathered the momentum of a speeding bullet. The last nine yards had receded into the distance, and I felt as if I were behind the starting line. Panic set in. My lower back went into permanent spasm—sciatica was mentioned—and lateral movement of my neck was no longer an option. When I tried to rise from my bed, the pain was so severe that my breath stopped, and I fainted. I lay four days in a stupor, half-dreaming, without the energy even to anguish over my dilemma. I had no desire to use my voice, since nothing seemed worth the effort of speaking. On the fifth day, no longer able to afford canceling another class, I arose and hobbled to the subway.

The distance was daunting in my painful condition. First, I had to cross Columbus Avenue and then traverse the park surrounding the Planetarium side of the Museum of Natural History. It was a hot day, and sweat ran in rivulets down my rigid neck. At each step, I feared that my back would seize up. I could see myself unable to breathe, falling into a dead faint—near the dog run. Since I'm always telling everyone else to breathe, I had just enough presence of mind to apply a little of my own medicine. I thought about my lower back, just above the right buttock—where the pain was acute every time I moved my leg. I loosened my jaw, which was appallingly tight, and allowed the breath to make its fullest, natural expansion. By concentrating on this "action," rather than the length of the walk, I managed to get to the subway.

Once on the train, I closed my eyes and continued to concentrate on breathing, loosening the jaw and connecting the energy of the breath to the painful area. I also started to make tiny stretching movements with my lower back. Since all parts of the back are connected to each other, this means that the whole back was involved in the stretch. I imagined a perceptive person watching me, aware that I was not just sitting with closed eyes. They would notice the unusual breathing, the facial play of tension and relaxation, and the slight movement of my torso as I stretched. If one imagines this on a movie screen magnified hundreds of times, here is a character with a back problem. For theater drama, you would intensify it until it "reads" to the back row, and for comedy, the old bag would be unable to get up when the train stops, and she would have to be carried from the car by four stalwart youths. As these thoughts passed through my mind, a very slight giggle aided my stretching motion. All of a sudden, I heard an unusual sound. I decided to keep my eyes shut and try to figure it out. It was a peculiar kind of singsong voice, accompanied by a shuffle and step. The words of the song escape me, but it went something like this:

> I'm walkin' and I'm playin' my beat
> Lookin' for the Lord ain't no easy street
> I'm so damn' tired and I'm so damn' hungry
> Broke inta pieces like that good egg Humpty
> I need a cuppa coffee and somethin' to eat
> Help me git offa' these poor ol' feet.

I couldn't face the effort of pulling my bag off my shoulder, searching for my wallet, and digging for change, but I did look up when the singing and musty odor had passed by. I expected to feel pity for some miserable creature, but instead, I saw a black hat set at a purposeful angle and a black and gray striped shirt, distinctive although too hot for the weather. A little homemade drum hung about the man's neck, which he punched to the beat of his song. I was suddenly appalled at my earlier lack of charity, and as penance for my laziness, I began to "think" myself into his life.

"Think" isn't the right word. My training and research have made it impossible for me to "think" myself into a person with my mind alone. Ever so slightly, I picked up the sway of his body, as I adjusted my breathing to the beat of his song. I could feel the sticky warmth of his striped shirt and guessed at the trajectory of his downward gaze from the angle of his hat. Every time someone gave him money, he tapped a little drumroll and his head bobbed. But his eyes never left the ground, and that gave me the key to his character. By his dress, dignified demeanor, and tone of voice, I could see that he was gentle, an artist of some kind, perhaps in a time long gone by. There was no arrogance in his shuffle step, no "attitude." It wasn't hatred that kept him from looking at people who gave him money, and it wasn't shame; you could tell from the jaunty way he delivered his plaintive song. *No, it was out of shame for them.* They had failed him, and the money they gave him was supposed to assuage their guilt. He was embarrassed for them, for the sorry state of their souls.

I left the train and proceeded to the studio, where my students were waiting for class to begin. They looked at me in amazement as I rounded the third flight of stairs. To be sure, I was huffing and puffing, but walking fairly normally, which was the last thing they expected after being subjected to an endless litany of complaints about my back. I was also surprised. When my students expressed their pleasure at my improved health, I thought back, remembering that the instant I looked up and saw the man in his striped shirt, I *felt* a weight lift from my body, and my breathing changed. (Anything that happens to us affects our breathing and causes an energy shift in the body. More about this later.) This *feeling* caused the *thought* to cross my mind that I had found the solution to my writing problem, hence, my sense of liberation. As I listened to the old man's voice and the sound of his little drum, I started making little grunting noises, which engaged my *voice*. From the breathing change and the vocal involvement, it followed naturally that my *body* started swaying in time to the music. Later, as I was walking from the subway to the studio, my right foot tried out the man's singular shuffle step, which interested me particularly, as it reminded me of the Manitulian Walk Step I'd learned from one of our guides when I was working with Grotowski in Poland. Therefore, my feeling, mind, voice, and body were fully occupied; they consumed me and left no energy with which to remember my back pain.

If, however, I had ignored the old man's refusal to make eye contact and been unaware of the reason behind it, all this information would not have held my mind sufficiently to supplant the consciousness of so gnawing a physical discomfort as my back pain. *It was my profound shame at not having given him money, at having been too self-involved to grasp the essence of the man's courage and superior behavior in the face of extreme hardship, that made the experience meaningful enough to command my full attention.* One could call this piece of the equation intuition or soul awareness, but in an attempt to be as scientific as possible, I will simply call it the *x* factor. It is what gives the artist an all-consuming passion for his subject and makes him bond with it. (This is not to be confused with an artist "merging" with his subject. I knew that I was not the old man in the subway, but *I focused all aspects of my attention on the part of myself that identified with him.*)

THE *x* FACTOR

Let us return to the football analogy to give a fuller explanation of the *x* factor. In the "game of acting," the pieces of leather and string that compose the "football" are the elements of mind, body, voice, and feeling. However, in the "game of acting," the actor projects herself across the footlights or transfers the totality of her own being onto film. In other words, "football" and "player" are one and the same. An actor depends on a particularly strong involvement of voice and body in the total equation. The reason for this is obvious: Player and ball are rolled into one. In other words, the actor is his own instrument. He must supply his own energy from within, and also be available to be moved by the other people and the forces around him. The "actor artist" has no paint to put onto a canvas, words written on a page, clarinet or violin to project his feelings in notes. He is paint, words, clarinet, violin, as well as the intention, and on top of it all, the realization of how those intentions are used!

So, back to me again. How else can I explain anything this complex, except by refracting it through the prism of my own being? Here I am in my studio, back pain vanquished for the moment, students lying prone on the floor and silent, except for a few giggles and coughs. Once again, it's opening night, a journey of fantastic proportion to be embarked on, full of hairbreadth escapes and dramatic twists with the outcome always uncertain. I know how ridiculous this sounds, but that's the amount of excitement I still feel about a relaxation exercise that I've done probably thousands of times. We're about to enter a land in shadow with occasional bursts of light, nothing less than a trip through ourselves from the inside out. This always reminds me of something Robert Wilson said about performing: that the actors should be so well rehearsed in the pattern of a play that they become "free" to create in performance. I feel that way about the "performance" of my relaxation exercises. I have done them for so long now that I can retain the pattern and stay on track in spite of the disturbing memories or wild imaginings that drift across my consciousness or how far afield I might wander in my improvisational embroiderings.

The usefulness of this relaxation depends initially on one's ability to focus on the breath. I cannot say often enough that all performing depends on breathing as the point from which one departs and to which one returns whenever there is a need to focus or center oneself. At RADA, breathing was constantly discussed in voice classes, but was taught in such a way that my body completely "misunderstood" what it was supposed to do, and as a result, I regularly lost my voice in performance. On the other hand, the Polish voice and movement workshops freed my voice, but I had no idea how this miracle had been accomplished.

As in my encounter with the man on the train, it was through a process of coincidences, great and small, that I stumbled on the extraordinary importance of the breath, an awareness that grew to become the cornerstone of my artistic experience. For example, I probably would never have started teaching voice if an old friend, who was Head of Acting at C. W. Post University, hadn't asked me to come on board midterm. As I was cramming Linklater and trying to formulate a lesson plan, I asked for some pointers from another old friend who was an established voice teacher at NYU. She shook her head gloomily: "It's all in the breathing. No one ever goes far enough." I had absolutely no idea what she was talking about. It irritated me that I didn't understand, but that irritation produced a pearl of wisdom. She was right.

After years of trial and error, I began to breathe my way into effective voice work, and eventually into understanding its integration with body, mind, and feeling. Every sound or utterance, every expression and gesture, is based on breathing. In short, the slightest action, even thought, is breathed. It would follow, therefore, that acting is composed of actions. In everyday life, we don't have to research breathing, unless asthma or some breathing-related illness is involved. Breathing and the actions that follow either flow naturally from the unconscious or we repress them. Acting is far more complex than "being ourselves"—which is not simple to begin with! Acting is an art form: It involves playing a character and revealing very private feelings before an audience or camera. An actor has to match the complexity of acting by having a far deeper and more thorough understanding of breathing than the average person.

In spite of the fact that breathing is the all-important basis for the actor's art and craft, most actors haven't the patience to learn to allow the breath to enter the body correctly, nor discover the impulse of the breath as it moves throughout the body step by step, encountering tension and, at times, almost unbearable resistance. Why, my students ask, should we pursue a task that is so incredibly tedious in its initial stages? I asked myself the same question years ago. Work on it, and you'll see, is the only answer I know.

THE STUDENTS' JOURNEY

Let us return now to the moment when I was about to start my class—it was a voice class. The reader may remember that this was the day that I had shifted the entire focus of my body into an awareness of the homeless man on the train. And in so doing, I had physically displaced the pain in my back. (I assume that I was able to do this because the pain was caused, not by an organic problem, but by an emotionally based set of muscle spasms.) As I began the relaxation exercise on this particular day, I heard the old man's haunting refrain and felt him accompanying me like a "doppelganger." I could almost see his striped shirt moving among the students, who lay motionless, like vessels waiting to be filled with inspiration.

When my voice students begin this exercise, they are requested to separate from the thoughts of the day by concentrating on their breathing. Then, on the incoming breath, they draw their minds down into the center or diaphragm area. This is followed by the direction to "breathe with their minds." From there, they focus on spoken directions and physically feel or visualize the movement of energy throughout the body. By energy, I am referring to oxygen and the effect of oxygen as it is processed by the lungs and circulated through the blood. I try, however, to stay away from anatomical language, as it interferes with the intuitive flow of connections between visualizing and physically feeling. By using two senses instead of one, the experience becomes more real. I suggest that they observe the energy as a color, any color that appears to them. If color doesn't work, then they may use another visualization. It is important to make the concept of air being drawn in by the diaphragm as concrete as possible. Since we are unable to see it, the general conception of air is that it is something insubstantial. Nothing could be further from the truth. Oxygen is an essential source of energy without which we cannot live for more than seconds, and yet we are seldom aware physically of how this vital "fuel" enters and energizes our entire system.

At the same time as the intake of energy is felt and visualized, the students are instructed—and constantly reminded—to drop and stretch the jaw. This serves several purposes. When the jaw is dropped or stretched, it creates a "yawn feeling" and suggests to the diaphragm that it needs to take in more oxygen. I believe that everyone would benefit from increased oxygen intake. After all, there are vitamins, even drinks nowadays, that claim to supply oxygen. Babies, unless they have been severely traumatized, are the only humans who fill their lungs sufficiently and make sound without inhibition. Breathing problems usually begin when babies become little children and start trying to make meaningful sound and form words. Even the most enlightened parents will encourage their child either to "speak up" or "quiet down," depending on the particular dynamics of each family's interaction. The social environment, outside the home, picks up where the influence of the family leaves off. The child's jaw tightens in response to these cues, and its developing muscles frequently absorb and physically memorize tension, fear, anger, and confusion, among other emotions. If the message is clearly "speak up," then a habit of "pushing out" the words will begin. The opposite would be "repressing" or "diminishing the volume" of the words or sounds that need to be expressed. The mixed messages that occur in almost every family or social environment cause even greater guilt, confusion, and tension. But whether the outcome is "pushing out" or "repressing" or a combination of the two, the physical symptoms are similar: a tense jaw and inadequate diaphragm support.

The chest muscles tense when the proper coordination between jaw and diaphragm is lost. Learning to reexperience the proper balance between them is impeded by the chest muscles, which should remain passive, but take on a "sympathetic" tension because they are positioned between these two active areas. A child's first encounter with speech is looking up at her parents'—or other adults'—heaving chests and rapidly moving mouths. So naturally children assume, as they begin to articulate, that the energy for speech comes from the area around the mouth and is supported by the chest. Quite the contrary. The mouth is passive like the chest, except for the formation of certain consonants. (I am not talking about singing here, with its sustained vowels and heightened resonance, which require more chest involvement.) Most people, however, are unable to differentiate any of these muscle groups; they under-use the diaphragm, fail to drop the jaw sufficiently, and tense the chest or muscles of the facial mask. The greater the need to be clear and make a point, the more clenched the jaw becomes and the tighter the chest. If an actor does not relearn and consciously feel the correct way to use his breath, he will tie himself up in knots whenever he has to play an emotional scene. The louder and more impassioned he becomes, the stronger the support from the diaphragm needs to be and the greater the flexibility required by the jaw. If there is even the slightest tension in the sets of muscles that should remain passive, it's like the Gordian knot: With each attempt at loosening up, it only gets tighter.

RESISTANCE TO RELEASE

One of the most notable things about this tension is the intensity with which the body fights all our attempts to let it go. Like an unruly child, it battles our efforts to bring in more than the energy to which it is accustomed. This is to be expected, since the body has been conditioned over the years to repress feelings by denying itself oxygen. Of course, these feelings have been repressed because they are painful, often very painful. Our body-and-mind connection is programmed to automatically steer us away from an overload that could result from too much awareness of pain. I've heard every excuse in the world not to do this work:

"Relaxing is a waste of time. When are we going to learn something real? . . . I just go to sleep. . . . This is never going to work. . . . I can't concentrate, I go blank every time. . . . When I'm tired, this just makes me more tired. . . . I stay depressed all day. . . . I keep thinking about all kinds of things, and I'm not accomplishing anything. . . ."

Students often forget that apart from showing up in class, a major part of their artistic progress comes from doing homework. The successful pursuit of any artistic vocation is a lifelong process of learning to concentrate and exhibit follow-through in the face of resistance. But more than any other kind of artist, how can an actor, who is expected to embody and speak for all humankind, make a career for herself when she lacks even sufficient character to break through her initial resistance! Yet many actors, particularly in America, ignore the need to focus on and control the use of their physical being, both voice and body. This leads to severe limitations in their work, and by the time they become bored with the narrow spectrum of roles they are able to play, it is usually too late. They are unable to overcome their laziness and put in a double amount of effort, since that is what is required. They must retrace their steps to the origin of their tension, and then re-integrate a major physical adjustment into the considerable knowledge of acting they already possess.

Let us return to my voice class. After some minutes spent working on the connection between diaphragm and jaw, the students are instructed to "send" energy to all parts of the body. In order to do this, they must continually focus on the "impulse" that comes from the incoming breath, which is used to move the energy through all parts of the body. Probably "relaxation" is a misnomer for this process; "energizing" would be a better word to describe it.

The next step is complex and difficult to describe. At this point, the combination of voice and movement can be viewed finally from the outside, as well as "felt" within the actor's body. The class is directed to make an open "ah" sound on any pitch and at any volume. Attention must again be paid to breath support and dropping the jaw. In addition to the "ah" sounds, the students have memorized some lines of Shakespeare or a piece of dramatic poetry. At some point during this part of the exercise, they will switch from the "ah" into their fragment of text. Finally, the actor is given an objective. He is told to use the impulse for the sound—the breath—and the sound itself to raise his body from the floor. He can visualize or feel how this direction works for him, individually, as he encounters vocal, physical, emotional, or mental tension and resistance and tries to overcome them and get to his feet. This process might be compared to a three-dimensional, physically active Rorschach test. You are the inkblot, which is moving and making sound. It becomes conscious of itself as it struggles toward its objective, which it cannot obtain without using its physicality—both voice and movement—to rise up. Getting up off the floor has the connotation of going from something less desirable to something more desirable, so the expectation is already built in that one is attaining a positive objective, and therefore, it is physically and metaphysically worth pursuing. The students are not expected to think out what they are doing, but just to involve themselves in the physical and vocal aspects and to be aware of their thoughts and feelings as they go through the work.

Sometimes, students remain lying on the floor. They are breathing, certainly, and making sound, but it doesn't extend far enough to engage the energy. If the energy is not engaged, then it remains dammed up, unable to flow throughout the body and move it into an upright position and ultimately move forward. Likewise, my students often continue on with the "ah" sound, but cannot find sufficient impulse to break into their memorized speech. I counsel them to make every effort they can to work through their blocks, but not to force results. Once an actor forces any sound or movement, it is an opportunity missed to breathe deeper and find the energy to solve a problem. The inability to locate an impulse when one is lying on the floor seems a small thing, but it will reappear, greatly magnified, when the actor is upright, spouting text.

On the day of this particular voice class, I struggled to raise myself off the floor. I could feel the tension in my lower back returning, with all the nagging doubts and fears that it represented. Most of the time, I partially follow my students in the exercise and then turn my full attention to them. But I found myself obsessed by the man on the train and the sort of "twinship" I felt with him. I had to find out about him, as I would a character in a play. My voice wasn't coming out right, and my body had a deep sorrow in its center that wouldn't let me up. The back pain was camouflage for leaden despair. It occurred to me to try the old man's song:

> I'm walkin' and I'm playin' my beat
> Lookin' for the Lord ain't no easy street

I felt stupid. What right had I to these words? I, who had never missed a meal in my life unless I was sick or on a diet. I heard a tremulous little sound nearby. A young Korean student, Yanni, was flailing on the floor. I crawled toward her, and putting my head near hers, tried to make some kind of strong, centered sound. I felt as if I were acting. What was a woman my age doing on the floor making weird noises with a young person? Then, I listened to her again. Long years of training have taught me to listen to sound with my body. Suddenly, my body sprang into action and these words flew from my mouth:

> I'm so damned tired, and I'm so damned hungry,
> Broke' inta pieces like that good egg Humpty . . .

I'd found my motivation. I was telling her that she wasn't so badly off, struggling there on the floor trying to make a good sound and push herself up off the floor. We all have our sorrows and a sense of inadequacy about the tasks that confront us. It was one of those rare moments when the body, voice, mind, and feeling coalesce, and we are one with the character, whoever he or she may be.

Yanni didn't manage to get off the floor that day, but her voice had grown in strength and purpose as we worked together. She told me later that she realized for the first time that she never felt as if she had a reason to say anything to anybody unless they dragged it out of her. To motivate herself to get off the floor was totally beyond her scope. She realized her limitation, which is the beginning step to broadening her horizon—today, the breath to respond, tomorrow, the motivation to initiate an action of sound, and somewhere down the road, the breath, the sound, the impulse to stand up.

A FINAL WORD TO THE PLAYERS

As we draw to a conclusion, let us consider Hamlet, truth, and a newborn baby. When Hamlet exhorts the Players to "speak the speech, trippingly on the tongue" and not to "mouth it, as many of our players do," nor "saw the air too much with your hand," but "to suit the action to the word, and the word to the action," he is not concerned with mere aesthetics. The Players are professionals and follow through on all counts: voice, movement, feeling, and thought. This integration renders their acting truthful, and Hamlet manages to "catch the conscience of the king." Conversely, Rosencrantz and Guildenstern go to their deaths, because they do not dissemble convincingly. Hamlet accuses them of trying to play upon him "like a pipe." They may be technically proficient, but they are unable to reach into Hamlet's mind and heart—as the Players did when they shook Claudius into revealing his guilt. Not only do they lack skill in pretending to care for Hamlet, but they also lack motivation. Perhaps they need the money Claudius offers them to spy on Hamlet, or they may feel coerced by Claudius's power. In any case, their entire "performance" lacks conviction, they are not true to themselves as human beings; hence, their performance is false.

If art is truth, then the artist must be truthful, willing to use any means at hand to convey the conviction of his character. Ultimately, all the actor has is a body and the confusing paraphernalia of thought and feeling it contains. A baby announces its entrance into life by taking a breath, crying, and flailing its limbs about. Its survival depends on sound and movement, in which it indulges freely, as it has no choice. All human activity is a myriad of variations on this same theme, even if it is pared down to a desire reflected in the diaphragm and spread imperceptibly throughout the body. If Rosencrantz and Guildenstern had combined the ferocious survival techniques of a baby with the skill of the Players, they might have convinced Hamlet of their friendship and deprived the world of a great play.

All characters believe in something. If you pare all of us down to our essence, no matter how tiny or nihilistic it may be, our belief is what keeps us alive. If it were up to us, we would probably all choose to die eventually, either for something we believe in or because we no longer believe in anything. Belief is hope. Hope is action. Babies, characters, actors have hope. Where there is hope there is life. Life is based on breathing. Through the guise of characters, we breathe ourselves into acting.

Transformations

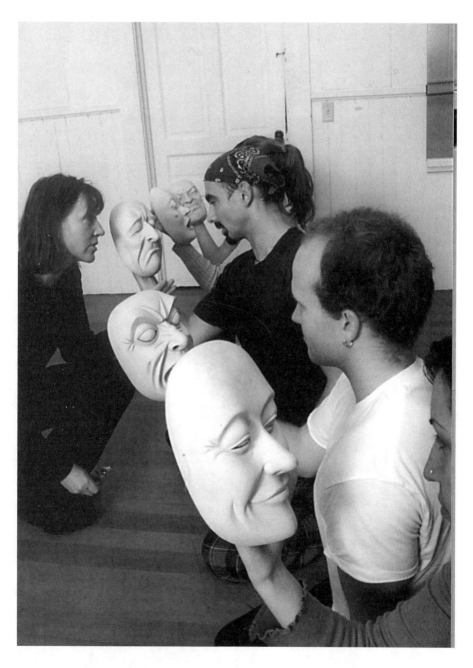

Mask and Ritual

Shelley Wyant

T he mask is a powerful and ancient tool for ritual and transformation. Ancient high priests, shamans, and medicine people have used the mask since the Stone Age for festive occasions and ceremonies. Many cultures employ masks for ritual in hunting, fertility, burial, admonitory, and disciplinary rites. It is believed that through a mask journey, information can be gathered from the spirit world to solve problems in the real world. Information collected in the mask dance can then be incorporated into sacred wisdom or lore or utilized for rituals against unknown forces in the universe. When the mask dances, it can encounter a variety of supernatural and spirit powers as it passes gracefully between ordinary and extraordinary reality.

As a theatrical device, masks can be found in the religious traditions and practices of the ancient Greeks. The Middle Ages saw the development of the mystery plays in which biblical devils, demons, and goblins were brought to life by masked characters. Fourteenth-century Japanese Noh drama developed a still-vital mask tradition. The fifteenth century saw the evolution of the masked characters of the Italian Commedia dell'Arte. Sacred ceremonial dramas in Nepal and Tibet still use masks today. In Bali and Java, mask characters entertain the gods and clown at religious ceremonies, as well as safeguard against calamities. Masks have protected ancient warriors, as well as modern-day baseball catchers, welders, fencers, and skiers. A mask can disguise and change one's appearance, so as to conceal identity. This "hiding" is ironically an exposure of some other aspect of the psyche. There is an exchange between identity and possibility. There is a marvelous freedom inherent in this revelation of the deeper self, a conversion between an individual's identity and the void. The mask invites a surrender of personality and illuminates elements of unconscious realms. It provides glimpses of qualities of supernatural beings, ancestors, gods or goddesses, or archetypal mythological creatures.

To a great extent, masks lost their importance as a theatrical convention in much of twentieth-century drama. With kitchen sink realism the mode of the day, the special magic of the mask as an usher into fantastical realms was not needed in drama. Aside from performances of the Greek plays that would often employ masks in the chorus, only a few brave twentieth-century playwrights attempted incorporating the mask. William Butler Yeats in his *Four Plays for Dancers*, Eugene O'Neill in *The Great God Brown,* and Terrence McNally in his 1993 production of *A Perfect Ganesh* are a few playwrights who tried to include the mask as a convention. Even they were not entirely successful.

The twenty-first century, with all its challenges, may have a new place for the magic of the mask. Recently, Julie Taymor reintroduced the Broadway theatergoing public to masks and puppets in her productions of *Juan Darien, The Green Bird,* and the triumphant *The Lion King.* Peter Schumann and the Bread and Puppet Theater Company have used the mask as a revolutionary political force for larger-than-life statements for over twenty-five years.

My initiation into the mask world came in 1981 during a trip to Bali. I was traveling with a book by Genevieve Stebbins entitled *The Delsarte System of Expression*. The work of François Delsarte (1811–1871), creator of the Delsarte system of expression, had always intrigued me. As a young actress working on Sam Shepard's *Melodrama Play*, I was introduced to Delsarte as a means of exploring my thirty-minute part as a recently dead body. I learned that in one study, Delsarte visited morgues and witnessed life energy visibly leaving the body, as he watched the thumbs of a recently deceased man curling inward. So, I took my time curling my thumbs inward, as I imagined the life force seeping out of my body.

Delsarte also speaks of "body thermometers" telling the emotional temperature. He speaks of the shoulders and hips as thermometers of passion, the elbows and knees as thermometers of will, and the ankles and wrists as thermometers of vitality. Delsarte is recorded to have categorized excitement, explosive anger—strong and violent aggressive emotion—as expanding motion, and thought, meditation, fear, concentration, suspicion, and repulsion as contracting motion. I wanted to know more of his theories, and as Delsarte never wrote about his work, I took Ms. Stebbins's fat book to Bali.

Delsarte, a contemporary of Darwin, examined the minute details of human gesture and classified them. His system divided the body into three zones: the mental or intellectual zone, the moral or spiritual zone, and the vital or physical zone. In the body, the abdomen and legs represent the vital zone. The head, hands, and feet represent the mental zone, and the chest and arms represent the moral zone in the body. In the mask of the face, the forehead and eyes are the mental zone, the nose and cheeks are the moral zone, and the mouth and chin are the vital zone. While in Bali, I asked my teacher, Idi Bagus Anom of Mas, to make three masks for me featuring these three zones. These three masks guided my exploration. While working in Anom's workshop, I met Islene Pinder of the Balinese American Dance Company. She invited me to use her loft studio to explore the world of the mask, and I began. In a variety of workshops and residencies at universities and conservatories over the past twenty years, I have had the privilege to witness players, in cooperative collaboration with the mask, discover unique and original ways to fully express their mythic imaginations.

The Transformation Exercise

While I was working as a guest artist at Skidmore College in 1983, my students expressed an interest in exploring my masks. I had given several lecture demonstrations for the Bond Street Theater Coalition and had been researching my masks in a private workshop since my return from Bali. I was anxious to try some things with a group. At Skidmore, we had a large, bright, wonderful studio. I was given two very large free-standing mirrors on wheels, and we were off.

Why did we need mirrors? As westerners, we tend to be culturally oriented with an outside-in point-of-view. If we see something, then we can understand it. We rarely operate on feelings or intuitions, which are great parts of pure creativity. If we begin with looking at the mask and its mirror image, then we are less apt to get lost. The reflection helps open the channels of imagination. Gently, students become familiar and secure within the world of the mask. The workshop environment is very important; it must provide a safe place for exploration. Once the quality and depth of exploration possible has been safely introduced, this creative zone can be revisited more easily without the mirror.

The group forms a large circle, with the mirrors facing each other at either end of the circle. Several pairs of partners are selected and asked to choose their masks from the mask table. We use full-faced neutral masks, as the neutral mask has few obligatory characteristics to specify and define personality, providing a blank canvas for exploration. The remaining participants select instruments.

Initially, my Skidmore introduction to acting class had been exploring the five senses. We were working on hearing when I introduced a "kitchen orchestra," which I had "borrowed" from a Bread and Puppet performance. As the kitchen utensils broke, I observed an abundance of empty Tide containers, old shower curtains, egg cartons, and assorted household items ready for the trash heap. These were easily accessible and free, so the "kitchen orchestra" evolved into the "garbage orchestra." The orchestra now plays a very important part in my introductory mask exercises.

In this initial collaboration, the ensemble forms a ritual orchestra. Some groups find the evolving rhythm difficult and need to be guided to "talk and listen to each other," supporting their masked classmates. They discover that playing less can indeed be more, and they eventually tune into the same channel. Some classes create record-quality orchestras, and others remain "rhythmically challenged." The music serves a high calling in this exercise. It is the shaman guiding between the real world and the world of invention. While the orchestra builds, those wearing masks are given instructions. The music entertains and dominates the ordinary thoughts of the masked players as they are coached to face and greet their partners.

The pairs are instructed to stay seated and observe their reflection in the mirror without judgment. The suspension of judgment is the first significant hurdle of the exercise. They are directed to study their own face, the face of the mask, the two together, and then, with breath, they don the masks. With the inhalation, the mask goes on, and the exhalation breathes life into the mask. As the players sit, the spine, crowned by the neck and head, reflects the changing persona, as it curves or straightens to accommodate transformation. Partners are then instructed to face each other, observe, greet, and beckon to one another. Participants enter a world that is like a dream, and as in a dream, linear thought vanishes and nonsequential abstract thought prevails.

There are guidelines to observe. All must stay seated and allow the connection to the floor to affect their interactions. They must not use their voices, allowing the language of gesture to evolve. In the next part of the exercise, the pair is instructed to face each other, to greet, beckon, and give and take imaginary objects. The whole group witnesses the exchange, as conjured wind and dust and daggers are tossed across the room. Finally, it becomes time for the partners to disengage. They are advised to blow a kiss or to "tell" their partner where to go and eventually to wave good-bye. In the end, they have traveled a huge distance together and have shared a profound and moving experience. The exercise concludes with each pair sharing their experiences with the group. A journal is brought to subsequent workshops; the first entry is a written record of the events experienced in the transformation exercise.

Explore the Room

Exploration follows transformation. Explore the Room is adapted from an exercise in Libby Appel's book, *Mask Characterization.* The focus of this exercise is a deep and unique investigation of objects. For this exercise, the whole group selects masks, puts them on in front of the mirror, and enters the workspace at the same time. This is the first time the masked players can walk and move about the room while privately exploring and relating to the objects from the garbage orchestra.

There is a huge leap between transformation of character to this individual, often profound state of concentration. Students experience this leap as a 180-degree shift in consciousness. In the Transformation exercise, they are encouraged to be guided by their imaginations. Now, they are asked to be driven by their activities, actions, and interests. Initially, participants are instructed to work by themselves and to feel no obligation to engage in any form of social contact or socially correct behavior. They are encouraged to find out what interests them in an object through the use of their senses. Does sound, sight, or touch fuel their exploration? Do they like to build or destroy? How driven by story or costume are they? They are instructed to change their personal rhythm and to explore and vary the tempo of their movements. Participants respond to suggestions of hopping, skipping, jumping, and rolling as a means of moving from one place to another. They are encouraged to engage with a particular object only as long as it holds their interest. When their interest wanes, they move on to explore another object. Some come to recognize for the first time their fascination for color or texture or sound. All actions are generated by the exploration of the objects in the room.

In the second part of Explore the Room, students may interact in their exploration of objects, and they may continue to explore solitarily. All interactions are nonverbal. Students invent wonderful games. They tie shoeboxes to their feet with speaker wire and ice-skate on catalogues; they jump rope with extension cords and play craps with bottle caps. They create a huge variety of unique new games and reinterpret old ones.

The exercise comes to a finish with my countdown announcement, followed by my request that all actions be completed. The masks are lifted, and all participants are asked to go directly to their journals and record their reflections and insights gleaned through their journey. Journal entries are recorded as soon as an exercise is completed and before conversation about the exercise occurs. Individuals learn to honor their private musings before diluting them with the reactions of others.

FURTHER EXPLORATIONS

First, there is *transformation*, an introduction into the mythic world of the mask. This is followed by *exploration*, which integrates moving in space, exploring movement, and interactions with objects while inhabiting the world of the mask. The neutral mask series continues with a selection of "appetizers" designed to further explore the safety and performing power of the mask. In *Chairs*, another exercise based on a Libby Appel model, an extremely familiar object is utilized in a completely new way. The conscious use of balance and weight shifts integrates with the imaginative mask-world to further expand and enrich the instrument.

The notion of energy centers motivating the body is not a new concept to modern-day acting teachers. Shakespeare says in *As You Like It*, "One man in his time plays many parts, his acts being seven ages." Tantric yoga defines seven chakras or energy centers of the body. With the neutral mask, in *The Four Stages of Man*, we explore four of the seven ages or energy centers of man: toddler, adolescent, adult, and elderly. The inspiration for this exercise is generally based in the work of one of my mentors, Pierre LeFevre, formerly of the Juilliard School. We begin with the introduction of a speculative theory about gravity, vital energy, and how in the aging process, energy journeys through the body in the course of a lifetime. We begin by focusing energy at the top of the head, the crown chakras, to find the buoyant energy of the very young. The "place" for this improvisation is a warm preschool environment. Then the students are instructed to direct their energy into the zone of their heart chakras as they rediscover middle school and the mercurial life of the adolescent. The energy for the third zone, adult, is placed in the large diamond formed by placing pinkies on hipbones and thumbs on the ribcage. Profession becomes the motivating engine of this stage of mankind. Finally, the slow steady weight of gravity on the elderly is explored by focusing energy on the root chakras, at the base of the spine. In scales, the final section of the four stages of man exercise, there is a family reunion. In this activity, students revisit each of the four zones in a random fashion and interact with other "family" members. The experience precipitates profound insights, which students record in their journals.

Once the mask performer has become accustomed to the limitations and possibilities of the mask, it is then possible to build specific tools. The tools of concentration, breath, and focus are further refined in Hinge Moments. Here, we examine mythology, the bible, fairy tales, history, and Shakespeare and look for the actions, which reconstruct the world of mythic characters. When Icarus flies too close to the sun or Medea slays her children or the tortoise is victorious over the hare, we see the changes in all of their unique range. Transformation is now fully realized and presented in space. The hinge moment is a studied, developed piece of choreography, complete with a beginning, middle, and an end. With the transformation of the hinge moments, we come full circle with the neutral mask work.

A series of workshops exploring the character mask follow the neutral mask work. For these workshops, a different set of masks is utilized. Their design, without mouths and chins, enable the masked performer to speak and engage in dialogues, adding voice and words to their physical transformation.

The mask encourages exploration of savory, nonlinear creative thought while providing direct access to the imagination. Students experience a sense of profound liberation that seems to be inherent in mask work. The unique creativity of the mythic imagination brings subconscious notions into consciousness. The theater has had a deep awareness of the significance and power of masks since Thespis first cloaked Dionysus in a mask. In my work, this exploration continues.

The Smallest Mask: The Red Nose

Jean Taylor

Ministers of nonsense. Delight makers. Purveyors of the illogical.

The clown has been with us for as long as we can remember. He is found in theaters and on street corners, in circuses and in ancient rituals. He is a ubiquitous performer, appearing in all corners of the world.

What is it about the clown that makes him such a universal character? And what can the clown teach a contemporary actor about himself and his craft? Societal rules of behavior vary from culture to culture, but the clown can be consistently counted on to present "other" or "contrary" ways of being and perceiving. Often within ritual performances, the clown's behavior actually borders on the taboo and yet carries an official sanction of the culture. In the Hopi and Navajo cultures, as an example, the clown's role is "to keep the people in touch with everyday reality while fulfilling the need for a connection to the sacred. While ostensibly mocking an entire performance, he also supports and embellishes it. This concept of burlesquing the sacred while also supporting it is repeated in most North American Indian cultures."[1]

This concept also exists in other world cultures, from the Ostyak of western Siberia to the Ashanti of Africa. In her article titled "The Clown's Function," Lucile Hoerr Charles utilized the Cross-Cultural Survey of the Institute of Human Relations, Yale University, to compare the role of the clown in primitive cultures. In all, she examined data from fifty-six cultures and came to the following inspired conclusion:

> In his race-long effort to achieve his full stature, to become more conscious, to come to grips with his own real potentialities, mankind frequently has become too absorbed in fine and high flights of intellect and power, and has neglected the humdrum, humble, everyday, earthy side of life. Such neglect is true of very primitive man as well as of so-called civilized man.[2]

Charles goes on to describe how this lack of balance, this lopsided perspective in man, eventually causes a stir in the unconscious, as the neglected functions call out for some relief, for an antidote. Enter the gifted clown, who "comes along and intuitively seizes upon these hidden elements in his audience and bodies them forth in dramatic play; his audience is held, led, released, and delighted. Once more, life is served."[3]

In addition to his role in ritual performances, the clown has, for centuries, been a potent theatrical presence. His antics and unique logic fill the comedies of Greece and Rome, the plays of Shakespeare, the "lazzi"[4] of the Commedia dell'Arte, and in our own time, the brilliant clown shows of Bill Irwin and David Shiner. Clown characters can appear in many guises, but they can always be counted on to embody our most human foibles.

So, what is the value of clown work for the contemporary actor? At the heart of clown work is the acceptance and celebration of human imperfection. On a personal level, it is learning to see our seeming limitations as a source of creativity and humor. As Jacques Lecoq, the influential acting teacher, said, clown work is "the discovery of how personal weakness can be transformed into dramatic strength."[5] What a gift for any actor, and what an incomparable compliment to any acting technique.

A BEGINNING CLASS

Our teacher begins the class by explaining that the small red nose, like other masks, is a tool for transformation. The clown is about presence, simplicity, vulnerability, and moment-to-moment experience—all things helpful, indeed essential, to the actor. She emphasizes that our study of clown is theatrical in nature, encompassing a full range of expression, from the very subtle to the exaggerated. Our clown work, she says, is a distant cousin to the circus clown and an even more distant cousin to the balloon-sculpting birthday clown. She asks us to let go of our preconceptions about clowns and approach the work with an open curiosity, which will allow the experience itself to inform us.

Our teacher continues: A clown arrives on stage free of past history. No parents, no siblings, no psychological baggage. He lives in the present and is fed by his connection to the audience. He moves from dilemma to solution, ad infinitum, revealing his innocence and resiliency. Which is precisely why we find him so delightful—he shows us that survival is indeed possible and that our own shortcomings often produce the next solution.

This first exercise, our teacher explains, will serve as a touchstone for all the successive clown activities. The Three-Second Wait, or Going to My Spot, is a wonderfully ridiculous high-stakes exercise. Our teacher credits her discovery of this game to a long-ago workshop with Vincent Rouche, a Belgian performer. Over the years, she has developed and expanded it. Like clowning itself, the exercise is both profound and absurd.

The Three-Second Wait

On the floor are two T marks, one further upstage than the other. These are our "spots." One at a time and in self-selected order, we are asked to announce to the group a series of simple actions: "I am going to stand up," "I am going to look at the pooblic,"[6] "I am going to go to my spot." The added stipulation is that once the statement is proclaimed, the actor must wait (hence the three seconds) before fulfilling the action. The space created by the "waiting" breaks an actor's habitual stimulus-response pattern and allows room for something new to happen. Drawing a clear comparison to the Alexander Technique, our teacher refers to positive inhibition, wherein physical patterns are held in check while the body learns a new way of responding.

The Three-Second Wait exercise also teaches us to establish and maintain a connection with the audience. We are reminded that the clown uses focus and eye contact to keep the "fourth wall" open. We find ourselves fully engaged as each actor attempts the announcing and waiting. The various strategies to "get it right" make us laugh with recognition. Our collective desire for perfection is exposed.

In the discussion following this exercise, many students comment on the difficulty they had in slowing down; others comment on their need to entertain by doing more than was required; and still others admitted their feelings of vulnerability when they allowed a genuine connection with the audience. All good things, our teacher assures us, as we move into finding our own clown.

Finding Your Clown

We sit in a circle and are given our small red noses. Like most masks, it has a thin elastic cord to stabilize it during improvisations. This is a simple exercise, our teacher says, meant as an initial encounter with the mask. Endowing this small object with a sense of ritual will only serve to increase its transformative power. We are instructed to turn away from our fellow students as we put on our masks and to complete any adjustments to its placement before turning back around. When we do turn around, our task is to simply look at each member of the class, allowing our responses to surface freely and releasing ourselves from the need to "show" anything particular. We are struck by the change in our classmates' faces. Each little shift in focus and subtle adjustment becomes fascinating and filled with nuance. The nose makes us look at familiar faces with a new curiosity. Even in relative stillness, much is being communicated. Spontaneous laughter erupts as we catch sight of an expression, a deep sigh, or a hilarious profile.

The next fifteen minutes of the class are spent in individual exploration. Wearing our "smallest mask," we begin the discovery of our own clown. The teacher reminds us that once the mask is on, the body becomes the clown's primary tool for expression. "How does your clown find comfort?" "What Olympic sport is he an expert in?" "Does he have an eccentric dance move that pleases him no end?" These questions encourage us to play, and as we play, we unscover our own wonderful ridiculousness. The insights gained during this group exercise will help us as we take our solo turns in the "walk-arounds."

THE WHITE CLOWN AND THE AUGUSTE

Although initially a circus term for a brief bit around the ring, in theatrical terms, the walk-around includes the entrance of the clown, the clown's discovery of the audience, his playing with the audience, and his exit. The teacher explains that clowns fall primarily into two categories: the "authority" or "white" clown and the "auguste" clown. The "authority" clown loves order, and the "auguste" clown can't help but bring chaos. It is the dynamic interplay between them that is the source of much humor. We are assured that through a series of improvisations, we will begin to have an inkling of where our clown fits into this continuum and are encouraged to discover this truth through our playing.

Walk-Arounds

To begin the walk-around, one student steps outside the room and is instructed to put his mask on and enter. He needs to enter simply, with openness and a sense of availability. As Philippe Gaulier, the internationally acclaimed acting teacher, says, "the clown must have great pleasure in the playing and it is his pleasure that charms the audience." The student-clown slowly pushes the door open; we see only a hand. Gradually the masked face appears, and the student shifts his focus directly to the audience. Contact has been made. As the clown enters the room, the teacher helps create a useful dilemma, a predicament for the student-clown: She acts as an authority figure, providing playable paramaters. "We have been waiting," the teacher says, "and are so looking forward to your demonstration." We see the panic on the clown's face and can't help but laugh. It is that universal feeling of being caught off guard, of feeling inadequate. But here is where the clown saves himself and us. He allows himself to believe he can handle this situation, that he is up to the challenge. In this walk-around, the challenge is "the bird call of the russet-breasted sparrow-hawk." The student-clown puckers his lips, swallows, and emits a strange whistle that quickly dissolves into prolonged lip flutter. The class laughs, enjoying the struggle. The clown tries again with renewed determination. He puckers, licks his lips, puckers again. This time, no sound emerges at all. Despite the effort, after a moment of quiet panic, the clown surrenders to the lip flutter, and we are charmed! The bird-call demonstration is followed by a "dance of the volcano spirits" and a "love song of a Scottish clan." Each clown is encouraged to stay connected to the "pooblic" throughout his walk-around. Our human and actor impulse is to "go away" from the audience when we don't know how to accomplish the task and to "return" when we have the solution. In clowning, it is the journey from panic to idea that we want to see most. We are reminded of the day's first exercise, "Going to my Spot," and understand the importance of direct connection with the audience.

We laugh as each new clown attempts to master his particular task. The individual humanity of each student-clown is brought forth, and the fear of failure becomes something to play with rather than reject.

It is the end of our first class. Each new improvisation, our teacher says, will give us valuable information about our individual clown. Next session, we will play with specific techniques that guide two or more clowns performing together, the essential tools of focus and rhythm, followed by the challenge of "moments in clown history." For the present, we are excited to have made our first foray into the world of the smallest mask and to have reacquainted ourselves with a sense of play and pleasure.

NOTES

1. Towsen, John H. *Clowns*. New York: Hawthorne Books, 1976, 8.
2. Charles, Lucile Hoerr. "The Clown's Function." *Journal of American Folklore*, 58 (March 1945): 32.
3. Ibid.
4. "Lazzi," as defined in *Lazzi, the Comic Routines of the Commedia dell'Arte* by Mel Gordon, are "comic routines that were planned or unplanned and that could be performed in any one of dozens of plays."
5. Lecoq, Jacques. *The Moving Body*. New York: Routledge, 2001,145.
6. "Pooblic" is the phonetic spelling of the word "public," as pronounced by the Belgian teacher-performer Vincent Rouche. It is entrenched in my being, since it was part of my early training. "Pooblic, Jean, Pooblic!" he would yell, as I tried to hide from the audience. It has become a regular part of the exercise, adding a wonderful playfulness to the proceedings.

Discovering Ensemble and Impulse through Improvisation

Paul Urcioli

On the first day of any improvisation class I teach, a survey of the students usually reveals them to represent one of two paradigms: First, there is the student who has never had any sort of improvisation class, who has been intimidated by too many "funny" people in prior training and too many episodes of *Whose Line Is It Anyway?* and lives day to day with the paralysis-inducing fear of "improv inadequacy," terrified of getting up to create theater in front of an audience with nothing prepared. Second, there is the student who has been part of an improvisation company either in college or high school, happens to be one of those intimidating "funny" people (at least in his mind), has also seen too many episodes of *Whose Line . . .* , suffers from delusions of grandeur when it comes to his ability, but sadly, usually has a limited idea of exactly what a truly great improvisation ensemble can accomplish.

IN A PERFECT WORLD

What I hope for is that by the time a course has ended, the students will not only have freed their impulses and had fun learning about the craft of improvisation, but more importantly, have discovered the joys of being part of a great team. That every member of the ensemble will have the desire to continually expand his range as an improviser, not only in becoming more mentally acute but also in accepting the stylistic challenges—that is, to dutifully portray the audience's suggestions and to be able to raise himself up to the demands of any scene, not only mentally but also *physically*, with a mind and body prepared to fully create in the moment.

I've been lucky enough to have been a part of, worked with, and witnessed the work of several remarkable ensembles. It has always been my experience that great improvisers are courageous, altruistic, smart, prepared, and most importantly, work together. They will throw themselves headlong into a scene, knowing that high risk means high return and that even if they don't succeed, people will respect a noble failure. They know that scenes will work or they won't, but they have to give up control and the desire to stand out and be the best or funniest. They know that the only thing that matters is the scene being created and that it's amazing what can be accomplished when no one cares who gets the credit. They have read more books, newspapers, and magazines; seen more kinds of theater, movies, plays, and TV; taken in more painting, sculpture, and photography than people usually do; and know what's happening all around them, in every facet of the world and in the community around them. They have continually drilled and improved their skills and still are not happy with the level they have reached. They are at their best executing spontaneously, performing with the coordination and grace of a great dance ensemble, the woven fluidity of the Princeton Tigers under Pete Carrill, the desire and commitment of a baseball team in the stretch drive, and the interconnected response and logic of a great jazz ensemble. They know each other's moves and tendencies as well as their own.

In addition to these characteristics of commitment and teamwork and, of course, full command of the tenets of improvisation—good storytelling skills, acting chops—I always tell my students they must understand how they can help the scene physically. A good improviser must know how to create characters through movement, direct himself with clarity, move specifically when playing various styles, and must be aware of the fact that his command of his body, sense of himself on the stage, and the physical choices he makes are as much a part of the craft as knowing what to say to push the story forward.

Of course, a great deal of time is required for an ensemble to grasp the fundamentals of storytelling and scene building. Hours of group work and drilling must be put in if a group of actors wants to improvise well. Since the focus of this book is movement, I won't dwell on the myriad of ensemble-building, acting, and storytelling exercises a group must undertake and commit to before setting out to bravely take the suggestions of an audience. (Hopefully, a mostly sober one.) Suffice it to say that just bringing a group of really funny people together and letting them do their stuff in front of an audience is not only a constant contest in one-upmanship and a dangerous experiment in ego fulfillment, but a complete disservice to the craft. In time, it will also most likely lead to the disintegration of the group. For an ensemble to flourish, there must be a shared commitment to something larger than the self.

A TEACHING ENVIRONMENT

Regarding improvisers' movement skills, with commitment and practice, they will develop along with the strength of the group. Members of an ensemble learn from and inspire each other to take risks. When I was with my first improvisation troupe, my partner and I received the suggestion "ice skating" for the activity in our scene. I chickened out. I chose to focus on playing our given relationship and play my half of the scene without the activity, thereby letting him deal with the problem. To this day, I am still inspired by the memory of him gliding around the stage with total commitment, giving total credence to the illusion. I felt at once awed and ashamed. I had decided to let him handle the difficulty of the suggestion. Later that night, while the entire ensemble exchanged war stories at the bar, I listened to the accolades he received for his commitment and realized the depth of possibility and rewards for fearlessly throwing oneself in are inestimable, that an improviser with command of his body can be a force onstage. We were a strong group, committed to our process, rehearsing our skills constantly. More importantly, our director recognized that sharing our experiences would make us even stronger. It's often been said that a chain is as strong as its weakest link. But every member of every ensemble I've worked with always brings his or her own strengths to the group. The environment should be such that members of the group are free to bring their knowledge and experience to the group, even teaching each other in a very formal way. Acting exercises, group games, and fun warm-ups are readily shared, so why not movement experiences?

If, for example, there is a member with Suzuki training, why not let that person lead the group in some of those techniques and increase the members' control, explosiveness, and strength? Someone with experience in Commedia dell'Arte could help teach the status and storytelling value in these stock characters. A member with training or experience in seventeenth-century movement could add to the group's knowledge of movement within a social structure. Laban could give actors a way to break down their characters' movement into simple descriptive words. In fact, I often use this language in concert with basic scene-building exercises. I give the actors a suggestion to get started—for example, two friends meeting for a drink—and assign each a word from the Laban vocabulary. Person A's movement, conversational style, methodology for perusing what he wants must all be "light and indirect." Person B gets something like "heavy" or "press" to describe how he goes about his business. The conflict may be heightened by the way A deflects responsibility for lateness, for example, and the way B takes control and a high-handed approach from the force of his suggestions. A good ensemble should take advantage of and be willing to experiment with all forms of movement contributed by its members. Any background a player has can increase the ensemble's physical specificity and, in the long run, help to increase their movement skills onstage.

GETTING STARTED

Since improvisation is all about going with and committing to the first thought, actors must get in the habit early on of fully expressing these impulses not only vocally, but also physically. At the outset of a new class, I would hope that an actor with some prior training would possess a sense of basic stagecraft: know stage right from left and up from down. He should also know how he could benefit from how and where he stands and moves onstage and in relation to the other players. Knowing that ¾ position is stronger than profile or ¾ back is a start, but he should also be aware of how his position on the stage and his physical relationship to the other actors can affect the scene. At the beginning of training, I always stress making strong entrances and exits, planting your feet, and taking stage. This, of course, is a dual responsibility shared by not only the performer making the choice but by the other performers, who must respect and give focus to the entrance and or exit.

Early on, I make actors do a daily drill. Two actors take the stage and improvise the first two lines of a scene and nothing more. I put the focus on getting off to a good start every time, teaching the actors to make strong choices to begin their scenes. After the initial frustration over not getting to continue their scenes, students begin to see that even with only two lines, when they concentrate, they can communicate so much about the relationship between the characters, the story, the activity, or location and sow the seeds of conflict necessary to drive the story forward. Even concentrating on these scene-building basics, I always stress the importance of making strong physical choices that support the acting choice. Actors must take the stage and get in the habit of planting their feet and placing themselves in a strong ¾ position. As they get freer and their work becomes more polished and filled with nuance, a reliance on ¾ isn't always necessary, but it's important to create and reinforce these habits early on to strengthen their physical choices. If an actor, for example, chooses to begin a scene where he attempts to get his money back for something, his tactic or approach should be reflected in his body. If he comes to the complaint department breathing fire and unwilling to take "no" for an answer, his posture must support that. If he chooses to play the character as spineless but still determined to reach his goal (the money), that impulse must appear in his body as well. Too often, I only *hear* the variations. The volume and pitch of the voice and even the chosen vocabulary tell me a lot, but I want to see the impulses explored and heightened in the bodies.

Often, at this level, it is important to cure actors of "wandering." Even when teaching my scene study classes, I find that young or inexperienced actors lack the necessary skill of stillness. It can be difficult to keep them rooted, even when they have rehearsed and know their lines. It's even more difficult to create stillness on the spot. Too often, rambling, unfocused dialogue is accompanied by rambling, unfocused movement. Short of stapling the feet to the floor, another point of focus can cure happy feet. It is about this time I begin to bring activity into the scenes. Keeping hands on a task (especially ones that require specific tools or props) often teaches actors to root themselves and gives their presence on stage a specificity they wouldn't otherwise have if they relied on what I call "talking heads"—that is, having the conflict, story, and characters' relationships develop only through verbal justification. Quite often, I've found that putting attention on *where* a scene takes place and *what* the activity is frees the actors in their creativity more than verbal skills alone. If the scene, for example, is "two roommates arguing over a phone bill" and the two actors simply stand there and fight it out, they are under pressure to push the events of the story forward using only the argument at hand. If, on the other hand, they choose or are given an activity or a specific location to justify, the possibilities are expanded, and writing the scene is made easier. It is not even necessary that the added choice have anything to do with being roommates or a phone bill. For example, if the suggested activity is "icing a cake," the activity will not only prove to be a useful obstacle to the argument, but could perhaps be connected to it—"you know I had to make all those long distance calls to get people here for your party" or "I had to order these ingredients from Belgium; you're the one who wanted a special Flemish birthday cake." The fact that the scene probably takes place (but doesn't have to) in a proper cake-icing environment will give both actors a more specific sense of how to stage themselves. A kitchen provides endless opportunity of where to go, where to stand, or what to do.

ADVANCED EXERCISES

When an ensemble has begun to master the basics of improvisation—heightening conflicts, developing relationship, location, and activity—I try to further develop their movement specificity by doing exercises to explore their physical creativity in creating characters. The very nature of improvisation is creating something from nothing in the moment in the sparest of environments. Actors must be encouraged to develop their ability to make specific character-related movement choices as well. There are many exercises to develop characters from the outside in as well as the inside out. A simple one I learned in an early movement class and have adapted to my improvisation classes is based solely on walking. I have an even number of actors walk in a circle. The actors work in pairs. Every other actor just walks. The actor behind him slowly and meticulously "puts on" his own leader's walk, copying that walk step-by-step. I coach the actors, so that they can focus on the specifics of the walk: Begin with the length of stride and weight of the footfall. Does the walk have purpose, or is it somewhat timid? Does is have grace? Stealth? Arrogance? Move on to the swing of the arms. Is it broad and long or close to the body and constrained?

The sway of the hips, the position of the head are all slowly adopted. Eventually, the leaders can step into the circle and see their walks being "worn" by their partners. I'll periodically ask the actors still walking to drop their new walk completely and then pick it back up to see if they have mastered it technically. I'll then ask them to tell me what the walk feels like on them. What kind of person walks like this? Does it remind them of a specific status, profession, or age? If a choice comes to them and they are adept at putting the walk back on like a costume, we can throw these newly developed characters into a scene, give them a suggestion, and see what arises. Hopefully the movement alone will develop the characters and help push the story forward.

I'll also encourage students to create a character from the inside out. The actors choose a piece of paper with a profession written on it. I then side-coach the actors as they simply stand and wait in a given location—for example, a bus stop. I'll ask them a series of questions about this person. While there are no right or wrong answers, the first thoughts that pop up begin to inform how the actor sees his character and then how that character moves. I'll ask the actor his name, age, address; annual income, what kind of car he drives (if he has one), marital or relationship status, number of children (if any), what he's wearing, what's in his pockets, etc. Once the actors have decided on some basic information, I'll ask them to begin moving through the space. The initial choices they've made always inform how this character walks and how he relates nonverbally to others while doing so. As with the previous exercise, these characters can then be placed in scenes. Implementing these exercises is fun for the players—and useful in the long run, because exploration time is a luxury you don't have when making choices the moment after the suggestion comes.

Another exercise I do involves asking the actors to play a scene with a specific physical limitation or irritation to affect their movements. For instance, I'll seat someone casually on a park bench and have her play the scene with absolutely no movement whatsoever. Justification can be up to the actor—"I'm sitting for a portrait," "I've been glued here"—or never even come up. It could just add a great obstacle to the scene. I mean "obstacle" in a positive way. This is because circumstances that break routines or make routines difficult usually result in good storytelling. Sometimes the limitation drives the scene all by itself. A hidden adjustment or "irritation" can also inspire specific movement as well—"play the scene as though your pants were far too tight," "walk around as though your head weighed twenty-five pounds," "move as though you always feel tingling in your feet," and so on. It's not even necessary for the suggested impetus to be revealed during the scene. What's more important is how the effect changes the movement and inspires justification. Often it creates great characterizations and status between the players. Using the twenty-five pound head as an example: Perhaps it will remind one player of feeling hung over, and a scene will arise where coworkers discuss the shocking events of the previous night's office party. The tight pants could give rise to a character that acts uppity and standoffish.

I also enjoy giving actors the freedom to concentrate solely on their physicality by doing games and exercises where the primary focus is movement. Often, control of the physical choices can be left up to others. The most famous of these exercises is the Freeze exercise and all its variations. At its most basic, two actors begin by moving randomly around the space. At any time, someone can call, "freeze!" The actors do so and then try to begin a scene that will somehow justify their body positions. At any point in that scene, "freeze" can be called again, and the process continues. Contrary to what one might imagine, the most common difficulty is not coming up with a great justification, but avoiding the retreat back to "talking heads." Too often, actors think of a proper justification, thankfully jump into the scene, and gradually forget all about the importance of continuing the movement and activity. If that happens, every subsequent scene is frozen in the same position: two people standing around talking—*riveting*. The actors have to be reminded to keep their activities alive and, more importantly, to vary and heighten them—better still, keep them alive and connected to their partner's activity. If this happens, each call of "freeze" will give the actors new positions and the scenes cohesion. The possibilities will be limitless. At each freeze, the bodies will remind the minds of something and give the actors their next justification.[1]

A variation on the Freeze game gives the responsibility of calling "freeze" to a facilitator and the justification of position to the audience. Hopefully the audience will not be motivated by the desire to entertain themselves and give suggestions that are actually related to what they see. For example:

"Freeze! What's Joy doing?"
"Beating her clothes on a rock."
"And what's Sasha doing?"
"Splitting the atom."
"Okay, go!"

What makes these scenes enjoyable is each actor's total commitment to the task and attempt to justify exactly how these activities can not only be connected but taking place in the same location. This exercise is not only enjoyable for an audience but also useful to return to as a rehearsal exercise for keeping actors' movements specific.

If an actor is having trouble taking risks with movement or shies away from larger physical choices, I'll often try exercises where the movement is not up to him. In simplest form, the actors playing the scene cannot move at all unless their bodies are pushed and manipulated by a sort of puppet-master partner. The "puppeteer" can push the back of her puppet's legs to make him walk, manipulate his arms for gestures and activity, and even turn his head or manipulate his face for focus and expression. It goes without saying that for this exercise to work well, a high level of trust and responsibility must already exist within the ensemble.

At a higher level, Dubbing is also a valuable exercise. Two actors play the scene onstage, while two actors off supply the dialogue. While the actors onstage have their anxieties alleviated by the fact that they are only responsible for movement and the other actors get to sit relaxed and worry about dialogue only, all four are always responsible for the story being told. Actors doing movement have to keep their mouths moving and justify what the voices say, and the voices have to justify all movement. Initiation can come from either side. For example, if an actor onstage suddenly moves as if reacting to a noise, his offstage voice could justify it with the sound of a loud clap of thunder and then initiate in his onstage partner a move to a window to check the weather.

Fraught with peril and frustration, the Double Dubbing exercise is even harder. Instead of four players dividing the responsibility for the scene, each player's responsibilities are doubled. It can really help to discipline an actor's stillness, specificity, and concentration on movement. In this exercise, only two players are required onstage, and each dubs the other. Clarity and proper give-and-take are required in the dialogue. For example, the scene is a babysitter and child, and each actor supplies the other's voice. The actor playing the child speaks for the babysitter, "For the last time, it's after ten, get to bed, or I'm calling your mom and dad at the restaurant." The Actor playing the babysitter has to attempt to mouth that dialogue with required expression and make specific physical choices—for example, a gesture toward a watch or clock, an authoritative gesture toward the bedroom, and a cross to the phone. The actor playing the babysitter then holds the pose, responds with the next line for the child to physically justify, and so on. Performing the exercise well takes tremendous concentration. Needless to say, the skill level is extremely high, but mastering it provides so many benefits: An actor will be able to be physically specific justifying choices made by someone else, while simultaneously creating the dialogue for another character.

STATUS AND BLOCKING

The knowledge of status transactions between individuals and how to best manipulate or play with them is one of the most effective skills an actor can possess. Getting what you want (or a character what he or she wants) is more readily accomplished when the player is a master of the constantly changing status seesaw. Adjusting one's status is achieved in one of four ways: raising the self, lowering the self, raising the other, or lowering the other. It's easiest to accomplish this when we communicate verbally, and it's incredibly easy to throw oneself into scenes where there are maximum status gaps—for instance, master–slave, CEO–janitor, quarterback–water boy—but good improvisers know how to communicate and exploit more difficult minimum-status gaps physically and often with subtle choices. Very often, words

In the photos, notice how the position of the actor on the left (legs crossed, arm splayed along the back of the chair) seems to give him a higher status then the actor on the right. In the second photo, notice how a simple adjustment of where the actors put their focus seems to suggest something new.

aren't even necessary. How we sit and stand when near each other speaks volumes about how we feel about ourselves in relation to the other(s) in the room. Picture two people sharing the same bench or sofa. The actor stage right sits relaxed, legs crossed, facing downstage, arms splayed along the backrest. The actor stage left also sits relaxed, but with feet on the ground, hands folded in his lap, and his focus on the other actor. Before we even assign a relationship, conflict, or situation, the first actor seems to have a higher status. Simple choices like where an actor puts his attention (eyes up or down), his focus (on or off his partner or the activity), or how he stands in relationship to the other actors (upstage of him or down, profile or full front) can sometimes communicate more than words.

Playing a game I call Japanese Rock Garden can be helpful in illustrating these subtleties. I developed it with a friend after we had been exposed to a lot of Viewpoints work. It's a nonverbal exercise where a group of actors go into the designated playing space and form a series of tableaux. I ask the actors watching to close their eyes between the pictures to maximize the effect of seeing only the tableaux, leaving the transitions the business of the players only. First, I limit the players' physical vocabulary to standing or kneeling neutrally and choosing to have their arms either at their sides or crossed in front of themselves. I tell them they can put their focus wherever they wish. The players choose an opening picture, and I call "lights up," so the audience can open their eyes. The actors hold the picture for a few moments then move to the next. I'll coach, "Everyone moves together and stops together." This helps to strengthen their awareness of each other and commit to their choices simultaneously. When they have stopped, I then say, "Lights up," and the audience members see the next tableau, and so on. Usually, the audience begins to read into the pictures. I often hear interpretations of tribal or religious rites, gang war, dysfunctional family dynamics, stories from history, etc., to which the players are, of course, oblivious. Discussion after each round lets the students see how small, specific adjustments, such as footing, angle of the body, and proximity, go a long way to helping the pictures become even more specific than they had been. Let's say, for example, one actor simply stands facing full front with his arms at his sides and another actor chooses to work with him by standing slightly upstage. If the second actor "sort of" stands nearby with no specificity in his position, physical relationship, or point of focus, then the picture is muddy. If, however, he chooses a strong ¾ position, upstage but in the clear of the first actor, arms crossed on his chest with his focus strongly on his partner, something specific is communicated. My first thought is that of higher status, a kind of disapproval of the other. Imagine for a moment the second actor if he stands upstage, yet in the clear, arms at his sides, and focusing on the same point as the downstage actor—what do you see? I imagine him now as lower status, a sort of follower, submitting himself to the wishes of the first actor. Imagine if they could translate these ideas onto the stage when they improvise. Actors could begin to make physical choices in the moment that *specifically* represent what they are saying. They begin to see the information communicated merely in how they stand or sit, how to make physical choices of stillness that help tell the story, and how to use the space itself to their advantage.

In rehearsal sessions, this exercise can be returned to and augmented again and again. When the players learn specificity, the restraints on the physical vocabulary can be removed, as long as players know they are responsible for using and reincorporating all the vocabulary introduced. Being grounded in these principles makes actors better directors of the moment as well. They eventually translate the skills from this exercise into their movement and blocking choices when they improvise. They begin to learn how best to balance and share the stage, how good movement and blocking tell the story as well as dialogue, and how best to put the audience's focus wherever it may belong.

PROCESS

Too often these days, a group of funny people decides that their gift of humor is reason enough to form an improvisation troupe. The ubiquity of comedy clubs, good and mediocre comedians rewarded with their own series, and million-dollar movie careers built on two-dimensional characters developed on sketch television has given rise to a seemingly endless parade of improvisation and sketch comedy groups. And why not, when a good show or performance in front of the right person can lead to a development deal? Sometimes, these ensembles contain a former student of mine eager to have me see his shows. Sometimes I'll go, and sometimes I enjoy myself. The work is energetic and exciting, and some of the sketch writing is both funny and daring. More often than not, however, I am disappointed. The performers are out for themselves; the results are ordinary, the writing predictable.

I see improvisation as an art form in and of itself, not just a springboard to "better things." There's no reason that these must be mutually exclusive concepts. Why couldn't an improvisation ensemble commit to the idea of art for art's sake? Couldn't they create work that excites, inspires, and moves people without thinking of where it might get them? And if success came their way, wouldn't it be exciting if a skilled and gifted group of artists became a source for popular entertainment? They could show us some incredible, beautiful things, raising the bar for us, instead of pandering to the least common denominator. They could show the public creativity that comes from the power of a group and its skills and gifts, instead of theater, television, and movies that stem from an aesthetic based solely on looks and the desire to titillate and shock.

If that sounds heavy-handed, embrace this: You've purchased this book because you are interested in learning more about and improving one of your necessary skills. You want to do better. Remember, nothing replaces the investment of time. Embrace your process, and accept that sometimes, the road is the goal.

NOTE

1. I should mention that whenever two people improvising have to share the same activity, total specificity is required. Remember, there are no actual props, and nothing gives the scene a lie like competing realities. Viola Spolin's Space Substance exercises can be incredibly useful in honing these skills.

PART FOUR

Beyond Glove and Fan

Bringing the Past into the Present: Period Dance on the Stage and in the Curriculum

Nira Pullin

The past is a foreign country; they do things differently there.

—L. P. Hartley, *The Go-Between*

Dance is one of the oldest arts. However, the investigation of the development of early social dance is a somewhat more recent field of study. In the world of dance, it is much easier to show than to tell. Unlike music, theater, and costume history, there are limited readable and accessible "how to" materials available on the subject. Actors, directors, and choreographers who want to study period dance in a practical studio setting have even fewer options. This chapter examines period dance and its role as an aesthetic and teaching discipline in academic and professional theater. It includes questions and answers by period dance teachers, considerations for putting period dance on the stage, exercises for the classroom and rehearsal hall, a timeline of period dances, and resources for further study.

In America, the discipline of dance and movement in the theater world is usually placed at the bottom of the list, if it is addressed at all. Most schools do not offer a course on period deportment and dance in their curriculum. By contrast, European theater professionals give much more consideration to period movement and dance in the production process and in the classroom. Although there is much interest and respect for its value among American teachers and directors, finding sources of information is a big challenge. As a result, too many directors and choreographers just do guesswork when it comes to period dance. Directors and production teams pay close attention to costume renderings, scenic design, props, and music, carefully connecting them to the style of the play and the production concept. But what about the dances?

Many directors, when asking for a dance in a period play, are not aware of what kind of dance is appropriate. They often assume that all choreographers and actors know how to dance period dances— wrong! There are only a handful of choreographers who specialize in historical dance. Choreographers are often further challenged by the rehearsal schedule. Directors tend to schedule dance rehearsals late in the process, expecting the choreographer to teach the dance in the same amount of time it takes to block a scene. Actors are expected to move and dance in costumes that are foreign to them with only a week of dress rehearsal to practice.

Published plays are also a challenge. Texts clearly delineate who each character is and their respective lines, and even suggest blocking. By contrast, most scripts indicate "a dance" without even naming it. How many theater people know the difference between a minuet and a mazurka, a farandole and a fox trot, a pavane and a polka, or even know what a galliard is?

Our contemporary culture, however, seems to have more nostalgia for the past and more of a desire to learn about the manners and social graces of ages gone by. There are the beautifully researched films of Merchant-Ivory and others appearing at movie theaters. The Stratford Festival productions in Canada demonstrate keen attention to the period details. And history comes alive via Internet and recent CD-ROM technology. Audiences are beginning to expect this same integrity in theatrical productions as well.

New York–based arts writer David Finkle, in an article entitled "CALL 1-800-THE HOOK," states the problem wonderfully:

> Here's a brash proposal. How about calling a moratorium on American productions of classic plays until there's a substantial pool of homegrown actors who can do them effectively? While we're at it, why not establish a federally funded Classical Theater Quality Control SWAT team (CTQC-SWAT) licensed to travel cross-country to shut down productions of Sophocles, Shakespeare, Kleist, you-name-'em, when they're not up to snuff? . . .
>
> Under Movement, sub-category Walking: Are the female members of the cast able to negotiate the stage in long skirts with bustles, skirts with panniers, hobble skirts? Are the men able to wear tights and not blush? Under sub-category Gestures: Can cast members bow or doff plumed hats with the appropriate panache?

So, what is period dance (also known as early dance, historical dance, and vintage dance)? I define period dance as social dance practiced through history for entertainment and recreation by the middle and privileged classes. This also includes theatrical dance until the mid-eighteenth century, when it became a professional activity. Here, period dance is classified as the social dances performed in what we loosely term "classical" plays, which includes plays from Shakespeare's age through the Victorian era.

How different were these dances from the dances of today? Today's dances and music differ from those of Shakespeare's time, but the reasons they were danced are much the same—and some dances are not as foreign as they seem. The two-step, popular at the end of the nineteenth century, came back as the country-western dance craze, and the waltz is still with us. Later dances, such as the lindy hop and jitterbug, are back today as swing dances, and the revival of the Argentine tango is still growing. There are country dance and contradance societies all over the world and vintage dance and early dance companies performing internationally.

And how does one approach the staging of these dances? I do not believe one can be a purist. Theater, after all, is "illusion." I do not teach period movement but movement of people in period clothing. People were human and had bodies just like ours today. They moved and danced differently because of the clothing they wore and the strict rules of decorum (for instance, unmarried women were always chaperoned, and touching intimately in public was never permitted), but to make uneducated guesses doesn't work. I break many rules of the era, but by choice, because it helps to tell the dramatic story today.

In the past, dance was part of a courtier and young lady's education and a necessary social grace. Dancing and deportment lessons with a dancing master began at a very early age. Many of today's actors aren't as quick or eager to learn, and many actors have never had dance or movement training at all. Though some actors may have initial fears, they become confident with practice, and even excited about how this work supports their creative process.

As an actor, I'm not just interested in knowing the lines in a play. I need to know how these people moved and what they felt, socially and privately. Learning period dance does just that—

brings to life a historical time emotionally and viscerally so the character becomes more than just words on a page.

—Kristopher Yoder, third-year actor, Hilberry Repertory Theater, Wayne State University

Dances of any period are a sign of the times—what would the 1920s be without the Charleston? They characterize the attitude, dress, and customs of the people of that era. By learning the dances you have an immediate physical glimpse into the social scene and life, because it takes into consideration the social standards, behaviors, and relationships of that time. It's a visceral way of learning history, and since dancing is universal, it's a fun way to learn.

—Trisha Miller, third-year actress, Hilberry Repertory Theater, Wayne State University

I find that the study of period movement and dance in the classroom and rehearsal hall brings history to life and enriches our understanding of the play. If you can dance the dances of a particular era, you will move better and be more comfortable in the period costumes. Actors' imaginations as well as their bodies are empowered by dance.

Period movement and dance is a great tool for building an ensemble. Actors develop so many important skills: concentration, balance, grace, confidence, and real awareness of one another.

—Alan Litsey, Ph.D., Associate Professor of Theater, Birmingham Southern College

When you sit in a classroom and talk about period dance in a scene, you don't experience it. But when you dance and move to the music, you get a flavor of the era. Some people think Shakespeare dull and lifeless, but when you dance a galliard you understand it wasn't. Men were looked well upon if they could dance well and do the athletic dances and swordplay. Period dance is an easy way to introduce things the actor should know, like rhythm, working with a group or partner, and how to communicate to your partner with your body . . . actions speak louder than words.

—William Wilson, Professor and Director, Rhode Island College

Each production presents its own set of problems. I tried to think back to all the problems and challenges I have encountered when choreographing dances in over one hundred productions. I interviewed other period dance specialists, teachers, and choreographers and asked them to share some of their expertise and experience. The thoughtful answers to the questions below come from John Broome, Director of Movement, Royal Shakespeare Company, England, and Stratford Festival Theater, Canada; Elizabeth Aldrich, Director, Dance Heritage Coalition, dance historian, teacher, and choreographer; Peggy Dixon, Director, Nonsuch History and Dance, England; and Virginia Freeman, director, choreographer, and lecturer in Movement and Historical Dance, University of Maryland Opera Studio.

QUESTIONS FOR THE EXPERTS

1. *What is most important, "movement-wise," when doing a period play?*

JOHN: To capture the essence of the age in the manner of walking, standing, sitting, and dancing and to appreciate the way these activities are in harmony with the costume of the period.

ELIZABETH: Carriage of the body—especially the upper body. (This is assuming appropriate costumes are utilized.) Next would be gestures of handling things and greetings (salutations and bows).

PEGGY: I'd say, primarily, establishing a good posture before you begin to develop the features particular to the character.

VIRGINIA: Of course, the word "style" seems right up there with learning your lines, motivation, life in that period, etc., but "style" can get confused with a careful approach, in such awe of history that it makes actors walk, stand, sit, woo, and die as if they are in a foreign land wearing strange clothes. When style is approached by focusing on the amount of "turnout" of the leg in the stance and walking; or changing the length of step, most often shortening it; or introducing something from that period early in rehearsals, this may be enough to help the actor find gestural aliveness. Simplicity in movement choices . . . the usual "less is more" approach.

2. How do you look real and not affected?

JOHN: By having the confidence to maintain a poised and natural dignity that does not strain after effects. By inhabiting your own body and not that of a "fancy-dress" person of a previous age.

ELIZABETH: This probably depends on how good one is on stage. I believe the most "affected" and unreal visual sights are when amateurs participate in what they call "period" balls; this is especially true of those who don quasi-nineteenth-century garb. They all look ridiculous, because they try to become part of the period, to become a nineteenth-century lady or gentleman. This is not possible. A good actor knows who he is and where he is in time and simply undertakes to interpret a role.

PEGGY: You need to feel comfortable and relaxed. Practicing some of the dances of the period should help. Getting used to audience eyes being focused on your movements as opposed to speech. I would particularly recommend practicing some of the very earliest dances in the historical dance repertoire.

VIRGINIA: Anything in a fabric, meaning tangible, way that can help . . . any hat, scarf, box, fan, walking stick, etc., can help the actor find his way into the period movement. Sometimes, to loosen up and "modernize" the movement in rehearsal seems to help.

3. What are the challenges in turning social dance into performance?

JOHN: Many social dances are repetitive and their enjoyment private. To transfer them to the stage, it is necessary to first capture their quintessential quality and then display this in choreographic sequences which dazzle rather than depress.

ELIZABETH: Once social dance is placed on a stage, it ceases to be social dance and, instead, becomes a theatrical dance. Very few of the qualities one might find in a social dance (namely spontaneity) can exist on the stage. I think many people try to maintain their images of social dance, and this usually fails. These dances need to be treated as any other theatrical dance. For example, all gestures must be "choreographed." One challenge is those dances that are not presentational (English country dances, quadrilles). They work fine for background dances but rarely work on stage as "featured" dance.

PEGGY: That it could be very boring. The dances of any one period are alike, and some of them go on and on and on. I recommend picking and mixing, putting audience appeal before authenticity, though obviously with reservations.

VIRGINIA: Safety and comfort . . . working levels, stairways, costumes, etc., from the beginning of the rehearsal period, so the performers grow in confidence with whatever is being asked of them, rather than presenting tentative examples of what the choreographer has in mind. All this means extra time and effort staying in touch with set designers, costumers (especially to get your hands on the footwear earlier than scheduled!), and stage managers in order to squeeze in more time on a complicated set.

4. What helpful hints would you give to others?

JOHN: Two cardinal rules: Avoid affectation at all costs, and move with an ease that disguises out all effort. Further, perform dances of each period with respect until the spirit of the age sinks into the body and is there cherished.

ELIZABETH: I think that there is too much emphasis on "authenticity." There are informed and uninformed performances. Sometimes, the ideas of a director, or the venue or amount of space, or perhaps less-than-authentic costumes must be taken into consideration. In these cases, it is better to create movement that fits these circumstances, rather than trying to force authenticity into something that will look silly. For example, Agnes de Mille's choreography for the Hollywood film *Romeo and Juliet* (1936) is completely inauthentic in terms of current scholarship on Renaissance dance. However, in examining the quasi-Botticelli costumes, the Hollywood interpretation of Verona, Italy, the style of acting, and the music, it is clear that, in fact, what de Mille did was completely appropriate and quite wonderful. On the other hand, had she presented "authentic" Renaissance dance, I am quite sure this would have been absolutely stupid. My general advice: Use your good sense and be aware of the various resources (books, primary sources, videos, people) that can help.

PEGGY: Keep it simple. Don't try to turn actors into dancers. There are certain characteristics that belong to particular periods, and you can show what they are, but don't try to get actors to perform the actual recorded dance steps. Find what they can do that has something of the right flavor.[1] Keep in mind some of the basic conventions. The left-foot start is one, but if they get that wrong, it doesn't matter so much as starting with aplomb. More important is being at one with the music, not just keeping the rhythm but continuing the movement to the end of the phrase. (Skill in slow motion is something that could be practiced usefully.) Also—perhaps I should have put this first—courtesy. In dancing, this means being very aware of your partner and of the other dancers in a set, making eye contact with them, never unnecessarily turning your back on someone. Practicing this in the context of a dance might help in observing the ordinary courtesies, as they were observed in the past.

VIRGINIA: Be extremely flexible in your expectations and approach. By that I mean to have several alternative things to do that might simplify the dance and satisfy a director and the cast, rather than take so much learning and rehearsal time. You can judge very quickly whether the amount of "drill time" is going to be worth it or counterproductive.

5. What resources have you found valuable?

JOHN: I believe that a fine source to be the scholarship of Belinda Quirey, best seen in her small book, *May I Have the Pleasure?* (See the section on Period Dance, in Training, at the back of the book.) Anyone seriously engaged in period work should read it at least once a year. The BBC series to which this book relates is also valuable.

ELIZABETH: The primary resources for dance and etiquette are located in every major repository throughout the world. The best dance collection is at the Dance Division of the New York Public Library. Excellent etiquette collections can be found at the New York Public Library, the Library of Congress, the Arthur and Elizabeth Schleslinger Collection at Radcliffe College, and Boston Atheneum. A very handy resource is the Library of Congress's online American Memory site: "American Ballroom Companion,

c. 1490–1920." (See the section on Period Dance in the Training appendix.) It contains over two hundred dance manuals that are cross-searchable and downloadable. The site also contains a long narrative on western social dance and is accompanied by seventy-five video clips of Renaissance, Baroque, nineteenth-century social dance, and ragtime dance.

VIRGINIA: The obvious books describe the period, occupations, political climate of the period etc. I find pictures of the artwork of that period to be so helpful . . . the same with music of that period, even if not to be used in a production, but the tempo and style of these sources help get in the mood. To learn the games of the period, the manners, and the flirtations also helps. I have also found that making collages of Xeroxed pictures from old dance books and magazines to look at on downtime becomes more than just interesting. . . . You may be doing some of the dramaturge's work, but it helps. I found Lyn Oxenford's *Playing Period Plays* [see Resources] to be very helpful.

AUTHOR'S NOTE: I did not ask Peggy this question, because her books are such excellent resources themselves. They include *Nonsuch Early Dance,* Volumes I through IX, plus cassette tapes. The books contain both detailed instructions and "quick crib" notes, as well as advice for teachers, performers, choreographers, and students. They cover dances from the courts of Europe from the twelfth to nineteenth centuries. For more on how to obtain these volumes, go to the Period Dance section in Training.

SOME IMPORTANT CONSIDERATIONS
WHEN PUTTING PERIOD DANCE ON THE STAGE

Make sure the actors are comfortable with the costume, set, and music: If the actors are comfortable, the audience will be also. The play will come alive and not be a chapter in a history book. It is difficult for an actor to feel at home in constricting clothing that is alien to him. But when an actor rehearses in it, knows why he's wearing it and how to move in it, the actor can appear perfectly at ease and unaffected.

If you imagine it miles away and in the past, then it gives you no connection. But if you believe that the past is now and in the present, it comes alive for you. —John Broome

Immerse the cast in the time period. Use visual aids, such as paintings, photographs, diaries, novels, and especially the music of the era. Don't say merely, "This is how they dressed"; give the actors a flavor of the age. Let them know why the people wore what they wore—whether for social, religious, economic reasons, or because of climate.

A period play or dance is not about showing off the costume the actor is wearing or using fans, hankies, swords, or snuff; it is about knowing the world from which the play came and the theatrical and physical demands on the body the clothing presents.

Style is knowing what kind of play you are in. —John Gielgud

Remember that the characters are human. Even though there were rules to follow, not everyone had the same relationship to the rules. Many rules—especially rules of etiquette—were broken, and sometimes that is what the plot is about. Each cast member must know where his character is in the hierarchy of the social class. How does his character adapt to his place in that hierarchy? Who, in the world of the play, has the most power, and who has the least? Who bows to whom, who sits and who stands, who can dance with whom, and in the dance, who is the highest-ranking couple? In social dancing, each performer dances as his character's circumstances dictate (that is, old or young, graceful or awkward, aggressive or shy). Social dances should not look like virtuoso chorus numbers in a musical comedy, nor should they be danced with the cookie-cutter precision of the Rockettes.

Make sure the pacing is not deliberate or self-conscious. If, for instance, you do all the appropriate bows at the beginning of a minuet as part of the "spotlit" business of the scene, it will become ponderous to an audience. These might happen in the background or during dialogue. If you are doing a quadrille or cotillion that requires a set of four couples (like a square dance), let the head couple do half a figure, then the sides, instead of each one doing a full figure. Don't let the movement slow down the dialogue or get in the way of telling the story. Many seem to think that all period dance is slow and there is lots of bowing. Just like today, there were dances requiring a variety of tempos and athleticism. Suit the dance to the mood or spirit of the play. You are allowed to take artistic license. The play's the thing.

Include movement as part of the audition process. If someone is cast to play a powerful character and then cannot do the required dance, it will weaken the performance considerably. If there is no choice in casting, let him sit out the dance. Someone can bring him an important message, or have a servant bring him a goblet of wine while he sits and watches.

To be or not to be authentic? As I stated earlier, I do not believe one can be a purist or be completely authentic. We are not re-creating history but presenting what the playwright wrote. Go for audience enjoyment and be creative, but be careful about your guesswork; make informed decisions. Besides, if you're talking in terms of theater, authenticity is as important as the director thinks it to be.

Most dances began and ended with a bow and a curtsey. Bows and curtsies should be practiced until they are as natural as hugs and shaking hands are to us today. They do not always have to be timed exactly to the music. One can linger at the end. Many pieces of contemporary music do not include music for these; if not, do the bows right before the music begins, or leave sufficient music for the courtesies before you start the choreography of the dance.

> *Actors always get rather hectic about bowing and curtseying . . . So bows and curtseys must be well practiced until they are completely unself-conscious. Everyone bowed and curtsied as a social reflex, as it is today, and always has been, in Japan. It was simply part of their natural self-expression for persons of quality.*
>
> —Simon Callow, *Acting in Restoration Comedy*

Keep the steps simple, and use interesting figures. If doing a dance with a long line, put it on the diagonal, cast off, and come into a vertical line from upstage to downstage, then cast again and end in a horizontal line across the stage.

If in a square formation, put it on the diagonal to the audience instead of square. It opens it up more to the audience. Go from a square to a circle formation, and then maybe to a line. Vary the formations as much as possible. It makes it more interesting, and the audience can focus on different actors. If space is a problem, separate the sets or couples around the stage. After dancing several bars, have a leader wind a line around the set pieces, stopping at various places to dance in place again.

Last, but certainly not least, communicate with the production team. Decide on a dance that will fit the production, that the actors can do, and that can be done on the set and in the costume, and agree on music with the director well before rehearsals begin.

EXERCISES TO PREPARE FOR PERIOD DANCE

Because an "upright but relaxed" posture is essential for period plays and period dances, the choreographer or director should begin posture work immediately and continue giving it attention throughout the rehearsal period. Otherwise, the actors will look lost in the costume. There is a lot more weight and material on the body, and a good posture and center is necessary for a command of the stage.

Exercises to Improve Postural Alignment from John Broome

I.

Stand and allow the body to roll down to hanging forward position.

Slowly roll up, feeling movement first in small of the back, then between the shoulders, and finally the back of the neck, until upright, shoulders dropped and relaxed.

Repeat, but when the upright position is reached, tilt the head and upper body back a little, then pull to upright again, feeling the lift through the top of the head.

Walk anywhere, freely observing each other.

From stillness again, roll the head effortlessly each way.

II.

Work with partners, one behind the other. The back person places palms of his or her hands a little below the shoulders on the outside of the partner's arms and lifts, holds, and drops the partner's arms with no assistance from the partner. Immediately stroke down from top of shoulders to elbows, and repeat the relaxed lift.

Eventually, the back person shakes the partner's relaxed shoulders freely up and down.

III.

Individually again, recline on backs on the floor, legs extended.

Lift the head and look at the feet.

Lower the head slowly, keeping it forward, and have the sensation of putting the nape of the neck on the floor. Let the tension go when it's down. Repeat several times.

Lift the knees, and place the feet on the floor. Reach with both hands toward the feet along the floor, lift the head and look at the knees and again slowly lower the head. Relax. Repeat as before.

Maintain this position, lift the hips just a little, and rotate the hips forward, lengthening the lower back along the floor (this can be assisted by a forward movement of the hands below the hips). Lift the head, and lower again. Sense the whole back of the body spread along the floor. Maintain this position, and slowly lower the legs to the floor. Relax.

IV.

A similar result can be found by working against a wall but with the advantage of being able to walk immediately afterwards:

Stand, feet a comfortable distance apart. Prepare the body, and fall back against the wall.

Discover which areas of the body make contact with the wall. Consciously adjust, so that the small of the back and the space between the shoulders touch the wall. Make sure the knees remain flexed. (The back of the head does not touch, but is a couple of inches away.)

Now slide the body up and down slowly, keeping contact. (Contract the abdomen if necessary to achieve this.) On finally coming up, leave the knees slightly flexed, "push off" slightly and walk freely, looking around so that the neck is not too rigid. Find that the arms will hang toward the front of the thighs and not by the sides.

It is important to allow the body to remember this position as walking continues. If lost, go back to the wall or the floor.

V.

Walk with a high, buoyant, easeful feeling.

Introduce a steady drumbeat (fairly slow), and allow the walking to follow this. The walk should remain dignified, free, and easy. If this is difficult, think of the walk as a step and a swing, and let the drum mark this at the same time. The walk should be continuous in motion and not halting. The "step-swing" almost always cures this. Continue, but gradually reduce the tempo until almost impossibly slow. The action should continue, smooth and flowing.

VI.

Walk beautifully, and lead a partner, arms low and forward. Share the walk.

Introduce slow and fairly solemn music, and walk in pairs, as in a procession.

You are now ready to dance!

Period Dance Classroom Exercise

The following exercise is a favorite of mine. It helps students to understand that the character is doing the dancing, not simply the actor.

I.

Teach a simple English country dance (see Playford, *The English Dancing Master* or Millar, *Elizabethan Country Dances*) or choreograph a dance using simples and doubles in various patterns:

- Simple = one step and a close
- Double = three steps and a close
- Pattern suggestions: (1) forward and away from partner, (2) changing sides with partner, (3) man does a pattern then the lady repeats, and (4) holding both hands and circling around each other

Remember to do a reverence (bow or curtsey) before and at the end of the dance. Do the dance flat-footed at first, until alignment and flow look good, then add a rise and fall to the footwork. Once the dance is learned and performed gracefully, work on the exchange between partners and others in the set.

II.

While dancing have partners say the alphabet to each other as conversation. Whenever they have eye contact, one whispers to the other. Example: The man says "A B C," then the lady replies "D E," and so on, alternating back and forth. They must get to the end of the alphabet by the end of the dance and not before.

III.

Do the dance again, but this time, the actors must make conversation.

Appropriate topics for ladies and gentlemen would be: the latest fashions; a new opera or play, or the latest concert or novel; the health of the family; the news of the day.

IV.

Practice the dance with different physical qualities, but without losing perfect precision.

Suggestions: aggressively, shyly, flirtatiously, a bit tipsy, a bit too energetic.

V.

Each member of the set now chooses his own quality. It is important that not all of them do the same one. (My students like to draw suggestions out of a hat, for instance.) Now, the dance tells a story: the relationships of the members of the dancing ensemble.

TIMELINE OF PERIOD DANCES: WHAT TO USE WHEN

This is not a complete list of historical dances, but a compilation of the more well-known dances. For a description of dances (steps and patterns), see *http://memory.loc.gov.ammen/dittml.html.* See the section on Training for more helpful information.

Medieval
- *Branle* (Fr.); also known as "branle" or "brawl" (Eng.)
- *Carole*
- *Farandole*
- *Saltarello*
- *Zarabanda* (Sp.)

Early Renaissance
- *Bassadanza* (It.); also known as *bassedanse* (Fr.)
- *Tordion* (Fr.); also known as *tordiglione* (It.)

Late Renaissance
- *Almaine* (Fr.); also known as "English measure" or "almain" (Eng.)

- Canary; also known as *canario* (It. and Sp.) and *canarie* (Fr.)
- English country dances
- *Galliard*; also known as "cinque pace" or "sink-a-pace" (Eng.)
- *Passo e mezzo*
- *Pavane (Fr.);* also known as "pavan" (Eng.) *or pavana* (It.)
- Volta; also known as *volte* (Fr.)
- Coranto, courant (Eng.); also known as courante (Fr.)

Baroque

- Allemande
- *Chaconne* (Fr.); also known as *chacona (Sp.), ciaccona* (It.), and "chacoon" (Eng.)
- Contradance (Eng.); also known as *contredanse* (Fr.), *contradanza* (It.); *Kontretanz* (Ger.)
- *Cotillion* (Fr.); also known as "cotillon" (Eng.)
- English country dance
- *Gavotte*
- Gigue (Fr.); also known as "giga" (It.) and "jig" (Eng.)
- Minuet (Eng.); also known *as menuet* (Fr.)
- *Passacaille* (Fr.); also known as *passacaglia or passacaglio* (It.)
- Saraband: also known as *sarabande* (Fr.), *zarabanda (Sp.)*
- *Courante* (Fr.); also known as coranto, courante (Eng.); courento (It.)

Nineteenth-Century Dances

- Cotillon; also known as *cotillion* (Fr.), the "German cotillon," and the "German" (Eng.)
- Galop
- Mazurka
- Polka
- Quadrille
- Scotch reel
- Waltz (Eng); also known as *valse* (Fr.) or *walzer* (Ger.)
- English country dance

See the section on Period Dance in Training, at the back of the book, for more helpful information.

NOTES

1. I wonder what I mean by "the right flavor." On reflection, I'd suggest quiet self-confidence for the medieval period; more assertiveness, even flamboyance in the sixteenth century; perhaps a little mannerism in the seventeenth (though "languid elegance" is the term that is bruited about for the earlier decades of it); unaffected grace for the eighteenth century; and I don't know what for the nineteenth century; perhaps just honest-to-goodness vigor.

My grateful thanks to: Jessica Chavex and Alan Litsey for their constant help. Elizabeth Aldrich and John Broome for introducing me to period dance and to all the teachers who have shared so much knowledge with me—Elizabeth Aldrich, Lieven Baert, Carlos Blanco, Ingrid Brainard, John Broome, Paule Dene, Peggy Dixon, Willie Feuer, Charles Garth, Ron Gursky, Wendy Hilton, Richard Powers, Patri Pugliese, Dieter Raab, Cathy Stephens, Julia Sutton, Carol Tetan, Catherine Turocy, Joan Walton—and to my dance partners, Dennis East and Bill Wilson.

Shakespeare Honors the Three Centers of the Body

Susan Dibble

or years, I trained to be a dancer and a choreographer; I became both of these. After performing and finding a way in which to make dances about animals, nature, human beings, spirits, and objects, I began to work in the theater. I became a choreographer for plays as well as for movement and dance theater. I was drawn to actors' sensibility, inspired by the actor's ability to make dances come alive in an organic way. I wanted to combine my work in dance with theater. I began teaching in theater schools and teaching movement for actors, and it became a lifelong mission.

Actors can be creators, poets, and performers who have access to their imaginations and passions, and ultimately bring life to the words of Shakespeare. I am drawn to the way in which Shakespeare honors the human being in its beauty and ugliness and the three centers of the body.

SHAKESPEARE AND THE THREE CENTERS OF THE BODY

Shakespeare honors the mind in *Richard II,* Act V, Scene v:

> KING RICHARD: I have been studying how I may compare
> This prison where I live unto the world;
> And for because the world is populous
> And here is not a creature but myself,
> I cannot do it; yet I'll hammer it out.
> My brain I'll prove the female to my soul,
> My soul the father; and these two beget
> A generation of still-breeding thoughts,
> And these same thoughts people this little world,
> In humours like the people of this world.
> for no thought is contented. The better sort,
> As thoughts of things divine, are intermix'd
> With scruples and do set the word itself
> Against the word:
> As thus, "Come, little ones," and then again,
> "It is as hard to come as for a camel
> to thread the postern of a small needle's eye."

He honors the heart and feeling center in *The Life and Death of King John,* Act III, Scene iv:

> KING PHILIP: O fair affliction, peace!

CONSTANCE: No, no, I will not, having breath to cry.

> O, that my tongue were in the thunder's mouth!
>
> Then with a passion would I shake the world;
>
> And rouse from sleep that fell anatomy
>
> Which cannot hear a lady's feeble voice,
>
> Which scorns a modern invocation.

CARDINAL PANDULPH: Lady, you utter madness, and not sorrow.

CONSTANCE: Thou art [not] holy to belie me so;

> I am not mad. This hair I tear is mine;
>
> My name is Constance; I was Geoffrey's wife;
>
> Young Arthur is my son, and he is lost.
>
> I am not mad; I would to heaven I were!
>
> For then 'tis like I should forget myself.
>
> O, if I could, what grief should I forget!
>
> Preach some philosophy to make me mad,
>
> And thou shalt be canoniz'd, Cardinal;
>
> For being not mad, but sensible of grief,
>
> My reasonable part produces reason
>
> How I may be deliver'd of these woes,
>
> And teaches me to kill or hang myself.
>
> If I were mad, I should forget my son,
>
> Or madly think a babe of clouts were he.
>
> I am not mad; too well, too well I feel
>
> the different plague of each calamity.

And the body or sexual center in *Romeo and Juliet* in Act III, Scene ii:

JULIET: Come, night; come, Romeo; come, thou day in night;

> For thou wilt lie upon the wings of night,
>
> Whiter than new snow [on] a raven's back.
>
> Come, gentle night, come, loving, black-brow'd night;
>
> Give me my Romeo; and, when [he] shall die,
>
> Take him and cut him out in little stars,
>
> And he will make the face of heaven so fine
>
> That all the world will be in love with night
>
> And pay no worship to the garish sun.
>
> O, I have bought the mansion of a love,
>
> But not possess'd it, and, though I am sold,
>
> Not yet enjoy'd.

I have structured the courses I teach that correspond with working with Shakespearean text to keep an active, consistent relationship between these central parts of the body. How I work with actors who are studying Shakespeare is directly related to my experiences as a choreographer and movement director for Shakespeare plays. The language is full of imagery that is filled with movement possibilities, and the stories include dances and rituals that play a significant part in the journey of the play. The wide range of characters that Shakespeare creates is rich with interesting challenges for physical choices. In my classes, I try to create an environment in which to explore and stretch the boundaries of the imagination and to begin to understand the creative process. By offering an opportunity for the actors to make their own work, I hope to enhance their experience of Shakespeare's language in order to find an enriched and intelligent way in which to tell the story of the plays.

WORKING WITH OPPOSITES

I begin the work with students in Movement, Dance, and Shakespeare workshops by introducing the importance of being aware of opposites. How do opposites live in the language of Shakespeare, the characters, nature, the world? John Barton, in his book *Playing Shakespeare,* says that "all questions of handling Shakespeare's text are to do with 'balances' between various extremes."

To begin this work with opposites and to explore the extremes, I teach exercises that focus on image, gesture, and symbol or metaphor connected to the Middle Ages and the Elizabethan period. The dances of these periods were often created out of a desire for form and order, and their purpose was not only to create unity in the social structures but to create harmony and balance in the universe. In practicing the bows, reverences, gestures, and manners of these periods, the actor can also become more conscious of the everyday social rituals and manners. The approach to this work is not to strive for perfection but to develop a natural balance in the body.

By honoring the body, the actors can find a healthy and unrestricted relationship to their alignment and physical structure. *Spine* and *breath* are the key words I focus on in order to help the development of an open and flexible core that offers support to the performer's stage presence and imagination. I work to create a sense of ease, poise, grace, and a strong connection to gravity. Simone Weil, in her book *Gravity and Grace,* says, "all the 'natural' movements of the soul are controlled by laws analogous to those of physical gravity. Grace is the only exception." In understanding how we can move from one extreme to another, the value of being conscious of both is crucial. "All life fluctuates between resistance to and yielding to gravity," Doris Humphrey wrote in *The Art of Making Dances.*

In many ways, grace and gravity can correspond to heaven and hell, or rise and fall. By developing an "aware" body, the actor can begin to be less stiff and rigid when moving on the stage and can have a body that is more receptive and available for impulses. Sensitivity and thought are actively balanced once the actor practices both equally, and this heightened physical awareness is what I work toward, so that the actor can be able to occupy the theater space and change it, change how it is perceived, and draw the audience in.

MOVEMENT AND LANGUAGE

Movement leads somewhere when the actor has a relationship to the story being told. Consistent stamina and energy are crucial for connecting to the rhythm of the language and the flow of the many changing moments and thoughts. Without this energy, this discipline, and informed action, the words cannot be heard at the level at which they are meant to exist. Volume alone cannot fill the demands of the text. The body must be engaged fully in order for the voice to communicate and tell the story clearly.

The language of Shakespeare must be given a place to live and breathe freely. The body of the actor must house this energy, so that it can be used efficiently. By articulating and shaping the free imagination and by bringing breath into the action of the text, the actor can begin to make the offering, tell Shakespeare's tales of the universal experience of human beings. In doing this, actors can have a shared experience with Shakespeare—who he was and who he *is* as an artist.

In the classes that I've designed, there is an ongoing theme, a thread that ties together the many different areas of study. This thread is called *desire*. It is simply a desire to offer the possibility to see the world, and the space we inhabit, and honor it, fill it, and change it by making something new.

FINDING A SENSE OF BALANCE

The first series of exercises described here are designed for finding a sense of balance, with an emphasis on poise, grace, and the ascending power in the body, while being conscious of and connected to the opposite, gravity.

Balance Exercise

Standing with your feet about twelve inches apart, allow your head and neck to be free, with a sense of floating upward, and feel the connection to your feet on the floor, with a balanced, relaxed, and focused presence. Open the palm of the left hand, and lift the arm out to the side, led by the hand. Let the arm float back down, and repeat with the right hand. Now open both palms, and acknowledge this simple movement as a gesture of offering. Lift both arms out to the side about 90 degrees, or shoulder height, with a gentle curve, so that you can see both hands peripherally. Bring the arms down to your sides. Repeat by opening the palms again, and lift the arms, reaching up to the ceiling. Lift the head and sternum without leaning back too far, and look up, as though looking beyond the ceiling up into the imagined sky, universe, or heaven. Bring the arms into an open V-

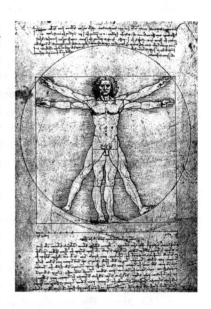

shape position. Be conscious of the five points of the body: the two hands, the two feet, and the head (much like Leonardo da Vinci's *Human Figure in a Circle*, Illustrating Proportions, c. 1485–1490).

As you bring your arms down, bring your head to a balanced position on top of the spine, and focus forward with your eyes. Now, lift your left palm forward as though offering a gift, and then let it float down. Repeat with your right hand, and then lift both hands forward at the same time with the same offering gesture. Let your arms float down, and then lift both hands up to the ceiling, with your focus high again. Open the arms out to the side, and bring them down, with a gentle bend of your knees over your toes to finish the sequence with a small bow. While bending the knees, keep the torso lengthening, and think of the two forces existing in the body: gravity and floating. Straighten your legs without locking the knees, and repeat the "curtsey," thinking of this movement as a bow that is an acknowledgment of time on earth. Repeat this whole sequence from the beginning with music. (I often use the music written by Patrick Doyle for the film *Sense and Sensibility*, track #3, or Erik Satie's *Gymnopedie*.) This can be done with a partner, standing side by side or facing each other. To finish, stand with a consciousness of what is above you, below you, at either side of you, in front of you, and behind you.

Six Directions in Space

Some simple things that have great significance are the hands and the balance of all the parts of the body situated in the middle of the Six Directions in Space (left, right, up, down, back, forward). We begin with the left hand, because it corresponds to the belief that the left side of the body was honored, being the side of the body where the heart is, and because of its connection to the direction of the sun moving from east to west. By acknowledging the six points of direction in the space, we can have an understanding of the potential for order in our surroundings. First, reach upward to what we imagine being Heaven or the universe, then downward toward the image of Hell by kneeling or simply lowering the body in that downward direction. Rise up, and turn to reach to the back (in a lunge) to what is behind us or what we may think of as the Past. Turn back to face the front, and reach toward the forward direction, or what can be thought of as the Future, and then reach out to the left side and right side. Gather the hands toward the center of the body or solar plexis, creating a position of the hands much like holding a ball, or the Sun. This final gesture represents the Present, the time we have on earth. To finish, lower the hands, and bend the knees in a small bow. This can be done to Bach's *Air on a G String* or to Peter Gabriel's "Passion" from the soundtrack for *The Last Temptation of Christ*.

Simple Walk

Begin to walk through the space, conscious of the left side of the body and the left hand leading you through the space, lifted about 45 degrees. Extend the right hand behind you as though ready to take another person's left hand. Keep the body poised and at ease as you move through the space, taking even steps. (I use a hand drum for this part of the class to keep a nice, lively rhythm for the walking.) I often take this into more difficult patterns, and steps, to get my students used to moving rhythmically, so that they can be more agile when working with Shakespeare's verse.

Eventually, everyone is in pairs walking through the space, with the leader extending the left hand. I encourage students to keep an even distance between each other to create a V-shape, pointing out the design they are making with their bodies as they walk hand in hand. This balance between two people is important, because in the simple walk, they are creating a sense of harmony. The Elizabethans were passionate about creating a balance in the universe in order to ease the chaos in the world they lived in.

Creating a Country Dance

Now, get into groups of three or four, and continue the lively walk across the room, from corner to corner. I use "Bare Necessities English Country Dance" music for this. This can be repeated a number of times, switching the leaders for each group. Eventually, the groups expand to six or eight, and I ask the leaders to tell the group where they are leading "their people." These larger groups now create gestures that can be repeated, four counts for each gesture, and they do the gestures as they travel across the floor in the lines. At this point I use Putumayo Presents *Women of the World Celtic,* track #1. The groups are no longer holding hands, but walking and repeating the gestures. If the group is very large, I ask two groups to merge, with every other person repeating the gestures of her original group.

This kind of dance is similar to the farandole and was used in the country to dance through the villages or fields, and sometimes through the graveyards as the Dance of Death during the time of the plague. When the tempo gets faster, the steps can turn into skipping or running. Many variations and patterns were created, all for the pleasure and exhilarating experience of dancing as a way of affirming life on earth. From here we can move into the hay, farandole, branles, or circle dances of the Middle Ages. These dances joined people together to encourage balance and order in the universe.

Creating Ensemble Choreography

In another variation on this theme of dance, I choreograph thirty-two counts of movement and gesture that represent Power. Everyone repeats this sequence and then, in groups of six or eight, choreographs eight counts of movement and gesture and teaches it to everyone in the group, staying with the Power theme. Eventually, the group learns everyone's eight counts of movement and links them all together, beginning with my first phrase. They can perform these in a circle or move into different arrangements in the space.

If the class is large enough, we perform two groups at the same time, positioning the two groups in the space. For example, one group can be inside a circle, with the second group on the outer edges. They work together to create a final movement, sometimes repeating one or two of the movements to create the climax of the dance. *Oceania* by Jaz Coleman is very good for this, or Peter Gabriel's "Rhythm of the Heat."

The Pavane

Another dance that is simple and can be very moving is the pavane. The basic steps are called "singles" (in two counts, step and bring feet together) and "doubles" (three steps and bring feet together, in four counts). There are many patterns for these simple steps, and I add gestures and symbolic positions for the body to arrive in that can tell a story. The pavane originated in Spain and was adopted by the Elizabethans, who performed it as a processional dance during formal occasions. It can also be adapted into a dance for a man and a woman and can work well to deepen the relationship between characters.

MEANING IN ACTION: BALANCE OF EXTREMES

In Shakespeare, the pendulum swings back and forth between chaos and order, humor and tragedy, peace and war, corruption and joy, good and evil. The actor must be alive and ready take on the size of these opposites, these extremes. It is important to have a body that exists in space with a conscious awareness of these many extremes and to be available to the many changes in the text, in the life of the characters, in the rhythms, and in the stillness that comes after an explosion. By finding ease and fluidity in the body without stiffness or rigidity, the actor can begin to experience the value of her body as a source of energy and imaginative impulses. In a simple gesture like the palm of the hand opening, we can see this gesture and receive a message: "I want to be seen," or " I am not holding a weapon, therefore I can be trusted."

Gestures are metaphors and are as powerful as words. Daniel Nagrin, in his book *Dance and the Specific Image,* says, "Every action, in or out of art, can be seen as a metaphor for something else." The actor can find a wealth of ideas, an open door to her creative self by exploring the many possibilities in gesture, symbol, and metaphor. By working with asymmetry and understanding its opposite, symmetry or order, we can explore the world of the chaotic and find inspiration in the many directions it takes us as creative people.

Louis Horst talks about the medieval world and its connection to asymmetry and parallelism in this way:

> The Catholic church, great unifying force in these centuries, gave shape and substance to the arts of the Middle Ages. It met almost every human need—social, moral, and intellectual—and so, strongly affected the inner mind of the times. Human ideals all found their seat in Heaven. Earthly experiences were profane. The devil was termed "Prince of this earth." For the individual, the Christian philosophy held ideas of meekness, self-abnegation, denial of physical satisfactions, disavowal of bodily appetites. These were to be foregone in this life for the promise of a sure reward in a life after death . . . to continue successfully in these trying and unnatural habits of living it was necessary constantly to practice penitence, to mortify the flesh to save the soul. . . . The strongest element of design in all the medieval arts is that of parallelism. The pull and stress of *opposition . . .* connotes strength . . .

The meaning behind the words of Shakespeare, what the words hold, what possibilities they offer to the thinking and feeling human being, is brought to the actor's attention after working with the elements of design and style in the Middle Ages. By looking into this period, students can understand the Renaissance as a time of separation from this parallelism and realize how the Elizabethans broke the mold of the tension and restriction experienced in the Middle Ages. Men and women played different roles, and the emphasis that had been so much on the "collective" changed to the "individual."

Metaphor

By exploring the possibilities in Shakespeare's language, we can then return to the form that he has created and ride on the vehicle he has designed for moving with his images. To begin this work, I offer an exercise using metaphor.

In this first series of exercises, I focus on the importance of finding balance and harmony, order in the body and in its place in the surrounding space, which to me is a metaphor for symmetry. The next step is to explore the possibility of creating images, through movement and gesture, and to fill space with these ideas. The patterns, designs, and movements are not necessarily balanced or ordered. The creative expression can come from breaking away from what makes sense or is defined in the dictionary. First, we begin by writing a list of sentences. I ask the actors to write the following incomplete sentences:

- This day is a _____.
- This journey is a _____.
- This place is a _____.
- This heart is a _____.
- This time is a _____.
- This life is a _____.

I ask the students to fill in the blanks and try to write the first thing that comes to their mind, without worrying about making sense. After they complete these sentences, they work with a partner and read their sentences to each other. I ask them to take each sentence and create movement and gesture that can bring these images to life. They teach these short pieces to a partner. They work with each sentence and connect all the movement with simple transitions, so that there is no break between the parts.

An example of this is as follows: "This life is a running brook with many rocks." The actor could choose to move her hands by shaking the fingers. The gesture could move back and forth in the space in front of the body, with the feet doing little sporadic jumps. The next four or five images are created in the same way. It is best to make them very simple. With the last images, the actor creates the ending. Example: "This journey is an open book, with a torn page." Here, the actor does a simple gesture of opening the arms with a gentle sigh of sound, and then moves with a sudden contraction in the chest. These gestures and movements may be repeated and are often slightly different each time.

These little pieces are performed with the writer-creator off to the side speaking the sentences as his or her partner performs the movements and gestures. Another way of working with this is for each person to learn the other's movements and perform them together in unison, making adjustments to create a duet or physical dialogue.

A small digression: Often, I am asked what I mean by *gesture* or *movement*, how are they different. To me, a gesture is an isolated movement of a body part—head, arm and hand, foot, or a combination of these parts—with an unconscious or conscious message. It usually has an emotion or intention connected to its delivery. A movement is an action created by the whole body, often traveling in the space. In the dictionary, the definition that is useful in acting is "a particular manner of moving." A movement can also be very subtle, and almost unnoticeable, but usually involves the body as a whole.

In the next stage of this exercise, we take the sentences and create a new sentence, a new metaphor or image, out of the original one. For example: "This life is a running brook with many rocks" can become "This running brook with many rocks is rushing to its mother" or ". . . is chasing me." This is where action comes in. And as in Hamlet, Act III, Scene ii, "Suit the action to the word, the word to the action," the emphasis is put on how words are given life when they are explored through action, movement, and gesture with symbolic meaning. By working this way, the part of the actor that wants to be safe and secure in the obvious meaning of things can begin to experience a new way in which to look at images and words.

THE CHAIN OF BEING

The Elizabethans focused intensely on the human body, the human being, and its relationship to God and the lower orders. They wanted to create a place for the human being to exist that would give a sense of place and belonging, and therefore establish an order in the existence of man in relation to the other powers of the world and universe. The Chain of Being was created for this purpose. Man and woman were placed in the chain to define their role and place in the order of beings existing in life. In *The Elizabethan World Picture*, E. M. W. Tillyard describes the links of the chain:

> In this order hot things are in harmony with cold, dry with moist, heavy with light, great with little, high with low. In this order angel is set over angel, rank upon rank in the kingdom of heaven; man is set over man, beast over beast, bird over bird, and fish over fish, on the earth, in the air and in the sea so that there is no worm that crawls upon the ground, no bird that flies on high, no fish that swims in the depths, which the chain of this order does not bind in most harmonious concord. Hell alone, inhabited by none but sinners, asserts its claim to escape the embraces of this order.

Along with the creation of the Chain was the passionate awareness of the devil, or the Prince of Darkness. In the Middle Ages and Renaissance, much attention was paid to the image of Hell and to death. As Clifton C. Olds writes in *Images of Love and Death in Late Medieval and Renaissance Art*, "The Black Death which decimated the population of Europe in 1348 . . . was not the only factor in the late medieval fascination with death, but it lay at the heart of the obsession. . . . Certainly The Dance of Death, which stresses the fact that death comes to all ages and social states, reflects the broad swath cut by the pestilence of the fourteenth century." As a way to explore the darker images in Shakespeare's plays I ask my students to create a Dance of Death.

The Dance of Death

The work on this assignment is done in the class. My instructions are simple:

1. Make a short (two to three minutes) dance about Death with a beginning, middle, and end.
2. Design clear movements and gestures to express your experience, thoughts, images of Death.
3. Work with a simple and clear vocabulary, and be prepared to show this to the class.
4. Remember to develop a clear beginning, middle, and end.

The music I often use is Beethoven's *Moonlight Sonata*. After twenty minutes or more, everyone shows her piece. We finish the class with the gestures from the first exercise described in this article.

Images of Hell, Images of Heaven

Another approach to working with the darker images is in a series of classes that focus on images of Hell. Each student makes a list of her own images of Hell and is asked to work with her classmates to create four images of Hell, chosen from her list. Each student directs or choreographs the group using her four images, making transitions between each one. Eventually, if there is a class of ten, the group has created a forty-image piece of Hell. Suggested music for this project is Peter Gabriel's "Passion" from the soundtrack to the motion picture *The Last Temptation of Christ*, Henryk Gorecki's *Symphony No. 3*, and *Lamentation* by Tunde Jegede. Each choreographer stands in a significant place, outside the group, acting as an observer of her work. The image of this single figure is representative of the devil, or Prince of Darkness.

To work with the opposite of dark, I take the students into the image of Light. They paint or draw their image of Heaven and write words that describe the images in their pictures. From these images, they can create gestures and movements that are easily fit into the form of the pavane. Each student will teach a few of her gestures or movements to a partner and add steps and measures to create an interesting version of the pavane. Eventually, the entire class will learn each other's phrases and join them together to make a complete dance.

HONORING RELATIONSHIPS

Another direction I take while my students are working on Shakespeare scenes in their acting class is to develop a connection with the relationships and their physical awareness to each other, and telling the story.

Discovering Relationship through Action

I give the couples, or groups of three characters, a list of actions:

Two looks	Hands touching	A sudden turn away
Walking in a circle	A laugh or gasp (or both)	Running toward or away (or both)
A bow or reverence	Fall	Suspend

I usually hang a few copies of the list on the wall, so that students can refer to this list while they are working. The list of actions can be worked with to create a pattern of movements. They create gestures, a few sounds, and physical moments between the characters. Before I work in this way, I teach the bows and reverences of the Elizabethan and Medieval periods. While teaching the bows, entrances, exits, hand gestures, and so on, in the Period Styles section of my course, I encourage the students to value the idea that the body is to be honored, that life is short, and that how we acknowledge another human being is to be considered with great care.

The actors take the list of actions and arrange them in an order of their choice. They pick and choose from the list to make the actions fit together in the best way for their scene. I encourage them to be open to the possibility that it might not always make perfect sense and try to steer them away from being too literal. By using the actions, they can tell the story or part of the story of the relationship and make new discoveries about their characters and the scene. It is a way in which to find the "essence" of the scene.

I give the actors enough freedom so that they can work from a response to the movement and their bodies in relationship to each other. I also invite them to use the pavane form, if they want, to give some structure to their "silent scenes." In the end, they are creating a physical dialogue that is unique and, ultimately, has a beginning, middle, and end. When the students have worked for about twenty minutes, I ask them to perform their pieces. I choose music for each scene. In the list, there is potential for exploring the opposites. For example: going toward each other and separating, being lower or higher, moving slowly or quickly, laughing and weeping. The next stage of this exercise is then to move into small groups, two couples together, for example, and find a way to combine the two pieces in the space and find the places they connect. The students can edit and adjust in order to create a deeper connection to Shakespeare's characters. If I am working with a large group, I often put them into groups of six and experiment with mixing scenes up as an extension of this exercise: tragedy with comedy—*As You Like It* with *Romeo and Juliet*—or tragedy with tragedy—*Othello* with *Macbeth*, etc. Inevitably, the space is charged with life that comes from the moments created by these actions and connected phrases. In working with these "silent scenes," students discover that the language can be enriched by the experience of the movements and gestures and by how their bodies move in the space. The actors are conscious of when they touch, how close they are, when one moves forward, and when one moves away—eyes and hands are given a chance to speak.

TEXT IMAGES

Another way in which I work with Shakespearean text is to take images directly from the text and create movement and physical relationships. I often use a scene between Desdemona and Othello, Act III, Scene iv, lines 30 to 95, or Romeo and Juliet's love sonnet, Act I, Scene v.

Image Exercise

I ask the students to read the text and listen to each other, and then write down the words that catch their imagination or interest. They look through the lists, choosing four or five, and create a sequence of movement-dance to illustrate and illuminate the text. Each couple is responsible for four or five counts of eight, which fits into a dance form, in honor of Elizabeth I, who was so passionate about dance. I also give each couple a handkerchief to work with for the *Othello* scene, which they incorporate into the dance. They teach each other their phrases and combine them all into a group piece. These dances are often very beautiful and have a depth that is often directly related to the story of the text. There is a balance and harmony in this work, and it is a wonderful way for the actors to gain courage and a positive relationship to their bodies by working with the essence of the scene and the symbolism in the gestures that they create.

SHAKESPEARE'S VISUAL WORLD

The visual world in Shakespeare's plays is the final piece to this chapter. How to bring all of these exercises into one final "event"? I present an assignment that gives the actors an opportunity to look at paintings from periods beginning with the Middle Ages. Some examples of painters include Signorelli, Botticelli, Breughel, Bosch, and on through the ages to Picasso, Miró, Chagall, Gaugin, and Dali.

Painting Exercise

Students are asked to choose one or two paintings to work from. I ask them to look for images of light and dark, heaven and hell, love and war, order and chaos. I also encourage them to begin to name their visceral response to the painting. What attracts them to the chosen painting is the most important thing, because this will give them material to work with in the movement-dance theater piece they will create. I ask them to talk about their ideas, and what they want to do for their final piece, by giving examples of themes and images they have taken from their paintings. They discuss their choice of music, props, simple costumes, and set pieces. I also have a lighting designer from the design program work with them to light their pieces. The actor and designer meet and discuss ideas, thus creating a final project performance that is a collaboration between actors and designers.

This project is a way to give the actors an opportunity to work as creative artists. It is also a way in which to practice editing one's work, in order to say what one wants to say clearly and directly. Often, the simplest pieces are the most powerful. I call this final project Heaven Hell–Light Dark. It is directly related to the world of Shakespeare, for example in *Hamlet*:

> What a piece of work is a man!
> How noble in reason!
> How infinite in faculty!
> in form and moving how express and admirable!
> in action how like an angel!
> in apprehension how like a god!
> the beauty of the world!
> the paragon of animals!
> And yet, to me, what is this quintessence of dust?

PASSION AND PRECISION

The actor is an artist, a human being who can create something unusual, beautiful, surprising, and magical out of the ordinary. I am interested in guiding the individual out of a mundane existence and experience of the world into the life of the creator, the artist, where all the senses are inspired to receive and respond to what is around us. In *Art and Beauty in the Middle Ages*, Umberto Eco says:

> . . . a work of art . . . is beautiful if it is functional, if its form is adequate to its scope. . . . The human body is beautiful because it is constructed with an appropriate distribution of parts. . . . man is beautiful because of his erect posture. . . . man is erect, and is thus enabled to use his most noble sense, the sense of sight, "to freely acquire knowledge of every kind of sensible object, both in the skies and on the earth." He can cast his eye at will over the earth and its beauty.

By opening our eyes to life and its details, color, light, texture, symmetry and asymmetry, beauty and ugliness, and by gleaning from Shakespeare's rich language, we can expand the horizons of our work as theater artists. In *The Tempest*, Prospero says in the epilogue, "Now I want spirits to enforce, art to enchant . . ."

At the core of my teaching is the desire to find balance between harmony and discord. By exploring the opposites, the extremes, the negative and the positive, the actor is given the opportunity to stretch imaginatively. The challenge is in finding trust in one's intuition, sensibility, and the magic that is deep within us. Courage becomes a part of the experience. And what is often thought of as untouchable, incomprehensible, or too difficult becomes available to the individual who works hard to face these obstacles. The actor can begin to claim the text and have authority. The words of Shakespeare become an integral part of the actor's body. Physical ownership is developed. The visceral, emotional, and mental experience all come together and can make the language come alive by maintaining a consistent relationship to structure and rhythm and meaning.

My mentor, John Broome, said it in two words: Passion and Precision. Without passion, the detail, exactness, specificity and form will most likely be cold. And without precision, the emotional, heartfelt experience of the words will most definitely be difficult to understand, and the story will be lost or unclear. If the story is not told clearly, then Shakespeare's words are not honored. The mind and heart must be balanced in the actor's work with the text. The actor is blessed and fortunate to be able to stand on the stage, to be in a sacred and powerful space, and give the offering. It is the actor's body we see and the actor's voice we hear. The words and the body create the spine from which the story is told. The body and the voice meet—sound and silence meet, and movement and stillness meet in the same place, in the performing space—and the balance of these words supplies the energy for the actor by creating tension and release, passion and precision.

Some Rehearsal Notes for Molière and Restoration Comedy Style

Rod McLucas

A s soon as we say the word *style*, certain difficulties emerge. All but the luckiest of us need only reflect back on our first introductions to Shakespeare in performance to be brutally reminded that actors attempting to play some supposedly "classical" style for its own sake should be drawn and quartered—as much to end their misery as ours. Indeed, focusing on any perceived "style" often takes actors so far from the realm of what they should be doing that the very term *style* provokes in many theater people—and understandably so—at least sneers, if not conniptions. Still, there clearly are style issues that legitimately come up in translating a text of any period, including our own, into performance. Obviously, a company focusing its psychic energies on a Greek tragedy will come up with very different modes of behavior than that same company preparing a contemporary romantic comedy. The distinction will derive from the artists' interaction with the works' themes and the characters' psychologies. In other words, a theater piece's style, in the positive sense, is a natural outgrowth of modes of thought. On the same principle, people's personal styles are also organic outgrowths of individual mind-sets—both on the stage and in real life—and those personal styles unarguably manifest themselves physically. Humans in all eras have used gestural vocabularies that identify them as belonging to a certain subsector of society, often in direct and purposeful contrast to other sectors. We can see this readily in our own culture—devotees of urban hip-hop and club members of the corporate power elite providing example enough.

Molière and the Restoration playwrights parade across the stage characters *very* strongly allied to a sense of their place within a social hierarchy. The qualities that distinguish one group of people from another are not only a major preoccupation of the playwrights, but also frequently constitute the subject of conversation among characters. As a result of directing a number of Molière plays and teaching several courses in Molière and Restoration scene study, I've come to believe that exercises in implementing the physical style of the period—gleaned primarily from the graphic arts—are extremely empowering and illuminating for actors approaching these works, and that, far from constituting an arbitrary imposition of "style" for its own sake, such physical exercises greatly inform actors' understanding of characters' inner lives.

The greater part of the fun in these plays lies in an ongoing, antler-locking power play between characters who are, to a greater or lesser degree (often a very lesser degree), masters of an aristocratic game of wit—and of wit as a domination strategy. In Molière, many bourgeois characters choose to act like nobles, and in Restoration comedy, many nobles fail miserably at implementing the tactics of their class. In any case, our joy in the material lies largely in observing people of varying degrees of skill pitting themselves against each other in a verbal gladiatorial combat—and watching the fallout. Although characters vying for status has been a staple of theater comedy since its earliest swaggerings onto the ancient stage, in seventeenth-century comedy, a specific awareness of aristocratic values is essential to understanding the nature and psychological underpinnings of the status-wrangling between characters. Since, despite the importance of wealth and privilege in our society, we don't have an aristocratic class, the mind-set and physicality of the nobility comprise a genuine obstacle for most modern actors. Very few contemporary Americans need special work on the physicalities and corresponding psychologies of middle- and lower-class characters.[1] We immediately recognize our own relaxed physical demeanor in artists' depictions of common people of the era. By sharp contrast to such relaxedness, aristocrats of the period, though they highly valued grace and ease, had no aspirations whatsoever to evince the casualness most of us cultivate today—and cultivate so habitually that considerable practice is usually needed to overcome it. Aristocrats, in a most conscious effort to distinguish themselves from others, were anything *but* casual in their physical deportment—and this was drilled into them from their earliest childhood, as can be seen in countless portraits of aristocratic children as young as three or four.

These people were raised to be obeyed, to exert authority over others; the principal psychological foundation of their physical mode is the need to command respect at all times. And as anyone who's ever taken on a leadership role knows, the least commanding trait of all is to seem to be working at being authoritative. Real command requires an unquestioning and easy ownership of the status to command. Both a scrupulous physical self-control and an unflusterable mental self-possession were consciously and rigorously cultivated, in the service of effectively controlling others. The physical aspect of that self-mastery led to a stringent conformity to a conventional gestural code. The psychological self-mastery, based in a zeal never to appear less than enormously self-confident and untroubled, required a constant repression of what even greatly self-confident people know to be universal frustrations, fears, and insecurities. The resulting injunction against giving voice to primary emotional responses, along with the strict limits on gestural expression, form the psychological foundation of the signature aristocratic devices of wit and understatement—both of which entail getting across information in coded form, in such a way that only other people equally attuned to the code will be able to decipher.

That injunction against expressing real, often very strong, emotions also lies at the heart of the comic aspect of the plays. Hundreds of years after imposing its dominion over others by sheer, unsophisticated, barbaric physical force, the European aristocracy had by now created a code of behavior that looked down on open expressions of aggression and prescribed a constant appearance of good humor. Meanwhile, the characters in Molière and Restoration comedy spend the bulk of their stage time antagonizing each other—and there is inherent comedy in people who are actually extremely ill-disposed toward each other, and who are, in fact, engaging in a sparring match, being psychologically married to presenting to the world a completely breezy and untroubled front. Wit and understatement, then, are *necessary* devices in this world, to express antagonistic sentiments while also effecting a kind of "plausible deniability" in maintaining one's aura of composure and apparent good nature.

The second act of Molière's *Misanthrope* is an excellent resource about the aristocratic mind-set and code of behavior. The entire act consists of a house party hosted by the leading lady, Célimène, who's renowned for the biting astuteness of her character assassinations. In the course of lambasting a series of absent courtiers, she delivers a de facto primer, by negative examples, on the qualities aspired to by her fellow socialites.

About Cléonte, a prominent "fool":

It's true. He's always thrilled you notice him first,
but that's because he's *bizarre*. The poor man's cursed!
And when next you see him—after some time's passed —
he's always still more bizarre this time than last.[2]

Bizarreness is in direct opposition to the rule of conformity to basic parameters of behavior and dress—in other words, being in fashion. Cléonte's eccentricity betrays a finger squarely off the pulse.

About the "pedant" Damon:

> He's quite a talker. He's got such a way
> of making nothing take all day to say.
> All his *ergo*'s, *nothwithstanding*'s and *therefore*'s
> make him the reigning prince of unearthly bores!

Although education is highly valued, boring longwindedness is antithetical to the positive quality of sparkling pithiness.

About Timante, who lurks conspicuously about the court:

> A shadowy figure 'ndeed, who seems to want
> dark mystery in all things. He looks sidelong,
> peers, points, recoils; you ask if something's wrong;
> he answers with secr'tive grimaces so rife
> with innuendo, you fear for your life!
> Then his eyes take on that glow; he looks both ways,
> and tells you "secrets"—that th' whole town's known for days.
> Or else he beckons you aside; you go;
> and then he whispers furtively, "Hello."

Timante's seeming anxious and worried, and believing himself to be in the know when, in fact, he's not, run up against the principles of always being at ease with oneself and others and of being in the loop.

About the braggart provincial, Géralde:

> . . . I wish he wouldn't preen!
> He thinks we peasants haven't ever seen
> a count or duke. And someone should convince
> him he's not the first one ever to meet the Prince.
> Nobility obsesses him! And he founds
> his monstrous, huge conceit on hunting hounds,
> horns, horses—and he thinks that we don't know
> he's been hunting *once*, and several years ago.

Bragging about one's noble rank, being overly impressed with others of higher rank, mistakenly valuing country-estate pastimes like hunting as equal to urbane pleasures, and what's more, telling self-aggrandizing lies it's easy to be caught in—this poor specimen does *everything* wrong. The ideal is to have sufficient confidence in one's reputation not to have to inform others of one's worth, to be secure enough in one's own rank not to be overawed by others', to be urbane as opposed to provincial, and never to leave oneself open to easy ridicule.

About Bélise, who "never was too clever":

When she calls here, I suffer martyrdom.
Try though one may with her, words just won't come.
And her dim, blank, sterile, vacuous expression
kills any mildly humorous digression. (. . .)
And though one minute with her's hard to bear,
she stays for hours! I want to tear my hair!
You ask the time, yawn—any insect could
grasp these signs. She sits there like a block of wood!

Being boring by dint of stupidity—even more heinous than by dint of pedantry—is strictly against the rules of wit and good conversation. And not being able to grasp coded communications—especially those that are not very deeply encoded—betrays a shocking absence of the paramount *decoding* aspect of wit, whereby one gleans what people really mean from indirect clues.

About the notorious complainer, Adraste:

The man's so filled with self-love he might pop!
He spends his life complaining. On this earth
some fail, it seems, to see his valiant worth.
And each time—which is always—he's denied
a royal grant, we hear the court decried.

Making an inaccurate estimation of one's value to the court shows an egregious lack of self-knowledge, and being a moaning curmudgeon breaches the code of always being in a good humor (the literal meaning of "de-bon-air"). Both traits leave one greatly vulnerable to ridicule.

About Damis, who Célimène concedes does have some shred of wit:

But he *works* so hard at it, he makes me furious!
His wit's belabored—each morsel is hewn
so strenuously he'll rupture himself soon.

Seeming to *work* at being witty ruins the critical effect of breezy effortlessness.

The ideal, in other words, is a state of being at once very much in control and vibrantly alive mentally while also appearing completely at ease, even jovial, both physically and psychologically.

Such a state manifested itself in a very specific set of physical manners. A study of portraits of seventeenth-century European aristocrats shows a remarkable uniformity of opinion about the ideal physicality.

RESTING POSITIONS, STANDING

For males, the weight is always on the back foot, and the front foot is posed with the heel raised to present to the world a flexed calf. There is an energy line from the floor up the back of the standing leg, up the back, and on up the back of the neck (as in many martial arts—and these men, despite what appears to us a rather frilly fashion sense, were all highly trained martial artists). For females, the weight is always on the front foot, creating an energy line from the floor up the front of the standing leg and the front of the torso and presenting the bust to the world.

Actors attempting to assimilate this physicality will immediately see the value of working in rehearsal clothes—for men, hard shoes with a thin sole, breeches (or rolled-up pants), big-sleeved shirts, and vests; for women, pumps, floor-length skirts, and bodices or corsets. This last—doing something to cinch the upper body—is especially helpful for women, because the clothing design of the time incorporates a completely different notion of the bust from our fashion sense. Rather than pushing the breasts forward, as our women's clothes do, the clothing of this period presses them back against the chest to create maximum cleavage—which will feel, well, very different and quickly transform any actress's bearing with little conscious effort on her part.

It's interesting to note, in this context of clothing design, that in the various fashions of the period, one constant is that the calf is the only place where observers could make a truly accurate judgment of the shape of men's bodies, and, similarly, the bust was the only part of the female anatomy that was not left to general conjecture—so as far as sexual display, those are the body parts "presented."

RESTING POSITIONS, SITTING

Males are almost always shown sitting on the edge of the seat. Often, this is to accommodate a sword. In any case, the calf is still always presented, either in front or behind the body, and the torso remains straight (not bent at the waist). The principal energy line is still up the back of the spine and neck. For seated females, the bust is still always presented, the principal energy line still running up the front of the torso. Note that, with the yardage of fabric on the lower body, there is no injunction (as with proper ladies of the nineteenth and twentieth centuries) against sitting with the legs apart—sometimes very far apart—and even resting the hands between them. Both men and women are typically portrayed "sitting up"—rarely leaning back against the back of a chair.

In resting positions both sitting and standing, for both sexes, the arm positions are elegantly breezy—often rather extravagantly "at ease." The energy lines up the legs and torso, standing, and up the torso, sitting, permit a port de bras that is relaxed. The arms fall easily off the shoulder. Note that men who carry staffs rest their hands on top of them (rather than holding them like a walking stick), both in standing and sitting positions.

WALKING

The key to walking in these costumes is simplicity of movement, avoiding wasted energy, and keeping the upward energy lines activated at all stages of step-taking. It's useful for both sexes to think about stepping from a straight back leg onto a straight front leg and to keep the weight moving consistently forward, taking the entire weight of the body, as one piece, onto the new leg with each step. Walking backward is an effective way of feeling that physical principle—when taking steps backward, it's impossible not to take the whole weight of the body, as one piece, onto the new leg. The challenge is to implement that as-one-piece note when walking forward.

REVERENCES (BOWS AND CURTSIES)

The purpose of all reverences is to give respect. Some reverence gesture is generally made on all meetings and partings. The idea underlying the gesture is conventionally meant to be "I am your servant" (regardless of the true psychological dynamic between characters). The basic thrust of the reverence is, therefore, backwards, giving the objects of the reverence room, rather than crowding them.

Men's bows should be thought of in two parts. First, the preparation consists of sending one leg back, then the back leg bends, in a "sitting" motion, while the front leg remains straight, and the body inclines forward, breaking at the hip joint—not the waist—so that the torso remains straight. It's always a step backwards onto the back leg, rather than putting the front leg forward. Most men find it more natural to step back on the leg on the opposite side of the sword. (So, right-handed men will tend to step back on the right leg.) The port de bras for the bow holds nearly infinite possibilities. It should be thought of in two parts, though, like the leg gesture. Some common ones are: Both arms out to the sides, then one arm bending in front of you; both arms out to the sides, then both arms bending in front of you; both arms up in front of the face, then both arms to the side; one arm out and one arm up, then dropping the raised arm in a series of circles.

Women's curtseys are also in two parts. In preparation, one foot circles around to the back, and then both legs bend, while the head dips forward. Except in the case of unusually deep curtseys, the torso does not incline forward. Like the bow, it's primarily a backward gesture, giving room. The port de bras consists merely of grasping the front of the skirt during the preparation and lifting it so the hem stays even with the ground as the legs bend.

Some Exercises for Resting Positions, Walking, and Reverences

At first, it's no small task—abiding by these principles—to merely walk around the room, stop in standing resting positions, and then reembark, find one's way to sitting resting positions and back up to standing, and to give reverences to actors one runs into. To start, go on the assumption that all characters in the room occupy the same social rank.

To complicate things a bit, try making an arbitrary distinction—like shorter or taller, or shirt color—to define higher rank, and vary the depth of the plié according to relative status. For those of higher rank, play with how small you can make the reverence and still not be accused of not having done it.

Vary the subtextual take on the reverence. For example, the other person is of higher rank, so you must give an appropriate reverence, but in fact, you have no real respect for the person. Investigate how the reverence can differ toward someone you find very attractive or repulsive, toward someone you know finds you attractive but who revolts you, toward someone you've just humiliated, toward someone who's just humiliated you, or toward someone who's just rescued you from humiliation.

Physicalizing the "Good Humor" Principle

As we heard from Célimène's gleeful disdain of unsuccessful courtiers (and from many courtly etiquette publications of the period), it's essential to always appear good-natured, never to betray negative feelings, and never to seem inwardly flustered by other people's behavior. In other words, it's strictly bad form to ever let on that anyone else has "gotten to" you. In light of that, do all of the above exercises with the injunction to smile at all times, whatever the power dynamic that's transpiring. Play with the communicative powers of the eyebrow, while still not leaving yourself open to the accusation that you've resorted to nastiness. Test the difference between making normal, pleasant eye contact, making insistent eye contact, and refusing eye contact. Try searing the unspoken truth (for instance, "You've won this round, but I'll get you yet" or "How does it feel to be a laughingstock?") into the eyes of your scene partner—still without opening yourself to the charge of having been less than affable.

Adding Text

A fruitful seventeenth-century-comedy version of the "inside-outside" exercise: Two actors improvise a jovial small-talk scene, while two other actors, representing their inner lives, vocalize a highly contentious subtext (such as, "I know you're trying to seduce my spouse" and "And what's someone of your superlatively limited appeal going to do about it?"), which the first two actors take in as the truth, but are forbidden to display in any overt way. Once actors begin speaking, a note that's often needed is, "Make the world come to you"—that is, maintain the integrity of your physicality, keeping the lift up the torso, neck, and head, resisting the impulse to jut the head and neck toward your scene partner in an effort at emphasis.

Physicalizing the "Wit" Principle

Have the first two actors do the same improv again, without the "inside" actors but using the subtext they invented, with both actors trying at once to sear their real meaning into the other's eyeballs and to glean the other's real meaning while outwardly remaining models of cordiality. To increase the difficulty, do a similar improv with two actors inventing their own contentious subtext beneath the affable chitchat—so they don't know each other's real agenda—and trying to glean as much as possible and to respond, within the code. Actors will quickly feel that, if the ideal is never to let anything get past you—to listen and observe very actively and grasp every tiniest nuance of text and body language—while also maintaining at all times a breezy nonchalance, the result will be a physicality that's at once highly energized and very easy-seeming, even if this last comes at considerable inner cost.

Clearly, the fun of these psychological convolutions comes from seeing that there are winners and losers—and the "considerable inner cost" just mentioned is a special comic gem, sparking a laugh doubtless partly sadistic, at the expense of the "loser," but which is also a laugh of recognition: We've all squirmed in discomfort under conditions that prevent us, for whatever reason, from expressing our inner distress. Though characters in Molière and Restoration plays are endowed by their creators with wildly unequal skill levels at engaging in the airy cockfight of aristocratic wit—and very occasionally, some decline to engage in it—extremely few are entirely oblivious to the rules of the game. (And the comic fuel of those that are oblivious lies in their very cluelessness.) An understanding of the noble ideal of genial imperturbability, and of the psychological constraints that make wit necessary in the first place, is therefore essential for actors taking on these works. Rehearsing under the self-imposed physical constraints described above—even if those constraints later become more relaxed or, as is so common in the case of Molière, directors choose to reset to the present or a more recent past—I've found to be an effective technique to help actors viscerally experience the highly energetic nature of the subtle verbal frays that form the heart of seventeenth-century comedies. I've also found it to be greatly entertaining.

NOTES

1. Molière's peculiar borrowings from the Commedia for some of his servant roles form a special case—and a fascinating study—that would make more than a subject for an entire essay of its own.

2. Excerpts are taken from my translation, © 1991. The corresponding passages from the original follow:

> Dans le monde, à vrai dire, il se barbouille fort,
> Partout il porte un air qui saute aux yeux d'abord;
> Et lorsqu'on le revoit après un peu d'absence,
> On le retrouve encor plus plein d'extravagance.
>
> C'est un parleur étrange, et qui trouve toujours
> L'art de ne vous rien dire avec de grands discours;
> Dans le propos qu'il tient, on ne voit jamais goutte,
> Et ce n'est que du bruit que tout ce qu'on écoute.
>
> C'est de la tête aux pieds un homme tout mystère,
> Qui vous jette en passant un coup d'œil égaré,
> Et, sans aucune affaire, est toujours affairé.
> Tout ce qu'il vous débite en grimaces abonde;
> À force de façons, il assomme le monde;
> Sans cesse, il a, tout bas, pour rompre l'entretien
> Un secret à vous dire, et ce secret n'est rien;
> De la moindre vétille il fait une merveille,
> Et jusques au bonjour, il dit tout à l'oreille.
>
> . . . Ô l'ennuyeux conteur!
> Jamais on ne le voit sortir du grand seigneur;
> Dans le brillant commerce il se mêle sans cesse,
> Et ne cite jamais que duc, prince ou princesse:
> La qualité l'entête; et tous ses entretiens
> Ne sont que de chevaux, d'équipage et de chiens;
> Il tutaye en parlant ceux du plus haut étage,
> Et le nom de Monsieur est chez lui hors d'usage.
>
> Lorsqu'elle vient me voir, je souffre le martyre:
> Il faut suer sans cesse à chercher que lui dire,
> Et la stérilité de son expression
> Fait mourir à tous coups la conversation. (…)
> Cependant sa visite, assez insupportable,
> Traîne en une longueur encor épouvantable;

Et l'on demande l'heure, et l'on baille vingt fois,
Qu'elle grouille aussi peu qu'une pièce de bois.

C'est un homme gonflé de l'amour de soi-même.
Son mérite jamais n'est content de la cour:
Contre elle il fait métier de pester chaque jour,
Et l'on ne donne emploi, charge ni bénéfice,
Qu'à tout ce qu'il se croit on ne fasse injustice.

Oui; mais il veut avoir trop d'esprit, dont j'enrage;
Il est guindé sans cesse; et dans tous ses propos,
On voit qu'il se travaille à dire de bons mots.

Molière, *Œuvres complètes*, vol. 2, ed. Georges Couton. Bruges: Gallimard, 1983, 169–71.

PART FIVE

Schools of Thought

The Williamson Physical Technique: The Physical Process of Acting

Loyd Williamson, Jr.

I have always been a teacher. Even when I was six years old, I was teaching the neighborhood buddies how to build the best dam across our local creek. I was senior troop leader in Boy Scouting, the idea person behind endless church-related organizations—in three different denominations, no less—a summer camp teacher and counselor every year from age fourteen through twenty-one. Finally, at twenty-three, I landed my first official teaching position, in a public high school, teaching American literature and English grammar to sixteen-year-olds—in the early 1960s, formal grammar was still important and fun.

As I was growing up, I also had a passion for theater and was always creating some jazz ritual for the local Methodist church or coaching friends who were doing school plays. During the time that I taught in high school, I began to direct the school plays, in the basketball gymnasium. In spite of their humble setting, they won the various state literary festivals, and I was offered fellowships to several graduate schools of theater—I took my M.F.A. in scene design and lighting.

I spent several seasons acting, appallingly, with no acting training—I was from Georgia, complete with the accent. I acted for nine months at the Oregon Shakespeare Festival (February to September of 1970), in repertory at the McCarter Theater Company in Princeton (fall of 1970), and in summer stock at Shawnee, Illinois (1969, 1971). Realizing that I had no idea what I was doing, I did what many actors do: I came to New York to study. I worked with several master teachers, until I finally found the right person for me: Sanford Meisner. I asked for his help. He accepted me, and my formal training began, a two-year (1971–1973) immersion in his professional class. Though I was unaware of the process at the time, the founding principles of the Williamson Physical Technique were evolving during this period—from my own study as an actor, from observing my fellow actors learning their craft, and (later) through coaching them in plays and film. While many of the specific epiphanies I had regarding the training needs of actors occurred in Meisner classes (more about that later), it was the study of both acting and dance that led to my understanding of the physical process of acting.

THE PHYSICAL PROCESS OF ACTING

I did not create this technique; I watched it emerge. The route that led me to this method of training actors' bodies has been very personal. Because I did not study in a conservatory environment, I never had the broad education in international styles of bodywork and in vigorous vocal study that accompanies many acting classes. My personal approach to physical technique came from New York City acting training in the 1960s and early 1970s, when study of the various versions of American Method preceded all other forms of study. In fact, for many of us in the New York training schools, the acting was (*and is*) everything. All other study was peripheral, even haphazard. In the classroom, Harold Clurman often bemoaned the lack of work in voice, carriage, and diction in our New York actors.

However, dance is an integral part of the professional theater, and to me, at the time, completely at one with the art of acting. Dance in New York was at the highest level of performing arts, and fine dancing had the same clarity and truth as did fine acting. Because of my respect for its integrity, dance became the venue through which I studied physical technique. From ballet training with Maggie Black, I learned the physical mechanics required of the body for a professional level of performance: alignment, freedom of the entire respiratory system (which supported remarkable sound), muscular fluidity. Anna Sokolow, the original movement teacher for the Actors Studio, the Lincoln Center School, and the Juilliard Theater School, was a mentor, who, to this day, remains the mother of my artistic soul. From my work in Dramatic Movement for Actors with Anna, I discovered the aesthetics of movement, the expressive beauty of another art. For Anna, movement must grow from an actor's inner experience. She taught actors how to awaken that inner experience by listening with their entire bodies to other artists: musicians, composers, poets (and for me, painters, singers, and dancers).

The relationship of the body to acting and dance guided me to one concept: The actor's body, his sensory contacts with other actors in his imaginary world, his connections and expressions, his experiences and behavior, are all part of one self-contained instrument. There should be no separations of any of its parts.

I am often asked, "What is the relationship between the body and the voice? How do you integrate the two?" The body and voice in this technique have no separation. They are already one instrument that is activated by the same source with one result: the production of behavior. Integration is not an issue. As a physical specialist, I am sometimes asked by directors or other colleagues to "just deal with the actor's body." Experiential life and physical life, acting impulses and physical impulses are all a part of this single relationship. Sensory contact, experience, and behavior are all parts of one event occurring in one indivisible place, the actor's body.

Interestingly, this physical technique relates to each of these art forms, acting and dance, from opposing points of view. In acting, the *body* is a support system, and the technique came from seeing how the body functioned when acting. Since acting is the root of this physical technique, the actor's physical life needs to facilitate essential aspects of acting. The acting situation demands a physicality that is as spontaneous and instinctive as the acting. Physical technique should be a *servant* to acting; enhancing, inspiring, yet unobtrusive. (This physical technique does not teach acting technique; furthermore, if an actor does not have an understanding of the craft of acting, this physical craft has nothing to be supportive of.)

In dance, the opposite occurs: *Dance* serves the actor's *body*. Certain approaches from ballet supply actors with an effective physical technique. Yet my early physical training with Anna Sokolow showed me that the physical technique of dance could actually parallel the physical process of acting: The actors discovered their own inner life experiences, through the master teacher's use of dramatic themes, through music, and dramatic images. For Anna, movement was the master artist's expression of the actor's inner life. Beautifully choreographed motion taught us how to express inner life experiences. We went beyond the ordinary, the mundane. All the rich inner life came flowing out into something beautiful and more fully realized than we thought possible.

THE BODY AND ACTING

The body has many tasks in acting, but perhaps the highest and most sacred of them all is *processing* the life that flows though actors' bodies when they are acting. The physical instrument is entrusted with the artist's creation. Imagine that a rare event occurs: The actor's body falters in processing his creation. We, the audience, then, may miss out on an experience that might have stayed with us through our lives. The actor creates the world in which we live during the play or film; the job of the body is to process the life that flows from that world.

The processing begins as the actor begins making contact through his five senses with the people and the place surrounding him. He must have an almost animal focus and allow that sensory life to permeate his entire body. The phrase we will use is, "the actor's inner life is activated by his sensory contact with the outer world." That activity sends the life out of the body into behavior. Processing is *taking in, activating*, and *sending out.* An actor with an effective physical technique will spend his life working to process more effortlessly.

Imagine the smell and touch of a special rose in your hand. Because of the smell or touch, perhaps your breathing flows deeper into the torso, or your pulse rate changes slightly. The smell and touch of the rose are the stimuli that affect the respiratory system (breathing), the circulatory system (pulse rate), and the muscular system (physical freedom and deeper relaxation). The activation of the inner life has begun. Processing has begun. The activation of the body's inner life can be very gentle, but no matter how gentle or simple, this activation will produce the flow of behavior.

Contact through the Five Senses

Through our five senses, we make contact with the *people* (and other living begins) and our *surroundings*; we become aware of our world. Consider Juliet Capulet from *Romeo and Juliet.* Her senses are filled with the smells, sights, and sounds of her surroundings: a summer night of beauty, as she stands on her own balcony overlooking the most beautiful of gardens. Her sensory contact is alive with the *sight* of the young man, the *sound* of his voice, the *touch* of his hand, the endless looks into each other's *eyes* as they speak, and most of all, the *smell* of this young man in full party doublet at a ball in summer, lit with a thousand candles. When all of these sensory contacts are alive in Juliet, we can assume that her inner life is fully engaged by the intensity of her passions. The most natural of behavior flows from her: long, passionate sighs. They emerge from her, shaped into repeated *O* sounds that carry the purest of sensory ecstasy: "Oh Romeo, Romeo, wherefore art thou Romeo?"

The phoneme *O* is practically sung through one long, sustained sound that is almost primitive, like the song of a beautiful young animal. No consonant sounds break this flow into an intellectual thought. The entire line is behavior that is pure, honest, and true. Her five senses in contact with the person and the surroundings are the origins of the moment. The actor's craft (her homework and rehearsal) has created the meanings of the place and the people, but the moment comes to life through the contacts of her five senses.

Contact via the five senses with surroundings has a special function in theater. Sensory connection with place is the foundation for all period style, whether for *Crimes of the Heart* in the contemporary American South or *The Way of the World* in Restoration England. The senses stimulate actors' fantasies of what their life would be if they lived with the people, places, and things of that other time and place. Without this sensory contact, the play will be a mishmash of varied contemporary behavior. (See the section Period Style: The Salon Project at the end of this article.)

Experience

The activation of the inner life by the five senses is what we call "experience." Experience is the moment that the body's inner life comes alive. Therefore, in the actor, such aspects of the physical body—breathing, blood circulation, muscular freedom, ease of posture—are all in some way susceptible, receptive, or vulnerable to stimuli from the contact of their senses with people, places, or things. In my opinion, an actor who experiences his world is a courageous person. In contrast, an actor with a respiratory system (breathing) that is consciously held in control or a tense muscular system will be unreceptive to experience, to "feel" a sunset or take simple pleasure in her teenage son's accomplishments. The tightness of her inner life will thwart any spontaneous interaction with her outer life, the world around her. In fact, if the respiratory system, already muscularly incapable of spontaneous movement, receives any further stimuli, she will probably tighten the breathing further. Someone places a hand on her shoulder, and she may flinch, driving that person away, her tight body becoming tighter. In the actor, it is bad acting, and it will tighten the audience as well. Internal activity is kept out. The way I like to phrase this is, "this actor *reacts* instead of *interacts."* Reaction is defensive; interaction is experiential.

In mediocre acting, stimuli from whatever the actor sees, hears, etc., does not make the journey into the inner life of the body. Classically trained actors often fall victim to this external problem. Often, the vocal training is intense and rigid; even the physical training is disconnected from the needs of acting the play or film. The actor's line readings are predicated on exactly how to accent certain words. The actors become skilled at delivery of text, using impressive vocal range and volume that has no source in spontaneous experiences and certainly does not produce spontaneous behavior. The actors' behavior is in line readings and gestures that have never made the journey to the inner life of the body. Their acting most often is reactive to what they hear. They do not take the time to allow themselves to connect with the sensory world of other people and their surroundings, absorb its meanings.

We also see nonexperiential acting on some fast, mass-produced situation comedies or in certain "action films." The acting here is also reactive.

Behavior

Inner activity finds a physical outlet: behavior. Our sensory contact with the rose caused increased inner activity in the circulatory system: an increased pulse rate. The actor's expression (behavior) of this experience might be a little redness in the face, a blush, and even some moisture in the eyes. This is behavior that is very simple. In this technique, behavior has two parts: motion and/or sound. Behavior may be as simple as an actor's face turning red. A moment such as this, at the climax in a movie or even a play, might be a turning point of the production, no dialogue (i.e., sound) needed. Or behavior may be sound, as in the magnificent form of words: "Oh, for a muse of fire. . . ."

THE PHYSICAL CHANNEL OF PROCESSING

I will use a metaphor for the body that Martha Graham used, but to a different end. The body is a *channel* through which the actors process physical life. Behavior is both the end of processing and the beginning. Behavior's function is unique. Receptive and sensually interactive, behavior is the key to continuous communication of experience between one person and another. For example, if you say something to me that enrages me, your comment will go to the depth of my inner life, affecting all my vital systems. The behavior—words and gestures—that comes out of my experience must be clear and true. However, if my behavior uses humor, disgust, threats, and so on, my sensory contact will be far more effective with you than one note screaming. My range of sensual behavior will force you to a new sensory contact with my experience—my rage, in this case—and take you to a new level of experience. Each time our behavior

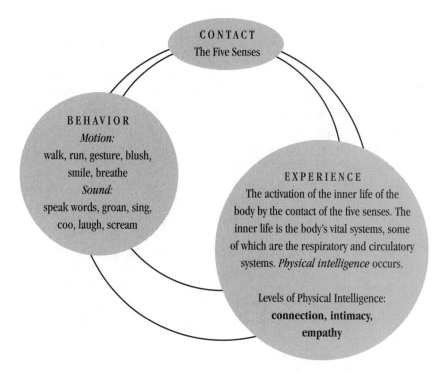

reestablishes the sensory contact on a new level, the meaning of the relationship moves on to unexpected discoveries.

If, however, the actor's expression of his love, hate, jealousy, or joy overwhelms his ability to maintain sensory contact with the other actor—the classic example is shouting—then all communication will stop immediately, including the communication with the audience. Our behavior, when expressing an intensely felt truth, must leave us open to receive all experiences from the person with whom we are speaking.

Because behavior reconnects us to the beginning of our channel, the actor's physical process becomes a circular channel, through which the actor processes physical life.

Experience is the most important event in the Physical Technique: the activity of the body's inner life. The question is, what exactly is this activity that takes place in the inner life?

THE VITAL SYSTEMS AND PHYSICAL INTELLIGENCE

Why do experiences between actors occur? We often hear such comments as, "We just seem to connect," or "We have similar vibes," or "We really can relate on stage." Trying to find an explanation for connection, Stanislavsky used the term "rays of energy." For our purposes, the activity in the inner life is specific

The Physical Process of Acting

The physical life of an actor begins with:

- CONTACT (AWARENESS) Through the body's five senses, actors make contact with the people, surroundings, and things of their world. Awareness comes from contact.
- EXPERIENCE Experience is the activity of the body's inner life that is stimulated by the contact of the five senses with the world around us. The inner life is composed of the vital systems (twelve), among them the respiratory, circulatory, and skeletal. The life in our own vital systems recognizes the activity occurring in the vital systems of another person's inner life: That is the beginning of an interaction that is pure physical connection. This is instinct bypassing intellect. We will call it *Physical Intelligence.* Three Representative Levels of Experience (Physical Intelligence) are *connection, intimacy,* and *empathy.*

  The inner activity of the body, experience, flows out of the body, creating:
- BEHAVIOR Behavior is the spontaneous expression of experience. Behavior has two parts: motion and sound. Motion is gesture, such as the rush of blood to the face, as in a blush, or fists thrust into the air in anguish. Sound can be speech, laughter, screams, song, or a simple sigh.

  Behavior must be sensuous and receptive, because it must interact with the five senses, whose stimuli create new experience followed by new behavior. Behavior must never overwhelm the contacts of the five senses. The interaction produces the beginning of a new experience and new behavior.

  This creates the summary term:
- *The Physical Process of Acting (of Communication)*

  Behavior is receptive to the actor's sensory contact with the person, place, or thing, transforming the contact into a new experience, creating new behavior, creating a deeper contact, and that sensory contact leads to a new experience, creating new behavior . . .

and happening in specific places, the vital systems of the body. These vital systems receive stimuli from the five senses to become activated, which create experience. Of the twelve vital systems, we will discuss only a few, some of the most accessible, such as the respiratory, circulatory, nervous, muscular, skeletal, and auditory systems.

In infancy, we learn Physical Intelligence. The infant absorbs it from the body of another human being whose own vital systems—respiratory, muscular, and circulatory—are totally open to the child. This person unconditionally allows the life in his or her vital systems to be absorbed by the child. This is the *nurturer.* The moment the giving nurturer and the receiving child absorb the complete connection, producing intimacy—and we should probably add, strength in one another—the infant's body begins a physical recognition of the sensations in his or her inner life, specifically the vital systems, the inner life of the child and nurturer that are absorbing and interconnecting on levels that only they experience. The infant's body is taking on a Physical Intelligence. Very soon, the child, like any actor, will respond to the activity in the same systems in another person and can recognize when the receptiveness is or is not present.

If a child has very little human contact, ample documentation tells us that the child's physical development may become seriously impaired, possibly for life. The vital systems or part of them may never become fully receptive.

Recognition is the central word in Physical Intelligence. When our body can recognize the activity in the vital systems at work in another person's (or actor's) body, our vital systems are exercising Physical Intelligence. A physical recognition such as this bypasses intellect. Physical sensation in a vital and working part of our body can recognize physical sensation in the same part of someone else. We see another person, and we feel that there is something about him that we do not trust. Our bodies respond to the activity of the same part of the vital systems of that person that are withholding or distorting what we feel is honest communication—experiential activity. This feeling comes from our Physical Intelligence. Or shall we call it intuition?

Three Representative Levels of Physical Intelligence: Connection, Intimacy, and Empathy

Connection is the simplest and least intimidating form of Physical Intelligence. Connection, simply put, is the actor allowing his or her vital systems (inner life) to be activated by the surrounding world. As with any experience, connection must begin with a receptive body. Connection does not require reciprocation, but only reception and activation. An actor must be connected every other actor in the play, but he or she can, and quite often must, connect with another actor who is connected to no one—not even himself.

Second, after connection comes *intimacy*. When actors feel "chemistry" onstage, their connection is not only reciprocal; the activity of the vital systems is in perfect harmony. For Romeo and Juliet, intimacy is mandatory.

The final component is *empathy*. An actor must be very serious about her art to have the courage to be empathetic. Empathy requires receptivity. If the actor is communicating with a beggar on the streets, she actually allows her own vital systems to become activated by the same conditions, in the same way that the beggar experiences those conditions. The actor does not just connect with the beggar, or become intimate, she allows herself to experience life as the beggar experiences it. The actor, to a certain extent, becomes the beggar.

THE EXPERIENCING PROBLEM

While studying with Sandy Meisner, I had ample opportunity to study the way in which some of my fellow students approached the work, and through that observation, I had an epiphany concerning the nature of communication and the actor's body. I won't attempt to describe the Meisner Technique; it is a beautifully structured method that should be used only by gifted teachers who have apprenticed themselves to a master Meisner teacher for the years necessary to learn the system. I offer my observations of Sandy's technique with respect, not with authority, and to demonstrate how it served as an inspiration for my physical process.

Reaction versus Interaction

In Sandy's class, our work began with the now famous Repetition Exercises. The basic Repetition Exercise is done in pairs. One student speaks a simple phrase, such as "That is a blue (or whatever color) shirt you have on." And the other answers: "This is a blue shirt I have on." The repetition goes back and forth until one actor is moved to change the text because of something he saw or heard in his partner. The new word or phrase is repeated until another change occurs.

I saw actors who could execute this exercise with physical freedom and who had a Physical Intelligence that could experience the inner life activity of one another. They were expressing through the words of the repetition, "picking up impulses from the other person." A sense of humor was usually in these actors' exchanges, as well as a wide range of other experiences (anger included).

However, I began to observe a very different element in many of my fellow actors when using Meisner's directive to "pick up impulses off another person"—a negative aspect. As the exchanges passed back and forth, some actors would inevitably start using the repetition text so that it sounded sarcastic, sometimes hostile. Without any stimuli, this negativity would begin. The other actor would mirror the hostile delivery and, most often, try to sound more hostile.

The possibility of the actors' inner life absorbing what they were seeing or hearing was out of the question. The repetition would turn into a contest of who could respond more negatively. For no reason, the actors would allow the repetition exchanges to evolve into defensiveness, anger, or finally, rage. More often than not, the actors would resort to screaming their exchanges at each other. From my observation, these impulses had no basis in the reality of the relationship. Nothing that the other person had done or said would trigger the beginning of these hostile exchanges. In fact, both actors were participating in an exercise where neither actor was required to have an opinion of the other. These negative responses seemed to me to be self-generated. The actors seemed to be filled with a restlessness, which could also be called nervous discomfort. The actors looked self-absorbed.

As the defensive aspects grew, the actors were hopelessly talking *at* one another, exactly the *opposite* of the connection of the inner life to one another that the exercises were designed to produce. The only experience one actor had of the other would be a defense against the other person's attack. Each actor's defensiveness would stimulate the defensiveness of the other, and the exercise became increasingly intense, tense, and loud.

One of the sources of the problem seemed obvious: When the actor stood in front of the class to do his work, he was in a place of extreme exposure that, in many cases, bordered on terror. The actor's self-consciousness produced a type of behavior that had nothing to do with anything other than with the *experiences* trapped in his or her body. An explosion of some kind was inevitable. When this occurred, the actor usually started shouting and lost contact with the other actor.

Perhaps another cause of the explosive behavior was that one or both actors felt an obligation to produce "big," emotionally charged behavior, so that they would force the repetition to be intense, full of energy, and involved. But I came to feel that this was not an expression of honest emotion or real experience. In fact, it was the opposite: a defense against connection. It was a banging of tensions together. More to the point, if this *reactive* behavior became a part of the actor's vocabulary, it became destructive, because it infected the actor's work for years.

My observation of this particular behavior was not limited to my fellow Meisner students. I have often spotted the phenomenon in Repetition Exercises through the years, in fact, it seems to be somewhat common.

So, by a few months into the second year of the Meisner training, most of the teachers begin their campaign to address this "tension issue." Sadly, at this point, the actor's body is half-trained (one or two semesters) or completely untrained. His neck is out of alignment, along with a tight and swayed-out back.

Unbelievably, one of the most popular suggestions is that the actor should take voice training; this is because his voice is strained. I have many wonderful colleagues who are voice teachers; this is not to criticize them. The point is that the screaming or tense voice is not the issue. The pushed and driven behavior, and no comment ever being made on physical technique, is the issue. The actors have come to believe that they should be emotional, with no obligation to process their experiences through a vulnerable, receptive, and exciting instrument.

The Repetition Exercise requires some simple rethinking to avoid this problem of reactive, rather than interactive behavior. All actors need time at the outset of the training to absorb the inner life of the actor from whom they are receiving the behavior to which they are reacting.

What I am about to suggest does not need to damage the value of the actor's "doings" or the kill the impulses in "picking up impulses off the other fellow" (Meisner's words). Why not select one declarative sentence and repeat until the actual meaning of the text exchange becomes meaningless? Through the essentially nonsense lines, allow the connection between the two actors to merge into a meaningful flow. Do this for four classes, until the actors can begin to be affected by the *life* in the other actors.

Many of the greatest acting teachers discovered the importance of stimuli germinating in the actor's fertile inner life; the actor's experiences then spontaneously flow into behavior. Meisner proposed what no other teachers had: that the actor should activate behavior by focusing on "the doing" and on "working off the other person." Sandy kept "self-involvement" and "self-indulgent emotional introspection" as far as possible from acting. Experiential connections, Physical Intelligence, and sensory stimuli can be incorporated into this work without encouraging self-indulgence; they will, in fact, render self-absorption nearly impossible.

Experiencing the inner life of the other actor not only enhances the flow of actor to actor, but extends to the performance itself. An audience will experience in their bodies only what the actor experiences in his. The audience's body has its own Physical Intelligence that recognizes the inner activity of the actor. The audience wants the actor's experiences first, because the whole internal life of the audience comes alive only when they can experience the life in the actors. The internal activity of the actor's body is the source of gestures and or sounds. Vivid experience will produce vivid behavior that brings the body of an audience member to full life. Sandy said, "An ounce of behavior is worth a pound of words." I would amend that to say, "An ounce of experience is worth a pound of behavior."

THE CURRENT CURRICULUM

The following material is an introduction to the Williamson Technique and to the specific physical methods used in *processing* actors' experiences when acting. Through a masterful physical technique, an actor is more sensually connected to the world around him—more spontaneous, with a vibrantly alive inner life, which in turn produces vibrant behavior that is clear, direct, and true. At first each class begins with creating a fantasy world with vivid sensory contacts that bring the body into *motion*. This opens the body for later *intimacy* exercises. Our final semester ends with variations on these same studies, but they are addressed through period style.

The Open Choreography: The Movement Vocabulary of the Technique

Movement and action, which take their source in the recesses of the soul and follow an inner pattern, are essential to real artists in drama, ballet, and other theater and plastic arts.

—Stanislavsky[1]

This quote summarizes much of this article. I had been teaching this combination of experientially motivated movement for several years, when I discovered Stanislavsky's *Building a Character.* Imagine my excitement on reading the great teacher's material on this subject. As a teacher, finding my way with no colleagues, before discovering this book, I had felt very much alone.

The Open Choreography is the movement vocabulary of the Williamson Technique. There are two parts to the Open Choreography:

- The external world, through which sensory contact activates the vital systems of the actor's inner life
- The internal world, through which the activity of the actor's vital systems produces external-world behavior

We begin our discussion by addressing the second word in the title and saying, "yes, the movement is *choreography*"; therefore, the actor will *not* begin by creating his own movement patterns to express what is in his soul. A further constriction is that the movement phrases have clear structure, developed around a central movement theme, and the structure of the phrases is reprised in four variations: on the floor, seated, kneeling, and standing. The actors must master the form—twelve to sixteen phrases in each of the variations, physical balance, sequence of the phrases, and an effortless flow of the movements. Therefore, the movement itself is a vocabulary that requires commitment.

But the other word in Open Choreography is "Open." The movement is called "open," because its very composition is such that, once the actors master the balance, form, and order of the phrasing, then gradually, the teacher nurtures the actors to begin a free combination of several phrases, i.e., a standing turn flowing into a floor rolling motion. Finally, every physical aspect of the Open Choreography can flow in any sequence, in any rhythm, dictated only by the connection or intimacy that the artist has with the world around him. This is "movement and action" following an "inner pattern," which has its source in the "recesses of the soul" of which Stanislavsky speaks. This is "open." The form becomes each actor's unique freedom of expression.

Next, we need to go into a studio where we can train the entire body with no interference from everyday events that might occur on our city streets.

What awakens the soul? When an acting teacher uses the term, it is not merely poetic and pretty; it is helpful. The *soul* in our work is an objectively described instrument. In this work, the soul awakens when we have contact with the world outside of our self: with a favorite fantasy place, or with music that has emotional depth, or with the harmonies of sound that an ensemble of actors brings forth when they share their voices in tones or songs. These are all ways of activating the vital systems as fully as possible. For Walt Whitman, in the opening pages of *Leaves of Grass*, it was, "I breathe the fragrance of myself and know it and like it."

What is the central area of the body where the truth of this contact occurs? Actually, all gestures, all responses, all behavior, indeed all of the body's experiential activity emanates from the body's inner life, which is housed in one particular area: the total expanse of the torso, or as we term it, the *total torso*. In the skeletal system, it is the area from the bottom (the coccyx) to the top (the vertex); the length and balance of the spine is mostly here. Practically the entire respiratory system is housed in the total torso. When the senses take something in, the vital organs that first respond are central to the activity of the total torso, especially that of the respiratory system, breath.

The movement of the Open Choreography is a based on a circular motion of the total torso. Why? Try and see what happens to you when you imagine being alone in a comfortable, familiar room and the door quietly opens, and suddenly standing there is one of your oldest and most loved friends whom you have not seen in five years.

You jump up from your chair . . .

"What th' . . . I'm not believ'in this."

You race into each other's arms.

What happens in your torso? Notice the (most likely) complete expansion, followed by a lifting of the arms in order to reach out to your friend. The arms lift because your torso activates and wants to extend itself further than just its expansion.

The Open Choreography works in this same way, only the fantasies, or images used, are different and more involved with the five senses. The sensory contact causes the total torso to expand, which in turn causes the extremities—arms, legs, hands—to flow into motion spontaneously because of the inner activity of the torso.

The First Variation: Floor

This is a good place to introduce the simplest of the variations, the floor variation. The exercise begins with the students fantasizing about a *favorite outdoor place*. The sensory contact begins with sensual experience of the air of that place flowing into the body. Then, the contact moves to a sense of *touch* of the surface on which, in the students' fantasies, they are lying: the ground, the earth, the sand, or the snow. The touch begins to activate the body. The teacher guides the touch to extend to the touching of the floor, or fantasy

surface, with the sides of the body, the belly, and so forth. The opening phrases of this first variation have little form. The sense of touch is making contact with the external, in this case, the fantasy place and the surface on which the students are lying. This activates the inner life. The exploration of their "field at night under the stars" produces external behavior. The torso begins to activate increasingly; its muscular, circulatory, respiratory systems all become more fully involved. The teacher can say, "As the air leaves your body, let the vocal folds vibrate. The sound can even be so soft that no one else has to hear it." As the activity of the torso area increases, the arms and legs will flow into almost balletic positions. The legs will circumscribe two individual arches, extending to their fullest length. The teacher almost never has to comment on any one manipulating any part of the body.

The Second Variation: Sitting

As the sensory involvement increases in the floor move- ment, the inner activity and the sensory involvement will instinctively lead the actor into more full movement, which in this case is swinging up into the first phrase of the seated variations. The bended legs tuck, one behind the pelvis, and one across the front, parallel to the pelvis.

The body swings out over the front leg and hangs there, gently swinging back and forth over the leg, with the head, neck, and remainder of the spine free and relaxed. The stretch of the spine begins to open the lower back. This is a variation on the "bottom of the circular swing" that we will use in a few moments. Between each phrase of the Open Choreography, the actor slides out into the floor using legs at a 90 degree angle to the floor to change the body to the other side. The advantage of changing sides between each phrase is that both sides of the hips are opened.

The second phrase of this variation is rolling up the spine into the first fully aligned spine, legs tucked as before, then rolling down and into the same movement on the other side. The third phrase comes in three movements: (1) the spine rolls up from the floor and hangs, gently swinging over the front leg, (2) the spine rolls up into an alignment, and (3) the upper chest stretches into an *upward arch* by the arching of the

upper spine. The arms are activated, swinging in any direction they spontaneously wish. They activate from the middle of the torso. This is a seated version of the standing circular swing, with all motion coming from the connection of the torso to the harmonies of sound and motion in their fellow actors. This introduces the main physical theme in the Open Choreography: the circular motion of the torso.

The Third Variation: Kneeling

The most difficult movement of the third variation is the side arches done from one knee. Then comes the turnout of this one-knee side stretch which ends with the actor in a prayer-like position.

The Fourth Variation: Standing

The full range of movement is not required yet. With a rather demanding transition to the fourth variation, the actors' bodies are propelled to the top of the circular swing, extending the body into a *relevé*, led by the upper spine, with the chest at its fullest upward arch, which to my instinct tells me is the most powerful gesture the body can make. Our expressions of reverence, anguish, ecstasy, grief, all happen in this gesture. To be casual is the one thing that an upward arch will not tolerate. The torso circles over in a full side arch and contracts down into a bottom curved spine, similar in appearance to a Graham contraction, but very different in physical execution. This is actually called the "bottom of the circular swing." When the actor is standing, the point where the arms connect into the shoulders is the balance point over the center of the foot. The spine goes into downward curve. The head and knees are forward of the balance point, and the lower back is behind that point, giving the body a perfect unrestricted balance and uninhibited down stretch. The actor swings through this point and then begins the torso's assent up the other side into the side arch, climaxing in the next upward arch.

The standing variations go from the circular swings into turning, running, wherever the actor's instinct takes him. Usually, just before the actors come into the full standing variations,

the teacher begins to gently use recorded music. The musician is selected because she or he plays with a physical fullness that is clearly inspiring to anyone. The actors can easily *hear* this musician with their *bodies* and not just with their ears.

The physical involvement of the inner life of the musicians should be immediately obvious. One example (among many) in recorded music that carries wonderful power to the actors is the *Andante* section of Rachmaninov's *Sonata for Cello and Piano in G Minor* with Emanuel Ax and Yo-Yo Ma (Sony Records). In the Rachmaninov, the performance musicians and composer are activated so intimately that they sound as if they are one body. Ax and Ma have a total sensory connection to the music and to one another. Their Physical Intelligence allows them to bond as completely as two human beings can. They become completely activated by the experiences in one another; they nurture the physical interaction between them.

Actors are transformed, because the contact between the duo of the piano and cello causes the actors to experience on the level of a truly great artist. The actor processes the music and the musicians with the same fullness. This connection sends the actors into expressiveness that embodies the same fullness that they hear. Physical Intelligence is truly at work. Listen to the actor who says, "I feel as though my body disappeared, and the music was all that was present."

That is the body's experiential and physical life in summary.

The actor takes this prepared body to rehearsal, to performance, or back to class.

STRUCTURE OF THE TECHNIQUE

There are four levels of the technique, with two classes each week for fourteen weeks.

Level I

The first "opening" semester: the body opening to experience the imaginary world of the actor's fantasy; to connect with and experience relationships with another person; the body opening its muscles to free overall motion; activating the inner systems, such as the respiratory system to allow for a spontaneous flow of breath; the activation of the five senses, so that they may take in whatever they contact. It might also be called the "taking in" semester. A receptive body is one of its major goals. A physical technique called *the circles of energy* introduces alignment and physical balance in basic activities of standing, sitting, and walking. The actors also begin their study of the first two Open Choreography variations. The following Level I exercise is Ten Minutes That You Give to Yourself in Which to Do Nothing. Some version of it remains as the opening of every class throughout the entire technique. The actors use this exercise before acting class or before a performance. Within the technique, this exercise is the most basic level of sensual contact and experience. The activation of the five senses, the resulting experiences, and the first motion and sound come at the conclusion of this exercise.

Ten Minutes That You Give to Yourself in Which to Do Nothing

This a time for being with one's body in quiet and stillness. Do nothing is a simple concept. It means that the actor is free from having to move or make sound. Once there is quiet and stillness, the exercise becomes a guide to connecting with and experiencing the sensations that are in one's own body.

How to Begin the Open Choreography: Teaching Instructions

(*Spoken to the class at the conclusion of the Ten Minutes.*)

Now, very gently, let's add that wonderful and necessary ingredient of the actor, the *imagination.* Imagine that you are on vacation and have been able to sleep for a long, beautiful night. (Even if you have trouble sleeping in life, just forget about that, and imagine that you have had a wonderful night's sleep.)

Imagine that, on this vacation, you have been able to sleep for ten hours. Now, imagine that, if you like, you can sleep two hours beyond that. Let the air flow into you, and let a sound flow back out as the air flows out.

Now, imagine that you are sleeping in a wonderful bed with luxurious 300-thread-count cotton sheets, the most luxurious of cotton. You are dressed or not dressed any way that you like.

Now, let your whole body snuggle into those sheets. Let a sound come out. Roll over into those sheets.

(*Give time. Add music—something simple, pleasant, with no emotional demands, such as the piano of George Winston.*)

Snuggle your sides into the sheets. Roll onto your belly, and snuggle into the sheets.

Let the morning air flow into you, and let a sound vibrate out of you as the air comes out.

Let your arms and legs go wherever they want to go. Let them move in ways that they don't get to move in life.

Just nurture your own body; enjoy your own body and its freedom.

Let out a sound: *ahhhhh.*

Repeat it over and over. Enjoy the sensation of your own sound: *ahhhhh.*

Now add in the sound: *eeeeeee.*

Let it flow out again and again: *eeeeeee.*

Now, put them together: *ahhhhhhh eeeeeeee.*

Now, add in the phonetics: *Ieeeee feeell.*

Say it again and again: *Ieeeee feeell.*

Now, fill in the blank with a long, completely silly sound, the crazier the better: *eeeee feeeel ahhheeeahwaaaafoooo.*

Rolling and snuggling in the sheets, let out your nonsense sound: *Ieeeeefeeeel-ahhheeeahwaaaazaaaaap.*

Swing up, and toss the sheets up into the air: *Ieeeee feeeel ahhheeeahwaaaa.*

(*Music volume more full.*)

Now, swing up any way that you want. *Ieeeee feeeel ahhheeeahwaaaa.*

Come up onto your feet. *Ieeeee have noooo apologies!*

Just let it flow!

Say *yes!* Say *yes!*

I celebrate my self! I celebrate myself! Say it five times, differently than anyone else!

Yes, yes.

I celebrate my self! I celebrate myself!

(*Music slowly begins to come down and very softly out.*)

Now, gently let yourself come into quiet, lying on the floor any way you like.

Let a sigh come out.

(*Silence . . . then add . . .*)

Whenever you experience one moment, you begin to experience all moments.

When you experience what is happening in your body or experience one moment of your body connecting to the world around you, then in that moment, you are completely *in the current moment,* no past or future. It is an essential ingredient in the art of acting, called "being in the moment."

The more you experience your own body, the more you can experience the world that surrounds your body, the people, places, and things of that world.

Level II

This is the second "opening" semester. Continuing the work of Level I, it is a deeper and more expansive opening of the body.

The exercise called Creating Drunk is especially important. Whether or not someone has ever tasted alcohol is irrelevant for this exercise. In fact, actual drinking can produce a withdrawal that is antithetical to the heightened sensuality that is the foundation of this exercise. Establishing sensory contact with the surrounding world and its people (the outside world), Creating Drunk is a part of the Physical Technique that helps develop a method that releases all physical resistances. When the inner life activity slows down, sensual contact with the other actors, and with the environment, becomes more vivid. The actors have more time to connect. More expansive involvement creates more expansive behavior, and more physical resistances fall away. Speech becomes more expansive, because the longer sound flows into longer vowels. The actor has much more time to experience when his speech is considerably slower. Once an actor learns it, a slower inner activity stays in the body, ready to be used for any play or film in the future.

Other areas of Level II concentrate on the physical technique of the Open Choreography, with emphasis on the unrestricted vibration of sound (the end of Level III will be the completion of the entire Open Choreography system).

Level III

If the previous semesters have been for bringing the five senses into full aliveness, contact, opening the systems of the body, and taking in stimuli, then the second half of the technique is for a flowing-out of behavior. The major concerns are (1) a basic mastery of alignment; (2) the mastery of the basics of the entire Open Choreography variations; (3) a body that is fully connected through the five senses and expressive in both gesture and sound; and (4) extensive exercises in the flow of sound with full use of poetry text, selected by the actors.

The final character exercise is the summary sensory project, the "Luxurious Primitive Animal" project, utilizing all of the sensual freedom of the actor's body and the openness of his sound. The fantasy begins in an imaginary forest at night, with animal-like creatures crawling through the woods and emitting a primitive full range of sounds while meeting other animals. The actors eventually put their animals on their feet and become human primitive people, with names and countries in which they live, and who share their sensual fantasies: "And what I like most in life to taste is_____," and so on, through all the senses.

Level IV

Level IV is the master semester, or professional semester. One-half of the class is a movement class that is a summary of the entire movement technique. The second half is various projects that integrate the technique into readings from contemporary writing, orations, and in the case of fully trained actors, scenes, monologues, and other acting projects.

Period Style: The Salon Project

In the Physical Technique for Period Style, the actors achieve a historically accurate understanding of the following areas:

- *Deportment, etiquette, and protocol*—the grace with which one carries (deports) oneself in walking and sitting; execution of bows, kissing of hands, handshakes, and social conventions; understanding one's rank in society and politics, and the behavior that is appropriate to that rank.
- *Clothes usage*—the specific skills required when using such items as the corset (particular to the style of each era), the train of a dress, various foundation garments specific to the era, heeled shoes for men and women, fans, gloves, hats, wigs, canes, handkerchiefs, snuff boxes, etc.
- *Furniture usage*—the posture and carriage required for the period regarding chairs, sofas, etc.
- *Social dancing*—this serves the identical relationship of the body to music as it does in the other sections of the technique.

In the dancing, the actors once again are encouraged to listen with their bodies, not just with their ears. However, in this Period Style Project, the actors are building their characters by interacting with music of the particular era. The actors select their dance partners according to their social-political-sexual relationships to one another. The actors usually learn four dances for each era, many of which are danced several times in the course of The Salon.

We use three eras in which many of our most wonderful plays are set: the Late Renaissance, Restoration England, and Victorian England. The following is an example of the era, the circumstances, and the cast. Before the semester begins, a list of the characters, with a brief version of the complete biography, is displayed. The actors are encouraged to select the character that they wish to play. If they do not know or would rather have help, the faculty assigns the character.

The Late Renaissance
TIME: 1586, two years before the Spanish Armada.

PLACE: England, Court of Elizabeth Tudor, Elizabeth I, Queen of England.

EVENT: This is an international gathering arranged by Elizabeth and her Privy Council to possibly deal with the succession to Elizabeth's throne. The fantasy includes Mary Stuart, Queen of Scots.

RENAISSANCE CAST:

Queen of England: Elizabeth Tudor, Elizabeth I.

Her ministers: Lords Burghley, Walsingham, Hatton, and Leicester.

The English Courtiers: Earls of Essex, Raleigh, Sidney, Drake, Blount, Throckmorton, and Babbington.

Ladies of Elizabeth's Court: Countesses of Pembroke and Throckmorton; Countess of Shrewsbury, Arabella Stuart; Countesses of Essex and Leicester; Lady Rich; and so on.

Invited Members of Other Courts:

Scotland: Mary Stuart, Dowager Queen of Scots; James VI, King of Scotland.

France: Henri III, King of France; Catherine de Medici; King of Navarre; Marguerite de Valois, Queen of Navarre; Henry, Duc de Guise.

Spain: Isabella Clara Eugenia, Infanta of Spain; Don Bernardino de Mendoza, Ambassador to France.

Ireland: Grace O'Malley, Irish Chieftain.

CONCLUSION

Even as a preteenager, I felt that how we respond to our world was as important as the specifics of the world that we were experiencing. Walt Whitman opens his mighty *Leaves of Grass* "observing a spear of summer grass." We can see Venice and experience nothing. We can hear the person across from us as he is talking and find a universe in just the sound of the voice. In theater and film, the body must process major issues of life, whether comic or tragic. The actor's inner life grows from these experiences, and he is able to process more than he did before the performance began. His experiences open his audience to those same abilities to process their world. The audience will become more alive to the world around them, and they will become expressive of their own experiences—because of the actor's art.

NOTE
1. Stanislavsky, Konstantin. *Building a Character*, trans. Elizabeth Reynolds Hapgood. New York: Theatre Arts Books, 1949.

An Introduction to Margolis Method™: A Dynamic Physical Approach to Actor Training

Kari Margolis

From the time I could walk, I felt my personal calling was to be an actor. Yet, as a young acting student, I did not particularly excel in my acting classes. Most frustrating was the fact that I did not know what to practice or how to begin to improve. I craved for acting to have the same sense of discipline and tangible techniques I found in music and dance. I was misguided at first by the actors I saw on late-night talk shows, who spoke proudly of never having taken an acting class. "Well!" I thought, "I guess I just wasn't born one of the lucky ones." Over time, I realized luck had nothing to do with being the kind of actor I wanted to be. I wanted to be an artist. And so began my search for an art form, a way to hone my instrument and master my craft. For what I unconsciously knew as a young theater student, and concretely know now, is that the theater experiences that impassion me most always have at their core the actor: physical, expressive, and totally engaged.

For the past twenty-five years, I have spent the good part of most days in the studio, exploring and working with theater artists to create an articulate language for the creation and performance of theater. I have been inspired by the generosity of spirit these artists have brought to the work, and it is they who now compel me to formalize my research and share what has become a comprehensive theater training methodology. I believe the "magic ingredient" great works of theater possess lies in the heart and soul of the actor—the actor who can synthesize the instinctual with the intellectual and the visceral with the technical. By doing so, the personal can become universal, and acting can become art.

In working to create a new modern theater, I look to ancient theater forms and find myself yearning for the reintegration of the actor as primal animal self. If you trace theater back to its ritualistic roots, you will find a performer who embodies both the actor and the dancer. Theater was a transforming and communal experience in which one could not separate the experience of the viewer from that of the performer. Theater today must reclaim its roots, its sense of ceremony and celebration, its ability to provoke and to empower. Only modern Western theater has so drastically separated the expressive human instrument into what we now call the actor (mind) and the dancer (body).

Similarly, the actor's training in Western theater has become a series of disconnected experiences. Students often do text work with one teacher, train the voice out of dramatic context with another, and take dance classes that do not connect to their other training. The student must then try to synthesize this information in order to emerge a whole and better actor. This disjointed method of training is like a flautist studying the fingering of the instrument with one teacher while learning to blow into the flute from another. Impossible! Margolis Method™ is an organic process that creatively links the training of the actor's body with the voice.

Not only must the actor's body and voice be trained as one, they must also be trained within a dramatic context. The ability to project oneself into imaginary situations is one of the actor's essential skills.

The brain, like a muscle, needs to be flexed and stimulated in order to grow. In response, Margolis Method trains actors to hone their thinking process to recognize the poetry and metaphors in everyday experiences. By delicately balancing physical, intellectual, and emotional expression, an actor can work in what I call the "creative state." In this state of hyperawareness, actors can access their deeper levels of creativity. The actor working within this state of integration has the power to engage audiences, stimulating their creative state as well.

Theater that speaks to an audience on a deeper, more metaphorical level engages the audience in a creative, living ritual experience. It is here that we can communicate in the universal language of all humanity, a language that goes beyond culturally specific gesture to speak to the souls of the spectators and stimulate their imaginations. It is this interpretive "underbelly" that makes theater a living communal art form and not simply a literary one.

Actor training must go beyond the idea that acting is only about exposing one's vulnerable self and being "real." An articulated technique allows actors to depersonalize their effort and approach their own bodies with the same egoless connection that a sculptor can approach an unformed mass of clay. Technique then becomes the link between the soul of the artist and the mind and heart of the audience.

In seeking to create a universal theater that speaks to all people, I continually rediscover the laws of physics as fundamental building blocks of all communication, intrinsically connected to everything we do. The laws of physics are universal, not idiosyncratic; tangible, not esoteric. By giving weight, force, and time to emotions, an actor can embody the laws of physics. We can look at an object and assess if it is too heavy for us to lift, moving too fast to reach, or leaning too far to keep from falling. In the same way, we can assess people's moods. Perhaps they seem too stuck in their ways to bring up a new idea, too vulnerable to hear bad news, or too far gone to receive any help.

By learning to embody the laws of physics, the actor will develop a more sensitive instrument with which to communicate emotions and psychological states without having to gesticulate or indicate. For example, it is the expression of gravity that imbues the actor with a sense of life. As gravity is always flowing through the body, even a character at rest is "active." Just the act of standing still would require the actor to express energy in at least two directions—a downward force expressing the gravitational pull and an upward force expressing the character's will to remain standing. Void of will, the actor would fall to the ground. Therefore, an actor standing onstage while not expressing at least these two directions of energy is merely indicating—the actor may be standing onstage, but not acting!

Margolis Method encompasses many exercises for the actor to develop the skill of "muscular physics," as well as structured improvisations to learn to apply this knowledge within a specific dramatic context. The end result is an actor who can more freely access creativity and commands a greater vocabulary of dramatic possibilities.

While this chapter only serves as an introduction to the overall Margolis Method, the exercises included do cover a wide spectrum of concepts. What they all share is a philosophy fundamental to Margolis Method—acting is a tangible art form with guiding principles and concrete skills. Each of the exercises can be practiced and, over time, have a profound affect on an actor's craft.

THE NEUTRALITY OF VERTICAL

Before actors can create characters, they must first be able to express total neutrality. Clearly, any physical habits we possess in daily life will affect every character we play. A head that juts forward or a pelvis that tips backward is already telling a story. The same is true if an actor holds tension anywhere in the body. Actors who bring their personal habits to the characters they play not only are limited, but often confuse an audience by unintentionally expressing extraneous ideas.

Physics and gravity dictate that the most neutral state is absolute vertical. If a weight is attached to a string, it will, of course, fall perfectly on the vertical. A simple dramatic demonstration involves picking a spot on the ceiling directly above you. If you keep your head vertical and simply tip it back, an audience will see a person looking at something. Repeat the exercise, but tip your head back and incline it slightly to the right. Now, an audience will not only see a person looking but will sense a person thinking or dreaming about something. The inclination of the head off of neutral suggests a more abstract meaning. If you took the exercise one step further and inclined your head past a 45-degree angle, the audience would no longer sense a character who was dreaming but someone who was straining to see something. The audience can sense that an object inclined past a 45-degree angle would certainly fall. A person holding their head in this position seems unnatural and awkward.

Now, imagine a character is revealed standing in a relaxed vertical position center stage. You don't know anything about this person or why this person is there, but you can sense that nothing dramatic has happened. Now, let's start again. The curtain rises and a character is revealed standing in a contorted position in the upstage corner. You don't know anything about this person either, but you can feel that something has happened prior to your arrival. The character is off "neutral" and has been affected. Something or someone has caused a change.

The actor must be somewhere to go somewhere. We must sense neutral in order to sense change.

MAKING THE PSYCHOLOGICAL PHYSICAL

It is the actor's responsibility to make the psychological world of a character physical. By expressing emotions physically, the actor can make a character's "inner world" tangible. An audience can feel when they have been included in the character's intellectual and emotional journey and will ultimately be more impacted by the choices a character makes. Void of this physical expression, the actor must resort to facial expressions, gimmicks, or gesticulations to explain a character's actions.

An actor is like a vessel that is full of an emotional state. In a dramatic exchange, an outer stimulus enters the actor's vessel, interacting with the character's present inner state. This interaction transforms the character's inner world. By physically expressing this transformation, the actor involves the audience in a character's dramatic transition from one emotional state to another and ultimately justifies a character's outward action.

The Inner and Outer Worlds of a Character

The inner and outer lives of a character always exist in parallel realities. Therefore, there is always an inner life behind every outward action. Void of this inner-outer dialogue, the actor can not express a dramatic transition, and an audience will experience only the outcome of a character's action without understanding its cause.

> Example: Imagine a bottle filled to the brim with water. Water in this example represents a character's present emotional state. At this moment, the character is full of this state. Now, imagine a bot-

tle of oil being slowly emptied into this same vessel, the oil representing a new (outside) dramatic stimulus. As oil enters into the bottle, water will be forced out. This is a physical representation of an acting transition. The amount of oil allowed to enter into the vessel will ultimately affect the actor's newly transformed state.

Exercise: Crossing the Desert

This exercise will allow the actor to practice dosing out[1] the change of a state of being.

* Start in vertical, with weight over the left leg.
* Feel that your inner space is full with a feeling of vigor and well-being.
* You are going to take three steps forward. With each step, feel you are losing some of your present state and are slowly filling with a downward feeling of fatigue.
* By the third step, you will have made a complete transition.
* For the next three steps, reverse the acting beats, and slowly dose out the change from fatigue to vigor over each step.

Photos of actor Gregory G. Schott. Notice the actor remains vertical with gravity falling through the entire body.

Improvisation

* Start neutral, sitting in a chair.
* Allow a feeling of hope to slowly build inside you.
* When the feeling has built enough to physically manifest change in your body, start to count from one.
* Continue to count to ten, moving up this number scale as you sense the feeling of hope growing inside you.
* As the feeling grows, allow it to justify rising out of your chair.
* When you are out of the chair and the feeling of hope has consumed you, you will be at number ten.
* From this state of being, allow a feeling of despair to slowly creep in.
* When you can connect to this feeling, you will once again start to count from one. Remember,

you must hold on to the history of your last acting beat! Therefore, you would now be at one of despair, but nine of hope.

- Allow yourself to feel this transition from hope to despair. The feeling of despair will pull you back down into your chair.
- Continue to repeat the process, finding new aspects of hope and despair each time.

EXPRESSING INNER AND OUTER WORLDS THROUGH "LINES OF FORCE"

Now that we have discussed the concept of the inner and outer life of a character, it is important to establish specific techniques to support the actor's effort to be clear and specific in interpreting a character's actions. By learning how to control the flow of energy through the body, the actor can guide an audience's awareness as to whether a character is sharing his inner state or making an effort to change others around him. An actor can accomplish this by relating to one of two "classical lines of force." The first classical line of force is the *center meridian* (the line tracing gravity falling through the body). No matter how complex the body shape of a character may be, it is still possible to trace a straight line through the shape to find the center meridian.

A photo of actor Kym Longhi.

When an actor chooses to focus energy up or down along the center meridian, the audience senses the inner emotional life of the character. Imagine one character approaching another very aggressively. Now, imagine that the character being approached reacts by shooting energy up through the body. An audience is drawn into that reaction and senses the character has reacted, perhaps in fear.

A photo of actors Rebecca Surmont and Gregory G. Schott.

The second classical line is the one that runs *perpendicular* to the actor's center meridian. When an actor chooses to focus energy out the perpendicular line of force, the audience senses a character's desire to affect the surrounding world. Take the same example as above. When the character is approached aggressively, instead of shooting energy up the center meridian, the actor sends energy out the perpendicular toward the approaching character. The audience now senses that the character being approached is responding equally aggressively in an attempt to stop the first character.

A photo of actors Rebecca Surmont and Gregory G. Schott

Inner and Outer Voice

Our bodies are our instruments; rhythm, density, and form are the skills with which to "play" them. Through repetition and practice, actors can learn to play their instruments more eloquently. Building on the concept that the body is the actor's instrument, Margolis Method has developed dozens of dramatic breathing and vocal exercises that allow actors to increase their vocabulary of vocal-physical expression. The focus of these exercises is to practice creating the inner physical conditions that will produce the most effective emotional tones.

Visualize that surrounding your center meridian is a pipeline that carries the emotional signals up and down through the body. I call this pipeline your "core." Now, imagine that your core can expand or contract, depending on your dramatic state of being. Sound is produced by the physical conditions of the body, as well as the kind of stimulus (breath) that is affecting it.

The opening and closing of the core will directly affect the sounds the actor's instrument will "play," just as will changing the keys on a wind instrument. The same is true of the actor's voice.

When playing a wind instrument, three major factors affect the musical outcome:

- Restricting airflow by depressing certain keys
- The sum of breath being blown into the instrument
- The quality (or intensity) of breath

Change any one of these factors, and you change the emotional content of the music. For example, the same keys being depressed will not produce the same sound if more or less air is being blown into the instrument.

In the following exercises, I have applied the concept of perpendicular and vertical lines of force to the voice. The outside voice is produced by pushing the voice off the center meridian to project out and away. An outside voice expresses a command or direction. A character trying to directly affect another character or the surrounding world would be most supported by using an outside voice.

The inside voice is produced by sending the voice up or down the core and resonating it inside the actor. An inside voice expresses a character's inner emotional and psychological reaction to events. A character who was just informed about a terrible event and who is expressing a deep personal pain would be most supported by using an inside voice.

Core Exercise

- Actors are asked to raise their hands over their heads and physically feel as if their cores are open several inches in diameter.
- When they drop their arms, they are asked to feel as if the energy they are dropping is falling through their open cores and pushing a sound out of their mouths.

  Because the core was open, the voice will exit the body in an easy manner. If the exercise is repeated with the core now tightened to a small opening, the same energy can no longer pass through the actor as easily and will produce a much different sound.

Improvisation No! No!

PHASE I. This exercise takes the principles of inside and outside voice and puts them into a simple dramatic context.

Movement for Actors

- Two actors stand facing each other, about ten feet apart.
- Actor A approaches Actor B with a clear intention, not knowing if Actor B will react by saying "no" with an inside or an outside voice.
- When actor B responds, Actor A stops in her tracks, and both actors freeze the moment to feel what relationship they have created between them.
- Then, they slowly start moving back to their original positions, as they release the dramatic tension created. The exercise is then reversed, and Actor B approaches Actor A.

Note: If the actor approached (B) reacts using an outside voice, the audience's attention will go to Actor A to see how A will respond to B's command. If actor B reacts with an inside voice, the audience's attention will stay with actor B, as they are pulled in to B's emotional reaction to A's approach.

PHASE II: Breaking the scholarly A-B structure. In this phase of the exercise, either actor can reinitiate an advance toward the other. Both actors must still take the time to embody the relationship they have just created, but they will not withdraw all the way back to neutral. A potential script could go:

- A approaches B. B responds with an inside "No!"
- A insists and approaches B again. B responds with another inside "No!"
- Once more, A approaches, but this time, B summons his courage and responds with a sharp outside "No!" sending A away.

The team has just completed a "dramatic packet"[2] and will then return to their neutral positions to start a new packet.

PUBLIC AND PRIVATE

We have explored the concepts of energy having to travel in at least two directions to create drama, and that the actor's inner and outer worlds exist in parallel realities. While these concepts support an actor's ability to be *in* a moment as opposed to having to *explain* a moment, they do not, in and of themselves, create a total picture. An actor must be able to identify and express the difference between what is public and what is private. For example, if equal emphasis is placed on a character's inner and outer worlds, the audience cannot sense whether the character is being affected or is affecting.

EXAMPLE: Pulleys. I use the image of pulleys, because they are a perfect physical example of an actor distinguishing the public and private aspects of a given dramatic moment. First, pulleys clearly demonstrate energy traveling in two directions. Every time you pull down on one side of the rope running through the pulley, the other side of the rope will rise, and vice versa. Even though the rope through the pulley will move an equal distance, emphasizing pulling up or down on the rope will drastically change the results. The direction of the rope being pulled (or emphasized) is considered the public action and will draw an audience's focus.

Exercise: Inner and Outer

In the following exercise, the actor is emphasizing the inner emotional state of a character. The arm rising is only expressing the natural physical consequences of the inner action (for every action there is a reaction).

- Stand vertically, with heels together and feet turned slightly outward.
- Raise your right arm over your head.
- Use your right arm to express an emotion being pushed down your core.
- Feel how the compression of an emotion inside your body causes your left arm to rise (expressing the effect of the inner pulley).
- As you reverse and pull the emotion up through your core with your right arm, let it affect your left arm by causing it to be pulled down.
- Try reversing the public and private. Now, allow the arm representing the outer world to affect the inner world.

CONFLICT

As we discussed earlier, for an actor to be in an "active dramatic state," one must express "energy in two directions." Physically communicating more than one thing at a time is the basic expression of dramatic conflict. In training actor's bodies to express a dramatic life force through resistance, I use the concept of elastics. The more an elastic is stretched, the more energy it stores. This stored energy expresses resistance, as well as dramatic potential. A stretched elastic will snap back upon release more violently than a lax elastic. The more a character emotionally resists, the more emotion is stored. The

Notice how the actor being suppressed is still offering resistance in the opposite direction.

more emotion stored, the more the actor can dramatically justify a radical action or outburst of emotion. If an actor expresses more emotion "out" than an audience senses the actor has stored "in," the actor will seem artificial. By understanding this concept, an actor creating a character who is irrational might do just that—unpredictably react with too much energy—a reaction that, to the audience, seems to have come out of nowhere.

The beauty of the elastic image is that it also trains actors to build an emotion, instead of just arriving at one. An actor can focus on building an emotion while physically interpreting the stretching of the elastic. An important part of the actors' training is learning to dose out their energy through resistance and to be able to control the amount of resistance being expressed. In early training, actors confuse resistance with tension. Tension is the tightening and closing down of the muscles. Tension does not let energy or emotion flow through the actor's vessel. Resistance is expressed through the density of the muscles—how full of emotional energy they are. A well-trained actor can express a tremendous amount of muscular-emotional density and still be open and relaxed.

Exercise: Elastics

This exercise is fundamental to feeling the drop of the actor's weight into the floor and feeling dramatic resistance.

- Stand with your feet together, imagining they are holding down two elastics with the heels.
- Now, lift your arms, and reach back over your shoulders as if you are holding the loose ends of the elastics.
- Slowly start to pull the arms up, and imagine the elastics are being pulled taut. If you do not send more energy down into your heels in opposition the elastics will, of course, snap out.

A dramatic elastic is being created by the two actors.

Now, try the opposite. Without any resistance, simply let your energy rise up in the same direction as the pulling of the arms. Notice how much less physical and emotional energy you feel.

DRAMATIC TIMING AND PHYSICS

Imagine a character is standing in front of a large group of people and throws a penny straight up in the air. All eyes look skyward. Every person in the group, regardless of gender, race, or background, knows exactly when that penny will fall back into the character's hand. They all can feel it. It's visceral; they know it in their bones. They would be shocked if that penny took even a second longer to fall than they had predicted. If that penny were thrown harder, everyone would instinctively accommodate for the added force and know the penny would rise higher and take longer to fall.

How do they know? Weight, force, and gravity. It's physics, pure and simple. Physics is the universal language!

When an actor engages in an action, it is essential that he embody muscular physics and set up an anticipated timing for the audience (much as throwing the penny sets up an anticipated timing as to when it will fall). If no anticipation is established, the actor's dramatic timing will seem completely arbitrary. The audience will lose any visceral connection to a character's choices and will only be able to follow the action intellectually, and often after the fact.

Once an anticipated timing is established, the skilled actor can manipulate this timing to create humor or surprise. Imagine the penny did not fall when expected, but lingered for a long time before it crashed down unexpectedly, hitting the character on the head just as he was preparing to leave. The audience was set up to believe it would fall according to their instincts, and because it did not, they knew something odd had taken place.

In order to feel the natural dramatic timing of an action, or the expression of feelings, I often ask actors to feel the "pendulum" of the moment. By sensing the "weight of an emotion," an actor can practice sending or pushing that weight like a pendulum. Taking into consideration the weight of the emotion and the amount of force (dramatic intention) with which it is pushed (or pulled), the actor can feel how long the pendulum will hover before it swings back. If a character sends a pendulum to another character, the audience will sense how long that character has before he would naturally need to react. This is what directors mean when they say "your timing is off." The director can sense that your reaction is either too early or too late in relation to the natural swing of the pendulum.

Exercise: Pendulum

- Stand with feet spread about three feet apart.
- Bend slightly forward, and let your arms hang down loosely in front of you.
- Lift your left arm up to the side.
- Now, swing your left arm down as if it were a mallet trying to hit your right arm.
- Even though you do not actually make contact with your right arm, your right arm should get denser to express the moment of impact before it responds by being pushed up to the right.
- When the right arm reaches the top of its swing, prepare to let it swing back to push the left arm up. Feel the pendulum! How long does one arm hover before it returns to its swing?
- Try to speed up and slow down the rate of the pendulum by using more or less force.
- Try to speed up and slow down the pendulum by making it lighter or heavier.

In this series of actions, you started with your left hand creating a "cause," while your right arm expressed an "effect." Once the right arm reached the top of its swing, it had to make a dramatic transition in order to become the cause that will affect the left arm. In this exercise, the length of time the pendulum naturally hovers is the amount of dramatic time you have to make the transition from an effect to a cause.

Improvisation and Dialogue of Energy

This improvisation gives physical expression to a dialogue or conversation between two characters, allowing actors to feel the timing of the pendulum. It will also allow actors to practice making the dramatic transitions between sending an emotion (cause) and receiving one (effect).

Exercise: Pendulum Without Text

- Two actors start by facing each other, about eight feet apart.
- Actor A embodies an emotion, something she wants or needs to share with Actor B.
- Actor A sends this emotion to Actor B, as if she is setting off a pendulum. (Actor A is the cause.)
- Actor B receives this emotion and interprets it. How does he feel about what Actor A has just sent him? He must embody this feeling while not allowing the natural swing of the pendulum to die. (Actor B is the effect.)

- In the time the pendulum would naturally hover, Actor B will make a dramatic transition from effect to cause, as he determines what emotion he now wants to send back to Actor A.
- Continue.
- Now, try the exercise without using arms. Try to express sending the pendulum with the entire body.

Each time an actor sends the pendulum to his partner, it should reflect the weight, force, and intention of the emotion being expressed. If, for example, Actor A were to send a very light, softly pushed pendulum, it would embody a different feeling than if he pushed the same light pendulum with tremendous force. The combined weight and force of the pendulum would also affect its hover time, buying the receiving actor more or less transition time.

Exercise: Pendulum With Text

Maintain the physical principles of the exercise above, but add the text lines: "It's you!" . . . "No, it's you!"

- Actor A starts and says, "It's you," as he sends the pendulum to Actor B.
- Actor B receives and returns the pendulum, saying, "No, it's you."
- Actor A receives and returns the pendulum, saying, "No, it's you."

Now, maintain all the principles of causing, transitioning, and being affected, while exploring saying the text lines over any or all parts of the exercise. For example, an actor could say "no, it's you" while making the transition, and then send the pendulum in silence. Or an actor could start the line of text over the transition (noooooo), then finish the text on the cause ". . . it's you!"

Exercise: Adding a Second Phase of Text Lines

- Once the actors can sense and maintain a rich and interpretive dialogue, they may introduce the second set of text lines: "Based on what?" and the response: "Based on fact."
- Try to find the strongest dramatic moments to make the switch from the "it's you" text to the "based on what" text.
- Once one actor makes the switch, the partner must respond with the appropriate response, and the conversation continues in this loop.
- At the strongest dramatic moment, an actor can switch back to the original text lines ("it's you").

While exploring this exercise, actors should try to feel when they have resolved a situation. When a situation has been resolved, the actors should bring the pendulum to rest, bringing closure to the "dramatic packet." An actor now needs to justify restarting the pendulum in order to initiate the beginning of a new situation. In this exercise, actors can practice honing their ability to recognize the beginnings, middles, and ends of dramatic situations.

An important concept revealed in the dialogue of energy exercise is that of "cause and effect": For every action, there is a reaction. At the same time, the universe is always seeking a state of balance. Open an airtight vacuum, and air will immediately be sucked in to fill the empty space. Theater is the investigation of all the forces that are working to throw the universe out of balance.

The circumstances of a play throw the characters that inhabit its world off balance. Every character in a play is in some way working (consciously or unconsciously) to throw the other characters off balance. When we say "so and so seems to be acting out of character," what we mean is, we do not understand the forces that have caused this person to break away from what we understand to be their normal behavior patterns.

When characters are thrown off balance, we learn more about them. We understand them better, because we see how they absorb and react to outside stimulus. Characters are built on the influences and the effects of these influences on their "balanced" personalities.

DEFINING CHARACTER BY CHANGING THE ACTORS' PHYSICAL CONDITIONS

Where an actor places his center of gravity will affect a character's conditions by changing his physical relationship to gravity. If the actor has the technique to actually create the physical conditions of a character in each new circumstance (for example, lighter, denser, grounded, unstable), he can let the character simply "be," instead of "showing" how the character is feeling.

While a character is created in great part by maintaining a consistency of personality traits, characters are brought to life by the inconsistencies they expose as they interact with different characters or changing situations. We interact differently with our parents than we do with a love interest.

EXAMPLE. Perhaps, due to recent circumstances, a character is feeling very insecure. In this case, the character would probably have a high center of gravity, be quite light in density, not very grounded, and physically unstable. In this state, the character could be very easily thrown off center. For example, the boss calling the character's name could cause him to be very flustered and to overreact. On another day, the character may decide to take matters into his own hands. In this case, the circumstances are different, and the character would be much denser, have a lower center of gravity, and feel very grounded. The boss calling the character's name in exactly the same manner as the day before could elicit a response no greater than a slight lifting of the head.

As a character transitions from one emotion to another, the actor must be able to justify and control the changing physical conditions. Some of the basic tools actors can practice are expanding or contracting their core, changing the sum of energy affecting them, and moving the center of gravity to different places in the body.

Energy Exercise I : In Place

- Stand in a vertical position, with heels together and feet turned slightly outward.
- Allow energy to enter through the crown of your head and flow through your body to the floor.
- With very minimal movement, physically express exactly where the energy is as it flows down through your core. Try to keep the energy moving at a slow but steady pace.

VARIATION I. Now, explore allowing the energy to fall quickly through the body. To accomplish this task, the actor must focus on feeling that his core is more open and creating less resistance to the falling energy.

VARIATION II. Experiment with creating more or less resistance as you move energy both up and down your core. Make note of how changing the physical conditions of your core stimulates different feelings or emotions.

Energy Exercise II: Transports with Density Changes

These exercises help actors dramatically justify movement across the stage. We will start with the constant of a character traveling six steps forward in a straight line.

- Start walking, feeling very light. Get heavier with each step, so that by the sixth step, you are so heavy, you could not possibly take another step.
- Start by running. Slow down with each step, so that you have dissipated all momentum by the sixth step.
- Walk briskly, and suddenly get very dense on your sixth step, as if you just confronted a wall.
- Create three other approaches.
- Try the exercise walking backwards.
- Try the exercise walking in a circle.

Improvisation: Enter, Action, and Exit

This exercise synthesizes all the principles discussed in this chapter, allowing the actor to create a physically justified dramatic script.

Choose a prop and set it on a table center stage.

- Actors must consider all the poetic meanings elicited by the prop.
- Create a nonverbal script that justifies a character entering the space, relating to the prop, and exiting.
- Develop this script by consciously applying all the laws of physics (we have discussed to this point) to every intention and action.

Complete the exercise three times, each time changing the rhythm and dynamic and, ultimately, the meaning of the experience.

Examples of props that can be imbued with a wide range of poetic meaning are objects such as a wineglass, a book, a telephone, or a suitcase.

EXAMPLE: Wineglass

The Entrance. A character enters quickly, sees the glass, and suddenly slows down. Just this change in rhythm suggests to the audience something important has happened. Why? Because the laws of physics tell us that a body in motion will stay in motion unless another force affects it. In this case, the other force is the meaning this wineglass contains for this particular character. (Another character might have noticed it, but simply continued past, unaffected.)

The Action. The character reaches for the glass and suddenly hesitates before lifting it. Once again, the change in rhythm suggests this is no ordinary glass! The glass seems unusually heavy. The audience instinctually knows how much this glass really weighs and how much force it would take to lift it. Therefore, the glass seeming so heavy suggests the that it is full of "meaning." Perhaps this person has not taken a drink in years. Perhaps they believe there is poison in the glass.

In the example above, the actor is expressing the story through the "how" (interpretation) of the situation, not simply the "what" (action). By doing so, the audience is stimulated to ponder the "why" (that is, why did they slow down? why was the glass so heavy?). The audience is engaged and connected.

CONCLUSION

To reflect on life is distinctly a human ability; to embody and give physical expression to this reflection is the art of the actor. No small task to master. Just as opera singers, athletes, musicians, and poets must continually develop their unique skills to express themselves at their highest and most refined levels, so must the actor. It is my desire and life's work to actively participate in the ongoing research and development of the actor's craft—a craft for which I hold the greatest respect.

My search has brought me to many places, and I have had the honor to work with many brilliant artists. From the world-renowned to the beginning student, each has left an indelible mark on my soul. While Margolis Method provides the theater artist with a comprehensive technique, it is more than a finite technique. It is a philosophy, a way of thinking and approaching the practice, creation, and performance of theater.

It is, of course, not possible to learn acting from a book, and certainly not from one chapter. But a book can be the source of stimulation, food for thought, or the itch to look further and learn more. I can only hope that this chapter has inspired this deep-seated goal.

NOTES
1. Dosing out means not giving away the entire internal change of a character all at once but allowing emotional and psychological change to physically manifest itself over time and space.
2. A dramatic packet is the term for a group of ideas that introduce, explore, and resolve a dramatic conflict or situation.

Movement Training: Dell'Arte International

Joan Schirle

D ell'Arte International came into existence anchored in the great traditions of the European popular theater: Commedia dell'Arte, melodrama, the world of the circus, fairs and streets, pantomime, music hall. The long river of tradition includes actor-creators such as Shakespeare, Molière, Chaplin, and Nobel Prize winner Dario Fo; it includes literary masterpieces as well as a huge body of nonliterary theater that is topical, visual, nonverbal, and original.

The Dell'Arte International School of Physical Theatre was founded by Carlo Mazzone-Clementi and Jane Hill in 1975 to bring the physical training tradition to the United States and to develop actor-creators through training in mime, mask, movement, and ensemble creation. Originally called the Dell'Arte School of Mime and Comedy, the name was changed in the late 1980s as a result of the narrowing definition of "mime" and a desire to investigate a broader vision of theater and the work of the contemporary actor.

Don't let your gestures be false—work from the body. Does the body tell you what your feelings are? Or no?

—Carlo Mazzone-Clementi

CARLO AND THE DELL'ARTE SCHOOL

As a student at Padua University in the late 1940s and a member of the Company Parenti-Fo-Durano in the early 1950s, Carlo Mazzone-Clementi took part in the reinvention of Commedia dell'Arte in Italy following World War II. The movement to revive this Italian cultural heritage was centered around Padua University and involved Fo, Franco Parenti, Giustino Durano, Amleto Sartori, Jacques Lecoq, and Giorgio Strehler, among others. Carlo developed his way of teaching based on extended work with Lecoq during the eight years Lecoq spent in Italy as a teacher and choreographer. Carlo was also influenced by studies with Jean-Louis Barrault, with Etienne Decroux, by training as a fencer, by a lifelong friendship with sculptor and mask maker Amleto Sartori, and by his own grandfather, "who *was* the commedia dell'arte."

Carlo further developed his teaching after coming to the United States in 1959 and teaching in universities like Brandeis and Carnegie Mellon and for companies like A.C.T. in San Francisco. While his training approach was based on Lecoq's pedagogy, Carlo modeled his own school after Jacques Copeau's, by locating it in a rural area and developing a resident professional company.

Carlo and Jane moved their family to Humboldt County, California, in 1972 and, with a few members of the original company they had established during their years in the San Francisco Bay area, started a summer festival in Eureka, about six hours from San Francisco. They acquired our present school building in the nearby small town of Blue Lake in 1974.

I met Carlo and Jane in 1975, as they were about to open the school in Blue Lake. It was a fortuitous meeting for us all; I was already a certified teacher of the F. M. Alexander Technique, an actor with many years of dance and movement training, and was already committed to living in a rural area. I was electrified by Carlo's vision of the relation of theater to life, to nature, to the idea of ensemble, although the work with mask and clown was totally new—yet totally fascinating. The idea of an organic, improvisatory method of making theater was new. I had been educated in the psychological method as an actor-interpreter, where physical training had been regarded as useful, but peripheral to the "meat" of an actor's work and to the creation of theater itself. It was indeed Carlo and Jane's hope that the contemporary American acting method could be wed to the European popular tradition and techniques of movement training to arrive at new forms of theater expression and a new way of training actors. The offer to teach at the school in its early years opened the door to a laboratory for my own quest to understand the role of movement in the training of an actor. When we created a new company in 1977, it became a laboratory to create original theater as a member of an ensemble of artists.

WHAT IS STAGE MOVEMENT FOR?

My "quest" began when I moved to New York in 1966 with the desire to become a teacher of stage movement. Inspired by Isadora Duncan's vision of "the freest use of the most intelligent body," I thought there surely was a course of study, a place or places I could go to learn to teach "stage movement." I was only a year out of university when I arrived in New York, and I soon discovered that there were as many approaches to movement as there were to singing. In some theater schools, movement training consisted of dance or fencing; at others, it was mime or "glove and fan" classes in period movement. The fitness craze had not yet struck, and actors were not yet in the gyms sculpting their bodies toward a homogeneous ideal, and the systematic teaching of stage combat was in its infancy. I began taking modern dance classes (my earlier training had all been in ballet), mime classes from Paul Curtis and Tony Montanaro, and classes in creative movement based in the work of Laban and Delsarte. I also started private lessons in the Alexander Technique with Joyce Suskind at the American Center for the Alexander Technique (ACAT) and eventually completed a teacher-training program at ACAT New York.

In 1969, following my certification, I assisted ACAT director Judy Leibowitz with Alexander classes during the inaugural year of the new Juilliard School of Drama. Based on the model established by Michel St. Denis (Copeau's nephew) at the Old Vic school, the Juilliard program was one of the first in the United States to affirm the value of the Alexander Technique to actors, as well as to offer studies in mask and clown. That historic first class included Kevin Kline, David Ogden Stiers, Mary Lou Rosato, David Schramm, and Patty LuPone, and the reception to Judy's work from the start was very positive. The Juilliard program became a model for others.

Over thirty years later, the field of movement has evolved. Most serious conservatory or university M.F.A. acting programs and some undergraduate programs now include Movement for Actors classes based on Laban, Lecoq, Grotowski, Meyerhold, Suzuki, Viewpoints, the Alexander Technique, Feldenkrais, yoga, and others; the number of job postings for movement specialists grows yearly. There is a branch of ATHE (Association for Theatre in Higher Education) that is devoted to movement: ATME (Association of Theatre Movement Educators). But as of this writing, there are no graduate programs in Stage Movement or Physical Theater, *and what has yet to evolve in U.S. academic theater training is the role of movement as a fundamental basis for the creation of theater.*

With good intentions, movement classes are assigned the role of helping the actor improve her "instrument," as though there were an instrument (the body or voice) "controlled" or "played" by the mind of the actor, and that the instrument required a different kind of training than the "player" of that instrument. If we separate instrument from player, even as a casual frame of reference, we disorganize body, mind, and spirit, leading to a disembodied practice for the actor—a practice in which the body does not have to be intelligent or conscious, only obedient. "The freest use of the most intelligent body" requires an integrated training in which player and instrument are educated as one. The eye, the muscles, and the imagination must all be trained as a unity.

> *My teaching is based on improvisation. I believe the school therefore is a crucible for creativity. It is not just a school of interpretation, but also of creation. What is truly important is movement with a capital "M" and to understand "how it moves!" It is finally the point of departure and the point of arrival. In sum, it is the fixed point, beginning with and around which move both the theater and the actor—who is his body.*
>
> —Jacques Lecoq (translation, Bari Rolfe)

In an article in *Callboard Magazine*, "What Are Stage Movement Classes For?" Professor Edgardo de la Cruz of California State University at Hayward lamented, "It has taken me four decades of training in dance, mime, clowning, stage combat, etc., and many workshops . . . to arrive at a conclusion: Stage Movement teachers all want their students to be flexible, all want their students to have fun and be 'creative' (meaning to express themselves spontaneously with great gusto and abandon), all want their students to find shortcuts to characterizations or find physical ways to tap into their emotions. But no one has shown anyone the way to apply this to scripts, rehearsals, or productions. . . . Are physical agility, flexibility, and fun all that we can offer to students?"

De la Cruz goes on to say, "Theater art is not about spontaneity. No art is spontaneous: A lot of bad art is. It is about indirection, ambiguity, metaphorical expression. It is about symbolic representation in a production 'language' which combines all the other visual and aural arts and is built of a multiplicity of choices which create in the audience an experience that is recognized as theatrical. Stage movement is one of the most potent elements in that concoction, and as teachers, we have to train students to use such a tool creatively within the demands of production, not just exercises."

RELATED TO THE THEATER

The work of the Dell'Arte International School is movement as related to the theater, a theater that explores life-as-it-is—its chaos, beauty, messiness, pain, humor, and glory. We approach the work from many viewpoints, internal and external, always guiding the student to understand what the audience sees. Great theater, on a high level of play, puts the body at a higher tension level than that of daily life, so we train to achieve an extra-daily, heightened state of tone that can be adjusted in large or small increments to the demands of the work. The performing body differs from the athletic body in that it is available to play in the world of illusion, and the imagination, especially the physical imagination, must also be trained. We study the nature of play and the dynamic presence of the actor in the empty space. The training of an individual is the training of a *person*, brought into the context of the larger picture that includes how a piece of theater is developed, rehearsed, and performed in ensemble.

Our theater and our training reflect vital paradoxes—we train to be strong *and* flexible; we train to play with economy *and* abandon; we train to be *easeful* at a high level of *tension*; we train to be both

Donald Forest and Joan Schirle in the Dell'Arte Company's Mad Love. *Photo by Brandi Easter.*

analytic *and* intuitive; we train to have a wakeful internal eye, as well as to see and hear fully our partners, our audience, our space, our props.

Our work at the Dell'Arte School begins with the absolute fact of the body of the actor in the performance space. This is what the audience sees. No matter what the actor *feels*, the audience's experience is based on what they *see* and *hear*. The common language of the body needs no translation. The language of gesture has no borders, any more than music or the visual arts. Movement is life, life is movement, and everything moves. Even when invisible to the eye, from the subatomic worlds to the cosmos, the universe is in motion.

> *In his body and his life man is deeply aware of the earth and of the other elements, of the sun and of the star-filled sky.*
>
> —Mikhail Bakhtin

THEATER AND THE SHARED HUMAN EXPERIENCE

Our first education—sensory, kinesthetic, spatial—precedes the acquisition of language and formal schooling. In a network of stimuli that includes things, people, sounds, elements, and invisible forces, our universal human "original instructions" include survival lessons about falling, distance, comfort, even gestural codes—that the opening of the arms means "come toward," the stillness of a raised hand implies a slap.

> *The ground is your friend.*
>
> —Carlo Mazzone-Clementi

Movement for Actors

It is the work of the actor to link us to the first education, in order to establish a visceral connection to the audience through the deepest shared ground of human experience. Invoked in the greatest theater, the fullness of life, the size and excitement of great characters comes from the actor's ability to reveal to the audience what it means to "fall" in love, to be "moved" by an experience, to be "crushed" by defeat, or to be "thrown" off balance. The actor in the live theater exists not only in relation to the individuals who witness his performance but also in relation to the collective ancestral body of the audience. The universal shared ground of human experience is deeper than any psychology and permeates narrative and abstract forms, figurative and nonfigurative movement.

As we grow up, we forget our first "school." We may not even realize how much we know "in our bones"; we take for granted how well our movement and spatial education serves us—after all, we've survived, and we function in the world without having to think too much about how to walk down a flight of steps or close a door or take a breath. Except in progressive systems of childhood education, the education of our kinesthetic sense ceases once we begin our formal schooling. We acquire skills like swimming or playing ball, but we aren't taught to look at how we do these things. Our physical intelligence gradually becomes separated from our verbal, mathematical, and other intelligences. We learn to mask the play of emotion across the face, to control the physical manifestation of our feelings. Habits can develop that interfere with the actor's flexibility and ease at one level and with his availability and responsiveness at the level of invention.

THE USE OF THE SELF

One way for the actor to reconnect to the first education is through training in "the use of the self," as F. M. Alexander called it. Fundamental to all work on conditioning, on physical and vocal technique, is learning a constructive way of using the whole self. Good use permits the actor to find the ease and flexibility for a lifetime of creative work. Good use develops habits of appropriate tension.

An education that allows you to use yourself badly is almost valueless.

—Aldous Huxley

Walter Carrington, one of F. M. Alexander's early pupils who runs a teacher training course in London, uses as an example of good use the small wild African dogs that hunt much larger animals like the wildebeest, a kind of gazelle. The dogs hunt by chasing their prey, sometimes for incredibly long distances, until the large animal begins to tire. A dog will then attach itself to the throat of the animal—which continues to run until its strength gives out entirely—and the dog chews out its throat until the animal collapses from exhaustion and terror. During its wild ride on the wildebeest, shaken about, the dog's internal systems—circulation, respiration, digestion—continue to function at peak level. We might say the animal is practicing good use to illustrate that "good use" isn't limited to a state of calm. On the contrary, the most violent kinds of movements and actions can be carried out with the kind of flexibility, economy, and "high performance" found in animals in survival situations or when confronted with the unexpected.

Good form is the most efficient manner to accomplish the purpose of a performance with a minimum of lost motion and wasted energy.

—Bruce Lee

The example of the African dog points up the need for the actor to find the relaxation necessary for creative performance while maintaining a heightened state, even an uncomfortable state. Giulio Cesare Perrone, Dell'Arte Associate Artist and a designer-director who has collaborated on many Dell'Arte projects, insists that a costume that is too comfortable does not support a heightened state, or that a set design full of places to sit or recline dilutes the stage tension. My own studies in Balinese dance and mask work bear this out; the *topeng* dancer maintains a constant state of "un-balance," which reflects the Hindu cosmology, but also keeps the performance riveting to watch. The taut, painted surface of the Balinese wooden masks reflects the level of tone in the body of the dancer.

From the Greeks on, there have been few dramas about balanced, centered people, unless they are in trouble. Balance is not interesting, though stopping oneself from falling is. Excess is interesting, and the most interesting characters are often the least centered, the ones who are either physically or psychologically uncomfortable. Hamlet's internal obstacles, for example, play as great a role in our fascination with the character as his external obstacles. For an actor to physicalize the character's tensions, rather than his own, requires the ability to achieve an unmannered, economical, highly energized state— to practice "good use." What Lecoq called *neutrality*—a condition of pure action unburdened by psychology—and what Barba calls *pre-expressivity* share the economy and availability that accompanies good use. The study of one's own use helps an actor to observe and differentiate qualities of movement, encourages risk-taking, lengthens the career, and helps an actor deal with the stresses of a life in the profession, as well as improving his stage work.

> *Imagination is always related to the inner self. The neutral condition is essential to get there. Every exercise we do is for the dark, the empty space, the immobility.*
>
> —Carlo Mazzone-Clementi

The training progresses from the study of how we move to what movement means in the theater. The work of the actor is to see and hear, to justify the text, to reveal the essence as well as the form. Because masks reveal their meaning in movement, they are an ideal study for the actor. The actor must bring an object to life and reveal to the audience the mysterious link between the mask and life. Just as there are masks that are beautiful wall decorations, but cannot be played, so also our training resists falling into the aestheticism of movement, rather remaining faithful to the proposals of reality, enlarging the sense and not the forms. The techniques that are studied to develop articulation and analysis of movement do not stop with beauty of line; the work with gesture is not just at the extremity, but at the center and how it comes from the center, how the gesture relates to the passions, to anger, joy, sorrow, fear—what are the intuitive ways body responds to them.

> *The study of Gesture is not simply a matter of looking at the movement that the model makes. You must also seek to understand the impulse that exists inside the model and causes the pose which you see. The drawing starts with the impulse, not the position.*
>
> —Kimon Nicolaïdes (*The Natural Way to Draw*)

As our work moves into explorations of style and what Lecoq calls "the dramatic territories," it becomes clear that the work is really about the dynamics of theater and the imagination, as the movement work connects to creative acting, rehearsal, and performance. Investigations into rhythm, opposition, alternation, stillness, surprise, the use of the space, of flow, of minimum to maximum scales—these studies open the actor's expressive channel for impulses, passions, ideas, feelings and relationships. Director Anne Bogart proposes that the spatial quality between two actors should be alive with a tension, an energy, even a danger. The study of dynamics gives actors the confidence to be responsible for their use of time and space onstage and to understand the nature of partnership—with another actor, with an object, with the space, with the audience.

These studies are combined into compositions, challenging the actor to take responsibility for the time and space. With style work and work with text, the dynamic becomes more specific to different territories, from the heroic diagonals of melodrama to the resilient buoyancy of the clown.

You must take pleasure in your BODY, in everything you do. Image, idea, and concept. You must see, hear, and smell in your feet, for example.

—Carlo Mazzone-Clementi

A TRIUMPHANT, FESTIVE PRINCIPLE

It was never Carlo's idea to import the historical form of Commedia dell'Arte to the United States, though many sought from him "the gospel of Commedia." For him, it was a dead form, a museum to be looked at for inspiration because of its great influence on Western theater, but he had no interest in resuscitating the historical style. He was far more interested in its essence and in the New World descendants of Commedia dell'Arte in silent film, vaudeville, burlesque, jazz, and the American musical theater.

We continue to investigate the Commedia dell'Arte for several reasons: It is an ensemble form, celebrating invention and demanding a commitment by the actor to an extreme physicality. It provides the actor with the ability to play with physical characterization in situation and circumstance. Even though it became a literary form, the origins of Commedia were in what Mikhail Bakhtin calls "the carnival-grotesque" and, as such, "exercises the same function: to consecrate inventive freedom . . . to liberate from the prevailing point of view of the world, from conventions and established truths, from clichés, from all that is humdrum and universally accepted."

Historically, the body of the Commedia actor not only served as the primary décor; through both voice and movement, the Italian actors found creative ways to transcend barriers of dialect and language. Most importantly, the humor of its situations, the passions, follies, the human comedy, are enacted through the body, with its traditional contents: copulation, pregnancy, birth, growth, old age, disintegration, dismemberment. Though its images are ugly from the point of view of "classic" aesthetics and contrary to the classic images of the finished, completed man, in the carnival-grotesque forms, says Bakhtin:

The bodily element is deeply positive. It is presented not in a private, egotistic form, severed from the other spheres of life, but as something universal, representing all the people . . . it makes no pretense to renunciation of the earthy, or independence of the earth and the body . . . This is why all that is bodily becomes grandiose, exaggerated, immeasurable . . . this exaggeration has a positive, assertive character. The leading themes of these images of bodily life are fertility, growth, and a brimming-over abundance. Manifestations of this life refer not to the isolated biological individual, not to the private, egotistic "economic man," but to the collective ancestral body of all the people.

The material, bodily principle is a triumphant, festive principle.
— Mikhail Bakhtin (*Rabelais and His World*)

Over the course of nearly thirty years, the Dell'Arte teaching has been influenced by many people, including school directors Jon'Paul Cook, Alain Schons, Ralph Hall, Jane Hill, Peter Buckley, and Daniel Stein, and by guest teachers whose long-term involvement helped shape the training: Ronlin Foreman, Avner Eisenberg, Julie Goell, Ole Brekke, Geoff Hoyle. The teaching work of the core ensemble artists of the Dell'Arte Company—since 1978, Michael Fields, Donald Forrest, Jael Weisman, and myself—is the fruit of our own explorations into the collaborative creation of over fifty plays and pieces of theater, our travels to world festivals, and the exchange with international artists at our own summer festival. A new generation of teachers who are graduates of the Dell'Arte program are taking a role in the continuation of the School. The work of the School is continually tested through the making of theater, and the company evolves its ideas and maintains its skills through work as teachers of the School.

Carlo Mazzone-Clementi died in November 2000, but his legacy continues. The next step in the evolution of the Dell'Arte pedagogy will be the establishment of a degree-granting program leading to an M.F.A. in Ensemble Physical Theater. As this book goes to press, accreditation is pending for the program to begin in 2003.

There is only one right way to draw and that is a perfectly natural way. It has nothing to do with artifice or technique. It has nothing to do with aesthetics or conception. It has only to do with the act of correct observation, and by that I mean a physical contact with all sorts of objects through all the senses.
— Kimon Nicolaïdes

EXERCISES

"Go"

Carlo, who loved soccer, built many of his acting exercises related to mask and movement on the pivotal relationship between the foot, the pelvis, and the head. He called his basic exercises "The Showers," because "you are never too clean to do them." One of the most important skills of the Italian actors was knowing how to enter and how to exit, both equally important: to claim your moment, but to be equally willing to give over to the energy of another onstage. Carlo's series of exercises with a soccer ball have been widely used and adapted. Here is his basic ball exercise, which builds ensemble rhythm, the idea of serving the partner, and the basic relationship between the foot and the pelvis, the horse and the rider.

To play: Players form a circle. One stands in the middle with a ball. She passes the ball with an underhand throw to each player in the circle in a clockwise direction, and each player in turn passes it back to her. A group rhythm is established, with the impulse to throw coming from the pelvis through the arms. Once the rhythm has been established, another steps in behind her and says, "Go!" No matter where the ball is, the first player must leave in a way that makes it possible for the new player to easily catch the ball. The game goes on, as other players continue to step in and call "go!" until everyone has come in once or twice. When all can play in a relaxed, rhythmic way, without dropping the ball, add a second ball.

Two balls: The center (A) holds a ball, and one player in the circle (B) holds a ball. They toss at the same time, with B tossing to A and A tossing to C, the person to the left of B. The catches must occur at precisely the same time. Passing continues around the circle clockwise. Again, any player can call the "Go!"

Side Coaching

- Serve the center.
- Serve your partner by giving a good throw.
- Listen to the rhythm; look for the optimal timing to call the "go"; only the leader can change the tempo.
- Get "ready" without getting tense; breathe, relax, project your intention through the ball. Be patient, contribute to the rhythm.

Cutting the Space

I often give actors precise physical tasks unrelated to any psychological motivation: "As you move this chair, set it exactly two inches from the leg of the table." This practice develops spatial sense, kinesthetic sense, heightened focus, and brings truth to their actions. The following exercise also reveals how different bodies accommodate to spatial demands—some will use their legs, some their spines, and so on. There is no *right* way to do it.

A group of seven or eight students stand at one end of the space. They visualize a line running from a point on their foreheads to the floor along a diagonal that bisects the rectangle of space. They move along the line, keeping the point on their foreheads aligned with the invisible line. The goal is to create a smooth, unbroken line as they descend, eventually placing their foreheads on the floor at the other end of the room.

To play: Stand at one end of the room. Using your own height as the height of the space and the length of the room as the width of the space, visualize a diagonal line from your forehead to a spot on the floor at the other end of the room. Using your forehead as a "chalk," trace that line in the space, descending until you have placed your forehead on the spot at the other end of the room.

Reverse, beginning lying on the floor, visualizing the point at which you will be standing when you have arrived standing at the other end of the room.

Tempo variations: In slow motion, in fast motion.

Imaginary circumstances: Carrying an object (shoe, book). Imagine the object is of great value and that you have retrieved it for your clan from some faraway place. You are entering the great hall of your people to lay it at the feet of your leaders. It is urgent that you bisect the space exactly. Or, holding branches, you are Birnham Wood coming to Dunsinane.

Inside Out and Outside In

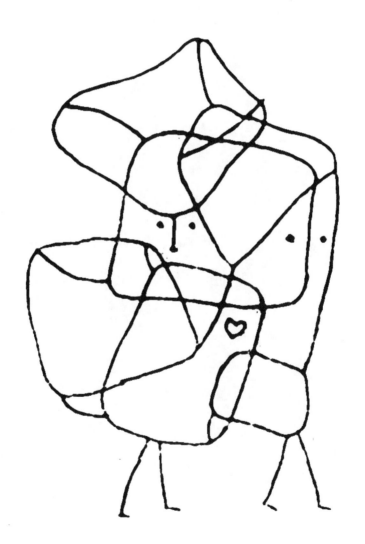

Synergizing Internal and External Acting

Jill Mackavey

A re you an innie or an outie?" My eyebrows shot straight up to my hairline, as I clutched the phone in disbelief. "An innie or an outie?" I asked back. "Yes," said the cheery voice on the other end of the line, after the telltale conference-call echo and time-lapse. "An innie or an outie (*Echo*) outie, outie, outie . . . ?" (*Pause. Sigh.*) "Is your approach to acting an internal approach or an external approach?" Of course, I knew what he was referring to. I was just a bit stunned by the Seussian cuteness of the question. "Both," I replied honestly, confident that I'd made it past the trick question. "Oh," said he. (*Silence, silence, silence, silence . . .*)

INNIE OR OUTIE?

That is an excerpt from a phone interview I underwent for a faculty position in a university theater program. At the time of the interview, I was finishing my postgrad studies in Movement Analysis at The Laban/Bartenieff Institute of Movement Studies in New York City. I was the mother of a feisty toddler, living in a fourth-floor walk-up in Brooklyn, and completely juiced about my studies, the mask work I was doing, and about teaching and directing. The interview had been scheduled for a set time, and I'd managed to procure a babysitter who would entertain my son during the call. The phone rang right on time, and I answered in my four-by-six "eat-in" kitchen. All was right with the world, until . . . "Are you an innie or an outie?"

As the interview continued, I attempted to explain to the disembodied mob on the other end of the line why I was both innie *and* outie, how I sought to integrate both schools of thought, blah blah synergy, blah blah Laban; but it was too late. To them (innies, it turned out), my position smacked of disloyalty to both camps, and they saw me rather like a sloppy stepchild who tries to get along with everyone and pleases no one. Naturally, I could sense their feelings, and by the end of the interview, I found myself, to my great surprise, standing with one foot on a kitchen chair and the other several feet away, on the edge of the sink. It was a disastrous phone interview but an absolutely stageworthy moment of inner and outer synergy. If only they'd seen it. Aloft in my kitchen, I was revealing physically the fullness of my inner passion. With optimistic energy and, I'd like to think, a certain comic nobility, I took my stand above the sink, as the interview went down the drain.

THE KING'S AND QUEEN'S VIEWPOINTS

Many actor-training programs, whether professional classes or university-conservatory programs, teach with a strong external or internal bias under the direction of a guru, be he live or be he dead, or one of the guru's disciples. In the United States, the bias is generally toward the internal. The split between camps is further emphasized by programs that offer courses in internal acting approaches, while the movement courses focus on external techniques (or vice versa), with little or no mixing of the two. To compound the problem, students often favor the approach they would benefit from the least. The setup isn't doing anybody any good, least of all the art of theatermaking itself.

The Feud at Court—The King

His majesty, the outie purist, emphasizes technical expertise and careful observation of behavior (movement) and speech patterns. He notes, for example, that when anxious people are behind the clock, they tend to sniff a lot, fidget with their clothing, and become rigid in posture. He then puts on behaviors appropriate to his character's personality, emotional state, and situation. These decisions are based on thorough intellectual and intuitive analyses. His majesty then crafts his performance around certain key moments—the double take, the laugh lines, the reversal of fortune. Emphasis in rehearsal and performance is on scoring and shading text and movement, mastering subtle and not-so-subtle technical choices, and their resulting effect on the audience. Dangers include lack of thoroughness in the preparation of a role, shallow, artificial, or dry performances, an inability to handle unexpected changes, imperviousness to scene partner(s), unfilled pauses, scene stealing, lack of momentum, posturing, and the chewing of scenery. Benefits may include attentiveness to the music and shape of the play and character development, entertainment value, connection to audience, and precision of delivery.

The Honorable King: There's More to Him Than Meets the Eye

Ironically, there is more to honor in the king's approach than first meets the eye. Many benefits proceed from properly employed externals. A clever or inventive choice is often the very thing that captures an actor's imagination and draws him into the internal journey of discovery. Sometimes an actor may have an idea that seems to pop up out of nowhere, that *appears* to have come from an external source. The queen's house of innie purists may say, "That's rubbish. It's contrived. It's inorganic," and discard it because they are unable to trace its lineage. I say that it's probably straight from his genius. Let it fly!

Flight from oneself. *Paul Klee, 1931*[1]

External aspects are also *necessary* to each and every role. These vital components include:

- The action(s) by which the actor manifests the character's desires; the visible intention or objective—*"to pulverize the bastard!"*
- External obstacles from the text, such as environmental obstacles—*my ankles and wrists are manacled*; and obstacles that are inherent in a given relationship—*I'm a woman in love with a gay man*, or *my daughter is insane.*
- Textual conditions, such as movement, manners, and clothing conventions of a particular place and time—*seventeenth-century France*; ensemble movement culture—*in* The Tempest, *how do the royals move as an ensemble that is different from the ensemble movement of the enchanted folk?*; ethnic-national-familial movement cultures—*how are the movements of the villagers in*

Gogol's The Inspector General *different from those of the Inspector General himself? In* West Side Story, *how are the movements of the Sharks different from those of the Jets? How are the sisters' movements in* Marvin's Room *similar?*

- Required physical adjustments, exaggerated or subtle—*Laura's limp, Richard's hump, Caliban's deformity;* or physical adjustments strongly implied by style, such as by Commedia dell'Arte stock characters. For example, Commedia's Coccodrillo most certainly deserves a phallus-powered walk.

External techniques can also be used to stimulate inner response. Using various *external* stimuli in order to call forth an *inner* response, and to heighten and develop *inner* responsiveness, is an indispensable way to generate organic physicality in an actor. Experiences of this sort also create deep trenches in the memory and forge surefire connections between stimuli, inner awakenings, and dynamic expression. External stimuli and experience are requisite to the development of a vulnerable, pliable heart, and a well-oiled responsiveness to real or imaginary situations.

The Buddhist monk and well-known author Thich Nhat Hanh says that smiling will generate an inner peacefulness.[2] In other words, the external practice of smiling leads to inner transformation, a transformation of the person's inner reality. External acting techniques include moving in a certain way in order to transform inner physical or psychological states. Robré, a former student, recently shared with me the following insight: "When I could shake myself out of my laid-back zone, as a result of running late or otherwise getting my heart racing, my performances were much more energized. During a recent performance I should have run around the auditorium a few times to get myself activated." The external practice of getting his heart racing by means of vigorous physical activity is essential to this actor being able to rise up and out of his casual style. External practice leads to internal transformation, which leads to vivid expression.

Need the actress playing Sonya in *Uncle Vanya* experience the rush of love? She needs a physical prep! Get her out of her dreamy mind-set, her ideas about love, and into her body. Have her run up and down four flights of stairs. Body overload! Racing heart, blood-filled organs, flushed and lively. Now, that's a place to start. External, yes. Mechanically induced, yes—and transformational.

The Feud at Court—The Queen

Her majesty, the innie purist, argues that once the inner life of a character is understood, and the actor makes personal and imaginative connections with the motivations, desires, needs, and personal history of the character, then appropriate and stageworthy behavior will naturally spring forth.[3] She knows all sorts of things about her character that the outie rejects as poppycock—what her character ate for breakfast, the disastrous effect mother's miscarriages had on her as a youngster, regardless of whether mumsey is mentioned in the play or not, her sexual quirks, and favorite sleepwear. The innie purist may even search for an appropriate psychological diagnosis for her character in the DSM-IV.[4] Emphasis in rehearsal and performance is on preparation, motivation, and working toward the revelation to the audience of the inner life of her character. Dangers may include self-indulgence, self-importance, submerged, inactive portrayals, generalization (all anger looks alike), inattention to style-appropriate behavior, lack of humor, and passive preparations for the rigors of physical or explosive scenes. Characterizations may be in the queen's own image rather than in the image of the independent spirit of the character. Benefits include commitment to authenticity, process, willingness to share inner life, and openness to inner surprises.

The Queen: Royalty Is in Her Blood

The internal life is how a character is wired; it is its heartbeat and very soul. It provides grounding for the actor and should awaken his compassion, interest, and fascination. It is the primordial bath where one steeps and brews the character.

Vital components of internal acting include:

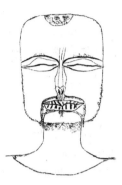

Absorption. *Paul Klee, 1919* [5]

- The motivation behind the action—*Lady MacBeth's intention in Act II, Scene i might be "to steel my husband's nerves," because her* internal motivation *is "my lust for power has set me on the rack," and her* inner obstacle *is "his cowardice repulses me!"* Motivations and obstacles are based on a character's psychological makeup—dreams, hopes, fears, and ambitions—as well as on several of the items that follow.

- Internal physical condition, such as robust health, or a *specific* illness—*George III's porphyria*[6] *in* The Madness of King George—and basic temperament—*lethargic, passive, nervous.*

- Internalized cultural or historic taboos and values—*Desdemona from* Othello *lives and breathes the culturally defined virtue of chastity and eschews all behavior, speech, and thought to the contrary.*

- Character's thought and intellect. Often, characters are driven by intellectual ideals, such as the many philosophizers that people Chekhov's plays. The intellect is at the core of who they are.

- Spirituality; the source of meaning and purpose in one's life.

- Physical appetites, such as drives for food, activity, rest, coupling.

- Relational appetites, such as the desire, or lack thereof, for solitude, romantic love, sexual intimacy, emotional intimacy, friendship, brother/sisterhood, etc.

- Inner tempos and rhythms that are discovered in the character's language and actions—*steady, emphatic, explosive, impulsive, swelling, fading.*

- Preferences and aversions to external, sensory stimuli. For example, a character may get physically ill when she *smells* whiskey, because her father was a drunk. When she takes a whiff, it opens the door to her woundedness and its behavioral manifestations.

- Approaches to conflict, whether direct—*confrontational, relentless, committed to truth-seeking, efficient*—or indirect—*avoiding, diplomatic, hedging, uncommitted.*

SYNERGY—THE ROYAL MARRIAGE

The word "synergy" is from the Greek *synergia,* meaning "joint work," from the longer *synergein,* "to work together." Synergy can be defined as the combined or cooperative action of two or more living, moving parts.[7] It suggests a dynamic relationship between parts such as those between the living organs of the body. So, too, with the external and internal aspects of acting. When taken to its fullest, one should always lead the way back to the other and, like living organs of the same body, work in dynamic cooperation.

Speaking to the inextricability of the internal and external, Saint Augustine in his *Confessions* states that the "soul knows itself through the senses." Shaun McNiff takes Augustine's idea further when he says, "the soul needs sensory images in order to experience itself."[8] Without the experience (outer manifestation), however subtle, there is no real soulful knowledge, no knowledge of one's deepest interior. However, once synergized with actual experience, the inner life has meaning. Until then, it is formless and unknown. It has no real experience of itself, and certainly offers no experience for an audience. Therefore, the expression of the inner life, the physicalization, actually *is* the experience.

Synergy's Face

What does external and internal synergy look like? Look for peak moments in people's lives. These moments are always felt in one's viscera and are immediately manifested in behavior. Spend time with a child right before his birthday and watch him, unable to contain himself within his own skin. Attend a ballgame and watch the fans rise *en masse*, holding their breath, physicalizing suspense as the possible homer heads toward the fence. Have a party on Super Bowl Sunday and watch a couch full of your usually mellow friends punch the air and pound their knees when the play is fumbled or the referee makes a bad call. Serve chocolate fondue to a chocoholic friend and watch her entire spine liquefy and transform into melted sweetness. Remember me on my kitchen chair.

In order to function synergistically in *imaginary* situations, actors must learn to respond to stimuli *viscerally,* as if having a peak experience. Take time to acknowledge your reactions to things. Where are these feelings located within your body? Grief, for example, has a *physical substance* that one can locate very specifically in one's body and that provokes response in varying degrees of intensity. In rehearsals and in offstage preparations, characters' inner lives must be similarly *physically* present within the actors.

Physical evidence of the inner state or conflict makes the internal life stageworthy, makes it worth sharing. If the inner life of spirit, thought, emotions, and physical state (congenital heart disease, consumption, for example) isn't incarnate, isn't able to be physically articulated and shared, but remains a private affair, it is nothing more than an exercise in self-indulgence, rather than the fuel of art.

Synergy—What For?

Shaun McNiff, in speaking about painting, writes, "The image belongs to the viewer as the poem is expropriated by the reader."[9] This leads me to ask, "For whom do we act?" We may answer that we act because we feel called to do so, or more simply, because we enjoy it. But ultimately, the creative act is to be shared and given away to the audience, who then assigns it a final meaning. The creative act cannot be shared until the internal and external are linked. There must be more at stake than personal significance motivating an actor to act in order to generate sufficient fuel for this synergy. In other words, you have to care about *communicating* to the audience more than you care about your own experience of acting.

We all must have a vision, a mythos to live by, but the ultimate question cannot be "where from," as all origins are a mystery, but wherefore, what for, for what's sake?[10] The ultimate answer, therefore, must respond to this ultimate question. It is not important *where* it comes from, but *for what's sake* it comes. In the case of acting, the answer must have something to do with communication and sharing. Be generous. Give it away! Through synergyzing internal and external acting, one is able to share with, and perhaps even transform, an audience. That is of ultimate significance.

FORMATION VERSUS PROCESS

Process speaks of time progression and is from the Latin *to proceed*. It suggests continuing development involving many changes and is a suitable word to use when speaking about artistic development. However, there is also a sense that process ends with the birth of some final product or package, such as "Opening Night" or "My First Broadway Show." Process's potency also has diminished, having become somewhat of a jargon word in the lexicon of creativity. The word I prefer is *formation*.

Formation comes from the Latin root meaning *to form* or *to shape*, as in the slow and ongoing formation of the earth. It also implies that we *are formed*. Our being formed into the artists we are called to be is a lengthy journey requiring great patience. In fact, it is a lifelong affair, with both the practical and romantic implications of the word "affair." Too often the assumption is that you must become "X" rather than to allow "X" to be formed within you. For example, many people wrongly believe they must become trained dancers in order to be fabulous movers or physically expressive actors. The seed of expressive movement is already in you, just as the seed of your artistry is already in you. You can block its development or, by allowing yourself to develop a finely tuned responsiveness, facilitate its formation.

Reminiscent of the unity that is so natural and evident in children and in peak experiences, somewhere in the course of one's formation, the internal and external begin to unite. Consistent internal and external synergy is part of the natural progression of artistic formation and is, in fact, its flashpoint. When the developing artist instinctively begins to express through a synergized internal and external vitality, thereby becoming an agent of transformation for the audience, the solely personal journey is left behind, and artistry begins.

Daimon—The Transcendent Aspect of Internal and External Acting

The original *daimon*[11] is a Greek word and has been explored extensively by Socrates, Aeschylus, Plato, Goethe, James Hillman, Nietzsche, Rollo May, Shaun McNiff, Thomas Moore, and countless others. With each discussion, the word reveals new dimensions. It is a roomy word, able to house significant and deep conversations within its chambers.

In Greek mythology, *daimon* refers to any secondary divinity that acts as an intermediary between the gods and mortals. Since antiquity, it has been referred to as a force of nature (Aristotle), one's character (Heraclitis), prudence or conscience (John Adams), or a spirit that claims a person at birth (Hillman).[12] Generically, it's been called the inner or inspiring voice and is linked to one's inner genius. It also has been linked to the word *demon*, as when one is seized by the darker aspects of the daimonic, such as by violent images or by unbridled aggression. For our purposes, it is important, however, to make a clear distinction between the daimonic force working within a person and the force of one's own personal power. James Hillman cautions that we must not reduce the daimonic spirit to anything other than its living presence—partnering it, imagining with it.[13]

The force of the daimonic, especially when experienced by artists during creative acts, is always experienced as if it is coming from a divine source, at least in part. This is in keeping with the original divine sense of the word. When seized by the daimonic, colors and other sensory input are experienced more vividly, and time opens up into eternal vastness. It is also experienced as synergy of internal and external expression on the deepest possible level.

Paradoxically, the daimonic seems to come from a divine source as well as from the *inner*most, most *particularly you* part of yourself. I liken it to an erupting volcano. The eruption comes over the lip of the volcano, involves the deepest parts of the volcano, demands its full participation, but the stuff of the eruption comes from a force deeper than the volcano, from within the core of the earth itself. Unlike volcanic eruptions, daimonic expression is not *necessarily* destructive. There is, however, always the presence of a force with the daimonic that feels powerfully right, as if one is seized by some Truth.

It is arrogant and illusory to believe that everything is under our control and direction. Our tendency to prize the personal too highly, to habitually sanitize and squelch powerful, disturbing, or absurd images and impulses, and to emphasize the importance of our almighty wills dwarfs our inspirited world. There is so much beyond our personhood! In many real-life situations, willpower and self-regulation are perfect choices. Personal control is also important in developing discipline as an artist. But beyond the personal, and beyond the boundary of what we call acceptable, is the stuff of transcendent art, and necessary for full, synergized expression.

Most discussions about integrating the external and internal elements of acting stop short of the transcendent. Once psychology and behavior are married, the case is closed. But what about the daimonic aspects of our art? Plays of all kinds have spirits embedded in their language and forms. Ugly spirits. Disturbing spirits. Dazzling, razor-sharp spirits. Characters have distinct spirits, too, of all sorts. Put on a mask; its spirits attend it closely. Artists, within their subterranean depths, have lively spirits, dark and strange, powerful and wickedly funny, hungering to collaborate and be made known.[14] If you truly seek to integrate the outer and the inner in your acting work, the spirits of text—its language, structure, and characters (external)—and the daimonic part of your artistry (internal) are essential elements that need acknowledgment and voice.

Undefended Presence—A Perk Along the Way

In the course of your formation as an artist, you may begin to notice yourself becoming more and more of an Undefended Presence. *Vulnerability*, *availability*, *receptivity*, and least inspiring of all, the state of *neutral*, are terms used frequently in training to describe desirable conditions for actors to achieve. These terms are related to Undefended Presence, but lack its radiance. Undefended Presence is receptive *and* responsive. Vulnerability and the others, especially the inert neutral, carry no invitation, offer no radiating energy, and lack the gift of charisma. Their energy tends to pull inward. Undefended Presence draws in *and* radiates out in a free-flowing, neurosis-free way. It doesn't carry the needy and apologetic implications that often attend vulnerability and is more animated than the somewhat passive availability. An Undefended Presence is ready and relaxed, and deeply compelling. Its doors swing both ways, an essential condition for synergy. Connections between psychology and behavior are possible, as are connections with the transcendent aspects we have just discussed. Undefended Presence is not a blank slate but a luminosity that exposes the transcendent. It is not artifice, but artistry. It is you as the artist revealed.

We all are able to recognize its opposite—the *de*fended presence. Symptoms include behavior that is guarded, needy, self-conscious, self-consumed, overly sentimental, manipulative, or exhibitionistic. Admittedly, defenses sometimes have charm, as in shyness, coyness, or adolescent experiments with bravado. But usually, we feel as if we can't really connect with defended people, as if they are "somewhere else," or wrapped in gauze.

When you experience yourself as an Undefended Presence, you feel deeply safe. You are not immune to trouble or fear, stage fright or slip-ups, but feel safe nonetheless. There is also a quiet joyousness that accompanies this sense of safety. All of your blemishes are completely visible to others, to the audience, and yet they contribute to the beauty of your Presence rather than detract from it. Again, you feel connected with, and supported by, something *other than you*. Undefended Presence is not a manufactured attractiveness, requiring knowledge of fashion or a well-toned body. It is beautiful, both because of and in spite of one's idiosyncrasies. Internal and external are synergized and energized. You are a fully responsive artist, efficient of energy, completely engaged and engaging. An Undefended Presence is able to hold everything lightly, to act without emotional muscularity (forcing, heaving, heaviness, generalities), sensitive to humor and irony, and is a conduit for Human Truth. Such persons have the power to transform audiences, and all who witness their work sense these actors' abilities to really "nail it." Truth will *always* equal specificity of expression, and an Undefended Presence is a vehicle for Truth.

ACTIVATING AGENTS

Activate, stimulate, get them going, galvanize;
Set 'em off, turn 'em on, fire 'em up, pressurize.
Stir, move, rouse, fuel, fan, coax, instigate;
Collaborate, motivate, electrify, and suscitate.

C'mon now baby, c'mon.
C'mon now baby, come-ON!

Teacher—Activator and Partner

Acting teachers, movement teachers, and directors need to do all of this and more. We need to be able to recognize and cultivate the fertility within our students and to be deeply concerned

About to take a trip. *Paul Klee, 1927*[15]

with their artistic formation. I particularly like the word "suscitate" in connection with teaching and directing. The most fundamental aspect of human movement, breath, is carried on the tongue of suscitate. By seeking to engage students on the deepest levels of their beings, we may be able to breathe life into the nascent artists that already exist within them. The students' job is to cultivate "suscitability"—the ability to be stirred awake—and to commit fully to their formation.

As a teacher, I begin with the fundamental belief that each of my students is an artist, uniquely talented, who shares my passion for our art. Meeting the artist in another person, encountering the daimon within her, is an *extraordinary* privilege. I seek to honor that and work to have students honor that in each other. It is a type of intimacy some surgeons must feel as they work within the body of a fellow human being, or that a priest must feel as she ministers to the spiritual needs of another. Teaching offers an opportunity for intense engagement with the essence of another person, the inner artist, the stirring daimon.

Initially, I work to intuit what might reach a given individual. It is not a one-size-fits-all approach. I attempt to discern how I can connect with that which I am striving to bring forth in each *particular* artist, without manipulating it into something it is not meant to be. I dance with it, listen to it, show it to itself, create an environment that it seeks or that it can't resist. If the structure of the course permits, I am inclined to begin with a session in Authentic Movement.[16] This allows the actors/movers to forge new connections and to explore what might be emerging for them as artists. It also allows me and the other students a chance to listen intuitively with our bodies to what is being spoken by the mover. I use this information as a starting place for our partnership.

In Authentic Movement, students witness each other moving. The witnesses simply are asked to "hold the space for the movers." As they watch, they stay connected to the movers' experiences by listening with their bodies and drawing on paper whatever comes from the sensations of connection. In the language of images, colors, shapes, words, and their own physical stirrings, they engage with the movers.

Right from the start there is no separation between inner and outer. The development of empathy and responsiveness is crucial to synergy and happens here. They are not to interpret or explain what they witness and are forbidden to judge. Unanimously, students are happy to honor this prohibition, and most are eager for their turn to move.

The movers move with eyes closed, the only restriction being a caution to open their eyes when doing anything that might cause a painful collision. Students who are arrhythmic or consider themselves to be lousy dancers discover that they are able to move exquisitely and expressively. This is often a magically transforming experience for them. Trained dancers are able to wrestle with the restrictions of their formal disciplines and can begin to let go of composition and style-bound movement, should they feel an impulse to do so. Many find it enormously freeing to discover the wide range of expressivity outside the confines of choreography. Authentic Movement is also wonderful for physically challenged students. Those who cannot hope to do a fa*lap*-ball-change or *pas de chat* are able to benefit from liberating movement experiences from motorized wheelchairs. They can experiment with time fluctuations, spatial pathways, and gravity as they lean into tight spirals or drop an unresponsive leg emphatically to the ground with the aid of an assisting arm. Still others are able to uncover a wide range of physical expression for inner impulses while stretching, traveling, and experimenting from the floor.

Many times, I'll have students warm up by improvising to music. I'll play a long piece to begin with, something outside the contemporary repertoire. Again, students begin with eyes closed. No one is watching except for me. The only rule is that they must enjoy themselves. I instruct, "If you aren't having fun, you're doing it wrong. Try something else." I am able to watch students actively engaging with their inner sensations and with the images that arise from the music, synergyzing the internal and external, and expressing themselves with joy. I watch for physical and emotional preferences and how each student approaches new experiences.

While the students continue to move to the music, I call out a movement term that I want the group to explore. I consistently use the non–style-based movement vocabulary of Rudolf Laban, which gradually becomes our common language. I keep a large music library on hand to pull from. To evoke directional or bound flow movement, I might play Philip Glass's *Knee 1* from *Einstein on the Beach*; for mid-reach space and emanating energy, Edith Piaf singing "La Vie, L'Amour"; for lightweight movements, Mandy Patinkin's version of "Always"; for breath-initiated shape variations, Lauryn Hill's "Nothing Even Matters" or Claude Debussy's "Claire de Lune." As they improvise, I join in from time to time, modeling the movements, fueling the spirit of experimentation and play, or partnering someone in order to call their attention outward, into a deeper exploration, or to reinforce something terrific that they are doing. I'll ask them to explore a given movement by traveling across the space, by leading with an underfunctioning body part—their abdomens or backs—to work as a group or in partners. I may gently touch them, on the head, for instance, asking them to take the movement through their spine, all the while actively seeking to draw them into meaningful relationship with the many dimensions of their physicality. In this, music is an indispensable tool.

As a course progresses, I design and reshape movement exercises to loosen deeply entrenched physical patterns and to reach the sleepiest, most inactive or defended parts of my students. I also pay attention to the materials the students are drawn to or avoid and to their vocal choices. For example, if a student is always trying to make things look orderly or controlled, it may be time to wake up the chaos in him. Exercises could include my having him create impromptu movement phrases that take him off-vertical into vigorous explorations of the horizontal plane. He could be required to work on flying and falling patterns or on exercises where he experiences dizziness before launching into text. I'd prescribe deeply conflicted roles for him to work on, such as Judas Iscariot from *Jesus Christ Superstar* or, for a female, Marquise de Merteuil from *Les Liaisons Dangereuses*. Romping, bawdy comedy roles would be appropriate as well.

A limitation I frequently see in students, particularly among those who take aerobic classes regularly, are avid weight lifters, or those who are heavyset, is the tendency to move their torsos and heads as single units, in symmetrical patterns. These students often need to work on cross-lateral movements, carving movements, and on exercises that explore subtle shape changes in their torsos—hollowing, lengthening, narrowing, bulging, etc. They benefit from working on oily, duplicitous characters and on characters that approach the world from an indirect point of view—Iago, Blanche DuBois, or almost any of Tennessee Williams' women. When students finally begin accessing these new movement possibilities naturally, bright lights switch on in their psyches, and amazing breakthroughs occur.

It is also important to listen for students' strengths. Notice, for instance, if they are intellectually awake and driven or connect easily with their partners. Listen intuitively, and dowse for opportunity to bring their artistry forth.

Perhaps this all sounds somewhat cosmic, as if there were a silver bullet that will pierce through to an artist's heart and magically synergize her acting. This is not the case. There is the Guru School of Acting that would like you to believe that there is a way that is The Way for all actors. But in reality, most often, that which will have the greatest impact on a developing artist is not cosmic at all. Rather, it is the right music, choice of material, partner, movement experience, or joke, at the right, or even the wrong moment.

Can, for example, an actress who is deeply cut off from her sensuality remain unaffected when she is encircled by a garnet-red, velvet stole and asked to partner the fabric, using carving movements, to strains of a Vivaldi cello concerto? Can an actor stuck in an emotional black hole resist sending his longings out into the far reaches of the movement space when a gritty rendition of Otis Redding pleading, "Try a Little Tenderness," calls to him from the studio boom box?

As a teacher trying to help students synergize the internal and external aspects of acting, you must participate as an artist. Question and challenge, engage and partner, not what you see on the surface, but that which you are hoping to bring forth, artist to artist. Model the movement for your students; inspire by *doing*. Take risks yourself. Sure, you need time to observe, to watch from an evaluative position, but you must, at the very least, participate enough to be able to lead the students into partnering each other. Tell stories—after all, that's what drama is about—that help them connect to certain movements. Use examples from dramatic literature. If you want students to be fully awake to smells, sounds, tastes, design elements, humor, people, and language, make sure these are built into the course structure and incorporated into your movement exercises. Integrate these things in your classroom and rehearsals, and the students will be much more likely to develop a holistic artistry.

The original Hellenic sense of *daimon*[17] had room for both the light and dark forces. The studio, too, is an arena that allows the full spectrum of images and expressions necessary to artistic formation to coexist. Teach to the whole student, and she will bring her whole self to her acting.

The Environment

Finding the right environment to explore your artistry is crucial to your formation. Environments can nurture and activate, or they can stunt and block. Students should seek out or institute performance venues and studio opportunities that support "degenerate art." Degenerate Art (*entartete kunst*) was a derogatory term used by the Nazis to describe art that was neither conventional, classical, nor a literal rendering of subject matter. In 1937, the Nazis held a show designed to denigrate this type of art and artists. Pictures were deliberately hung askew, and insulting remarks were posted next to the works. Marc Chagall, Max Ernst, Wassily Kandinsky, Paul Klee, and Max Beckmann were among the 109 artists shown. Paul Klee, whose drawings appear in this essay, wrote, "Art does not reproduce the visible: it *makes* visible."[18]

Actors frequently stop themselves from *making visible* their artistry in synergized expression by believing it degenerate, that is, somehow inferior when compared to performances by commercially successful actors whose style or popularity they may wish to *reproduce* or emulate. Their real artistry remains submerged and their external expressions lifeless. They resemble artificial flowers stuck in fertile soil. Actualization of synergized artistry is impossible, because any impulse toward expression thought to be wrong, unattractive, or unconventional is killed off before introduced into consciousness. We've all had friends who've wanted to be the next Harrison Ford or James Brown. Are any Elvis impersonators out there really exploring their own creativity? Fear of failing to live up to a narrow or conventional standard of art has kept many actors from risking the discovery of their genius. In honest formation, we may learn that it is only in the making of "degenerate art" that we will uncover the particularity of our artistry.

Another aspect of environment that is important in synergy is our ability to apply to our acting our inborn sensitivity to place. McDonald's is made of red and yellow plastic. No one can linger comfortably at Micky D's; you're not supposed to. It has been designed to do a volume business, to get people in and out lickety-split. The Museum of Modern Art in New York City has a very horizontal pull to it when you walk in. The architecture of the space encourages you to look all around and to enter into relationship with the artwork. Most cathedrals, on the other hand, do exactly the opposite. You do not look from side to side at your neighbors, but up to the heavens or forward toward the altar. Cathedrals are designed to inspire awe and facilitate your connection with God. Architects and designers take advantage of our sensitivity to place and atmosphere. So should we! We make decisions based on these sensitivities all the time, whether we're choosing a seat on the bus or where to buy our groceries. Why do we go numb when we act? Our sensitivity to environment must carry over into our acting by our being responsive to set, costume, and lighting designs. We must carry our sensitivity to body language and spatial relationships into our acting, just as we do when we send a nonverbal message to a talkative coworker that we're not interested in listening to her today, or when recognizing from across the room that the slippery guy with the hairy chest is about to make his move. We also must pay attention to how our inner shifts manifest themselves through our physicality into our environment.

Rehearsal clothing must be considered when discussing environment as an activating agent. We've all heard actors say, "Everything comes together for me when I get my costume on." This makes sense and indicates receptivity to environment and stylistic demands. Unfortunately, student actors frequently dismiss the importance of appropriate rehearsal and classroom clothing. Here is the proper place for the word *neutral*. Insist on neutral clothing in the movement studio. Students, your tattoos have intense personal significance. Cover them. Leave your jewelry home; ditch the ball cap. These things absolutely matter. If you are invulnerable to the influence that your favorite Bulls jersey and crack-revealing jeans have on you, then you will be invulnerable to everything that is worth experiencing in your classes and rehearsals.

Marital arts students bow each time they enter or exit their dojo. Whenever my children and I drive away from our home, we say, "Bye, house. See you soon," and upon our return, we offer a greeting. My husband begins and ends his visits to his parents' grave by gently patting the headstone. Each of these simple rituals warms the place through our attentions.[19] If we want to bring forth our richest creative work and set free the transcendent elements of our artistry, it is important that we likewise warm our studio spaces. Wouldn't you prepare your home by cleaning it, swabbing the bathroom, and removing clutter if you were expecting an honored guest to dinner? It is no different when we are preparing the space that supports our creative efforts.

TOOLS FOR SYNERGY

There is a trinity of tools that is essential for synergyzing internal and external acting: naming, language, and fun.

Naming—A Context for Meaning

Many cultures and religious traditions hold naming ceremonies to officially recognize and welcome children into a family, ancestry, or faith community; others recognize an individual's passage into the adult community. Naming practices also include the changing of one's name when one marries or when one joins an organization in which the individual identity is given in service to the greater goals of the group, as in religious orders (e.g., Mary Smith becomes Sister Immaculata) and militant organizations (e.g., Patty Hearst becomes Tania). In the book of *Genesis*, God Himself names people after they reach a certain depth in their relationship with Him. Sarai becomes Sarah, Abram becomes Abraham, and Jacob becomes Israel, the father of a nation.[20] Their lives, while still shaped by private concerns, thereafter are lived out *in a context of meaning* that extends far beyond the personal sphere. Far from being a limiting practice, naming enlarges and bestows great significance upon that which is named.

Study this line drawing:

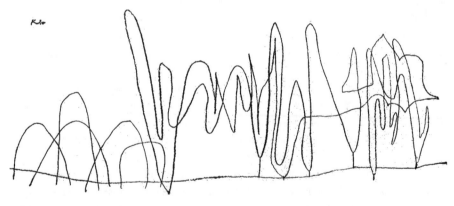

Paul Klee, 1934.

It may impart a certain feeling to you, you may like it or not, you may think it resembles one thing or another, or nothing at all. It may suggest a tempo, a type of energy, or simply irritate you. It may look like an EKG or polygraph test. But when I tell you that its *name* is "Avenue with Trees,"[21] you can begin to follow its line from west to east, as if you are traveling the tree-lined road. As a result of the naming, your journey into the drawing takes on form, and by your interacting with it, specific communication (art!) begins. You begin to imagine that the trees are poplars or cypresses, that you're in Paris or Greece, walking alone in the noonday sun. Naming the drawing has not limited it, or your experience of it, but rather, has released it from the subjectivity of your inchoate impressions by providing a greater context for its meaning. It retains its own spirit and also is animated by your dynamic imaginings.

Naming is the antidote for flabby thinking, sloppy feeling, and muddy acting. Be specific in the naming of your intentions.[22] The intention of "to get him to tell me" will *not* draw the inner life of a character into meaningful synergy with external expression. However, the intention of "to wheedle it out of the despot" suggests a *specific* internal attitude with regard to the other character, hints that the approach needs to be covert, aligns the actress with the style of the piece, and primes her physicality for specific, *playable* action. Only that which is playable has communicative power. I cannot play "to get." It is a first-grade verb and stylistically meaningless. I can, however, play "to wheedle." As soon as I ingest its name, my body responds. My knees bend a little, shoulders become activated, body posture softens. I move indirectly through space, sometimes playfully, sometimes furtively, in support of the secrecy implied by "wheedle." Perhaps, going into a rehearsal, "to get" is all I know. I can start there and rehearse several specifically *named* intentions—"to charm the snake," "to squeeze it out of the tyrant"—until I am able to bring the inner world of my character to life in a way that bears the unique mark of my artistry. The nonspecific, "to get him to tell me," has great meaning and communicative power once it is specifically *named*, "to wheedle it out of the despot."

Language—Action's Muse

Language is the energy, the life force, of a play. It is the incantation that carries the awakened spirit of a play to the audience or the incoherent curse that backfires in an actor's throat. Language is three-dimensional, having weight, proportion, volume, and energy. It is the architect of action, the blueprint of thought, the cupid of feeling. Get to know language as thoroughly and intimately as you would your desired lover. "To seduce" does not carry the same energy as "to tempt." The energy of Mamet's language is different from that of Noel Coward.

Language is an incurable tease to an artist. Allow it to romance you, to *form* you. Read poetry aloud to develop your language sensitivity—Galway Kinnell, Dylan Thomas, e.e.cummings. Whisper it. Sing it. If you can't connect with the soul of a word or phrase, it may reveal itself to you through movement. Dance your way through Langston Hughes's "The Weary Blues." Do you hear the daimon of the piece? What is its feeling, shape, action, muscle?

It is our job to rise and synergize ourselves with the spirit of a text as it is revealed through its language. How can we, for example, rise to fulfill and communicate the implications of the phrase, "I am undone?" Too often, actors wish to tame a phrase like this by translating it into safe and colorless contemporary language. Even while retaining the words, "I am undone," the energy of expression is more like a defeated exhaling of, "Shit." But "I am undone" is a complete descent into turmoil for she who is undone! How can we celebrate with our *physicality*, in movement, the magnitude of undoing, the implications of undoing? Undoing must not be reduced in the actor's mind to a common expletive he grumbles in traffic. "Shit" has the finite energy of a glob of dough being flung from a spoon. I can express the totality of its energy with a quick, direct, sagittal head toss. But *"Undone!?"* Oh, that *undone* carries a much different physical energy! It carries the energy of trembling fingers struggling to undo twenty tiny buttons on a tight bodice after a seven-course dinner, or the frantic buttoning-up of the same bodice after a lustful indiscretion. Undone has the energy of the desolate Rapunzel lowering her cascading tresses to the witch below, and of a brown paper bag, weakened by a soaking rain, releasing five pounds of gorgeous tomatoes onto the muddy floor of the #2 train at rush hour. It is a downward corkscrewing, a spilling. It is beyond repair.

Whether a text is written in contemporary, straightforward prose or is lilting with rhyming couplets, we must honor action's muse, language, by rising to animate its specific nature.

Fun and Celebration—We Do Not *Have* Bodies, We *Are* Bodies[23]

Children move all the time, and they wouldn't move a muscle if wasn't fun. They test their bodies and push their limits—*wow, look what this limb can do. I can balance on this wall, I can fling myself down this hill!* This is our heritage. We, too, need to find enjoyment in moving if we are ever going to employ in our artistry the enormous range of physical expression of which each of us is capable. The movement studio is the place to reconnect with just how much fun it is to *be* a body.

Another word for "actors" is "players." The movement studio is the place to play and celebrate how every inch of you moves. Find out what your limitations are, and work to move beyond them. Find out where you have free and unlimited access to physical expression, and work to develop control within that facility. If it is easy for you to work in deep space (low to the ground), try letting that go for an entire day. See if you can access high space. Women, try wearing high-heels; men, firm-soled shoes. Stand up straight. Instead of sitting on the floor, find a stool, and perch. Get your eyes off the ground. Look around. What do these physical adjustments suggest to you emotionally? There will be a change in your internal awareness. Your job is to sense, respond, and catalogue these changes.

We can experiment *within our present capabilities*, and whenever possible, seek to expand them. Let's celebrate what we can. My father, during the last year of his life, was rarely able to walk without forearm crutches, due to a cancer that was located primarily in his lower spine. He was a very tall man, and with his feet planted as the pivot point in the center of his narrow kitchen, he was able to accomplish many domestic tasks without crutches. Using the counter for support, he'd tilt toward the sink, grab a washed plate, dry it, and push off with his arms, tilting toward the opposite counter, where he'd put the dish away. He made coffee, prepared snacks for guests, and fed his pets by employing and *enjoying* the strength in his arms and chest and by taking advantage of his great length and the dimensions of the space itself. From the confines of armchairs, some old people use canes to push things, pass things, drag things closer, express delight and displeasure with taps, thumps, and whacks. The canes become extensions of their bodies, much like swords to swashbucklers or fans to the ladies of the Restoration. This is a celebration of mobility.

Celebrate that you *are* a body, complete with the challenges and blessings of your individual anatomy. Don't let the fact that you have a big gut keep you from enjoying movement. A good exercise for working through blocks that you might have about your physicality or movement ability is to dance your disenfranchised body part. Choose a body part that, for functional, expressive, or cosmetic reasons, you dislike. What is its dance? What is its song? What does it have to say to you? Let it have its say! Discover just how bulgy you can make that stomach. Paunch it way the hell out there! Now, laugh. Now, growl. Walk about the room. Roll on the floor. What character is suggested to you by having the loosest, jiggliest, most bulging stomach in the world? Activate that gut! Let it lead you about the space. Let it introduce you to a stranger. Are you power hungry? Fed up with the entire world? Now, let it passively, sluggishly schlump out before you. What inner changes occur for you? What does this physicality suggest to you emotionally? What feels good about it? Rotten? Sexy?

"The soul desires to dwell with the body, because without the members of the body, it can neither act nor feel."[24] As long as we live, we *are* our bodies. Let's make the most of it.

A CLOSING THOUGHT

Next time, when I'm asked if I'm outie or in,
I'll reply, "I am both, from my toenails to chin.
I am both, I am both, sir! from id to libido.
I'm both, decked in leather or when wearing my Speedo."
And if you insist I choose one o'er the other,
I'll protest, "In and out are the twins of one mother.
This brother and sister, inseparable twins,
If parted, I promise, sir, nobody wins."

NOTES

1. Klee, Paul. *the thinking eye*, New York: George Wittenborn, Inc., 1964, 296.
2. Hanh, Thich Nhat. *Living Buddha, Living Christ*, New York: Riverhead Books, 1997.
3. This is possible, but highly unreliable, even when an actor is well along in his formation as an artist. It is an ideal that needs the support of external practices.
4. *Diagnostic and Statistical Manual of Mental Disorders*. Washington, D.C.: The American Psychiatric Association.
5. Klee, 20.
6. Porphyria is an abnormality of the hemoglobin that, in the early stages, causes a number of horrible symptoms, such as abdominal pain, constipation, weak limbs, fever, fast pulse, hoarseness, and dark red urine. Eventually, the nervous system is also affected, setting off a whole host of other problems that result in behavior resembling insanity. George III, in the late 1700s, was diagnosed as stark raving mad.
7. *Webster's New Universal Unabridged Dictionary*. New York: Simon and Schuster, 1983, 1851.
8. McNiff, Shaun. *Earth Angels*. Boston, Mass.: Shambala Publications, 1995, 235.
9. Ibid., 226.
10. "Five Questions to James Hillman: An Interview with James Hillman by Fabio Botto," Milan, Italy: Spring Publications, Inc., July 8, 1999. See: *http://springpubl.com/jh-interview.htm*.
11. Like the Greek gods and goddesses who are a blend of good and not-so-good qualities, the Greek *daimon* refers to both light and dark forces. The Latin *daemon* generally refers to the lighter forces. The German *das Dämonische*, as described by Johann Wolfgang von Goethe (1749–1832), refers to each man's unique, inborn, developmental force, the unalterable law of his own individual growth. In a character, a *daemonic* figure is endowed with a powerful, uncannily attractive individual force that sweeps other people along in its violent destiny. (See *das Dämonische, Benet's Reader's Encyclopedia*. New York: Harper and Row, 1965.)
12. "Wod and the Damonic," Wednesbury Theod, Eric Wodening, © Eric Wodening, 1998. Originally published in *Idunna*, vol. 4, issue 4, December 1992. See: *http://www.geocities.com/Athens/Atlantis/2575/wod.htm*.
13. Rephrased from "Five Questions to James Hillman, an interview by Fabio Botto."
14. For a moving portrait of the artistry of Alberto Giacometti illustrating this principle, see: May, Rollo, *The Courage to Create*. Toronto: George J. McLeod, Ltd., 1975, 84–85.
15. Klee, 26.
16. For more on Authentic Movement, pioneered by Mary Starks Whitehouse, read Whitehouse, Mary Starks, Janet Adler, and Joan Chodorow, *Authentic Movement: Essays*. (Edited by Patrizia Pallaro. London and Philadelphia: Jessica Kingsley Publisher, 1999); or participate in an Authentic Movement class.
17. McNiff, 106.
18. Bachmann, Marie-Laure. *Dalcroze Today: An Education Through and Into Music*. Oxford, England: Clarendon Press, 1993, 180.
19. McNiff, 119.
20. *Genesis*, 17:15, 17:5, 32:28.
21. Klee, Paul. *Avenue with Trees*, pencil, 1934. From: Klee, *the thinking eye*, 100.
22. Obstacles and motivations also should be specifically named.
23. Foster, Richard. *Challenge of the Disciplined Life*. New York: HarperCollins Publishers, 1985, 117.
24. Leonardo da Vinci, source unknown.

The Actor as Athlete of the Emotions: The Rasaboxes Exercise

Michele Minnick and Paula Murray Cole

We can no longer think of emotions as having less validity than physical, material substance, but instead must see them as cellular signals that are involved in the process of translating information into physical reality, literally transforming mind into matter. Emotions are the nexus between matter and mind, going back and forth between the two and influencing both.

—Candace Pert[1]

ARTAUD, SCHECHNER, THE *NATYASASTRA*, AND NEUROSCIENCE: ORIGINS OF THE RASABOXES

One of the twentieth-century theater's greatest debates was over the question of the *direction* of the actor's work: Does one approach it from the "outside-in" or the "inside-out"? In his essay "Rasa-esthetics," our teacher and colleague, performance theorist and experimental theater director Richard Schechner discusses a related question: the *"location* of theatricality,"[2] bringing into dialogue what may seem at first an unlikely trio: the classical Indian performance text the *Natyasastra,*[3] contemporary studies on neurobiology and psychology, and writings of the twentieth-century theater theorist and practitioner Antonin Artaud. With a closer look, one finds that all three are concerned with the same thing: a theory of a circular, rather than a binary relationship between emotion and the body, inside and outside, which focuses on a visceral, gut-based mode of perception, rather than a solely visual-auditory one.

Fascinated with the classical Indian theory of *rasa* (see below for an explanation), encouraged by the findings of contemporary science, challenged by Artaud's demand that the actor be an "athlete of the emotions,"[4] and undaunted by the warnings of much Stanislavsky-based training that an actor should never "play the emotion," Schechner designed the Rasaboxes exercises, the practical component to the theoretical argument of *Rasaesthetics*. He began teaching this exercise, which trains the performer's emotional-physical-vocal expressivity and agility, in performance workshops at NYU each summer. Since we began teaching these workshops ourselves several years ago, we have further developed the exercises

---

Authors' Note: In our experience, the Rasaboxes exercise is a form of movement training that directly affects an actor's work, as it immediately engages the entire complex of emotion-body-voice-imagination-character, which an actor must access when actually working on a role. Not only does it *directly* train the emotions, but it integrates physical and emotional training in a deeply personal way.

The Rasaboxes do not necessarily, however, train the body directly in terms of relaxation, alignment, flexibility, strength, etc., the way that other forms of physical training do. We recommend that the training be accompanied by a yoga practice or other form of physical warm-up that stretches, opens, and relaxes the body in a deep way.

The Rasaboxes are not meant to supplant other forms of actor training. A Rasaboxes-trained actor is not necessarily going to do away with objectives, through-lines, creative improvisations, and other widely used approaches. If these methods are used to answer the "what" questions of acting, the Rasaboxes can be used, in combination with them, to answer the "how" questions. Qualitative changes can be made by applying the idea of rasa to a character, a scene, even an entire play. At times, it is useful to think of rasa as a kind of tonality, or rhythm of performance, that can be modulated as the pitch and key or the tempo and rhythm of a piece of music can be modulated for a piece of music.

and applied the training to our performance work. In addition to its function as training, the Rasaboxes provide us with a way of developing character, creating "emotional performance scores," and emotionally preparing offstage in a direct, embodied, present-tense manner.

BASIC PRINCIPLES OF THE EXERCISE

The most basic principle of the Rasaboxes is that every idea an actor wants to communicate must somehow be embodied, received by and expressed in or through the body, even if it is only on the level of the breath. Ideally, the exercises outlined below set in motion a feedback loop between inner and outer: As emotion courses through the body, it shapes behavior according to its demands, and in turn, refuels the imagination and sparks physical impulses. Doing and manifesting intertwine with receiving and responding. When one becomes completely connected energetically to emotion, one is working in relationship to it from the outside, until it is the inside, and back again. Rather than focusing on either the inside or the outside, the Rasaboxes encourage a holistic approach to the relationship between the inner and the outer aspects of an actor's craft, generating a fruitful dialogue between mind and body through its focus on what Candace Pert refers to above as the "nexus" between the two.

Serving as a bridge between psychophysiology and expressiveness, the Rasaboxes develop a conscious working relationship between the actor's individual, physical body and emotions and her emotional-physical relationship to the environment and other performers. The exercises train performers to use emotion as an objective tool with which to develop and negotiate characters, scenes, entire plays, and performance scores. They can help the actor to make choices that are not only seen and heard by the audience, but also palpably experienced, viscerally engaged. In addition, the Rasaboxes can serve as a multidirectional training ground where habits and patterns can be brought to light and new choices can emerge.

Whether as a result of our cultural or our theatrical training or our individual histories, many of us have limited access to the experience or expression of certain emotions. We have observed the power of the Rasaboxes to free performers (ourselves included) to experience and develop a vast range of expressiveness, from very subtle film-sized acting to operatic or grotesque histrionics, without sacrificing "sincerity" or "truth." In fact, because of its focus on physical embodiment and expression, Rasaboxes training can serve to deepen a performer's ability to find authentic emotional connections that might have otherwise seemed unavailable to her. This training encourages the actor to approach his craft as a conscious, body-oriented process to which he holds the keys and the tools for his own development.

WHAT IS RASA?

"Rasa" is a Sanskrit word meaning, literally, essence, juice, flavor and can be found in ancient Indian Ayurvedic texts to describe the six flavors found in food: salty, sweet, bitter, sour, pungent, and astringent. This *property* of food is then used in the mixing of foods to balance the humors of the body—fire, water, and wind—which, in turn, reflect the material makeup of the universe. Rasa also refers to the tastes that are *perceived* in food. In the *Natyasastra*, rasa is described as the experience transmitted through performance, which, in the classical Indian forms that make use of the *Natyasastra*'s rasa theory, is an inextricable combination of dance, drama and music. In a chapter dedicated to rasa, Bharata, the perhaps real, perhaps mythical author of the *Natyasastra*, says:

Because it [performance] is enjoyably tasted, it is called rasa. How does the enjoyment come? Persons who eat prepared food mixed with different condiments and sauces, etc., if they are sensitive, enjoy the different tastes and then feel pleasure (or satisfaction); likewise, sensitive spectators, after enjoying the various emotions expressed by the actors through words, gestures and feelings feel pleasure, etc. This (final) feeling by the spectators is here explained as (various) rasa-s of natya.[5]

In this context, the experience of rasa is generated by the enacting of nine basic emotions (termed the "bhavas" in the *Natyasastra*) and their many possible combinations. As Schechner puts it,

The sthayi bhavas are the "permanent" or abiding" or indwelling emotions that are accessed and evoked by good acting, called *abhinaya*. Rasa is experiencing the sthayi bhavas. To put it another way, the sweetness "in" a ripe plum is its sthayi bhava, the experience of "tasting the sweet" is rasa. The means of getting taste across—preparing it, presenting it—is abhinaya. Every emotion is a sthayi bhava. Acting is the art of presenting the sthayi bhavas, so that *both* the performer and the partaker can "taste" the emotion, the rasa.[6]

The nine basic rasas and their corresponding emotions, loosely translated, are: sringara (love, the erotic), raudra (rage), karuna (grief, but also pity or compassion), bhayanaka (fear), bibhasta (disgust), vira (courage, virility), hasya (laughter, ridicule), adbhuta (wonderment, surprise), and santa (bliss, peace). The experience of these emotions takes place *between* the performer and the spectator in the moment of live performance. This shared space between is the location of rasa. The concept of pleasure is key here, both for performer and spectator. In a sense, both are tasting the emotion performed. Although some practitioners of classical Indian dance will say that they don't experience the emotions they are portraying, what's important is that they perform in such a way that the rasa of a particular emotion is enjoyed—savored like a good meal—by the audience.

How does one achieve this shared experience between actor and spectator? In classical Indian dance forms such as Kathakali, specific facial expressions corresponding to the nine basic emotions are learned and memorized by the dancer-actors and performed in highly complex combinations of rhythmic footwork, gesture, and other body movement, all of which are codified and performed as "traditional" dance-drama, with only slight variation from one generation of dancers to the next. But how does this idea of rasa relate to Western performance practice? Is there, after all, a way for Western actors to make direct, physical use of emotion, not undermining, but rather enhancing other modes of Western actor training? Can performers be what Artaud only imagined—"athletes of the emotions"? The Rasaboxes exercises described below form the field of our exploration and experimentation in answering these questions.

LANGUAGE: WHY SANSKRIT?

Before we begin our description of the exercises themselves, it is perhaps necessary to explain our relationship to the Sanskrit terms and the complex theory they reflect. In creating a training exercise designed primarily for application to performance practices outside the classical Indian dance-drama complex, we use the term "rasa" (both as part of the title of the training technique and within the exercises themselves) in particular ways that do reflect its original usage in the *Natyasastra*, but more accurately express the particular way in which Schechner reconfigures the term in "Rasaesthetics."[7] As you will see in our description of the basic exercises below, we also maintain the original Sanskrit words for each rasa. Schechner says of his choice to retain the Sanskrit terms:

> For me the reason has been so as to help students—none of whom in my practice have ever been literate in Sanskrit—to come up with their own equivalents to the rasas. That is why the exercise begins with the writing of words and the drawing of pictures. To use English (or any language the participants know) from the start would be to depersonalize and limit the range of meanings/feelings associated with particular rasas. And doubly so if the translation were my own. My "sringara" is not your "sringara," and it is important to me that during the exercise your sringara finds its place. Also the exercise is exploratory. You may not know what your "sringara" is until you go through the process of writing it out, moving through it, vocalizing it, etc. Finally, your "sringara" of today may not be, certainly will not be, your "sringara" of tomorrow. Organicity and aliveness in the sense of developing new meanings has for a long time been central to both my artistic and my scholarly work.[8]

Indeed, we have observed this freeing up of individual and changing associations to be true. In practice, each rasa emerges as a category or "family" of emotion, such as raudra, which contains a range of related emotions. We loosely translate the Sanskrit word "raudra" as "rage," but in addition to the many personal associations one might have to the concept of rage, it also implies many levels of emotional intensity related to raudra as a larger category: irritation, anger, vexation, and so on. So, in our use of the word, raudra is a rasa, irritation is an aspect of raudra.[9]

Finally, rather than codifying the expression of emotion through particular gestures and facial expressions that are always performed in the same way (as in classical Indian dance), our method is improvisational. While the Rasaboxes may give one a sense of dipping into a universal pool of emotion, the way each person makes contact with and expresses each emotion is specific to the individual and may change each time she engages in the exercise.

THE BASIC EXERCISES

The Grid

We begin by making a grid on the floor using tape or chalk, leaving space around the outside for people to view the exercise. The perimeter of the grid is approximately 18' × 15', creating nine equal-sized rectangles of roughly 6' × 5'. We usually work in an empty black-box space.

Introducing the Rasas

First, we assign each of the eight rasas randomly to each of the eight outer boxes, leaving the center box empty. This box is reserved for santa, a rasa added by Abhinavagupta several centuries after the *Natyasastra* was compiled. Reflecting the Buddhist influence that led to its addition as the ninth rasa, we have often interpreted santa as a state of detachment from the other emotions. Spatially located always in the center box, it performs in a certain sense like the eye of the storm surrounding it. We will explain how we use the santa box later.

We write the Sanskrit word for each rasa in the boxes on the floor with colored sidewalk chalk. If an appropriate floor is not available, we write on large pieces of paper taped to the floor. When all the rasas are in place, we walk around the grid and talk about each one, giving basic descriptions of each rasa, based on its traditional Sanskrit context and meaning, but also on our contemporary understanding of these eight emotional states. For example, we might talk about sringara as love, erotic or romantic love, love of a mother for her child, love for god, but also as physical pleasure, such as smelling sweet odors, tasting savory food, and so on.

After this phase, the grid will look something like this:

SRINGARA	BIBHASTA	KARUNA
RAUDRA		BHAYANAKA
HASYA	ADBHUTA	VIRA

Word-Image Association

In silence, participants enter each box, drawing and writing (in whatever language they choose) in the boxes their personal associations to each rasa. These associations can be different from one day to the next. This phase of the exercise finishes when everybody has made their contribution to each box and stepped outside the grid. These associations may include abstract designs, quotations from poetry, evocative images, and all together create a kind of associative graffiti for the group for that day.

Embodying the Rasas

We've experimented with many ways of beginning the work of physicalization. We usually begin with still poses that embody each rasa to its extreme. The important thing is that the rasa be fully physicalized, from head to toe, the whole body engaged in its expression. For example, in raudra (rage), the teeth might be bared, the fists clenched, the belly tight, the toes gripping the floor, the eyes glaring, nostrils flared, spine in an attitude of readiness, about to strike.

Although the poses are "still," the body is active, alive. Usually, people begin by creating and memorizing still poses for three or four rasas. Once these poses have been memorized, participants practice moving from one box to another, switching instantly from one pose to the next. The idea is to do this without preparation or transition between the rasa poses, doing each rasa as "purely" as possible—although we eventually combine rasas to achieve mixed emotions, in this phase, it is important to switch as completely as possible, without allowing one rasa to bleed into the next. This switching is the core of the Rasaboxes exercise, as it develops psychophysical agility, allowing performers to transform instantly from rage to love, from fear to grief, and so on.

Breath and Voice

Once the poses are established, we bring them more fully to life by engaging the breath, sensing how it should fill and animate the shape of the body. Then, the physicalization of the rasa shapes the voice. (It's also possible to begin the exercises with the breath or the voice and go from there to the body.) As Schechner notes:

> The first poses/sounds often have the quality of social clichés—of the "already known," that fit the rasas as casually understood. Big Laughs for hasya, clenched fists for raudra, weeping for karuna, and so on. The distance between stereotype and archetype is not great. Sooner or later, the social stereotype/archetype will be augmented by gestures and sounds that are more intimate, personal, quirky, unexpected. Practice leads one towards these. The road from outer to inner = the road from inner to outer.[10]

A relationship to the rasa, which may begin from a stereotypical image of an emotion, develops into an intricate dialogue between the performer and her own physiology and associative imagination. One can enter a Rasabox and taste the emotion from a feeling in a particular organ, an evocative visual image or sensation—seeing a lover, holding a stone in the hand, feeling the floor to be made of sand, a breeze on the skin—a personal memory, the shape the body makes, the weight of the body on the floor. The Rasaboxes exercises work as a kind of imprinting process, developing a connection between mind, body, and emotion, whereby the performer discovers specific keys that will open and reopen the pathways between inner sensation and outer expression.

Sound and Movement Improvisation

Eventually, the incorporation of breath, body, and voice leads to open sound and movement improvisation in the boxes. It can be helpful to begin this phase from the still poses, allowing sound and movement to emerge from them.

Imagine each rasa as a substance that fills the three-dimensional space of each box and is taken in, absorbed into the body. It's like a kind of alchemical process, through which the body's constitution is altered on a cellular level, allowing the rasa to then emanate from the body, through skin, eyes, voice, gesture, etc. This energetic transformation is palpable—it has been our experience that just about everyone watching feels the change take place in the room. Not only do those on the "outside" become viscerally engaged with the emotion being performed, they often reflect that emotion physically on the face or other parts of the body. If the performance is truly "rasic," there is no longer an outside—both performer and spectator are on the inside, tasting and enjoying the same rasa. It is most often in this phase that the Rasabox becomes a charged environment from which character, situation, and relationship (to imagined or real objects or people) begin to emerge.

It is usually in this phase of the exercise that we introduce the possibility of entering the santa box. Schechner proposes this as an option only if one feels that one has been "cleared" by going through all the other boxes first. We have also worked without this restriction, treating santa at times as just another rasa to be explored. The santa box can also serve as a place in which to rebalance oneself neurologically, to clear, empty, or calm oneself, just as corpse pose might do at the end of a strenuous yoga practice. However, whereas corpse pose suggests an inner focus, the santa box is a place from which one can still relate to others and to the environment, but without relating through a particular emotion.

Relating

The next series of exercises focuses on the interaction between people in different Rasaboxes. First, two people enter, each in different boxes, say karuna and raudra. Initially, they ignore one another, focusing on the expression of their own rasas. Then, they begin to engage each other from their respective rasic points of view, responding not to stimuli in their own box or imagination, but to the other person. Once they have fully engaged with one another, either one of them can move to another box, so that two people might go from relating in karuna-raudra to sringara-bibhasta. Ultimately, the game opens to include the following choices for either player: changing boxes; staying in the same box while the other player changes; leaving the game to allow another player to enter.

Relationship opens up a complex dynamic. Both subtle and radical shifts in quality and intensity surface when two rasas are in dialogue. Because of the challenge this initially presents, we usually limit relating verbally to using first names, and perhaps an exchange such as the following:

PLAYER A: "I'm [*player A's name*]. Who are you?"
PLAYER B: I'm [*player B's name*]. Who are you?"

Invariably, once words are introduced, verbal improvisation enters the exchange.

Finally, we expand the possibilities of relating through the incorporation of memorized text (scene, monologue, or poem). In a group situation, we usually have everyone memorize the same six or seven lines, so that they can do Rasaboxes "scenework" in a round-robin format. If we are working with a scene from Tennessee Williams's *A Streetcar Named Desire*, for example, the group will have learned both Stella and Blanche's lines. Someone enters doing Stella's lines, another, Blanche's. After they have moved through several exchanges in different rasas, one person will exit the boxes, and another will enter, begin the scene again, and so on. The words are used as open text, focusing the exploration on how each rasa informs that text differently, rather than on character, given circumstances, or other elements of the play text. The text stays fixed, while the rasas shift. We have learned from this process that emotion is not necessarily psycho-"logical." Often, the least logical emotion is the one that makes the scene most interesting.

Layering

Whereas in all of the previous exercises participants have attempted to work with "pure," unmixed rasas, in this phase, they begin to combine them. There are several possibilities. One can work with a *baseline, core,* or *primary* rasa, over which other rasas are layered. A Blanche played with raudra (rage) as the core rasa would create a very different production than one played with karuna (grief), for example. The idea of a core rasa can imply several things: that there are *mask* rasas layered over it to hide or protect the core, or that there are simply momentary *surface* rasas, which fluctuate according to the play's actions and events. (See Paula Murray Cole's narrative below for a complete description of this process.)

Also, two or more rasas can be blended to create more complex combinations of emotion. For example, what would result if you were to combine 50 percent raudra (rage) with 50 percent karuna (grief)? Or 70 percent sringara (love) and 30 percent hasya (laughter)? The nine emotions represented as distinct, isolated states by the Rasaboxes by no means cover the whole range of human emotion. They can be thought of, rather, as a basic palette from which a full spectrum can be created.

The idea of layering rasas can be extended as an approach to scene work. One might set an entire scene in the "key" of a particular rasa (or combination of rasas), while individual characters or moments can be played in other rasas. In the third act of Chekhov's *Three Sisters,* for example, while everyone else is traumatized and operating in a state of emergency because of the fire (perhaps bhayanaka [fear] or karuna [grief or compassion]), Masha can do nothing but revel in her newfound love (sringara) for Vershinin. Sometimes, particular rasas seem to logically emerge out of the text, as if the playwright is working with a kind of rasic palette, but it is also possible to apply randomly chosen rasas (or combinations) to a text to discover what works.

BEYOND THE BOXES

Ultimately, a performer experienced in Rasaboxes training can internalize its structure and is able to transform from one rasic state to another without the physical map of the boxes. It is possible for such a performer to change the emotional quality of a moment, a speech, or a scene at any point without necessarily changing her place in space. Emotion, like space, time, and other elements of staging, becomes simply another tool to be used in the process of exploring and developing performance work. The Rasaboxes can free performers from questions about "motivation," allowing them to think of and use emotion in a more playful, adventurous way. Finally, emotion—which is so often blocked or internalized—moves into the body, where it can energize the space *between* one performer and another and between performer and spectator.

BUILDING CHARACTER AND SCORING PERFORMANCE: TWO NARRATIVES

Paula Murray Cole

In 1999, I played Ofelia[11] in Richard Schechner's adaptation of Shakespeare's *Hamlet*. I used the rasa work in a few ways in this production: (1) as a tool to discover the emotional content of the play through both text analysis and physicalized exploration in scene rehearsals, (2) as a way of creating the psychological structure of the character, and (3) as a mode of offstage emotional preparation and onstage performance.

Whenever I begin work on a play, I comb the text for clues about my character: I look at the given circumstances and how all of her relationships take shape.[12] I begin to get a sense of my character's objective (what she desires from others), the obstacles she faces in pursuit of those objectives, and the specific action she takes. Based on information culled from the text, I develop a biography for the character, which helps me to get a handle on her psychology: what and who has shaped her sense of self, her emotional needs, her connection with others and the environment, her behavior. This work helps me to consider the rasas I may want to use. I begin to get a feel for which rasic emotions are most accessible to my character, which will best support the text, my own interpretation of the role, and the director's vision for the production. Although I make notes about all this work on paper, more importantly, I do it in-body, out loud. It is my private rehearsal time and my preparation for group rehearsals.

I then begin to experiment with the rasas in scene rehearsals. One of the ways I began to incorporate this work during *Hamlet* was to play whole scenes in a single rasa, full tilt. For example, the scene in which Ofelia tells her father, Polonius, that Hamlet has frightened her by behaving in a strange manner, I first played in bhayanaka (fear), then karuna (grief or compassion), next sringara (love), then raudra (rage), and so on. I noted how each rasa affected the actor playing Polonius and how it informed the actions I chose. This kind of exploration helps me to discover the range of emotional and active choices I want to keep and to limit other choices that seem less useful.

Next, I experiment with *layering* rasas to create the internal and external conflicts that drive the character's choices throughout the play. For Ofelia, I chose to work with four primary rasas: two *surface* rasas to which, I felt, she habitually gravitated: bhayanaka (fear) and karuna (grief); one *mask* rasa: sringara (love), with which she deeply identified, but also strategically used to gain familial and social approval; and one *core* rasa: raudra (rage), which is repressed until her final scene. I used them in varying weights or levels of intensity, depending on the challenges Ofelia faced in a given scene.

The key element in my interpretation of the character was the way in which I used the *core* rasa, raudra: It founded the psychological base from which I built my through-line of action. I decided that Ofelia's survival at home with Polonius and her brother, Laertes (and later, by extension, her lover Hamlet), hinged upon her ability to suppress any degree of objection she felt in the face of what they wanted from her. From early age, I imagined, any jot of resistance was completely squashed by her father's disapproval and threats of rejection. Conversely, she was pleasurably rewarded for being lovely, kind, affectionate, and compliant. She understands, however subconsciously, that she must hide her *core* feelings of rage (raudra) behind the *mask* of loving affection (sringara) in order to survive or thrive in her relationships. So, I denied Ofelia full access to rage until her final scene (though it peeked out in quickly squelched flares at the end of the nunnery scene and in the player's scene, as her situation and relationships became strained). Raudra was, however, the rasa always creating the tension from beneath, shaping the others—the irritating grain of sand creating the pearl.

Given this psychological character structure, what happens to Ofelia when her father is murdered by her lover while her brother is absent and the whole thing is covered up by the king? What happens when she feels the "forbidden feeling" of outrage because her murdered father is buried without ceremony? What does she do when the relationships that necessitated the repression of her *core* rasa and adherence to her *mask* rasa are gone, violently stripped away? Luckily, Shakespeare lets us find out in Ofelia's famous and final scene: the mad scene.

In brief, my physical score and psychological action in the mad scene focused on (1) performing a funeral for my father, (2) punishing and humiliating the king and queen for my father's death, and (3) secretly warning my brother of their treachery. For Ofelia, the scene is quite logically motivated, but her psycho-emotional conflicts overwhelm her, displace and fragment her interactions. My four primary rasas were energized to the absolute extreme as I abruptly (but not illogically) switched gears between them. In this scene, I allowed Ofelia to fully experience and express raudra. The force of that rasa, finally unleashed, was exhilarating, giving rise to new rasas: hasya (ridicule) and bibhasta (disgust), all the better with which to blast and humiliate the king and queen.

Indispensable to the process of building this production was composer-choreographer Liz Claire. She (and the other musicians) created music that interwove throughout the fabric of both the rehearsals and performance of this production. Liz is trained in the Rasaboxes work, and I had the luxury of working with her on Ofelia's scenes, mostly scored to the sound of her solo violin. Between the two of us, we composed movement and music that supported, amplified, and greatly enhanced the rasic choices that were made.

Lastly, I used this work as offstage preparation before and during performances in order to gear up for scenes. While training in the Rasaboxes, I learned to locate places in my body that, when moved or held in certain gestures or rhythms, initiate the sensations and physiology of a particular rasa. For example, when I slowly and gently turn my forearms skyward in a gesture of helplessness, I feel, get involved with the karuna rasa. This happens in a matter of seconds. So, to prepare for my entrance into the mad scene, I engaged this rasa offstage in order to seem as if, feel as if I'd been crying inconsolably for weeks. My face would become red and puffy, tears streaked down my cheeks, long strands of rheum ran from my nose! This was easy and fun to do, not painful, not personal. As I hit the boards to play the scene, I sensed the audience felt the rasa, experienced it with me. Their response fueled me even further, fueled the rasa set into motion between us. The effect, it seems, was both persuasive and harrowing.

The rasa work helped me to plot Ofelia's journey throughout the play, to access her emotional and psychological behaviors, to shape the moment-to-moment action. In rasic terms, perhaps I will say the work helped me to discover my own performance recipe: which ingredients to mix together, how long to stir and cook it, to "taste" and make adjustments, and finally, to offer up my creation to be shared and enjoyed.

Michele Minnick

In addition to their function in performer training and building a role in a scripted play, it is also possible to use the Rasaboxes as a tool for the creation of choreography and performer-generated work, work that originates from the body rather than from the text. I am currently developing an original piece, to be performed by myself and choreographer-composer Liz Claire, about Russian poet Marina Tsvetayeva. We are using biographical and historical material, as well as poems, for the text of the piece and using the Rasaboxes as one of several ways of developing the physical-emotional and musical score.

The Rasaboxes have provided a rehearsal structure, a way for us to navigate possible emotional mapping to be used as part of the physical score of the piece, as well as providing a way for me to discover "character" choices. My use of the Rasaboxes in thinking about character is different than Paula's approach to Ofelia, in that I am not approaching Tsvetayeva as a unified character to be portrayed in a seamless way by me, but rather as a series of moments and personas that I can move through and between, also keeping myself present in the piece. Though I am still very much in the process of making the piece, and much of the "material" that has been generated so far may be discarded, I can talk about some of what I have discovered through using the Rasaboxes in rehearsal.

Working with Liz and with dramaturge Gisela Cardenas, I have used the Rasaboxes in the first phase of the rehearsal process as a general framework for exploration. Laying the emotional map out on the floor at the beginning of each rehearsal, I have assembled texts (poems), objects, costume elements, and many, many photographs of Tsvetayeva that Gisela gathered and labeled for me. These materials, when I begin to play with them in the different boxes, enter into a dynamic relationship with each other, with each emotion, with the background research I have done on Tsvetayeva's biography, and with improvised movement, sound, and text that emerge in the rehearsal itself.

Text and Movement

For example, one simple way of working has been for me to take a poem or part of a poem and simply work with it, sounding it in each box. So far, I have been working with the poems in their original Russian, occasionally improvising text "as Tsvetayeva," based on both what I know and imagine of her life, in both English and Russian. Just as the Rasaboxes give a framework for interpreting texts, they can also provide stimulus for the generation of new text, which emerges, as it were, from my emotional and imaginative body. This is a very different way of generating text than sitting at a desk writing (which is, however, also part of the process).

As I enter each box, I notice that I immediately associate that emotion with certain times, certain people, or certain aspects of Tsvetayeva's life. I spent one rehearsal simply moving from box to box, speaking sometimes to imagined figures, sometimes directly to Gisela. Hasya (laughter) brought me to childhood, karuna (grief) to the death of Tsvetayeva's mother, raudra (rage) to the sense of betrayal felt toward all of Russia, and bhayanaka (fear) at my return to a time of utter aloneness near the end of Tsvetayeva's life. Sometimes, the combination of the emotion and the aspect of her life lead me to speak, generating text, and sometimes just to move and make sound, generating a kind of emotional choreography made up of particular postures, gestures, and movements.

Objects and Images

One of the objects with which I developed clear, differentiated relationships over a period of two or three rehearsals is paper. It first entered into play in the sringara (love) box one day. We had a large roll of white paper on hand, mostly for the purpose of writing down the rasas. At a certain moment, Gisela brought it to me while I was working in sringara, with images in my mind of Tsvetayeva's first meetings with the man who was to become her husband. Suddenly, the paper itself became him, became a wedding veil, became itself—paper on which to write letters, poems to and for him.

This was the first entry of paper as both an object and an image into our process, one that made a great deal of sense, in view of Marina's lifelong relationship as a poet to the blank page. Later, it came into the bhayanaka (fear) box. I was in the process of making a discovery that fear, in the complex alchemy that is me + Tsvetayeva + fear, is about loss of memory, loss of meaning. I began to rip apart the paper on which "bhayanaka" was written. Each blank, white piece stared at me (as Tsvetayeva), representing parts of my life, of my past, that I somehow felt had slipped away from me, were beyond reach, beyond identification. I began, slowly, to name each thing, with simple, childlike words, like "mama," "Sergei" (Tsvetayeva's husband), taking each piece of paper representing these lost things and taping them together, in a string of blanknesses, terrified that the empty spaces of white paper would never be filled again, neither with the life they represented, nor the poetry that, in the past, had always come to me.

Later, in the raudra (rage) box, I suddenly found myself ripping paper again, but this time, angrily, raging in words the whole time at a Russia that had betrayed me. I shoved each piece of paper into my mouth and chewed on it. As the paper filled my mouth, the sound of my voice became more and more monstrous. This paper-eating image returned again another day, while working with periods of Tsvetayeva's life in each box, rather than with rasas. Facing the death of Tsvetayeva's daughter Irina, who starved in an orphanage at the age of two, suddenly, I found myself shoving huge amounts of paper into my mouth, until again, speech became a hideous, monstrous sound. The action and the image it produced represented for me the guilt at not having been able to feed my own child.

Music and Movement

Liz and I have begun to explore interaction between musician and actor in the Rasaboxes—she on her violin and me playing with text and movement. The music she creates, and the movement I do in the different rasas, creates a dialogue, which is opening new territory for both of us. Her playing stimulates my movement in a way that allows me to enter into a rasa very deeply and continue to discover new physical connections to it. I remember one rehearsal in which she played for me in karuna for a long time, and the sound of the violin seemed to open up my chest, as if my ribs were splitting apart. The movements that were generated in this session were quite powerful, and something we will probably return to. In general, following a musical impulse (and in a way, not having to continually generate my own stimulus for the rasa) frees me to go places I wouldn't ordinarily. Here, rasa becomes a terrain for dialogue between actor and musician, blurring the boundaries of our roles and the techniques available to us.

Eventually, as we move from this first exploratory phase of the process to a more compositional phase, I will discard the boxes, so that the actual physical score of the piece can emerge. How these images, movements, texts will come together, and whether or not the individual rasas as we use them in the boxes will figure in as a conscious compositional tool, I don't know. They have already been layered into the process, however—in a sense, my relationship to the poetry, to the objects, to all the materials I am using, including my own body and voice, are already "rasic." The Rasaboxes, though eventually they become invisible, deeply inform the trajectory of the whole piece.

These are just two examples of how one can apply the Rasaboxes to performance. The possibilities are endless. As Bharata says in the *Natyasastra*:

> It is impossible [. . .] to know all about natya since there is no limit to bhavas (emotions) and no end to the arts involved (in natya). It is not possible to have a thorough knowledge of even one of them, leave alone so many of them.[13]

It is our hope that in this spirit the practice of the Rasaboxes, as well as the Rasaesthetics to which it ascribes, will serve as an ever-broadening generative field of exploration for the purposes of performance training and composition, as well as for the general health of the body-mind.

NOTES

1. Candace Pert from *Molecules of Emotion*, quoted in Juhan, Deane. *Job's Body*. Barrytown, N.Y.: Station Hill/Barrytown Ltd., 1998, 370.
2. See: Schechner, Richard. "Rasaesthetics." *The Drama Review*, Cambridge, Mass: MIT Press, Fall 2001 (T136). In this article, he discusses the "location of theatricality" in a comparison of (Aristotelian) Western theatrical theory and practice with those of classical Indian dance-drama-theater. Relying greatly on studies of the enteric nervous system, Rasaesthetics suggests a gut-based, rather than a purely vision-based approach to performance practice and theory. The article outlines Schechner's theory of what he calls "rasic" performances, as well as giving a basic outline of the Rasaboxes approach to emotional training and composition for performance.
3. In addition to Schechner's "Rasaesthetics," (see note 1), see Kapila Vatsyayan's excellent study, *Bharata: The Natyasastra* (New Delhi: Sahitya Akademi, 1996), for an overview of the *Natyasastra's* history and interpretations, as well as Adya Rangacharya's *The Natyasastra* (New Delhi: Munshiram Manoharlal Publishers Pvt. Ltd., 1986).
4. See: "An Affective Athletecism" in *The Theatre and Its Double*. Mary Caroline Richards translates the phrase as "athlete of the heart," but Schechner's "athlete of the emotions" provides a clearer portrayal of our use of Artaud's idea.
5. Vatsyayan, 55. (See note 3.)
6. Schechner, 31. (See note 1.)
7. Were we to remain theoretically faithful to the *Natyasastra*, technically, we should call the exercise the "Bhavaboxes," as bhava refers to the emotions that are actually *performed* in order to *evoke* rasa. But we maintain the use of the word "rasa" both for simplicity's sake and also because of its other associations—with the pleasure and physicality of tasting, with the sense of something physical that is enjoyed between actor and spectator.
8. This comment was made to Minnick on a paper she is working on, which deals with the potential benefits and problems surrounding the aspect of cultural appropriation in the Rasaboxes.
9. When we teach the Rasaboxes, we use the Sanskrit words for the rasas to represent the nine primary emotions, although there are different, though related words corresponding to the bhavas, which, according to the *Natyasastra*, are the actual performed "emotions." We have limited the amount of Sanskrit language we use in our practice to avoid confusion; too much new terminology can bog down what are usually fairly short training programs. (See also note 8.)
10. Schechner, 41. (See note 2.)
11. This was the spelling used in Schechner's adaptation, a mixture of several versions of the play text.
12. Much of the following is a fairly compact description relying on the reader's foreknowledge of *Hamlet*. I hope not to alienate those unfamiliar with the play, but my intention is to be concise about how I used the rasa work in parallel with standard Western acting techniques in building a particular character or role.
13. Rangacharya, p. 53.

PART SEVEN

Moving Forward

Mind-Body Juggling for the Camera

Erika Batdorf

Intensive and extensive movement training is a crucial element in the education of any actor. This is a statement that I think most people in the field would acknowledge as true; and yet we rarely find American actors with extensive and detailed movement training, especially in the film industry. There are many reasons for this, some of which circle around the endless debate that has existed as long as film has existed. Must film actors be content with type casting, or is there room for character work? Is the ability to act for film something one does or does not "have," or, is it something that can be learned?

The art of film can exist with or without trained actors. However, the art of film *acting*, regardless of how or whether it is used by the producers and directors of film, is still within the control of the actor and can be perfected or ignored.

What, then, is the most relevant movement training for film and television actors? Training programs that address film acting typically value movement for overall fitness, relaxation and grounding, good breath and vocal connection, alignment, fight and choreography work. The need for these skills is accepted, hopefully, without debate.

One of the things I do with my students is have them develop an ongoing plan and schedule for their regular workout. An *actor* workout—not a purely fitness-oriented regime. This workout must include a balance between strength, flexibility, and endurance, awareness, alignment, and coordination. Each actor must take responsibility for her own physical practice and how it relates to her goals as an actor. Through this practice, skills should be continually expanding, and the actor should run into questions that can then be addressed by taking various classes. For example, if an actor has no idea what her alignment challenges are, or even if she knows what they are, but has no specific exercises to address them, then she needs some information about alignment. Alexander work, a Feldenkrais class, even a good physical therapist through her local doctor—any system that helps with alignment would be ideal, so that she is not type cast by the slump in her shoulders or her protruding chin.

However, beyond practicing one area of expertise at a time, the actor needs to include in this regime the art of juggling various skills simultaneously—exercises in advanced coordination. It is this aspect of juggling I will examine, particularly within two areas of movement training that are often problematic or questionable for film actors. It is now commonly recognized that our bodies hold emotional memory and deep core feelings and that physical improvisation and connection can help us source this information. However, I find most film actors find classes and exercises in this area abstract and confusing. This confusion is understandable, as most of the language used in this work was developed for dance, experimental theater, or therapy.

The other, even more controversial area of movement training has to do with character and range. I hear film actors and film-acting teachers all the time express concern regarding the loss of authenticity when external physical character work is discussed. We are afraid of the extreme ends of the pendulum swing. At one end of the spectrum we have the intense and challenging world of the body and emotions, often hard to explain and comprehend in words. At the other end we have the world of specific character body skill, requiring patience, practice, and control. We often perceive these two arenas as contradictory, especially for film work. I would suggest that they are both helpful and complementary.

BELIEVABILITY AND EMOTIONAL CONNECTION

We all want to be able to cry on cue, laugh convincingly from the belly, find our rage and then have it simmer like a slow steam through our words . . . or simply to be able to act without overacting. I assume that we already accept that a strong mind-body connection leads to easier emotional access. There are volumes of work and much in this book that already addresses this issue. But, how does a film student determine if a particular movement class is addressing her needs? What are the specific physical skills she is learning? How does she integrate such work into her acting?

There are a whole host of techniques that work with deep physical connection in the theater-therapy crossover community. Different versions of these systems are taught in theater schools and studios throughout North America. Each system is adapted by a particular teacher from the various perspectives of and integration with the other training of that teacher. I say this because I have experienced vastly different versions of, say, Grotowski's river work, sometimes profoundly relevant to film acting, sometimes less so.

I would like to make an attempt (brave or foolish) at delineating what I see as some basic physical skills that one should be gaining from movement work that is designed to help you act more believably from the whole body.

- Physical awareness—the brain's ability to go to a specific part of the body and feel it internally (proprioceptive awareness). This skill will help you discover your habits. (If you can't feel them, you can't change them.) It should help you feel parts of your body, so that your thoughts and impulses can travel to more places than simply your hands and your face (which most of us can feel more easily than, say, our back ribs). We often assume that we can change things if we "know" about them. Then why do we keep repeating the same bad physical habits? It is not simply a matter of our brain understanding that we overact with our eyebrows. We have to be able to connect the brain to the eyebrow to relax it or be able to redirect the impulse to another part of the body. Also, without the ability to feel the body, one cannot source emotional information from it. This takes practice in physical awareness.
- Kinesthetic awareness—by this I mean the brain's ability to recognize and respond to organic movement impulses. This is simpler than it sounds, and harder than it seems. It means noticing consciously your desire to stretch, your relationship to gravity, your breathing rhythm and impulses, your tension levels, and where these physical impulses want to go next, your physical response to temperature and other stimuli—including thought and feeling—anything that makes you adjust your physical position. It is your body's constant attempt to make itself comfortable. We move this way all the time—unconsciously. Unfortunately most actors actually stop moving organically when they are acting. One needs to learn to recognize and follow these impulses while performing, rather than unconsciously suppress them. (For those actors who forever are wondering what to do with their hands, this is one of the skills that needs to be expanded.)
- Sensory awareness—this refers simply to the senses: smell, taste, sight, hearing, touch. Your ability to consciously choose to notice your senses can help connect your ability to feel your body with your

ability to notice how the environment is affecting your body. Conscious awareness of the senses will also introduce new and varied stimuli and impulses. Working with the senses provides an excellent transition from being solely focused on the internal feeling of the body to simultaneously being able to see your scene partner and engage in a real mutual exchange with your fellow actors and your environment.

- Communication—now see and be seen while working on the other three skills; that is, look someone in the eyes without losing your conscious awareness of your body, movement impulses, and sensory information.

In other words, in a movement for actors class designed to teach an actor how to connect emotionally, one should be learning to feel one's own body; use impulses within one's body; connect, through the senses, to the room and others; and begin to simultaneously integrate thoughts and images. All this is unlikely to happen in a single class! But this perhaps gives one a road map of some things to look for. Some movement classes may or may not also work on text and voice integration, obviously a necessary step at some point. Some classes focus on certain areas mentioned above, and others may work on the challenge of juggling a few or several of these skills at one time.

How does all this help the film actor specifically? These skills offer the actor more immediate and extended emotional access and decrease overacting.

One thing that can cause overacting is "pushing"—forcing the feeling that we *think* the character should be experiencing into our bodies, perhaps flailing our hands unnecessarily, overexaggerating the face, and mugging in general. This tendency is exacerbated by our inability to consciously feel larger and deeper parts of the body. If someone walks up to you and tells you that you have won the lottery, your reaction will be a whole-body reaction. Your breathing pattern, your rhythm, your heartbeat, your tension levels will all change, to name just a few physical responses you are likely to experience. If you are trying to re-create this moment as an actor, even if you use the most profound psychological approach, if your body does not respond, your acting will misfire. If you put the thoughts and feelings that you find into the parts of the body that you can feel superficially (usually the hands and the face), you will find that the size of the muscles will be too small to contain the size of the thoughts that you discover. This causes these smaller parts to move faster or freeze with tension—the face will contort, the hands will flail, or the feet will pace. If you can access the larger, deeper parts of the body consciously, then you have a large enough container for these feelings. You can place those feelings into the muscles of the legs or the back, you can deepen the breathing, you can engage a more believable whole-body response.

Sometimes, we think of film acting as the same as theater acting, but smaller. What do we mean by smaller? More intimate? Less range of motion? More realistic? Taking up less space? In theater training, we are learning physically how to authentically fill the space, be dynamic and visually striking. In film training, we are focused on intimate and authentic emotional connection and articulate thoughts. I would suggest that the above skills can make an actor's work "smaller" in the sense that as your ability to consciously control your body grows, so does your ability to place your thoughts and feelings into breath, deeper muscle groups, and less obvious physical movements. (For example, a moment of frustration can be expressed in a slow lengthening of the spine, rather than through pacing.)

A good class in deep physical awareness will inevitably lead to emotional connection. If one feels ones body deeply, breathes well, and is in a safe environment, emotions will arise. Emotionally connected, movement-based improvisation extends the range and speed at which an actor can access emotional states and locate them in varied parts of the body. It is work that film actors need to study and continue to practice. Whereas theater actors can explore in the rehearsal process the emotions that pertain to the role they are working on, film actors need to access varied emotional states quickly and without a great deal of repetition or preparation. Therefore, I suggest that film actors need a regular whole-body, emotionally connected practice that exercises and expands their range. If this work is going well, a film actor should notice her acting work becoming more believable and less self-conscious. She should find that her superficial habits diminish and her emotional and physical range increases.

JUGGLING

At some point, an actor has to integrate the above principles into acting work. Memorized text, the scene partner, the subtext, and external information, among other things, need to be introduced, giving the brain even more to juggle. I refer to this as "juggling," because you cannot always be feeling consciously your hamstrings while remembering your lines, while taking direction, while achieving your objective . . . More likely, your brain is doing a circuit through as many of these things as it can manage.

When one is in early stages of memorization, the conscious brain has to take up more energy to source the text. One has less conscious ability to feel the body, its impulses, or sensory information. In the extreme moments of this, the actor's eyes will glaze over, and she will freeze her body as she looks for her next line. Most often, she will move from the head and the hands—unless she can consciously choose not to. So, she can either learn those lines incredibly well (and, let's face it, how often does that happen in the film industry?) or she can learn to consciously contradict the natural body-language tendency to move from the head and hands (or pace or freeze) when working with partially learned text.

In order to work against this tendency, a film actor has to have a thorough knowledge of this process of juggling. The more experience and the more practice you have, the faster and smoother the juggling goes, and the more balls you can handle. Instead, however, we often just drop certain balls. Many actors find themselves working primarily from pure thought. Actors find themselves in front of a camera physically paralyzed, not just because of lack of movement training, but lack of experience in juggling.

Somewhere, you must practice juggling and be allowed to fail! One way to practice this juggling on your own is by working with text and breath while engaged in a whole-body process. Simply practice advanced coordination; for example, try working on a monologue while doing a complex yoga or martial arts routine, and still notice all the sensory information you are receiving. One can add more or less complexity to such exercises. For example, try doing the text at different tempos in contrast to the tempo of the movement, focus on different breathing patterns, or choose a particular body part to feel while running the text and doing the movement.

RANGE AND EXTERNAL CHARACTER DEVELOPMENT

When an actor does physical character work, especially if it is done before he has learned the previously discussed skills, it will initially take him into acting that looks inauthentic. The camera will detect this inauthenticity, and the actor will likely be encouraged to drop some "balls"—the external physical characteristics—and "be himself," a good choice in most situations where the actor has little time and physical training. I would suggest that with the right training, those same balls would actually increase that actor's authenticity rather than decrease it.

There are certain principles that are crucial to the actor's development of range. This work is best done after the actor can already feel her body and impulses in her body while seeing and being seen; it consists of simply learning range within the basic elements of body language. I break those elements down as follows:

- Posture and gesture
- Tensions
- Space and shape
- Rhythm
- Breath
- Eye-head relationship

Most of us think of physical character work as posture alone, which is why it is often rejected. If you think creating a physical character involves changing the shape of your skeleton and then more or less freezing it in this new shape except for a few new gestures, I would agree with those who discourage external character work—be yourself!

Character development is much more complex than simply changing the skeletal shape, hand, arm, and facial gestures. It involves changing tension levels, spinal shape, extensive gesture change, subtle head-eye relationships, rhythm, and breath. Even changing all this is not enough. We then must find a new range of motion and feel the organic movement impulses within each of these areas, rather than inhabit a frozen image of each. We then must experience how this influences our thoughts and our emotional connection to our bodies.

Posture and Gesture

We tend to change only the superficial levels of posture. In the most superficial situations, the actor will change only the arms and maybe the face. Ideally, this change needs to happen from the floor up. The way the feet fall on the floor—Toe, then heel? Turned out? Wide steps or on the sides of feet? Bounce in the step? The variations are endless!—and the shape of the spine are crucial. If you change only the upper body, it will not be believable. In body language terms, we "read" the lower body and see that as the *truth* of a person, and then we see the upper body as decoration—especially the hands or arms. We lie with the face and the hands. We "are" the shape of our spine and our legs.

Tensions

Changing the muscular dynamics of the body will greatly affect how the character is perceived. Posture and tension levels are inextricably linked. If you change your posture and do not change your levels of tension, the posture will not be sustainable; it will be uncomfortable and will appear false. There are whole series of muscular range exercises that can be used to help actors explore tension levels through-out the body. Decroux technique has a marvelous system for muscular dynamics; systems like Laban help delineate various qualities that affect muscular range. Having a limber, flexible body is imperative. Simply practicing isolated muscular contractions while running text can help give the actor more muscular range and access. Daniel Day Lewis's character in *A Room with a View* is a strong example of tension and pos-ture choices that work together and are well articulated throughout the whole body.

Space and Shape

A conscious awareness of where you are in space in relationship to the camera can help give clear and strong shapes and character images. I have seen actors in film who create a clear shape with their bodies and use that shape in a variety of ways to establish who they are in a scene immediately. This idea is as old as Commedia dell'Arte. In Commedia, as the actor enters the stage, she makes a clear and recognizable shape with her body, so that the audience can identify her without any words and minimal costume. This can be done with long distance shots, quick sequences, and opening scenes. In *Rain Man,* Dustin Hoffman creates such a distinctive shape with his arms and his body and such a clear rhythm in his walk that in a scene shot at night from above, we clearly see his character—even though he is just a tiny, black silhouette on a road. Again, in *A Room with a View,* Daniel Day Lewis establishes his character immediately in each scene by always beginning with a tight, closed-leg posture, among many other distinctive physical choices. The overall shape of his body is distinctive and communicates his character instantly.

Working with space and shape is a real collaboration between the actor and the director. Choosing a strong visual relationship between your body and the set can make the difference between a striking scene and a dull scene. Try running some text in your kitchen, and find as many different and interesting places to be in the room as you can. How many shapes can you make while washing dishes, making dinner, holding a fork? Keep in mind a particular angle of the camera.

Rhythm

Rhythm is something that can turn a dull actor into a dynamic actor. I often encourage actors to watch good cartoons and visual films (*Max Headroom* has particularly overly dramatic rhythm) to help them understand visual as well as sound rhythm. Your rhythm is not just your words; it is also your movements in relationship to your words. Detailed rhythm exercises with text work and small props, such as cigarettes, pieces of paper, or cups of coffee, can be excellent exercises for creating drama through visual and sound rhythms. For example, try playing with a tissue (or other similar small prop) while running some text. Experiment with different rhythms and tempos. Play with the tissue quickly while speaking, and then suddenly stop moving the tissue while continuing to speak in the same rhythm. Speak slowly while moving the prop quickly, and vice versa. Simply play with your text and your subtext while consciously manipulating the speed and rhythm of the movement of the prop. It is surprisingly difficult to have a different speaking rhythm than movement rhythm, but it can create a subtle and dramatic affect. Most of us have rhythmic habits that we are completely unaware of, just as we have chronic tension and postural habits, especially when working with memorized material.

Breath

All of the above is going to dramatically affect your breathing. An advantage that film work has over theater is that you can actually make extreme choices with tensions and postures, creating interesting breathing patterns that, on stage, would make it impossible for you to be heard. When coaching actors for stage, I find we spend a great deal of time adjusting and experimenting with certain postures and tensions to allow for a fully supported voice. In film coaching, the issue almost never comes up. All of the above, without integration of new breathing patterns, will be unsuccessful or unbelievable.

Eye-Head Relationship

This is an exciting and relevant area for film. The stylized theater cultures that work with the eyes, largely Oriental theater cultures, have a lot to offer film actors. We often leave our eye work completely unconscious, except for the most obvious choices, like Anthony Hopkins's strong, but quite simple, choice in *Silence of the Lambs.* A more subtle choice is illustrated again by Dustin Hoffman in *Rain Man.*

Throughout the film, Hoffman never makes eye contact with his eyes centered in his head. Then, in the final scene on the train saying good-bye to his brother, played by Tom Cruise, he centers his head and his eyes for two brief moments, giving a subtle sense of change in the character. Our eye movements can be choices, ones that change the way we are type cast. Our eyes are full of habits. Eye habits are such that they are not as obvious as a bad spinal alignment, and yet they will affect how we are cast just as profoundly—and unconsciously. Perhaps your eyes tend to move a lot, or they get stuck looking up in one corner, or you always freeze your eyes center, or you look up from a tilted head. These things will cast you as "cute" or "angry" or "uninteresting." It is unlikely that a director will be able to identify exactly why he perceives you as cute or angry. You may repeatedly get the response, he looks perfect for the part—but he just seems too angry.

I use the phrase "eye-head relationship," but it should, of course, be eye-spine relationship. As with breath, everything you build underneath the eyes must then be integrated with the eyes. Poor line memorization is one reason we have limited use of the eyes. We use eye positioning to help us remember things. We may be using subtle eye shifts that will hopefully be read by audiences as searching for a thought, when we are actually searching for a line! Our eye movements will likely be telling the story of a power struggle with the director, our awareness of the location of the camera, our insecurity during the audition, or something as mundane as having forgotten lunch, instead of revealing the character's thoughts in the scene. To combat this, many of us make the easiest and least interesting choice—we freeze our eye movements. Try spending the day with a completely different head-eye position. Notice how long you can sustain it, in what circumstances you have difficulty sustaining it, and how it makes you feel.

PRACTICING BEING UNCOMFORTABLE

Changing all of these things takes practice. Some of that practice involves simple repetitive exercises in each area. Some of that practice involves changing something and then seeing what the internal reaction is to that change. Often, we make a change, and at our core, we will feel uncomfortable. This is where the work becomes interesting! If you are changing your body to the point where you *feel* like a different person, then you are acting. However, we often reach that point, and it will feel so unfamiliar or frightening, that we will resort back to our familiar posture, breathing pattern, rhythm pattern, and so on, or we will put a "layer" over it to make sure that we are not truly perceived as this "other" person. This will usually look like we are caricaturing the thing we are playing; it often happens unconsciously. Then, we can immediately justify not staying in this uncomfortable place, as we are convinced that it will not work—it is not "me." It is as if our body says, "Look, isn't this ridiculous? I could never be this strong or sweet or angry or handsome or sexy! And anyway, see how fake it looks?"

In order to get past this point, we have to examine what comes up emotionally when we shift our habits. It is in those uncomfortable places that new believable characters lie. If one does not find something that is both exciting and a bit scary, then one is probably working within one's familiar territory and superficially in the body. If you are looking to extend your range, you must be willing to let your self feel truly different. You will have to fight—internally and externally—your resistance to the discomfort. Internally, one needs to ask: Why am I unable to embody this? How and why does this threaten my sense of self? Externally, one simply needs to practice the new physical character enough to find it fully, with all the elements of tension, rhythm, breath, eyes, and posture.

After I work with actors on believability and emotional connection, we practice external physical manipulation of the body, and we analyze our own body language. This practice should help train the actor's brain to be able to consciously access specific parts of the body in specific ways. We then reenter the emotionally connected physical work and are able to analyze the emotional connection specifically and physically. Simply put: We learn to feel our bodies, we then learn skills to change our bodies, and we then learn to feel our bodies once changed *and* how to change how we feel by changing our bodies. (When I became angry, my head turned left, my breathing speeded up, my left arm got really tense, and that traveled up into my shoulders and down my spine, and I started pacing. My eyes seemed to mostly be looking down and right, against the direction of my head.) Through this analysis, we can then quickly recreate emotional states. (If I increase my breathing, turn my head left and my eyes right, slightly increase the tension in my shoulders, and tap my foot on the floor, I feel angry.)

If anything, I would advocate that film actors needs even more training than theater actors—if they want range. In theater, one can rehearse with the text for longer periods of time. With film, one's bag of tricks has to be large and immediately accessible. If you are content to play yourself and you are lucky enough to have the right look for the industry, then you may not need to be concerned with range.

As you age, however, you may find your lack of range limiting. If you are interested in playing outside your obvious look, juggling will have to be among your tricks of the trade. Sure, with the help of makeup, costumes, and special effects, film actors are "transformed," but if you really want to be able to access profound external and internal changes, you will need to put on different rhythms, tensions, postures, etc., to find other roles. In order to make these changes and maintain authenticity, actors need training, or practice and repetition—not for a particular role per se, but in general, as preparation for potential roles. One's instrument needs to be malleable on the subtlest levels and as organically as possible—meaning from the inside out *physically*—not just from thought.

Teaching Postmodern Choreography to Actors: Eschewing the Inebriation of Emotion

Nicole Potter Interviews Annie-B Parson

Annie-B Parson and I worked together for some years, she as a choreographer-director and I as an actor, at a downtown, permanent theater ensemble in New York City. She was (and is) an inspiring and demanding teacher. After leaving the ensemble, Annie-B went on to teach at NYU and to found Big Dance Theater, an ensemble that has performed her work all over the world.

Since she dissembled, asserting that she was incapable of putting her thoughts down on paper—which I don't believe for a minute—the only way that I could get her to participate in this book was to track her down at a Starbucks in Brooklyn Heights. Here is a bit of the conversation that we had, regarding actors, choreography, teaching, and avant-garde (or Postmodern) work.

PARSON: Thinking about what actually *I am thinking about* in the classroom . . . I should start by telling you about the makeup of the room, because it is the experimental theater wing [of NYU, Tisch School of the Arts], with students who are trained in voice, acting, and movement. And the movement training is what is called "developmental movement"; it's not like they are taking ballet and jazz.

POTTER: And your class is called . . . ?

PARSON: Choreography. Their acting training is Grotowski. And then they have Meisner for a year. And then, their voice training is very experimental voice work. And then, at the end of their training they do—bel canto?

POTTER: Isn't that straight singing?

PARSON: Songs. But everything comes from an experimental base. So, when I get the students, it's the end of their training.

POTTER: They're undergraduates?

PARSON: Yes, so, when I get them, they are twenty, twenty-one years old. Most of them have never had a dance technique class. They've all had extensive movement, extensive improvisation training. Lots of them have taken hip-hop, they've taken Afro-Haitian and other styles. But not ballet or modern dance. They've taken contact improv; they've had a lot of improv. They are really, really comfortable with their bodies, but they've never really made any dances.

So, I guess my first inclination when I was working there was to see what they had to say. But I kind of quickly closed that box, because it seemed that if we worked from the perspective of content, because of their age, you're getting into some really narcissistic stuff, which doesn't really lend itself to thinking about making work. Later on, of course, there's lots and lots of traditions of narcissistic work, which they are free to follow, but you need the base. I just felt really strongly that you need the base, almost like sketching a head from different angles. You really need to look at the craft of making things. That particular department is about making your own work, self-scripting, making pieces, and I thought, I really want to take it more from a more formalistic point of view. I am the only one there who teaches from that perspective.

So, a lot of the inspirations that I have are from the 1960s and 1970s, choreographers who were formalists. And I have found that when I work that way, the truth or the subject matter would come in the back door; it was there, it just wasn't in the lead. So, you don't make a dance about your summer vacation; instead, you're making dances about the elements of movement—space, shape, rhythm, time—and I started to get some really good results. These "elements of movements" were introduced to me by Mimi Garrard of Alwin Nikolais's company.

POTTER: And how were they at focusing on those things? I mean, they are sophisticated enough to focus on those things; those things aren't revelations to them?

PARSON: Well, it's varied. Some of them want to be very narrative. When you walk into my class, you can leave meaning outside the door. You do not need to worry about meaning. I often tell them this quote of van Gogh's, which is, "meaning comes in glimpses." Let meaning do its own work, because form has meaning in itself; it even has spiritual meaning. And if you let it do its work, then this idea of subject matter or story will work itself out. Most of the time, because we impose so much on everything that we touch, as viewers and as people making things, if you just get out of the way and really rigorously work out the forms themselves, your sense of truth will come in. Sometimes, it's very light. Sometimes, it doesn't come. But that's okay.

One student asked me the other day, "What are you looking at when you're looking at our work, because I am bored." That's a really good question. What am I looking at? I am looking at how the exercise is affecting their progress, how they changed (or didn't change) from the last time to this time. I'm looking at how the whole group is responding to this exercise, and I am thinking about what they should do next, and I am thinking about them on the professional stage and what's missing. But mostly, I'm just thinking about choreography and what makes it work.

The tricky part, and also the fun part, about teaching is that you're always thinking about how to reinvent your wheel. And so, what I'm doing is looking at abstraction and letting it have a voice, and there are thousands of ways to do that, and they have to do with who you are as an artist. So, it's a lot more manipulative than, okay, what does this student want to make, and how do I help them to say it, to support that. To create their own voice.

POTTER: You want to define your use of the word "manipulative" in that context?

PARSON: I am much more in the driver's seat. I give them an assignment, and they need to fill in the blanks, and they need to do it in a way that pleases them and that excites them to come into the room and show it, but they are not allowed to go outside of this structure that I create. In a sense, the opposite way to work would be like when I studied with Bessie Schoenberg: You bring in a piece, and she talks about that piece and helps you to bring out your own voice. This is *not* that. I don't think my students are ready for that. They are inexperienced. So I say, let's look at what structure and form can do for you and how you can work these tools of movement. And sometimes, we will start with just elements of movement: shape, time, space, rhythm, motion, and subsets of those things. Line, phrasing, musicality, dynamics.

POTTER: Can you give an example of an early exercise you might assign?

PARSON: Sometimes I work with a Bill T. Jones exercise about shape that I have altered through the years. If I was working with a very beginning group, I might say, okay, let's look at shape. And I'd say, bring in six shapes. And what you want to do as a director is to have the audience only think about shape.

You don't want them to think about how you moved from shape to shape, which brings up the notion of motion. You don't want to think about narrative—you want to be able to execute this in a way that we, the viewers, don't think about Nicole struggling in the shape or contemplating the shape; we just want to look at shape. It sounds kind of simple, but there is also the element of time, because dance is temporal, time is passing, so you also have to think about how long you can sustain the shape before it seems like you're there so long that the viewers are thinking about time, or you're there so short that they are thinking about rushing. So then, they take the six shapes, and I try to take it into a more choreographic place.

The shapes tend to be very cool; they give off a cool feeling—unemotional, not hot, not sweaty, not narrative—if they do them really purely. You can't actually do anything on stage, over time, that has motion, that is 100 percent shape. But you can really call the audience's attention to shape. It calls for a certain muscularity; it asks for specificity of thinking about shape. Then, I'll take them to step two: I want to warm it up.

So, I want to give them the sense of two contrasting elements, of warm versus cold, and how opposites and contradictions and complexities of dynamic actually add a little tiny bit of truth. So now we're letting art come in the back door, for just a second. And I think of the warmest thing I can think of. So, I might ask them to bring in a story of when they were little and they got lost. And that's very, very warm, because it has feeling, it has fear, it has emotion. It has connections to parents and disconnects and various opposites to the cool, icy pure shape. Then, I ask them to simultaneously tell the story as they perform their shapes—and we did this, Nicole, I remember Montana doing one.

POTTER: I don't recall. I'm just thinking about how bad I am at doing things that are cool.

PARSON: (laughs) We talk a lot about this in class, how everybody has their own temperature on stage.

In this study, the students can't change the shapes. They can't try to alter them to make them fit the story (the "story" part is derived from an early Bill T. Jones exercise). They can't change the time of the shapes. All they can do is perform these two parallel lines of shape and story and let the form work on it.

POTTER: And the story is vocal?

PARSON: Yes, and I ask them to let the story be infused with the quality that shape gave their bodies. The dynamics of shape: simple, spare, take out the umms, the adjectives, all the sort of decorative things, because shape doesn't do any of those things. So, I try to get the storytelling very spare. But the subject matter is very, very hot. Then they can decide: Do I want to tell the story, do a shape, tell part of the story, stop, do a shape? The only thing they can't do is change the shapes. They can phrase it any way they like. They can do five shapes and then tell the story in the sixth shape and leave. Usually, they do shape, story, shape, story. And then, I often use a very cool piece of music, like Philip Glass or some nonnarrative piece of music that's minimalist, that heightens the shape, because what happens usually is the balance starts to tip, where the story overwhelms. So, I need a little help on the cool end; I just try to maintain the balance of hot versus cold. There's this sense of fire and ice.

POTTER: There's a dynamic tension.

PARSON: Yeah. There's a dynamic tension. So, that would be the first step in looking at one element.

POTTER: How difficult is it for them to do that?

PARSON: It's really hard for people, who, in general, are not exposed to abstraction as viewers or as readers or in any way. Some people are naturally abstract thinkers; you get one of those a semester. But it's really hard for most actors to invest in this thinking at first. But the thing is that the way I assign this is so tight that there is basically nothing you can do to get out of the abstraction box. And then, they start to feel as performers, and watching the other students, what's going on, get excited about those elements. I do studies on time, on space, on motion, rhythm, dynamics. And then, with my more advanced students, I work with chance procedures. I give them dice, and we roll the dice to make movement, to make qualities of movement, to determine where the movement happens in the space. I've done a whole semester of chance work, and then you really have to get out of the way. It's very persuasive work.

POTTER: Do you decide on the elements before you begin the chance work?

PARSON: I do it all different ways. It's a really hard course to teach. You have to start (not to be coy) to almost meditate before you start. You have to clear your mind so much, because, as John Cage said, it's not about what you like and don't like. The inebriation of emotion is not possible. You have to get turned on, by the randomness, by the unknown, by getting out of the way; you have to get charged up by those things. That takes a certain openness and sophistication. That's why I don't teach it to beginning students. I'm doing a chance exercise right now with my students—well, they like the dice. That's fun.

How would I work with chance? I've done things where they go to the library and they take dice, like a dance library that has videotapes, and they pick a tape based on chance. And they have to learn a certain amount of movement, and then they apply chance elements to that movement once they learn it. The costume? They walk out the door, they time themselves; the first person they see in forty-five seconds, they have to dress like that person. Everything is up to chance: the movement, where it happens, what it looks like, how often it occurs.

What they find is, those who can sit with chance and let it work for them, and also stay out of the way but also be in very close touch with it—it's a little hard to describe—they get amazing results. The reason I like it—and it's not my training or background; I was literally exposed to it through watching the early chance work of Cunningham and reading little bits about Cunningham and Cage—but it's beautiful for students, because most of them don't have a subject matter yet, and they don't have a voice yet, so in all this stuff, all these exercises I'm doing, just like any other teacher, I'm trying to help the student find her own voice. You don't want it to happen too soon, because they just get so idiosyncratic and silly (and usually their subject matter is my parents' divorce, my abortion, so forth), and if you can get the narrative out of the way and really let them look at elements that could be interesting and supportive to that voice at some point, then they actually have something called "craft." I think. That's what I'm working on.

Sometimes, in the classroom, I have no idea what's going on . . .

POTTER: Because it's experimental?

PARSON: Right. Because I'm working as if I'm making a piece. I've found that I'm so allergic to formulas. I don't consider myself a teacher at all, in fact, and I don't even know if this stuff can really be taught. You have an artistic mind, a new potentially artistic mind, and you're feeding them a sensibility, and they can reject that sensibility when the class is over. They can say, I never want to do that again. Or they can let it affect their work.

POTTER: It just seems to me that it inevitably affects their work, if they get a chance to look at these elements. You say that dance is temporal. So is theater. Any kind of theater is taking place in time and space.

PARSON: Last term, I assigned a piece about Heidi. That character, or any character that has a lot coming off them, could be very cartoony, the big bad wolf, where they use these different dance elements to create a character on stage. What is the time of that character, what is the rhythm of that character, how does that character move, not realistically, but dance?

POTTER: I don't know exactly how to ask this question, but when you're working on a piece, how do you make a separation between the acting values and the movement? Wait, that's not exactly what I mean, let me try again. How do you approach the acting? Do you use some specific form of actor coaching?

PARSON: In terms of acting values that are going on onstage? I'm not really interested in making a performance that is based on acting values. To use the word differently: Everything that is going on onstage is valuable. A student might think that a transition moment between point A and point B is not valuable. And they will do it like a blind spot. And we'll work on creating that transition moment as a major moment. A thing of physical value. That goes back to Cunningham, who showed us that everything is of equal value.

That's the opposite of conventional theater, where certain things are very valuable and other things are a wash. And that's based on the story and the emotional track we're following. In my work and the work that I'm teaching, that's not a given at all. I'm very interested in transitions, and so sometimes, things that other people would consider to have less value, I would consider to have more value, and things that they think are very valuable, like peak emotional moments or catharsis, I consider less valuable. This is not intellectual on any level, it's just, that's what I feel in my body when I'm making it, and it seems to have more truth when I'm watching it. If something's very heightened on stage and asks for a dance or a song, an image, it may not be in the same place as where others might see it. And that's what I want to do for my students. I want them to find their own voice and find their own way to express their idea.

When I look at a piece of work, I try anything I can to express it, whether it's acting or dance or image. It never occurs to me, let's see, I think this should be an acting moment. It never occurs to me, it's more of a scramble. Desperation. How can I express this idea? Just try everything in the world, until it rings true to me or to everybody in the room. I try to get my students to at least feel that, that there's an equality between ways of expressing things. We're doing an exercise now about framing. I want them to understand that an event could be tiny and a frame could be huge. The frame is usually tiny, and the moment is huge, so we're working on the opposite. Create a frame, and we'll do a nonevent in the middle. A huge song-and-dance number, and then, the event is picking a penny off the floor, and then, the end of the frame is something equally enormous.

When I'm teaching, I'm thinking about what I'm interested in looking at. So, I guess that would say a lot about what I'm interested in seeing on stage. I tell the students to look at Richard Foreman, whose framing is so extreme, it's almost vaudevillian. He's a master framer. He'll throw a raw steak onto a bald head in order for you to hear a speech. Throw an egg at somebody, have ten guys come out and do a song and dance, and have the event take place inside of that. Whereas Cunningham would make the framing and the event the same. He would never differentiate. There are these different inspirations coming in.

So, I guess when I'm working with my company, the acting values are nurtured, but I'm never working on them as a separate issue. I like to watch acting grow over a period of years. Because of touring, my group has been lucky enough to perform stuff over a period of years, and performances do get a chance to grow. They also grow from piece to piece. When you see a piece at the beginning, it will have nowhere near the acting values that it does two weeks later. I get a stomachache from watching people push on stage and ask a lot of the audience. I hate that needy actor thing. I'd much rather see it much cooler and more detached in the beginning, and encourage the actors to slowly start to deepen and heat up what's happening where it's necessary. That's just a taste thing, because I literally cannot stand watching pushed emotion.

People sometimes say my work is a little cool. It's probably because it has a formal base. I trust form. I trust the structure of the piece, more than I trust the narrative of the piece; I'm more involved with it. If you really hang in there with it, it has more vertical depth. It has more layers than if you just trust the horizontal, if you just trust the narrative of the story, or even if you don't have a narrative, you just trust the horizontal, the temporal part of it.

My students say, well, how do I make my own structures and my own forms? When I described the first exercise, about the shapes, my focus in that was to find the balance between the cold and the hot, but to let them both be parallel and not let them get mixed up. But that's just a sensibility thing, not a formula. I can't say to you, okay, go out and make your own work, but make sure it has opposite temperatures.

POTTER: True, it's a sensibility, but it's also a skill. I think a lot of actors are resistant to doing that, because emotion is so highly touted.

PARSON: True. And in reaction to that, it's not wrong to act your way through this exercise, but it's just not what we're doing. And I had the same thing as a young performer. I acted my way through dances. And my teacher said, trust your body, see what happens, just let your body do it. And that was an incredibly important comment.

POTTER: I just have one more question. Why do you think your work is Postmodern?

PARSON: I don't really know what your definition of Postmodern is.

POTTER: No, *your* definition. You described your work to me as Postmodern, remember? A couple of months ago?

PARSON: Well, when I think about Postmodernism, to me it starts with Cunningham. Things are equal, the epiphany is equal to the transition. Twenty years later, Postmodernists are taking iconic figures and saying Elvis Presley has the same value as the Madonna, as Stravinsky, as the Mona Lisa—everything has equal value. In my opinion—this is just my observation, I'm not an academic at all—I say, okay, there are these boxes, and they're lined up, and they all vibrate against each other. And for a good practitioner of Postmodernism, those vibrations are very strong. And for a bad one, it's just eclectic and random, without keying into the synchronicity of the universe. Because, in order to do chance or Postmodernism, you have to believe that there is synchronicity there. And you have to be able to listen to it and work with it. It sounds like a big order, but it isn't really. It's just getting out of the way, letting things affect you, and seeing how they affect you. What you need, what you don't need, things like that. If that's true, I would say the work I'm teaching in class, based on that definition, is Postmodern.

SITI: Why We Train

A Conversation Between Anne Bogart and the SITI Company, compiled by Will Bond

T he SITI Company is an ensemble-based theater company whose three ongoing components are the creation of new work, the training of young theater artists, and a commitment to international collaboration.

In 1992 SITI was founded by Tadashi Suzuki and myself to redefine and revitalize contemporary theater in the United States through an emphasis on international cultural exchange and collaboration. Originally envisioned as a summer institute in Saratoga Springs, New York, SITI has expanded to encompass a year-round program based in New York City, with a summer season in Saratoga. SITI believes that contemporary American theater must necessarily incorporate artists from around the world and learn from the resulting cross-cultural exchange of dance, music, art, and performance experiences.

One of the most important aspects of SITI's work is the teaching of our training techniques to actors and theater artists throughout the United States and the world. Training, for the SITI Company, isn't a closed book. We are always exploring and expanding our horizons, both individually and collectively. Because of this, training is not just a platform from which we teach, but a forum within which we also learn.

The foundation of the SITI Company's training is comprised of two disparate yet complementary disciplines in both training and the creation of new work:

- The Viewpoints grew out of the Postmodern dance world as a way of creating structure for movement improvisation. I adapted the Viewpoints from Mary Overlie and expanded them for the theater to create bold and innovative new works. Through rigorous physical application of the Viewpoints, participants acquire an understanding of this unique vocabulary while aggressively exploring the boundaries of theater, movement, and music.
- The Suzuki Method is a rigorous physical and vocal discipline for actors, created by renowned theater artist Tadashi Suzuki and his company. The method is designed to regain the perceptive abilities and powers of the human body. Drawing on a unique combination of traditional and innovative forms, the training strives to restore the wholeness of the body as a tool of theatrical expression. As with many training traditions, the emphasis in the Suzuki Training is upon the lower half of the body, i.e., the hips, the legs, and the feet. Traditionally, the pelvic region houses the center of gravity, of breath, and is the seat of the emotions. The training seeks to challenge and strengthen awareness of the pelvic region and its grounding through articulation of the feet. One thing we know as artists from all over the world—indeed as human beings on earth—is that, if we share any common connection, it is through our connection to the earth, and the body is connected to the earth through the soles of the feet. And so the Suzuki Training involves a wide vocabulary of footwork, in particular, the rhythmic pounding of feet on the floor.

In the late 1970s I was introduced to the Six Viewpoints by Mary Overlie, who developed and articulated a unique approach to creation, analysis, and improvisation for the stage. Her new methods emerged at the tail end of the Judson Church Era—a time of great innovation in the dance world. The Six

Viewpoints (defined by Overlie as time, space, movement, shape, story, and emotion) addressed means of physically thinking about and working with time and space. I was immediately intrigued by this logical yet ingenious way of looking at movement for the stage, and I started to investigate her ideas with actors. The results were very exciting. In experimentation with the Viewpoints, I found a way to collaborate productively with actors in the creative process.

In forming my theater company, SITI, with Japanese director Tadashi Suzuki, we chose actors who had training both in the Suzuki method and with the Viewpoints. What we found was that the combination of Suzuki's training with the Viewpoints led to an astonishing demonstration of strength, focus, flexibility, and spontaneity that I find rare on the American stage. Because of these discoveries, SITI trains and teaches both approaches.

—*Anne Bogart*

Summer 2002 will be the ten-year anniversary of the SITI company. SITI was founded in Toga Mura, Japan, where its first production, Charles Mee's *Orestes*, was presented in the Toga International Arts Festival. That autumn, the company went to its U.S. home in Saratoga Springs, New York, and performed *Orestes,* while SCOT, the Suzuki Company of Toga, performed *Dionysus* with SITI company members and began the SITI summer training program at Skidmore College.

The following is a transcript of an interview that Anne Bogart did on June 20, 2001, with SITI company members Ellen Lauren, Stephen Webber, Susan Hightower, J. Ed Araiza (JEd), Will Bond (Bondo), Kelly Maurer, Akiko Aizawa, Leon Ingulsrud, Barney O'Hanlon, and Tom Nelis on the subject of training. Also in attendance were company member and technical supervisor Brian Scott and associate member Christopher Healey. The interview was done over dinner, after a long day of teaching and training, in the dining hall of Skidmore College in Saratoga Springs, New York, where the company was first established and where it has held its summer training intensive for the past ten years.

The company is gathered around a rectangular dining hall table littered with dinner trays and coffee cups. At the surrounding tables are the sixty-five SITI training participants from all over the world, having dinner and preparing for rehearsals of their composition assignments. In another section of the dining hall sit the dancers who are doing the David Parsons company workshop. Amidst the sounds of clinking silverware, falling trays, horseplay, laughter, and often very loud conversation, Anne begins:

ANNE: The first question is very general and dumb, but I think it will focus the other questions. So, the first question is: Why do you train?

(*Long silence.*)

STEPHEN: Stumped us!

(*Laughter.*)

LEON: We haven't got a clue.

(*More laughter.*)

KELLY: For me, it's a simple question with a simple answer. You train the body and the voice because it's the instrument you use to do the work that you do, and it's no less important than tuning a car, you know.

The SITI Company. Photographer: Richard Trigg.

ANNE: I think that answer's really important, and that's why I ask this question, because I think we need to answer, not esoterically, but just practically. I think that's a really brilliant answer.

JED: To become a better performer.

AKIKO: I train because I want to. I want to share the vocabulary with my company. Vocabulary means, about acting.

ELLEN: I train because I want to keep changing.

BARNEY: I train because the work directly addresses the work. You know. The training work directly addresses the work that we do on the stage. And we need to have one in order to have the other.

TOM: I train . . . to become virtuosic.

ELLEN: The alternative is unacceptable. To not train seems to me to be, first of all, just about as low on the gray cell evolutionary scale as you can go as an actor. For the stage, to not train . . .

KELLY: I think if you don't train, you're making a horrible assumption about what it takes to have the goods to get out there.

LEON: In one sense, the training isn't about . . . there is a component that is about learning how to act, but in terms of continuing to do it, it's about maintaining or furthering or exploring . . . that it's dynamic. That you don't look at the art as something that's static—that it's something you get once, and then you just keep doing that—but as something that keeps moving. And training is where you investigate that or encounter that.

JED: I train because it continues to interest me, and I find it pragmatic and accessible, while it's physically challenging and difficult.

KELLY: Why do you train, Stephen?

STEPHEN: Oh, thanks for asking, Kelly . . . *(all laugh)* . . . I train . . . actually, I train because it's very, *very* difficult to perform on the stage. And when you go on the stage, you need all the resources that you can get. You need all the help that you can get to be able to do that.

ANNE: How about you, Bondo?

BONDO: *(who is holding the mike for the interview)* I train for the experience. The experience of training is the experience of what it is to be in the day. And it is hard. And that is my experience of what it is to be on the stage. Just for the experience of it.

SUSAN: And it's also self-educational . . . a lot of information about who you are and what you can do.

BONDO: You can't have too much information about what you can do.

KELLY: And what you can't.

ANNE: I'm going to ask you another question now. By the way, the first two questions are about training in general and the last three are about Viewpoints and Suzuki. This question is: What are the best circumstances for training?

KELLY: A hungry group of people.

LEON: A context of high expectations.

BARNEY: Time.

ELLEN: Time. I was just going to say . . .

BARNEY: Space.

BONDO: Time and space . . .

BARNEY: Clean space.

ELLEN: And a group with whom you're going to go through it over a long period of time. A *company* for me is the best situation under which to train.

BONDO: Right. So, that's an answer in terms of why we train ourselves—we're in a context right now where we are training other people, too . . . but you're thinking . . .

ANNE: I'm just thinking, what are the best circumstances for training, which includes time and the kind of space, the kind of people you're with. Those things are all right; I think you should go on with that. What else makes for good circumstances in which to train?

ELLEN: I love training when you have an immediate project, or you're in rehearsal and you can contextualize the training toward the current work you're actually working on. It's not necessary, but I like that circumstance.

TOM: It's also great to train when you're teaching new people, so you get to ask the questions, the basic questions anew . . . face them for the first time.

BONDO: I also think of training in foreign places, like not at home, not where we live, training here in Saratoga, or training . . .

BONDO: . . . removed from . . . daily care . . . so to speak . . .

KELLY: Mmm.

BARNEY: Yes.

AKIKO: Yes.

SUSAN: Yes.

ELLEN: Yes.

KELLY: Seconded. Thirded.

TOM: And it's also good to train . . . to be taught by your mates. In other words, to keep hearing the underlying reasons from the training from various perspectives those being the various members of the company that you train with.

JED: I love training with people that are better than me, 'cause it's humbling and inspiring at the same time.

TOM: And it's also great to train—and somebody mentioned it already, but to expand on it—over a long period of time, so that you have the opportunity to train in different states—train when you're weak, train when you're energized, train when you're tired, train perhaps when you've got a nagging injury . . . only comes with time.

(After a short break to refill our dinner plates and coffee cups . . .)

ANNE: Number three: What specific issues has Suzuki training addressed in your work as an actor?

LEON: Good God.

ELLEN: They're getting harder.

TOM: The need to be onstage. How big or central to your work your desire to simply be onstage can be. And I mean, it's as central as anybody's idea of super-objective or anything like that. The underlying reason that you stand on the stage is the thing you need to know before you can do anything.

BONDO: Well, that was my first impulse, too. I mean, just the first time I did the training or went to Japan, I realized, oh, there is such a thing as this theater and there is such a conversation as a personal need and reason to be on the stage—how high that can actually be. That was my first impulse, too— and it's personal.

TOM: It's personal.

JED: Breath. Breath. Breath. Concentration. What is focus? And a lot more breath. And I'm still battling that every class.

KELLY: Energy. Concentration. Focus. Breathing. Rigor. Uh—will that do?

BONDO: Shall we go on?

ANNE: Yes.

ELLEN: I guess it's a fine line between this sounding self-righteous, but I believe, for me, acting as an act of heroism, or being heroic inside of your own body, your own psyche, and finding that joyful and expressive.

BARNEY: I would have to concur with that and just say, personally, when I first started doing the Suzuki training, hearing that, particularly from Ellen when she taught, and actually going for it inside as a student—trying to locate that hero, you know, in a person that I didn't find particularly heroic at the time—so that awakening that in me has not only profoundly, I think, affected my work on the stage, but in life.

AKIKO: For me . . . strength. Mentally . . . physically, as an actor and also as a human being.

STEPHEN: Presence. Presence.

LEON: There is something that . . . when you take away the costume, the play, the production, character, there is still acting—that there is something fundamental that an actor is doing that exists even when you strip all the trappings away from it. There is still that core of energy in the activity called "acting" that is discernable from daily life, and that is not dependant on the behavior of a character.

SUSAN: Yeah, mine's like that. It's about the physical expression of the imagination. How do you do that with your body?

JED: Yeah. Integrity. You can't fake the Suzuki training. You can see it very clearly when someone is not attempting—and that happens to me, that happens often—where you just don't have it, but you have to face that.

ANNE: I actually think you should go around one more time and go further maybe . . .

BONDO: . . . go deeper . . .

ANNE: . . . go deeper . . . one more round—everybody has to say something.

TOM: I realize through the training that it isn't about a character I'm playing, it's about me onstage and what I am doing and what I'm willing to face, and my, as you said, my personal need to be on the

Pictured left to right: Will Bond, Akiko Aizawa, Barney O'Hanlon, Danyon Davis.
Photographer: John Nation.

stage, not really my character's, and that the audience perceives character in my struggle. I gotta face myself.

ELLEN: In many ways, it's the most frightened I've ever felt—encountering that training, translating that training into performance, performing inside the aesthetic of that training, performing outside the aesthetic of that actual training but accessing it—and it's a rush for me. I'm addicted to that.

STEPHEN: Specifically, the issues that the Suzuki training has caused me to address as an actor are knowing which muscles to relax and which muscles I can use and put energy in, connecting the body and the voice, and knowing what the appropriate level of energy is from which to begin working. Those are three.

BARNEY: The word "energy" has come up. I really feel strongly that it teaches you how to create energy, and a great amount of energy, and I'm learning how to focus that energy in different ways, in different size containers, as Susie [Hightower] would say, you know, your expression, the body as an expressive being.

BONDO: It's the best example I've experienced of what it is to live . . . well, this is strange . . . a fictional life. To practice being fictional, which is larger than daily life and on a high experiential level of playing. It's terrifying, like Ellen said.

SUSAN: There are a lot of things in the training that we characterize as being impossible to do, impossible to achieve, but when you couple that with the infinite possibility that there is in your body and in its expression, then the only impossibilities are internal—are in you, it seems—so, it's fascinating to find that out when your life is filled with impossibilities that are habitual.

KELLY: I'd say that beyond the technical advantages that the training has—obviously, it makes you strong, it teaches you how to breathe, it teaches you how to focus energy, body precision, and the like—I think because the training is so difficult and because it demands that you step up to the plate with everything that you have on any given day, the thing that I love about it, the thing that I hate about it, the thing that I'm afraid of, and the thing that I also . . . what's the word that I want—celebrate—is that it exposes who you are on a daily basis.

STEPHEN: I think also it has given me a way to practice having an experience. That is a difficult thing to practice, but you can do it in the Suzuki training.

ELLEN: It just occurred to me, it's incredibly profound to me to be doing something that other actors did, that they learned from other actors before them, and to be part of a lineage passing from one generation to the other, and you feel that throughout history behind you and what lies ahead and where you lay in that chain. [That] is profoundly moving to me and influences . . . impacts my work.

ANNE: What specific issues has Viewpoint training addressed in your work as an actor?

BARNEY: The big realization about the Viewpoints is that it places the act of creation and the responsibility for creation back in the performer's hand, and for me, that's the most profound aspect of the Viewpoints.

LEON: . . . That's the sound of us all nodding.

BONDO: For me, it's the first time that the question or the conversation of freedom has really come up intelligently, and the emphasis on the amount of responsibility it takes to really have that conversation of what freedom is.

JED: It's very different in this country, I think, to have a training that asks you to celebrate your individuality, and yet to be a strong part of a group, to work in an ensemble. And that, to me, is kind of antithetical to what I—to how I had been trained before, and it's very liberating, because, I think, it does both.

SUSAN: I think this training tells you pretty quickly if you're not awake all the time. It's embarrassing. (*General laughter.*)

TOM: Because it puts, as Barn said, the creative responsibility back in the actor's hands, it ends up discussing the techniques or the reins that we hold as actors when we're on the stage—the techniques to explore the audience's sensibility of time and space on the stage. And as huge as those concepts seem, Viewpoints very pragmatically goes after elucidating how to manipulate time and how to manipulate space and how to speak with each other in terms of time and space, and I think once actors begin to relate to that, they feel an enormous sense of possibility in the stage picture, possibility that comes from them, as opposed to possibility that comes from being directed to do a certain thing.

ELLEN: For me, too, agreeing with all of this, it's the sense that the answer is always in the other—the answer to being on the stage, to the moment, the depth of the profundity of the moment on the stage, how to solve it, lies in the other partner or the player up on the stage with you, as opposed to something you've got to get yourself into or out of individually. And that sense of compassionately working toward revelation in the other has had big influence on me.

LEON: It deals with having a very refined and rigorous understanding and control of various principles governing time and space, and then taking all of that rigor and playing with it, which is not something that happens alone—it's a communal act of play. It is both selfish and selfless at the same time.

TOM: One of the huge revelations in Viewpoints is the collaborative nature of stage work. The possibilities that several points of view might add up to something much more complex, yet not complicated, but much more complex than a singular point of view. That's what the Viewpoints attempt. That idea.

ELLEN: I think you see yourself just as clearly in the Viewpoints work, just as objectively as you do . . . you have just as profound (that word again) a self-encounter as you do in the Suzuki training.

BARNEY: . . . clearly seeing your habits . . .

ELLEN: . . . having fun with yourself . . . clearly, clearly . . .

BONDO: I love, too, that you have as real a conversation as musicians have or as painters have, where notes are real and colors are real, and I find great strength and courage having the same conversation with those art forms as an actor. It's very encouraging and empowering, isn't it?

ELLEN: Good point. Yeah. Objectifying our work.

STEPHEN: I think one specific issue the Viewpoints has caused me to address in myself as an actor is the issue of space and my relationship to the space that I am in, my relationship to the space that I am occupying, and also the space on the opposite side of the room from me, the space of the audience and the space that is around all of that and how that relates to the issue of presence and my presence in the space.

AKIKO: Viewpoints . . . it's about listening, of course from my ear, and using my whole body—whole body surface—and listening [to] the information from the actors on the stage or the floor or the prop or the wall. The first time, I was so frightened, because . . . so much freedom . . . so much freedom . . . I was in the Suzuki Company of Toga, and first, I'm so . . . how do you say . . . restrict? (*confirming with Leon in Japanese*) . . . restricted . . . but Viewpoints is kind of free, and so, I couldn't move . . .

KELLY: Yeah. I would have to hearken to what Akiko is saying. I mean if the question is how has it affected me, I agree absolutely, just as a side note, with everything that's been said, but because my background, too, was deeply, *deeply* in the Suzuki training and the discipline and the rigor of that structure, which I adore and I think has great value, personally, the thing that the Viewpoints training has allowed me to do is trust my instincts and my sense of play and to bring back, not what is necessarily childish, hopefully, but get in touch with a childlike play inside of me that, you know, it's allowed to be fun, too. It doesn't have to all be pain.

TOM: Another thing that's very important to me is . . . it trains you to see what's really there, and this concept that Anne talks about, seeing without desire, becomes a basic tenet of how you will collaborate with a group toward building a piece that is going someplace that none of you can predict in the beginning, if you can look at it without desire. And so, one trains oneself to just see what's there, and when it's going in the right direction, we'll all recognize that fact, hopefully.

BARNEY: Maybe I'll just wrap it up . . . the Viewpoints, and also for me the Suzuki trainings, are fluid trainings . . .

JED: Are what?

BARNEY: . . . fluid trainings—the work never stops, you never stop discovering, you just get deeper and deeper and deeper and deeper. You can get deeper into space; you can go deeper into time; you can go deeper into your relationship with another human being. And the more you practice it, the more enormous and infinite it becomes, and that's why we do it, because it just keeps going; there's no end in sight.

ANNE: You've already started in on this last one, but where do these two trainings intersect?

BARNEY: On the stage in rehearsal . . . I don't know . . .

KELLY: In the center of your body.

ALL: In the center of your body!

TOM: Now, we used to say—and I don't if it's still true, but I'll throw that in—but we used to say that "we build them with Viewpoints, and we maintain the pieces with Suzuki . . ."

ANNE: I never heard that.

TOM: We used to explain it that way, and it's interesting, I think, just as a jumping-off point.

ANNE: That's great.

TOM: I wonder whether people still think that or not, because it seems to me they've merged very much. But I remember a student asking a questions last week about the Suzuki: "You're telling us that the Suzuki training changes because their shows change, and they need other exercises to address the points of the show. Does your training change that way?" And while our approach to the Suzuki work does not necessarily do that, our approach to Viewpoints seems to be very fluid . . . how will we start this show, or what's a good way to attack this show? So I wonder, I don't know, I wonder if anyone else still thinks that's true.

JED: I think that there's more of a blending. I would still say that's true, but it's not as distinct as when that was first said. Because I do think that, absolutely, in the maintenance of the show, we're still working on those issues of time and space and kinesthetics and all of that stuff, but I would say, that's the first step.

TOM: Time and space is so much a part of both of the trainings.

JED: Yeah.

STEPHEN: I think the two trainings intersect onstage, in performance, and in rehearsal.

AKIKO: I agree. And both of them are very practical. That's it.

JED: I think that that's a huge issue for me. I think these trainings are incredibly pragmatic. I came to them later, and I remember, the first time I saw the Suzuki training, the issues that the actors, the workshop participants, were dealing with were crystal clear. And what you can learn in one day, even though, as Barney says, it's fluid, you never stop learning. There are so many concrete issues you deal with, and if you're smart, can learn about them the first day, that it gives you a reason to keep studying for twenty years.

ELLEN: I think they both intersect in the quality and level of rigor and energy with which one approaches them. They both intersect, as we touched on before, in the mirror that they hold up to the self, to your foibles, and your pluses. I think they both benefit by doing them as a group. They are not solo sports. And finally, as Stephen said, in the moment, in the act of creation, is ultimately where they crash together.

LEON: I think both of them make two very basic assertions: one, that the actor is an artist engaged in creativity, and the other is that the human body—the expressive potential of the human body—is unbounded and that you just can keep exploring.

The SITI Company is comprised of: Akiko Aizawa, J. Ed Araiza, Anne Bogart, Will Bond, Susan Hightower, Leon Ingulsrud, Ellen Lauren, Kelly Maurer, Jefferson Mays, Charles Mee, Jr., Tom Nelis, Barney O'Hanlon, Neil Patel, James Schuette, Brian H. Scott, Mimi Jordan Sherin, Megan Wanlass Szalla, Stephen Webber, and Darron L. West.

The Problem of Movement Theater

Brad Krumholz

As soon as the actor is in front of the spectator, her body is no longer her own. Everything she does is under scrutiny and generates and acquires meaning, just as every word that passes her lips is heard, interpreted, and processed. For this very simple reason, it is clear why an actor must develop her body just as fully as her voice and skills of textual interpretation.

In our English-speaking, North American theater culture, the majority of plays require "realistic" acting styles. This means that the actor must appear to be going about her business in a normal, day-to-day style of behavior, in both body and voice. However, the actor is also required to heighten this behavior, so that she may be seen and heard from quite a distance, and also, so that the play can become something more than a cold reading of text. Choices are made, vocally and physically (according to clearly decided intentions and objectives), to convey information to the audience about character, character development, point of view (of both actor and director, if not playwright), and to sculpt the energy and flow of the spectator's sensorial journey.

It stands to reason that, in order to do all of this (and I realize that I am simplifying beyond belief), the actor must possess a balanced combination of physical and vocal control and freedom. If the spectator is supposed to "believe" that the character has a bad leg, which prevents him from doing something of import in the story, and the actor does not portray this physically, the point will have been lost. Likewise, if the actor overdoes it, the spectator will be jarred out of belief and will not experience the full potential impact of the play.

Why am I going on like this? In order to begin to elucidate the basic problem of "movement" in the theater. Why is it a problem? Well, it's not such a problem if you are dealing with the world of psychological realism. Granted, some actors are better than others—many overact, and many are imprecise, and so the theater ends up suffering from mediocre performers who cannot communicate anything substantial to their audiences, anything beyond the words—but there are some excellent and well-trained actors in the mainstream theater. No, the "problem" generally arises when people try to make theater that is somehow "different" or "new" or "groundbreaking."

Perhaps because they realize that the body is a major medium of the theater experience, or because they have a fascination with the abstract musicality of the flesh, or an aversion to text, or they just want to do something out of the ordinary, theater makers will often try to "incorporate movement" into their work. When, as in psychological realism, the movement form is more or less a version of "real" behavior, there's not much cause for the confusion of the creator—opening a window onstage is based on a daily and familiar behavior from life experience, even if onstage, it acquires additional layers of subliminal image, meaning, memory, muscular action, etc. But when the movement form is decidedly *not* based on "real" behavior, the referent gets lost. The visible movement of the body is left searching for a form, and the result is usually false, noncommunicative, imprecise, boring, clichéd, or banal.

Sometimes, the solution to the lack-of-form problem is to use a preexisting form of movement, like dance, inside the theater medium. "Dance theater" is just such a hybrid. There are dance theater companies whose work is mainly a very theatrical type of dance, and there are dance theater companies who attempt to blend the theater and the dance more seamlessly. Generally, however, there is a pretty clear distinction between the elements of a dance theater performance that are dance and those that are theater, even if these parts alternate with great alacrity (and if this distinction is not made by the artists, it is generally made by the spectators).

Theater makers who don't have the facility or desire for such interdisciplinary ventures end up searching for movement forms in all sorts of ways—truly, they don't know what to do with their bodies, but they feel that they must find *something*, or else they will be betraying a fundamental truth of theater—that the body must express in the space. So, some come up with "gestures," which can be repeated when necessary, in accordance with the effect desired in the play. Some create choreographies, either based on some actual daily activities (which become stylized and abstracted or else decontextualized) or based on the generalized pseudo-dance movement exercises they have invented. The result is generally incomprehensible.

Most of this kind of theater grew out of the "movement" classes that are offered to help actors in the world of "straight" theater.[1] The best actors in straight theater recognize the need for the delicate balance of form and freedom. So, they take classes that will allow them to strengthen, to become flexible, and to find freedom, both physical and psychological, with their bodies. These training exercises stay in the studio though, since no one in his right mind would, for example, begin to make strange, abstract spine undulations while portraying Biff in *Death of a Salesman* on Broadway.

But some actors enjoy their movement workshops so much that they want to find a way to work that way all the time. And why not? It's good for the body, it feels good, it's sexy, and what could be truer to theater than to expose its guts, the very primal stuff that lies beneath all that stage acting? And so, the movement workshop has found its way onto the stage and into the spotlight.

So now, you have heard my complaint. It is now clear that the theater's relationship to "movement" is problematic. What do I propose as a solution? I propose action.

What is action? Action is the attempt of a person to do something real. It sounds so simple, and yet, even as I conceive of such a thing, I become aware of the task's enormity. In life, to do something real is the norm—I eat, I pick up a pencil, I walk to the post office—at every moment acting upon inner impulse, to make the material world provide me with what I desire. But on the stage, the surrounding material world is fabricated, and so, if I am to do something real, I must find a way of dealing with the reality of my fictional, created surroundings, my given circumstances.

One problem is that the harder I try to act truthfully, the less truthfully I act. The craft of acting can be seen as the development of techniques to overcome this paradox.

For example, in my scene, I need to pick up a pencil, and at the same time, I need to let the spectator understand that I have just realized that my brother-in-law just told me a lie. So, I construct a series of mental and physical cues—of action, intention, memory, image—which, through repetition in rehearsal, become a part of my real circumstances. When I pick up the pencil in performance, I am actually doing something real for myself, which, if the scene is well-constructed, will read for the spectator without interference.

In relation to the aforementioned "problem," there should be no difference between this process in a realist situation and in a more abstract style of presentation. But as I said, when the source or referent of the form is not everyday behavior, the artists become confused, and they begin to create vague forms based on vague emotions, intentions, and images. Real actions originate deep in the body, and each engages the whole body in its own dynamic and precise way. Usually, when an action for the stage is created badly, the body fails to find this dynamism and precision and only approximates the outer form of the action, without the complex neuromuscular connections present in a real action. The consequence of this failure is the loss of the spectator's investment. Only if the actor is deeply engaged in action will the audience become engrossed and receive the communication on every level: intellectual, emotional, and visceral.

This does not mean that the actor must be involved in daily behavior on stage. Rather, it means that the actor must learn to create the verisimilitude of the life process of action inside everything she does, regardless of whether it is "realistic" or "abstract." In my opinion, there exists the greatest possibility of communicating something profound, ineffable even, by using the expressive and symbolic powers of the body. However, this can only occur if there exists the balance of impulse and form, of spontaneity and precision, that comes from real action.

We cannot rely on luck or faith in talent, and we cannot expect to achieve success by working sporadically and without continuity. The ability to create real action comes as a result of long, hard, unflagging work on that ever-disappearing craft of the actor as an expressive organism.

How is this possible? If you want to exist in the realm of traditional, non–movement-based theater, there are a number of conservatory programs that will provide the tools necessary to working well. But if you want to create work that is different, that seeks to communicate through the entire being of the performer, I suggest that you forget about working in the mainstream—and this means abandoning the structure of the mainstream theater as well as its forms. It means establishing a structure within which to investigate and develop craft, in a focused and long-term group, led by a collaboration of director and actor, in a search for expressivity through action.

It is essential that this work occur inside of a context that can support it. It would be useless to engage in this search without a director who can respect the actor's material, developing and molding it successfully into its final performance form, in concert with the material of the rest of the ensemble and the overall performance design. You must form a band of like-minded theater warriors, because without a group, the actor will lose the battle and become absorbed as a tool in someone else's ineffectual and short-lived vision-project in the world of theater as a business.

"That's not fair!" I hear someone say? "That's not practical," I hear another voice? Exactly so. The current situation of the noncommercial, nonmainstream theater in North America is incredibly cruel, bordering on impossible. But what choice do you have, if you really look at the available options? You can go to school, but you can't stay in school forever, and most schools will only prepare you for a career in the mainstream theater. Once you graduate, after a few years of studies led by a variety of teachers, of a variety of quality, with a total lack of truly focused development, what will you do? You can audition for shows—but no matter how "alternative" the show may be, you're still auditioning, which means that, in a very short period of time, you must find a common vocabulary of physical expression with your entirely disparate and temporary coworkers—a totally untenable situation.

The remaining options are joining a group that already exists or starting your own group. To join a preexisting group that works with the necessary consistency, rigor, and honesty is a very rare possibility, but it can happen if you search long and hard enough. If you start your own group, and you intend to work in a style that is not realism, then you must strive to develop a way of work that will actually allow you and your comrades to express individually and together, with honesty and rigor, and without hiding. This, according to me, is the only possibility of overcoming the "problem" of movement in the theater. And it requires an incredible devotion to a very difficult path, for which the rewards are anything but financially or publicly gratifying, at least for the first five or ten years of the group's life.

But listen: Dancers commit to the continuing development of their craft. How frequently and how hard does a good dancer train? How many hours per day? For that matter, how many hours per day does everyone just assume a musician needs to practice if he is to achieve any level of quality? So, why should it come as such a shock that an actor must also train daily (for many hours and years, along a clear and focused path) to be good?

It comes as a shock because: (1) In theater there exists the possibility of a career based almost solely on looks; (2) there is a commonly held belief that what makes an actor good is this thing called "talent"; and (3) there exists no possibility for a "job-to-job" actor to practice every day, because this actual practicable and applicable craft is missing in our culture. Sure, actors take yoga classes to remain healthy, strong, and limber, and they take an occasional Viewpoints workshop to have a good "learning experience"—but where are the scales to practice and the dance steps to master? And what do these have to do with the actual work actors can do in the rehearsal period, anyway?

Now, I understand that the business of theater will not likely be changing anytime soon, and that actors will continue to rely on looks and talent and connections and the occasional workshop to get by, or to succeed. But this article is about movement and its place in the theater. And I say that if you want to do "movement theater," you should have a training, whether it be codified or invented, you should work consistently with a group of committed coworkers, and most importantly, you must know (even if you can't articulate the knowledge in all of its complexity) that every action you create onstage exists for a purpose—to do something real. Then, and only then, might the public begin to have a need for your work, because they will receive from it something delectable and rare and electrifying, and available through no other life experience than theater.

NOTE

1. Musical theater actors are generally trained in dance, and they have a degree of mastery over the forms used in the dance sections of musical theater, but there is, more and more, a lack of Fred Astaire–like leading men, and more of a distinction between the discipline of actor, dancer, singer, etc. . . .

Contributors

Barbara Adrian is presently an Assistant Professor of Theater at Marymount Manhattan College, teaching voice, speech, and movement for the actor in the B.F.A. and B.A. theater program. She also coaches professional actors for television, film, and stage as well as freelances as a movement and voice-speech-dialect coach for productions throughout the New York tri-state area, working with such notable directors as Robert Brustein, David Rabe, Elisabeth Swados, and Tina Landau. Ms. Adrian holds an M.F.A. in Acting from Brooklyn College and is a CMA in Laban Movement Analysis.

Erika Batdorf has performed, directed, and choreographed original movement theater since 1983. Her solo works have appeared in such places as the Smithsonian Institute, The Fine Arts Museums of San Francisco, Landegg Academy for International Development in Switzerland, Harvard University, Trinity Repertory Theatre in Rhode Island, and P.S. 122 in New York City. Batdorf has taught at Brandeis University, Emerson College, the University of Alaska Anchorage, and at the Boston Conservatory. She runs The Batdorf School for Movement Theatre and teaches at York University in Toronto.

Will Bond is a member of the SITI Company, an ensemble-based theater company whose three ongoing components are the creation of new work, the training of young theater artists, and a commitment to international collaboration. The SITI approach teaches and trains actors in both the Viewpoints and Suzuki methods.

Paula Murray Cole is a teacher, actor, director, and New York State Licensed Massage Therapist. She has taught acting, voice, and movement at several institutions, including Ithaca College; the University of Illinois Champagne–Urbana; and New York University, where she teaches the Summer Performance Workshop with Michele Minnick. She played Ofelia in Richard Schechner's production of *Hamlet* and Natasha in his *Three Sisters*. Her recent directing credits include Benjamin Britten's *Albert Herring* at Ithaca College and Euripedes' *Trojan Women* at the Governor's Magnet School for the Arts in Norfolk, Virginia. She is currently conducting research on the applications and effects of therapeutic bodywork, for both professional performers and those in training.

Susan Dibble is a choreographer, dancer, and teacher. She graduated from SUNY College at Purchase with a B.F.A. in Dance in 1976. In 1987 Susan joined the faculty of Brandeis University, where she teaches Movement for Actors, Modern Dance, Choreography, Clown, Mask, Period Styles, and Historical Dance. Over the past twenty-five years, she has performed with her company, Susan Dibble Dance Theater, and has worked as a choreographer for theaters throughout New England and New York City. Susan is the resident choreographer and director of movement training for Shakespeare & Co. in Lenox, Massachusetts, where she has been working since 1981.

Mary Fleischer is an Associate Professor of Theater Arts and Chair of Fine and Performing Arts at Marymount Manhattan College. She holds a Ph.D. in theater from the Graduate Center of the City

University of New York, and her interdisciplinary interests have generated performance projects, articles, and a forthcoming book.

Dan Kamin is the author of *Charlie Chaplin's One-Man Show*. On film, he created the physical comedy sequences for *Chaplin* and *Benny and Joon* and trained Robert Downey, Jr. and Johnny Depp for their acclaimed starring performances. He also played the wooden Indian that came to life in *Creepshow 2* and created Martian movement for Tim Burton's *Mars Attacks!* Dan performs his one-man shows internationally. A frequent guest artist with symphony orchestras, his popular "Comedy Concertos" combine movement, comedy, and classical music. In recent years, Dan has directed several hit productions of classic comedies in Pittsburgh. Visit *www.dankamin.com* for more information.

Brad Krumholz is cofounder and artistic director of NaCl Theatre. Since 1997, he has directed *The Secret Storey, A Canon for the Blue Moon, The Passion according to G.H., ASPHYXIA and Other Promises, Arca Nova, The Time Cycle*, and *Invisible Neighborhood*. Since 1990, he has worked in the field of ensemble experimental theater, first as a student at the Odin Teatret in Denmark and then with Canada's Primus Theatre. Krumholz was a founding member of Cleveland's Theatre Labyrinth (now Wish*hounds*). NaCl produces The Catskill Festival of New Theatre at the company's work center in Sullivan County, New York.

Marianne Kubik has trained with Gennadi Bogdanov, protegé of the late Nikolai Kustov, and Nikolai Karpov at the Moscow School of Biomechancs. She was also a participant in the first United States workshop in biomechanics at Tufts University in 1993. She has been utilizing Meyerhold's pedagogy and technique as a tool for her training of contemporary acting students. She is currently Assistant Professor of Movement in the Department of Theater and Film at the University of Kansas.

Teresa Lee is a theater and movement artist-educator. She is an associate professor teaching performance in the Department of Theater and Dance at Appalachian State University. Ms. Lee earned her certification to teach the Alexander Technique from The Alexander Foundation in Philadelphia, Pennsylvania, in 1995. Since then she has been working privately, applying her Alexander work to actor preparation in professional theater workshop settings, and in college and university classes in the Southeast. She is also on the faculty of the Seven Oaks Alexander Technique summer residency course and serves on the Board of Alexander Technique International.

Jill Mackavey holds a B.F.A. in Acting from Boston University's School of Fine Arts, an M.F.A. in Directing from Brooklyn College, City University of New York, and is a Certified Movement Analyst from the Laban/Bartenieff Institute of Movement Studies, New York City. As a writer, award-winning director, teacher, movement specialist, and actress, she has worked in academic theater and dance for more than twenty years in the greater Boston and Orlando areas and in New York City. Jill also works in the area of Theology and the Arts. She and husband, Rick, have two sons and live in Ashland, Massachusetts.

Kari Margolis is a director, playwright, and actor and is co–artistic director, with partner Tony Brown, of Adaptors, Inc. (Margolis Brown Theater Company). Many of the multimedia theater productions she has created have toured nationally and abroad. She has also created site-specific works for such places as Coney Island, the Brooklyn Museum, and the Minnesota Science Museum. Ms. Margolis's work has been recognized with awards including six fellowships from the NEA, a Pew/TCG National Artist Residency, a "Bessie" New York Performance Award, a New York Foundation Performance Fellowship, three fellowships from the McKnight Foundation, and a Jerome Travel Grant.

Rod McLucas has directed and translated into rhyming verse Molière's *Tartuffe* and *Misanthrope* and has directed, adapted, and choreographed, among many others, Wedekind's *Lulu*, Schnitzler's *Fatal Question*, Lope de Vega's *Fuente Ovejuna*, and Molière's *Hypochondriac*. When other companies tire of his megalomania he masterminds the forays of the Colossal Theatre Company, a producing entity dually dedicated to classical and experimental work. A modern dancer during the Pleisticene era, he has taught his own movement-based approach to theater at NYU and Marymount Manhattan College—where he taught classical acting for several years—and currently coaches select victims in New York City.

Michele Minnick is a performer, director, teacher, certified Laban movement analyst, writer, and occasional Russian translator. She translated and performed the role of Anfisa in Richard Schechner's production of Chekhov's *Three Sisters* and played Rosencraft in Schechner's *Hamlet*. Her directing work includes *Julie Johnson, Cloud Tectonics,* and *The Gene Pool* at the Kitchen Theatre in Ithaca, New York, and *The Little Mahagonny* for the Ithaca Opera Association. Currently she is developing *Not I/Marina Tsvetaeva* with composer-choreographer Liz Claire. Michele is a Ph.D. candidate in the Department of Performance Studies at NYU, where she is working on, among other things, the relationship between performance art and self-transformation.

Annie-B Parson is artistic director of BIG DANCE THEATER, which was awarded an Obie in 2000 and has been presented for six seasons at Dance Theater Workshop, three seasons at Jacob's Pillow, two seasons at Classic Stage Co., two seasons at The Kitchen, two seasons at the Guggenheim Works and Process Series, at the Performing Garage, The Walker, and at the American Dance Festival, among other venues. BIG DANCE has performed at festivals in Italy, Germany, Belgium, Holland, France, and Tblisi. Ms. Parson has choreographed for film, television, and regional theater, as well. She teaches at the Experimental Theater Wing at NYU's Tisch School of the Arts.

Nira Pullin is the choreographer and period movement specialist for Wayne State University theaters. She has choreographed for the Utah Shakespeare Festival, Michigan Opera, Dayton Opera, Prince Street Players, national and international tours, numerous colleges and universities, television commercials, and industrials. She has taught period dance and deportment in England, Germany, Canada, and throughout the United States. She is a recipient of the President's Award for Excellence in Teaching, a member of the Society of Stage Directors and Choreographers, and a certified instructor in the Original Pilates Method.

Alan S. Questel is a Trainer in the Feldenkrais Method and was personally trained by Dr. Feldenkrais. He has taught at Princeton University, SUNY College at Purchase, the Institute for Transpersonal Psychology, the New York Open Center, and the New Actors Workshop. He lectures and teaches at hospitals, colleges, and Feldenkrais Professional Training Programs throughout the United States, Australia, Europe, Japan, and Canada. An actor before becoming interested in the Feldenkrais Method, Alan worked and toured with Jerzy Grotowski and Paul Sills. He makes his home in Santa Fe, New Mexico.

Floyd Rumohr is an award-winning director, author, and teaching artist. A leading arts advocate for children, Mr. Rumohr has worked with over eight thousand public school students and hundreds of teachers and has presented at conferences and served on panels for the Arts-in-Education Roundtable Face-to-Face Conference, Partnership for After School Education, and the Coalition of Essential Schools. He has served on the faculty of Arts Connection's Summer Institute, where he trained teachers to integrate arts processes into their teaching, and is currently a consultant to the New York Foundation for the Arts' Technical Assistance Program (TAP).

Joan Schirle is a founding member and Artistic Director of Dell'Arte International, whose unique physical style reflects over twenty-five years of collaborative creation. She is director of training at the Dell'Arte International School of Physical Theater and a senior teacher of the Alexander Technique. Her teaching includes movement, mask performance, Commedia dell'Arte, and physical acting. She has taught in M.F.A. programs at Yale, UCSD, University of Missouri Kansas City, and others. Her solo show, *Second Skin*, tours widely. She has directed at San Diego Rep, Houston's Alley Theatre, Bloomsburg Ensemble, and A Traveling Jewish Theatre. She heads Dell'Arte's proposed M.F.A. program and its Study Abroad: Bali Program.

In addition to her regional and Off-Off Broadway credits, actor and teacher **Jean Taylor** has collaborated on a variety of original plays, including *Fatesplay*, *Be An Animal/Don't Be An Animal*, *The Swim Meet*, and *Snatches*, featured at the 2002 Edinburgh Fringe Festival. Ms. Taylor is a teaching artist with Lincoln Center Institute and the Flynn Center for the Performing Arts. She teaches clown for The Barrow Group Theatre in New York City, and has been a guest teacher at The New School, The Stella Adler Conservatory, and Marymount College. Ms. Taylor studied clown with Philippe Gaulier, David Shiner, Ron Foreman, Vincent Rouche, and Merry Conway.

Caroline Thomas founded the Total Theatre Lab in the 1980s. Ms. Thomas is the creator of The Integrated Acting Process and is a director and playwright as well as a teacher. Ms. Thomas graduated from the Royal Academy of Dramatic Art in London, studied Meisner and Method in New York City. Later she became involved in Experimental Theatre and worked with Andre Gregory, Robert Wilson, and Jerzy Grotowski.

Paul Urcioli is an actor and director living and working in New York City. He has performed improvisation and educational theater in clubs and schools throughout New York and New Jersey with Good Clean Fun and as half of the duo Goodhead and Attitude. Paul has taught improvisation at NYU Undergraduate Drama, at Oberlin College, and in countless workshops for colleges and high schools throughout the United States. He is currently a Master Teacher of Advanced Performance Technique-Styles, Physical Comedy and Improvisation in New York City at the Atlantic Theater Company Acting School, whose technique is Practical Aesthetics, developed by David Mamet and William H. Macy.

Loyd Williamson, creator of the Williamson Technique, is artistic director of the Actors Movement Studio in New York City, which he founded in 1977. His technique has been taught at the Mason Gross School of the Arts, Rutgers University, since 1978 and in other acting programs. He has coached extensively on Broadway, Off-Broadway, and film. He holds an M.F.A. in scene and lighting design from the

University of Georgia. He completed Sanford Meisner's professional acting program, later studying with Harold Clurman. His mentor in Movement for Actors was Anna Sokolow, and he was an actor in her *Players Project*.

Shelley Wyant is a teacher, director, and performer. The mask has been Ms. Wyant's special teaching tool, and she has offered workshops at conservatories and universities such as Brown University, Smith College, SUNY New Paltz, and the Lincoln Center Institute. She is currently on the faculty of Bard College, the Stella Adler Conservatory, and the Actor's Studio M.F.A. Ms. Wyant is a founding member of Actors and Writers of Olivebridge, New York. In 1990, she founded MaskWork Unlimited, whose critically acclaimed works using masks and giant puppets have been performed in the Hudson Valley, New York City, and internationally.

Training

This list contains contact information for the contributors and their training programs, as well as for programs recommended by them. A good source for more extensive, current information is Theatre Communication Group's monthly publication *American Theatre* (355 Lexington Avenue, New York, New York 10017, *www.tcg.org*), which contains interesting articles on current companies, directors, teachers, trends, as well as extensive advertising for diverse training programs. I have found the training directories published by American Theatre Works, Inc. (P.O. Box 510 Dorset, Vermont 05251; phone (802) 867-2223, fax (802) 867-0144, *www.theatredirectories.com*) to be very useful. Although you will have to carefully sift through information provided by many different schools, contact information and Web addresses are provided, so you will be able to locate an array of options nationally and internationally, that fit your financial, training, and geographical needs. Must I add that the information in advertisements and school-provided copy would tend to be self-serving? It would behoove you to seek out personal contact with someone who has experienced the training before you commit yourself.

- Actors Movement Studio, 302 West 37th Street, Sixth Floor, P.O. Box 1098, New York, NY 10018; tel (212) 736-3309; *www.actorsmovementstudio.com*. Classes held at above address; offers full training in Williamson technique, Level I to Level IV.
- Atlantic Theater Company Acting School, 453 West 16th Street, New York, NY 10011; tel (212) 691-5919. Steven Hawley, Director; Brandon Thompson, Admissions. Movement classes include Laban, Suzuki, Viewpoints, and Committed Impulse (an advanced specialized movement and approach to character designed by Josh Pais).
- Brandeis University M.F.A. in Acting Program, 415 South Street, Waltham, MA 02254-9110; tel (781) 736-3340.
- Chekhov Theatre Ensemble, 138 South Oxford Street, Suite #1-B, Brooklyn, NY 11217; tel (718) 398-2494; *www.chekhovtheatre.org*
- CLOWN TRAINING: The Barrow Group, New York City; tel (212) 501-2545; *www.barrowgroup.org*; *barrowgroup@ earthlink.net*. Four- and six-week clown workshops.
- CLOWN TRAINING: Ecole Philippe Gaulier, Michael's Church Hall, St. Michael's Road, London, England NW2 6XG; tel 0208-438-0040; *gaulier@dircon.co.uk*. Month-long clown workshops.
- Dell'Arte International School of Physical Theatre, P.O. Box 816, Blue Lake, CA 95525; tel (707) 668-5663; fax (707)-668-5665; *www.dellarte.com*; *dellarte@aol.com*. Full-time one-year professional training program, summer workshops, and an M.F.A. program pending accreditation.
- The Feldenkrais Guild of North America, 3611 Southwest Hood Avenue, Suite 100, Portland, OR 97201; tel (800) 775-2118 or (503) 221-6612; fax (503) 221-6616; *www.feldenkrais.com*; *guild @feldnkrais.com*.
- Feldenkrais Resources, 830 Bancroft Way, Berkeley, CA 94710; tel (800) 765-1907 or (510) 540-7600; fax (510) 540-7683; *feldenres@aol.com*.
- Laban Movement Analysis, Integrated Movment Studies, 2525 12th Avenue West, Suite #1, Seattle, WA 98119-2116; tel (206) 849-4380; fax (206) 283-1838; *www.imsmovement.com*.

- Laban/Bartenieff Institute of Movement Studies, 234 5th Avenue, Room 201, New York, NY 10001; tel (212) 213-1162; *www.limsonline.org.*
- Margolis Method Theater Center, 3112 17th Avenue South, Minneapolis, MN 55401; tel (612) 722-2333; *www.margolisbrown.org*; *margolisbrown@aol.com.* The center offers three-, six-, and nine-week workshops in spring, summer, and fall, and a one-week intensive workshop in July.
- NaCl Theatre (North American Cultural Laboratory), Tannis Kowalchuk, Cofounder and Artistic Director, 110 Highland Lake Road, Highland Lake, NY 12743; tel (845) 557-0694; *www.nacl.org*; *nacl@nacl.org.* NaCl offers various workshops and schools throughout the year, both in New York City and at its theater center in the Catskills. NaCl offers a performer training retreat in the summer at NaCl Catskills, the theater and artists' residence in Highland Lake, New York. Set in the Catskill mountain region, the retreat allows for an intense immersion into a complete performer training that is physical, vocal, and creative. Each session is seven days long and led by NaCl founders Tannis Kowalchuk and Brad Krumholz, with guest directors.
- Shakespeare & Co. Training Programs, 70 Kemble St., Lenox, MA 01236; tel (413) 637-1199.
- SITI Company. *Mailing address:* Old Chelsea Station, P.O. Box 1922, New York, NY 10011. *Company address:* 49 Bleecker Street, 4th Floor, Suite 10, New York, NY 10012; tel (212) 477-1469; fax (212) 477-0564. For the New York City training sessions with SITI and the SITI summer program at Skidmore College in Saratoga Springs, New York.
- Total Theatre Lab, 118 West 79th Street, New York, NY 10024; tel (212) 799-4224; *www.totaltheatrelab.com.* Caroline Thomas, Founder. The Integrated Acting Process is a constantly evolving technique, involving a particularly supportive interaction among students, and between students and teachers. It focuses on balancing body, voice, mind, and feeling. Facets of the training are traditional: Classes offer the study of scenes or monologues, as well as technique. However, the features that particularize the Integrated Process are the importance given to breathing, voice, and movement, and the fact that students are encouraged to find their own process and make their own discoveries.

Coaching, Private Lessons, and Individual Consultants
- Jill Mackavey, M.F.A., CMA, 25 Hawthorne Road, Ashland, MA 01721; tel (508) 881-9221; *RTagliared@aol.com*
- Rod McLucas; tel(212) 362-8793; *RodMcLucas@nyc.rr.com.* Mr. McLucas offers private coaching in New York City and is frequently invited by membership companies and colleges to conduct workshops in classical theater techniques, self-generated styles, and movement and voice as methods of connecting.
- Alan S. Questel, 13 Reno Road, Santa Fe, NM 87508; tel (505) 466-3336; fax (505) 466-3334; *ASQUESTEL@aol.com.* In Europe please contact: *konradwiesendanger@swissonline.com.* Alan S. Questel has a series of CDs, recorded live at public workshops.

Period Dance
When researching any subject, I believe that primary resources are a must. However, to the novice, the primary sources on early dance can seem like a foreign language. In fact, most of our primary sources prior to the nineteenth century are in Italian, French, or Spanish. Some translations are available.

For the purposes of this book, I have listed secondary sources, because they are more readily available and easier to read. I have also listed where to buy books and some Web sites with helpful information.

For a more complete list of resources, including primary sources, additional secondary sources, videos, and workshops, log onto the Allworth Press Web site at *www.allworth.com*.

A Short List of Books on Period Dance That I Have Found Helpful

Aldrich, Elizabeth. *From the Ballroom to Hell: Grace and Folly in Nineteenth-Century Dance*. Evanston, Ill.: Northwestern University Press, 1991. Excellent information on dances, manners, fashions, and music of the 1800s.

Anonymous. *The Extraordinary Dance T.B. 1826: An Anonymous Manuscript in Facsimile*. Hillsdale, N.Y.: Pendragon Press, 2000. With analysis by Elizabeth Aldrich, Sandra Noll Hammond, and Armand Russell.

Brissenden, Alan. *Shakespeare and the Dance*. Atlantic Highlands, N.J.: Humanities Press, 1981.

Callow, Simon. *Acting in Restoration Comedy*. New York: Applause Theater Books, 1991.

Chisman, Isabel, and Hester E. Raven-Hart. *Manners and Movement in Costume Plays*. Boston: W. H. Baker, no date available. Covers medieval to nineteenth century.

Dixon, Peggy. London: Nonsuch Early Dance. Volume I: *Nonsuch: Dances from the Courts of Europe Medieval to Fifteenth Century French Basse Dance*.

———. Volume II: *Nonsuch: Early Dance. Italian Renaissance (Fifteenth Century) and Caroso and Negri (Sixteenth Century) Dances*.

———. Volume III/IV *Nonsuch: Early Dance. Tudor Dances and English Country Dances*.

———. Volume V: *Nonsuch: Early Dance. Later English Country Dances*.

———. Volume VI: *Nonsuch: Early Dance. Ballroom Dances of the Seventeenth and Eighteenth Century*.

———. Volume VII/ VIII: *Eighteenth Century and Nineteenth Century Ballroom Dance. Glossary of Eighteenth and Nineteenth Century Dance Terms*.

———. Volume I: *A First Supplement*.

Hilton, Wendy. *Dance of Court and Theater: The French Noble Style 1690–1725*. Princeton, N.J.: Princeton Book Company. 1981. History, steps, style, and notation.

Millar, John Fitzhugh. *Elizabethan Country Dances*. Williamsburg, Va.: Thirteen Colonies Press, 1985. Easy-to-read explanation of country dances and music.

Oxenford, Lyn. *Playing Period Plays*. Chicago: The Coach House Press, 1966. Excellent information: medieval to nineteenth-century deportment, props and costume, and the spirit of the times.

Papp, Joseph, and Elizabeth Kirkland. *Shakespeare Alive!* New York: Bantam Books, 1988. Discover the London of Shakespeare's time.

Playford, John. *The English Dancing Master,* ed. Hugh Mellor. Bath, England: Pitman Press, 1933. An unabridged reprint of the classic text originally published in 1651, this book is now available through Dance Books, Ltd. Excellent information from an expert on period dance.

Pool, Daniel. *What Jane Austen Ate and Charles Dickens Knew*. New York: Simon and Schuster, 1993. The facts of daily life in nineteenth-century England. Invaluable material.

Quirey, Belinda. *May I have the Pleasure?* London: John Blackburn, Ltd., 1976. The development of social dancing from its origins to the 1960s.

Styan, J. L. *Restoration Comedy in Performance*. New York: Cambridge Press, 1986. Excellent. History, deportment, acting style, mode of speech, handling of props, and the spirit of the times.

Wildeblood, Joan, and Peter Brinson. *The Polite World*. London: Oxford University Press, 1965. Revised edition, London: Davis-Poynter, 1973. English manners and deportment, thirteenth to nineteenth century. Excellent information.

Where to Buy Books on Period Dance

Drama Book Shop, 250 West 40th Street, New York, NY 10018; tel (800) 322-0595; fax (212) 730-8739; *www.dramabookshop.com.*

Dance Books Ltd., The Old Bakery, 4 Lenten Street, Alton, Hampshire GU34 1HG U.K.; tel (011) 44-1420-86138; fax (011) 44-1420-86142; *www.dancebooks.co.uk.*

Pendragon Press, P.O. Box 190, Hillsdale, NY 12529; tel (518) 325-6100; fax (518) 325-6102; *www.pendragonpress.com.*

Princeton Book Company Publishers, Distributors for Dance Books Ltd. and Dance Notation Bureau, Publishers of Dance Horizons Books, P.O. Box 831, Hightstown, NJ 08520; tel (800) 220-7149; fax (609) 426-1344; *www.dancehorizons.com.*

Stagestep, 2000 Hamilton Street, Suite C200, Philadelphia, PA 19130; tel (800) 523-0960; fax (800) 877-3342; *www.stagestep.com.*

For the Nonsuch/Eglinton books and tapes, send inquiries to: Peggy Dixon, 16 Brook Drive, London SE11 4TT, England; *pegnnsch@globalnet.co.uk.*

Web Sites

Society of Dance History Scholars, *www.sdhs.org.* Web page has a list of people teaching early dance.

Congress on Research in Dance, *www.cordance.org.*

The Library of Congress "American Ballroom Companion, Dance Instruction Manuals, c. 1490–1920," *http://memory.loc.gov/ammem/dihtm,/dihome.html.* This Web site has over two hundred manuals that can be downloaded, as well as a detailed narrative and seventy-five video clips.

Early Music and Dance, *www.panix.com/~wlinden/earlym.html.*

Renaissance Dance, *www.rendance.org.*

You can also do a search on the Web for "Historical Dance" or "Early Dance," and there is lots more information.

Suggested Reading

Balk, Wesley H. *Performing Power: A New Approach for the Singer-Actor*. Foreword by John M. Ludwig. Minneapolis, Minn.: University of Minnesota Press, 1985. Thought-provoking theory concerning the "perceptual modes"—seeing, hearing, and touching—as they relate to the performer's "projective modes," which utilize the body, the voice, and the face. Detailed explanation of and exercises for objectively isolating and exploring each of the aforementioned and reintegrating them into empowered performance.

Barba, Eugenio, and Savarese, Nicola. *A Dictionary of Theatre Anthropology: The Secret Art of the Performer*. Translated by Richard Fowler. London and New York: Routledge, 1991. An extensive and fascinating compilation of essays and pictures that focuses on the elements and crafts of an eclectic range of performance disciplines, specifically as they engage the body.

Brestoff, Richard. *The Great Acting Teachers and Their Methods*. Lyme, N.H.: Smith and Kraus, 1995. Brestoff takes acting students on a whirlwind tour through time, letting them peek into the classrooms of various renowned acting teachers of the ages (although mostly the modern age).

Chekhov, Michael. *On the Technique of Acting*. Preface and afterword by Marla Powers. New York: HarperPerennial, 1991. The classic introduction to the work of Michael Chekhov.

Hodge, Alison, ed. *Twentieth Century Actor Training*. London and New York: Routledge, 2000. An intelligent and inspiring collection of essays that provides overviews of various modern acting systems, from Stanislavsky to Eugenio Barba.

Johnson, Don Hanlon, ed. *Bone, Breath, and Gesture*. Berkeley, Calif.: North Atlantic Books, 1995. Not specifically for actors, a collection of essays and interviews on the principles and techniques of body awareness.

Johnstone, Keith. *Improv: Improvisation and the Theatre*. New York: Theatre Arts Books, 1979. Not as complete or as pragmatic as Spolin's *Improvisation for the Theater*, Johnstone's book contains inspiring (or inflaming) passages concerning the negative and dulling effects of education upon those who would be creative and prescriptives for overcoming the institutionally wrought death of the imagination. Although Johnstone focuses more on verbal than on physical agility, what is invaluable here are his exercises and techniques for exploring the concept of status.

Knaster, Mirka. *Discovering the Body's Wisdom: A Comprehensive Guide to More Than Fifty Mind-Body Practices That Can Relieve Pain, Reduce Stress, and Foster Health, Spiritual Growth, and Inner Peace*. New York: Bantam Books, 1996. A general-health book, not meant for performers in particular, but Ms. Knaster interviewed, studied with, or put herself into the hands of teachers and therapists in a wide variety of disciplines that will be of interest to the actor: Pilates, Feldenkrais, yoga, Laban-Bartenieff, t'ai chi, and so on.

Lecoq, Jaques, with Carasso, Jean-Gabriel, and Lallias, Jean-Claude. *The Moving Body*. Translated by David Bradby. New York: Routledge, 2000. "In my method of teaching I have always given priority to the external world over inner experience," writes Lecoq. It is a treat, especially for American, Method-trained actors, to read such a contrarian point of view, supported by an entire system of exercises (although I think the exercises would be difficult to experience without a knowledgeable teacher as guide). Those who never studied with the man will mourn his passing and envy those who did.

Richards, Thomas. *At Work with Grotowski on Physical Actions*. London and New York: Routledge, 1995. An autobiographical investigation of one student's growth through his work and relationship with Jerzy Grotowski.

Ruyter, Nancy Lee Chalfa. *The Cultivation of Body and Mind in Nineteenth-Century American Delsartism*. Westport, Conn.: Greenwood Press, 1999. A great history of Delsartism, for all those whose acting teachers led them to believe it was just a bunch of silly posing.

See, Joan. *Acting in Commercials: A Guide to Auditioning and Performing on Camera*. 2nd ed. New York: Backstage Books, 1998. Surprised to see this listed here? This is a serious and practical book about commercial work, one of the few I've seen that gives physical work its due.

Spolin, Viola. *Improvisation for the Theater*. Evanston, Ill.: Northwestern University Press, 1963. The classic "cookbook" of theater games, written by the mother of American improvisation. The great thing about Viola's book is that if you follow her instructions (including those concerning points of concentration and side coaching), the recipe will be a success, even if you've never made it before.

Stanislavski, Constantin. *Creating a Role*, and also, *Building a Character*. Translated by Elizabeth Reynolds Hapgood. New York: Routledge. Lest you think the grandfather of the Method would have looked askance at this exploration of physical approaches to acting, see *Creating a Role*, Part III, The Period of Physical Embodiment, and almost all of *Building a Character*.

Suzuki, Tadashi. *The Way of Acting*. Translated by J. Thomas Rimer. New York: Theatre Communications Group, 1986. An intriguing introduction to Suzuki's ideas, but also frustrating, because there is no entrée into practical application.

Wangh, Stephen. *An Acrobat of the Heart: A Physical Approach to Acting Inspired by the Work of Jerzy Grotowski*. Afterword by André Gregory. New York: Vintage Books, 2000. Lots of acting exercises, taken from or inspired by Grotowski, are included in a step-by-step breakdown and "demoed" through the experiences of a class of (fictional) students enrolled in N.Y.U.'s Experimental Theatre Wing.

Yakim, Moni, with Broadman, Muriel. *Creating a Character: A Physical Approach to Acting*. New York and London: Applause Theatre Book Publishers, 1990. Lots of exercises for finding character and emotional states through movement.

Zaporah, Ruth. *Action Theater: The Improvisation of Presence*. Berkeley, Calif.: North Atlantic Books, 1995. The exercises in this book are dynamic, well explained, and easily adapted to a variety of classroom and rehearsal situations.

Bibliographies

Biomechanics: Understanding Meyerhold's System of Actor Training

Braun, Edward, ed. *Meyerhold on Theatre*. London: Methuen, 1991.

———. *Meyerhold: a Revolution in Theatre*. Iowa City, Iowa: University of Iowa Press, 1995.

Coquelin, Constant-Benoit. *The Art of Acting*. New York: Columbia University Press, 1929.

Gladkov, Aleksandr. *Meyerhold Speaks, Meyerhold Rehearses*. Amsterdam, Netherlands: Harwood, 1997.

Law, Alma H. and Gordon, Mel. *Meyerhold, Eisenstein and Biomechanics: Actor Training in Revolutionary Russia*. Jefferson, North Carolina: McFarland, 1996.

Leach, Robert. "Meyerhold and Biomechanics," in *Twentieth-Century Actor Training*. Edited by A. Hodge. London: Routledge, 2000.

———. *Vsevolod Meyerhold*. Cambridge: Cambridge University Press, 1989.

Meyerhold, Vsevolod. "The Theater Theatrical" (1906), in *Directors on Directing*. Edited by T. Cole and H. K. Chinoy. Indiana: Bobbs-Merrill, 1963.

Rudnitsky, Konstantin. *Meyerhold the Director*. Translated by G. Petrov. Ann Arbor, Mich.: Ardis, 1981.

Ryan, Paul R. "Lee Strasberg's Russian Notebook," in *The Drama Review*, 17(1): 107–21.

Schmidt, Paul, ed. *Meyerhold at Work*, New York: Applause, 1996.

Vakhtangov, Eugene. "Fantastic Realism" (1939), in *Directors on Directing*. Edited by T. Cole and H. K. Chinoy. Indiana: Bobbs-Merrill, 1963.

An Introduction to Laban Movement Analysis for Actors: A Historical, Theoretical, and Practical Perspective

Bartenieff, Irmgard. *Body Movement: Coping with the Environment*. New York: Gordon and Breach, 1996.

Geisinger, Marion. *Plays, Players, & Playwrights: An Illustrated History of the Theatre*. New York: Hart Publishing Co. Inc., 1971.

Gleisner, Martin. "Movement Choirs." *Laban Art of Movement Guild* magazine, November 1979: 8–11.

Green, Martin. *The Mountain of Truth*. Hanover, N. H.: University Press of New England, 1986.

Laban, Rudolf and F. C. Lawrence. *Effort*. United Kingdom: Hollen Street Press, 1979.

Laban, Rudolf. *A Vision of Dynamic Space*. London: Falner Press, 1984.

———. *The Language of Movement: The Guide Book to Choreutics*. Boston, Mass.: Plays, Inc., 1974.

———. *The Mastery of Movement*. Revised and enlarged by Lisa Ullmann. United Kingdom: Northcourte House Publishers Ltd., 1988.

Martin, Roger. "Smooth Moves." *Explore: Research and Science at the University of Kansas*, Fall 1985: 5–9.

North, Marion. *Personality Assessment Through Movement*. Boston, Mass.: Plays, Inc., 1975.

Preston-Dunlap, Valerie. *Modern Educational Dance*. Boston, Mass.: Plays, Inc., 1975.

———. "Laban and the Nazis: Toward Understanding Rudolf Laban and the Third Reich." *Dance/USA*, August/September 1989: 18–23.

———. "Laban, Schoenberg, Kandinsky 1899–1938." *Traces of Dance*, ed. Laurence Lerippe. Editions Dis Voir, 1994.

———. *Rudolf Laban: An Extraordinary Life*. London: Dance Books, 1998.

Preston-Dunlap, Valerie and Charolotte Purkis. "Rudolph Laban—The Making of Modern Dance: The Seminal Years in Munich 1910–1914." *Dance Theatre Journal* 7 (3), Winter 1989: 11–17.

———. "Rudolph Laban—The Making of Modern Dance, Part Two: The Seminal Years in Munich 1910–1914." *Dance Theatre Journal* 7(4), February 1990: 10-13.

Seigel, Marcia B. "Profile: Irmgard Bartenieff." *The Kinesis Report: News & Views of Nonverbal Communication* 2 (4), Summer 1980.

Stanislavsky, Konstantin. *An Actor Prepares,* translated by Elizabeth Reynolds Hapgood. New York: Routledge, 1964.

Thorton, Samuel. *Laban's Theory of Movement: A New Perspective* Boston, Mass.: Plays, Inc., 1971.

Torporkov, Vasily O. *Stanislavsky in Rehearsal: The Final Years*, trans. Christine Edwards. New York: Theatre Arts Books, 1979.

Shakespeare Honors the Three Centers of the Body

Bachelard, Gaston. *The Poetics of Space: The Classic Look at How We Experience Intimate Places.* Boston, Mass.: Beacon Press, 1994.

Barton, John. *Playing Shakespeare.* London: Methuen Drama, 1984.

Eco, Umberto. *Art and Beauty in the Middle Ages.* New Haven, Conn.: Yale University Press, 1988.

Horst, Louis, and Carroll Russell. *Modern Dance Forms in Relation to the Other Modern Arts.* Princeton, N.J.: Dance Horizons Book Publishers, 1987.

Nagrin, Daniel. *Dance and the Specific Image Improvisation.* Pittsburgh, Penn.: University of Pittsburgh Press, 1994.

Stodelle, Ernestine. *The Dance Technique of Doris Humphrey and Its Creative Potential.* Princeton, N.J.: Princeton Book Company, 1990.

Tillyard, E. M. W. *The Elizabethan World Picture.* New York: Random House, 1959.

Weil, Simone. *Gravity and Grace.* New York: Routledge, 1997.

Index

Books from Allworth Press

An Actor's Guide—Making It in New York City
by Glenn Alterman (paperback, 6 × 9, 288 pages, $19.95)

Creating Your Own Monologue
by Glenn Alterman (paperback, 6 × 9, 192 pages, $14.95)

Promoting Your Acting Career
by Glen Alterman (paperback, 6 × 9, 224 pages, $18.95)

Career Solutions for Creative People
by Dr. Rhonda Ormont (paperback, 6 × 9, 320 pages, $19.95)

Casting Director's Secrets: Inside Tips for Successful Auditions
by Ginger Howard Friedman (paperback, 6 × 9, 208 pages, $16.95)

Producing Your Own Showcase
by Paul Harris (paperback, 6 × 9, 224 pages, $18.95,

Technical Theater for Nontechnical People
by Drew Campbell (paperback, 6 × 9, 256 pages, $18.95)

Technical Film and TV for Nontechnical People
by Drew Campbell (paperback, 6 × 9, 256 pages, $19.95)

The Health & Safety Guide for Film, TV & Theater
by Monona Rossol (paperback, 6 × 9, 256 pages, $19.95)

Clues to Acting Shakespeare
by Wesley Van Tassel (paperback, 6 × 9, 208 pages, $16.95)

An Actor's Guide—Your First Year in Hollywood, Revised Edition
by Michael Saint Nicholas (paperback, 6 × 9, 272 pages, $18.95)

Booking and Tour Management for the Performing Arts, Third Edition
by Rena Shagan (paperback, 6 × 9, 288 pages, $19.95)

Directing for Film and Television, Revised Edition
by Christopher Lukas (paperback, 6 × 9, 256 pages, $19.95)

Producing for Hollywood: A Guide for Independent Producers
by Paul Mason and Don Gold (paperback, 6 × 9, 272 pages, $19.95)

Making Independent Films: Advice from the Film Makers
by Liz Stubbs and Richard Rodriguez (paperback, 6 × 9, 224 pages, $16.95)